FREE Study Skills Videos,

Dear Customer,

Thank you for your purchase from Mometrix! We consider it an honor and a privilege that you have purchased our product and we want to ensure your satisfaction.

As part of our ongoing effort to meet the needs of test takers, we have developed a set of Study Skills Videos that we would like to give you for <u>FREE</u>. These videos cover our *best practices* for getting ready for your exam, from how to use our study materials to how to best prepare for the day of the test.

All that we ask is that you email us with feedback that would describe your experience so far with our product. Good, bad, or indifferent, we want to know what you think!

To get your FREE Study Skills Videos, you can use the **QR code** below, or send us an **email** at <u>studyvideos@mometrix.com</u> with *FREE VIDEOS* in the subject line and the following information in the body of the email:

- The name of the product you purchased.
- Your product rating on a scale of 1-5, with 5 being the highest rating.
- Your feedback. It can be long, short, or anything in between. We just want to know your impressions and experience so far with our product. (Good feedback might include how our study material met your needs and ways we might be able to make it even better. You could highlight features that you found helpful or features that you think we should add.)

If you have any questions or concerns, please don't hesitate to contact me directly.

Thanks again!

Sincerely,

Jay Willis
Vice President
<u>jay.willis@mometrix.com</u>
1-800-673-8175

Praxis

Health and Physical Education Content Knowledge (5857)

Secrets Study Guide

Exam Review and Practice Test
for the Praxis Subject Assessments

Written and edited by Mometrix Test Prep

Printed in the United States of America

This paper meets the requirements of ANSI/NISO Z39.48-1992 (Permanence of Paper).

Mometrix offers volume discount pricing to institutions. For more information or a price quote, please contact our sales department at sales@mometrix.com or 888-248-1219.

Mometrix Media LLC is not affiliated with or endorsed by any official testing organization. All organizational and test names are trademarks of their respective owners.

Paperback
ISBN 13: 978-1-5167-4026-0
ISBN 10: 1-5167-4026-2

DEAR FUTURE EXAM SUCCESS STORY

First of all, **THANK YOU** for purchasing Mometrix study materials!

Second, congratulations! You are one of the few determined test-takers who are committed to doing whatever it takes to excel on your exam. **You have come to the right place.** We developed these study materials with one goal in mind: to deliver you the information you need in a format that's concise and easy to use.

In addition to optimizing your guide for the content of the test, we've outlined our recommended steps for breaking down the preparation process into small, attainable goals so you can make sure you stay on track.

We've also analyzed the entire test-taking process, identifying the most common pitfalls and showing how you can overcome them and be ready for any curveball the test throws you.

Standardized testing is one of the biggest obstacles on your road to success, which only increases the importance of doing well in the high-pressure, high-stakes environment of test day. Your results on this test could have a significant impact on your future, and this guide provides the information and practical advice to help you achieve your full potential on test day.

Your success is our success

We would love to hear from you! If you would like to share the story of your exam success or if you have any questions or comments in regard to our products, please contact us at **800-673-8175** or **support@mometrix.com**.

Thanks again for your business and we wish you continued success!

Sincerely,
The Mometrix Test Preparation Team

Need more help? Check out our flashcards at:
http://mometrixflashcards.com/PraxisII

TABLE OF CONTENTS

Introduction

Thank you for purchasing this resource! You have made the choice to prepare yourself for a test that could have a huge impact on your future, and this guide is designed to help you be fully ready for test day. Obviously, it's important to have a solid understanding of the test material, but you also need to be prepared for the unique environment and stressors of the test, so that you can perform to the best of your abilities.

For this purpose, the first section that appears in this guide is the **Secret Keys**. We've devoted countless hours to meticulously researching what works and what doesn't, and we've boiled down our findings to the five most impactful steps you can take to improve your performance on the test. We start at the beginning with study planning and move through the preparation process, all the way to the testing strategies that will help you get the most out of what you know when you're finally sitting in front of the test.

We recommend that you start preparing for your test as far in advance as possible. However, if you've bought this guide as a last-minute study resource and only have a few days before your test, we recommend that you skip over the first two Secret Keys since they address a long-term study plan.

If you struggle with **test anxiety**, we strongly encourage you to check out our recommendations for how you can overcome it. Test anxiety is a formidable foe, but it can be beaten, and we want to make sure you have the tools you need to defeat it.

1

Secret Key #1 – Plan Big, Study Small

There's a lot riding on your performance. If you want to ace this test, you're going to need to keep your skills sharp and the material fresh in your mind. You need a plan that lets you review everything you need to know while still fitting in your schedule. We'll break this strategy down into three categories.

Information Organization

Start with the information you already have: the official test outline. From this, you can make a complete list of all the concepts you need to cover before the test. Organize these concepts into groups that can be studied together, and create a list of any related vocabulary you need to learn so you can brush up on any difficult terms. You'll want to keep this vocabulary list handy once you actually start studying since you may need to add to it along the way.

Time Management

Once you have your set of study concepts, decide how to spread them out over the time you have left before the test. Break your study plan into small, clear goals so you have a manageable task for each day and know exactly what you're doing. Then just focus on one small step at a time. When you manage your time this way, you don't need to spend hours at a time studying. Studying a small block of content for a short period each day helps you retain information better and avoid stressing over how much you have left to do. You can relax knowing that you have a plan to cover everything in time. In order for this strategy to be effective though, you have to start studying early and stick to your schedule. Avoid the exhaustion and futility that comes from last-minute cramming!

Study Environment

The environment you study in has a big impact on your learning. Studying in a coffee shop, while probably more enjoyable, is not likely to be as fruitful as studying in a quiet room. It's important to keep distractions to a minimum. You're only planning to study for a short block of time, so make the most of it. Don't pause to check your phone or get up to find a snack. It's also important to **avoid multitasking**. Research has consistently shown that multitasking will make your studying dramatically less effective. Your study area should also be comfortable and well-lit so you don't have the distraction of straining your eyes or sitting on an uncomfortable chair.

 The time of day you study is also important. You want to be rested and alert. Don't wait until just before bedtime. Study when you'll be most likely to comprehend and remember. Even better, if you know what time of day your test will be, set that time aside for study. That way your brain will be used to working on that subject at that specific time and you'll have a better chance of recalling information.

Finally, it can be helpful to team up with others who are studying for the same test. Your actual studying should be done in as isolated an environment as possible, but the work of organizing the information and setting up the study plan can be divided up. In between study sessions, you can discuss with your teammates the concepts that you're all studying and quiz each other on the details. Just be sure that your teammates are as serious about the test as you are. If you find that your study time is being replaced with social time, you might need to find a new team.

2

Secret Key #2 – Make Your Studying Count

You're devoting a lot of time and effort to preparing for this test, so you want to be absolutely certain it will pay off. This means doing more than just reading the content and hoping you can remember it on test day. It's important to make every minute of study count. There are two main areas you can focus on to make your studying count.

Retention

It doesn't matter how much time you study if you can't remember the material. You need to make sure you are retaining the concepts. To check your retention of the information you're learning, try recalling it at later times with minimal prompting. Try carrying around flashcards and glance at one or two from time to time or ask a friend who's also studying for the test to quiz you.

To enhance your retention, look for ways to put the information into practice so that you can apply it rather than simply recalling it. If you're using the information in practical ways, it will be much easier to remember. Similarly, it helps to solidify a concept in your mind if you're not only reading it to yourself but also explaining it to someone else. Ask a friend to let you teach them about a concept you're a little shaky on (or speak aloud to an imaginary audience if necessary). As you try to summarize, define, give examples, and answer your friend's questions, you'll understand the concepts better and they will stay with you longer. Finally, step back for a big picture view and ask yourself how each piece of information fits with the whole subject. When you link the different concepts together and see them working together as a whole, it's easier to remember the individual components.

Finally, practice showing your work on any multi-step problems, even if you're just studying. Writing out each step you take to solve a problem will help solidify the process in your mind, and you'll be more likely to remember it during the test.

Modality

Modality simply refers to the means or method by which you study. Choosing a study modality that fits your own individual learning style is crucial. No two people learn best in exactly the same way, so it's important to know your strengths and use them to your advantage.

For example, if you learn best by visualization, focus on visualizing a concept in your mind and draw an image or a diagram. Try color-coding your notes, illustrating them, or creating symbols that will trigger your mind to recall a learned concept. If you learn best by hearing or discussing information, find a study partner who learns the same way or read aloud to yourself. Think about how to put the information in your own words. Imagine that you are giving a lecture on the topic and record yourself so you can listen to it later.

For any learning style, flashcards can be helpful. Organize the information so you can take advantage of spare moments to review. Underline key words or phrases. Use different colors for different categories. Mnemonic devices (such as creating a short list in which every item starts with the same letter) can also help with retention. Find what works best for you and use it to store the information in your mind most effectively and easily.

3

Secret Key #3 – Practice the Right Way

Your success on test day depends not only on how many hours you put into preparing, but also on whether you prepared the right way. It's good to check along the way to see if your studying is paying off. One of the most effective ways to do this is by taking practice tests to evaluate your progress. Practice tests are useful because they show exactly where you need to improve. Every time you take a practice test, pay special attention to these three groups of questions:

- The questions you got wrong
- The questions you had to guess on, even if you guessed right
- The questions you found difficult or slow to work through

This will show you exactly what your weak areas are, and where you need to devote more study time. Ask yourself why each of these questions gave you trouble. Was it because you didn't understand the material? Was it because you didn't remember the vocabulary? Do you need more repetitions on this type of question to build speed and confidence? Dig into those questions and figure out how you can strengthen your weak areas as you go back to review the material.

 Additionally, many practice tests have a section explaining the answer choices. It can be tempting to read the explanation and think that you now have a good understanding of the concept. However, an explanation likely only covers part of the question's broader context. Even if the explanation makes perfect sense, **go back and investigate** every concept related to the question until you're positive you have a thorough understanding.

As you go along, keep in mind that the practice test is just that: practice. Memorizing these questions and answers will not be very helpful on the actual test because it is unlikely to have any of the same exact questions. If you only know the right answers to the sample questions, you won't be prepared for the real thing. **Study the concepts** until you understand them fully, and then you'll be able to answer any question that shows up on the test.

It's important to wait on the practice tests until you're ready. If you take a test on your first day of study, you may be overwhelmed by the amount of material covered and how much you need to learn. Work up to it gradually.

On test day, you'll need to be prepared for answering questions, managing your time, and using the test-taking strategies you've learned. It's a lot to balance, like a mental marathon that will have a big impact on your future. Like training for a marathon, you'll need to start slowly and work your way up. When test day arrives, you'll be ready.

Start with the strategies you've read in the first two Secret Keys—plan your course and study in the way that works best for you. If you have time, consider using multiple study resources to get different approaches to the same concepts. It can be helpful to see difficult concepts from more than one angle. Then find a good source for practice tests. Many times, the test website will suggest potential study resources or provide sample tests.

Practice Test Strategy

If you're able to find at least three practice tests, we recommend this strategy:

UNTIMED AND OPEN-BOOK PRACTICE

Take the first test with no time constraints and with your notes and study guide handy. Take your time and focus on applying the strategies you've learned.

TIMED AND OPEN-BOOK PRACTICE

Take the second practice test open-book as well, but set a timer and practice pacing yourself to finish in time.

TIMED AND CLOSED-BOOK PRACTICE

Take any other practice tests as if it were test day. Set a timer and put away your study materials. Sit at a table or desk in a quiet room, imagine yourself at the testing center, and answer questions as quickly and accurately as possible.

Keep repeating timed and closed-book tests on a regular basis until you run out of practice tests or it's time for the actual test. Your mind will be ready for the schedule and stress of test day, and you'll be able to focus on recalling the material you've learned.

Secret Key #4 – Pace Yourself

Once you're fully prepared for the material on the test, your biggest challenge on test day will be managing your time. Just knowing that the clock is ticking can make you panic even if you have plenty of time left. Work on pacing yourself so you can build confidence against the time constraints of the exam. Pacing is a difficult skill to master, especially in a high-pressure environment, so **practice is vital**.

Set time expectations for your pace based on how much time is available. For example, if a section has 60 questions and the time limit is 30 minutes, you know you have to average 30 seconds or less per question in order to answer them all. Although 30 seconds is the hard limit, set 25 seconds per question as your goal, so you reserve extra time to spend on harder questions. When you budget extra time for the harder questions, you no longer have any reason to stress when those questions take longer to answer.

Don't let this time expectation distract you from working through the test at a calm, steady pace, but keep it in mind so you don't spend too much time on any one question. Recognize that taking extra time on one question you don't understand may keep you from answering two that you do understand later in the test. If your time limit for a question is up and you're still not sure of the answer, mark it and move on, and come back to it later if the time and the test format allow. If the testing format doesn't allow you to return to earlier questions, just make an educated guess; then put it out of your mind and move on.

On the easier questions, be careful not to rush. It may seem wise to hurry through them so you have more time for the challenging ones, but it's not worth missing one if you know the concept and just didn't take the time to read the question fully. Work efficiently but make sure you understand the question and have looked at all of the answer choices, since more than one may seem right at first.

Even if you're paying attention to the time, you may find yourself a little behind at some point. You should speed up to get back on track, but do so wisely. Don't panic; just take a few seconds less on each question until you're caught up. Don't guess without thinking, but do look through the answer choices and eliminate any you know are wrong. If you can get down to two choices, it is often worthwhile to guess from those. Once you've chosen an answer, move on and don't dwell on any that you skipped or had to hurry through. If a question was taking too long, chances are it was one of the harder ones, so you weren't as likely to get it right anyway.

On the other hand, if you find yourself getting ahead of schedule, it may be beneficial to slow down a little. The more quickly you work, the more likely you are to make a careless mistake that will affect your score. You've budgeted time for each question, so don't be afraid to spend that time. Practice an efficient but careful pace to get the most out of the time you have.

Secret Key #5 – Have a Plan for Guessing

When you're taking the test, you may find yourself stuck on a question. Some of the answer choices seem better than others, but you don't see the one answer choice that is obviously correct. What do you do?

The scenario described above is very common, yet most test takers have not effectively prepared for it. Developing and practicing a plan for guessing may be one of the single most effective uses of your time as you get ready for the exam.

In developing your plan for guessing, there are three questions to address:

- When should you start the guessing process?
- How should you narrow down the choices?
- Which answer should you choose?

When to Start the Guessing Process

Unless your plan for guessing is to select C every time (which, despite its merits, is not what we recommend), you need to leave yourself enough time to apply your answer elimination strategies. Since you have a limited amount of time for each question, that means that if you're going to give yourself the best shot at guessing correctly, you have to decide quickly whether or not you will guess.

Of course, the best-case scenario is that you don't have to guess at all, so first, see if you can answer the question based on your knowledge of the subject and basic reasoning skills. Focus on the key words in the question and try to jog your memory of related topics. Give yourself a chance to bring the knowledge to mind, but once you realize that you don't have (or you can't access) the knowledge you need to answer the question, it's time to start the guessing process.

It's almost always better to start the guessing process too early than too late. It only takes a few seconds to remember something and answer the question from knowledge. Carefully eliminating wrong answer choices takes longer. Plus, going through the process of eliminating answer choices can actually help jog your memory.

Summary: Start the guessing process as soon as you decide that you can't answer the question based on your knowledge.

How to Narrow Down the Choices

The next chapter in this book (**Test-Taking Strategies**) includes a wide range of strategies for how to approach questions and how to look for answer choices to eliminate. You will definitely want to read those carefully, practice them, and figure out which ones work best for you. Here though, we're going to address a mindset rather than a particular strategy.

Your odds of guessing an answer correctly depend on how many options you are choosing from.

Number of options left	5	4	3	2	1
Odds of guessing correctly	20%	25%	33%	50%	100%

You can see from this chart just how valuable it is to be able to eliminate incorrect answers and make an educated guess, but there are two things that many test takers do that cause them to miss out on the benefits of guessing:

- Accidentally eliminating the correct answer
- Selecting an answer based on an impression

We'll look at the first one here, and the second one in the next section.

To avoid accidentally eliminating the correct answer, we recommend a thought exercise called **the $5 challenge**. In this challenge, you only eliminate an answer choice from contention if you are willing to bet $5 on it being wrong. Why $5? Five dollars is a small but not insignificant amount of money. It's an amount you could afford to lose but wouldn't want to throw away. And while losing

$5 once might not hurt too much, doing it twenty times will set you back $100. In the same way, each small decision you make—eliminating a choice here, guessing on a question there—won't by itself impact your score very much, but when you put them all together, they can make a big difference. By holding each answer choice elimination decision to a higher standard, you can reduce the risk of accidentally eliminating the correct answer.

The $5 challenge can also be applied in a positive sense: If you are willing to bet $5 that an answer choice *is* correct, go ahead and mark it as correct.

Summary: Only eliminate an answer choice if you are willing to bet $5 that it is wrong.

8

Which Answer to Choose

You're taking the test. You've run into a hard question and decided you'll have to guess. You've eliminated all the answer choices you're willing to bet $5 on. Now you have to pick an answer. Why do we even need to talk about this? Why can't you just pick whichever one you feel like when the time comes?

The answer to these questions is that if you don't come into the test with a plan, you'll rely on your impression to select an answer choice, and if you do that, you risk falling into a trap. The test writers know that everyone who takes their test will be guessing on some of the questions, so they intentionally write wrong answer choices to seem plausible. You still have to pick an answer though, and if the wrong answer choices are designed to look right, how can you ever be sure that you're not falling for their trap? The best solution we've found to this dilemma is to take the decision out of your hands entirely. Here is the process we recommend:

Once you've eliminated any choices that you are confident (willing to bet $5) are wrong, select the first remaining choice as your answer.

Whether you choose to select the first remaining choice, the second, or the last, the important thing is that you use some preselected standard. Using this approach guarantees that you will not be enticed into selecting an answer choice that looks right, because you are not basing your decision on how the answer choices look.

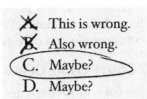

This is not meant to make you question your knowledge. Instead, it is to help you recognize the difference between your knowledge and your impressions. There's a huge difference between thinking an answer is right because of what you know, and thinking an answer is right because it looks or sounds like it should be right.

Summary: To ensure that your selection is appropriately random, make a predetermined selection from among all answer choices you have not eliminated.

Test-Taking Strategies

This section contains a list of test-taking strategies that you may find helpful as you work through the test. By taking what you know and applying logical thought, you can maximize your chances of answering any question correctly!

It is very important to realize that every question is different and every person is different: no single strategy will work on every question, and no single strategy will work for every person. That's why we've included all of them here, so you can try them out and determine which ones work best for different types of questions and which ones work best for you.

Question Strategies

⊘ READ CAREFULLY

Read the question and the answer choices carefully. Don't miss the question because you misread the terms. You have plenty of time to read each question thoroughly and make sure you understand what is being asked. Yet a happy medium must be attained, so don't waste too much time. You must read carefully and efficiently.

⊘ CONTEXTUAL CLUES

Look for contextual clues. If the question includes a word you are not familiar with, look at the immediate context for some indication of what the word might mean. Contextual clues can often give you all the information you need to decipher the meaning of an unfamiliar word. Even if you can't determine the meaning, you may be able to narrow down the possibilities enough to make a solid guess at the answer to the question.

⊘ PREFIXES

If you're having trouble with a word in the question or answer choices, try dissecting it. Take advantage of every clue that the word might include. Prefixes can be a huge help. Usually, they allow you to determine a basic meaning. *Pre-* means before, *post-* means after, *pro-* is positive, *de-* is negative. From prefixes, you can get an idea of the general meaning of the word and try to put it into context.

⊘ HEDGE WORDS

Watch out for critical hedge words, such as *likely, may, can, sometimes, often, almost, mostly, usually, generally, rarely,* and *sometimes.* Question writers insert these hedge phrases to cover every possibility. Often an answer choice will be wrong simply because it leaves no room for exception. Be on guard for answer choices that have definitive words such as *exactly* and *always.*

⊘ SWITCHBACK WORDS

Stay alert for *switchbacks.* These are the words and phrases frequently used to alert you to shifts in thought. The most common switchback words are *but, although,* and *however.* Others include *nevertheless, on the other hand, even though, while, in spite of, despite,* and *regardless of.* Switchback words are important to catch because they can change the direction of the question or an answer choice.

⊘ FACE VALUE

When in doubt, use common sense. Accept the situation in the problem at face value. Don't read too much into it. These problems will not require you to make wild assumptions. If you have to go beyond creativity and warp time or space in order to have an answer choice fit the question, then you should move on and consider the other answer choices. These are normal problems rooted in reality. The applicable relationship or explanation may not be readily apparent, but it is there for you to figure out. Use your common sense to interpret anything that isn't clear.

Answer Choice Strategies

⊘ ANSWER SELECTION

The most thorough way to pick an answer choice is to identify and eliminate wrong answers until only one is left, then confirm it is the correct answer. Sometimes an answer choice may immediately seem right, but be careful. The test writers will usually put more than one reasonable answer choice on each question, so take a second to read all of them and make sure that the other choices are not equally obvious. As long as you have time left, it is better to read every answer choice than to pick the first one that looks right without checking the others.

⊘ ANSWER CHOICE FAMILIES

An answer choice family consists of two (in rare cases, three) answer choices that are very similar in construction and cannot all be true at the same time. If you see two answer choices that are direct opposites or parallels, one of them is usually the correct answer. For instance, if one answer choice says that quantity x increases and another either says that quantity x decreases (opposite) or says that quantity y increases (parallel), then those answer choices would fall into the same family. An answer choice that doesn't match the construction of the answer choice family is more likely to be incorrect. Most questions will not have answer choice families, but when they do appear, you should be prepared to recognize them.

⊘ ELIMINATE ANSWERS

Eliminate answer choices as soon as you realize they are wrong, but make sure you consider all possibilities. If you are eliminating answer choices and realize that the last one you are left with is also wrong, don't panic. Start over and consider each choice again. There may be something you missed the first time that you will realize on the second pass.

⊘ AVOID FACT TRAPS

Don't be distracted by an answer choice that is factually true but doesn't answer the question. You are looking for the choice that answers the question. Stay focused on what the question is asking for so you don't accidentally pick an answer that is true but incorrect. Always go back to the question and make sure the answer choice you've selected actually answers the question and is not merely a true statement.

⊘ EXTREME STATEMENTS

In general, you should avoid answers that put forth extreme actions as standard practice or proclaim controversial ideas as established fact. An answer choice that states the "process should be used in certain situations, if…" is much more likely to be correct than one that states the "process should be discontinued completely." The first is a calm rational statement and doesn't even make a definitive, uncompromising stance, using a hedge word *if* to provide wiggle room, whereas the second choice is far more extreme.

⊘ BENCHMARK

As you read through the answer choices and you come across one that seems to answer the question well, mentally select that answer choice. This is not your final answer, but it's the one that will help you evaluate the other answer choices. The one that you selected is your benchmark or standard for judging each of the other answer choices. Every other answer choice must be compared to your benchmark. That choice is correct until proven otherwise by another answer choice beating it. If you find a better answer, then that one becomes your new benchmark. Once you've decided that no other choice answers the question as well as your benchmark, you have your final answer.

⊘ PREDICT THE ANSWER

Before you even start looking at the answer choices, it is often best to try to predict the answer. When you come up with the answer on your own, it is easier to avoid distractions and traps because you will know exactly what to look for. The right answer choice is unlikely to be word-for-word what you came up with, but it should be a close match. Even if you are confident that you have the right answer, you should still take the time to read each option before moving on.

General Strategies

⊘ TOUGH QUESTIONS

If you are stumped on a problem or it appears too hard or too difficult, don't waste time. Move on! Remember though, if you can quickly check for obviously incorrect answer choices, your chances of guessing correctly are greatly improved. Before you completely give up, at least try to knock out a couple of possible answers. Eliminate what you can and then guess at the remaining answer choices before moving on.

⊘ CHECK YOUR WORK

Since you will probably not know every term listed and the answer to every question, it is important that you get credit for the ones that you do know. Don't miss any questions through careless mistakes. If at all possible, try to take a second to look back over your answer selection and make sure you've selected the correct answer choice and haven't made a costly careless mistake (such as marking an answer choice that you didn't mean to mark). This quick double check should more than pay for itself in caught mistakes for the time it costs.

⊘ PACE YOURSELF

It's easy to be overwhelmed when you're looking at a page full of questions; your mind is confused and full of random thoughts, and the clock is ticking down faster than you would like. Calm down and maintain the pace that you have set for yourself. Especially as you get down to the last few minutes of the test, don't let the small numbers on the clock make you panic. As long as you are on track by monitoring your pace, you are guaranteed to have time for each question.

⊘ DON'T RUSH

It is very easy to make errors when you are in a hurry. Maintaining a fast pace in answering questions is pointless if it makes you miss questions that you would have gotten right otherwise. Test writers like to include distracting information and wrong answers that seem right. Taking a little extra time to avoid careless mistakes can make all the difference in your test score. Find a pace that allows you to be confident in the answers that you select.

⊘ Keep Moving

Panicking will not help you pass the test, so do your best to stay calm and keep moving. Taking deep breaths and going through the answer elimination steps you practiced can help to break through a stress barrier and keep your pace.

Final Notes

The combination of a solid foundation of content knowledge and the confidence that comes from practicing your plan for applying that knowledge is the key to maximizing your performance on test day. As your foundation of content knowledge is built up and strengthened, you'll find that the strategies included in this chapter become more and more effective in helping you quickly sift through the distractions and traps of the test to isolate the correct answer.

Now that you're preparing to move forward into the test content chapters of this book, be sure to keep your goal in mind. As you read, think about how you will be able to apply this information on the test. If you've already seen sample questions for the test and you have an idea of the question format and style, try to come up with questions of your own that you can answer based on what you're reading. This will give you valuable practice applying your knowledge in the same ways you can expect to on test day.

Good luck and good studying!

14

Content Knowledge and Student Growth and Development

Motor Development Processes

ANN GENTILE'S MOTOR LEARNING STAGES

Gentile's learning model has two stages. In stage 1, the learner is **getting the idea of the movement.** In stage 2, the learner focuses on **fixation**, or working on consistency and closed skills (e.g., executing the skill in isolation) and **diversification**, or working on open skill in changing environments. In stage 1, the learner is getting a grasp on the movements that are required for the skill. The learner decides on the regulatory and nonregulatory conditions needed to perform the movement. **Regulatory conditions** are important to the movement skill, whereas **nonregulatory conditions** are not. However, nonregulatory conditions, such as crowd noise, can be distracting. Regulatory conditions include things like equipment type, positions of players, and the proximity to the goal. These aspects must be considered before a learner can be proficient. Learners who are more skilled and have more experience are better able to ignore nonregulatory conditions. In contrast, it is difficult for novice learners to ignore nonregulatory conditions. Once learners are proficient, they move on to stage 2.

FITTS AND POSNER'S MOTOR LEARNING STAGES

Fitts and Posner's three motor stages of learning are the cognitive stage, the associative stage, and the autonomous stage. In the **cognitive**, or beginner, stage, the learner makes lots of errors, is inconsistent, and focuses heavily on the skill cues. During this stage, the teacher is more direct with instructions, which include both verbal instructions and demonstrations, to help the learner understand the movements. This first stage is similar to Gentile's stage 1 (getting the idea of the movement). In the **associative**, or intermediate, stage, the learner has a grasp on the skill and understands the skill movement patterns. This learner will start to become more consistent in movement patterns. As such, they will rely less on skill cues and begin to refine movement by trial, error, and feedback, which aids in the development of self-correction skills. During the associative stage, the teacher designs the practice activities after identifying the errors and providing corrective feedback. In the **autonomous,** or advanced, stage, the movements become automatic and the student can perform skills independently. The learner is able to self-correct during the autonomous stage. During this stage, the teacher should focus on motivation and design activities that refine the movements.

OPEN AND CLOSED SKILLS

While no skill is completely open or closed, **open skills** occur in dynamic environments where things are always changing, like during team sports. There are players, a ball (or object), coaches, and spectators, all of which create an unpredictable environment and impact performance. There are also closed skills within team sports, like a free throw in basketball or a penalty kick in soccer, that illustrate the open-closed continuum. **Closed skills** occur in environments that are stable and predictable, like golf. Closed skills are often introduced when teaching novice learners, so that they can focus solely on the skill, or when teaching a closed and controlled activity, like archery. Activities that are open in team sports are often taught in progression from closed (e.g., dribbling in isolation) to open skills (e.g., dribbling during game play) to increase competency.

15

BERNSTEIN'S DEGREES OF FREEDOM PROBLEM

Bernstein's motor learning stages focus on the **degrees of freedom problem**. The degrees of freedom problem refers to the variations that can take place in a **complex movement** because of the number of **isolated types of movement** involved in accomplishing a movement skill. For instance, when a pitcher throws a baseball, his feet, legs, torso, arms, and hands are involved in throwing the ball. Therefore, the goal is to reduce the number of problems that can arise from degrees of freedom that may impede success to achieve the desired movement. Two concepts integral to Bernstein's learning stages are the coordination and regulation of movement. Coordination is the ability to move fluidly with complex movement skills. In throwing a ball, a pitcher starts by winding up the upper arm and back and smoothly translating the throw through the whole arm so that all of the arm muscles involved can contribute to the motion. Regulation is the ability to control individual movements in joints, limbs, and muscles. This usually means working a particular muscle in isolation. To work on regulating motions involved in throwing a baseball, one might attempt to throw a baseball by only using the forearm, or work on the associated footwork without throwing a ball.

BERNSTEIN'S MOTOR LEARNING STAGES

Bernstein's motor learning stages revolve around breaking down motor tasks into smaller pieces to develop **regulation** of individual movements, then integrating them to develop **coordination** between those movements. **Stage 1** is freezing the limbs, which involves regulating as many degrees of freedom necessary to produce the desired movement. For example, the leg and foot action of an overhand throw might be restricted so that the novice learner can focus on the arm motion of the throw. **Stage 2** is releasing the limbs as degrees of freedom gradually increase as skills become more proficient. **Stage 3** is exploiting the environment, (expert stage), which is when the learner is able to perform the tasks in a variety of situations. For example, throwing at different speeds, throwing while running, throwing at various distances and levels, and throwing with defenders all exploit the environment in different ways. Developing skills on each of these levels helps to isolate inefficient movements and develop the fluidity of movements involved in a complex skill.

MOTOR LEARNING AND MOTOR PERFORMANCE

Motor learning is the study of skill acquisition processes and includes the factors that help or hinder motor skill performance. Motor learning can be a permanent or semi-permanent change. Once a person learns how to ride a bike, they will not forget—even after a long absence of riding. Motor learning cannot be observed directly. Instead, performance is observed over time to evaluate consistency and proficiency in a movement skill, which aids in making a determination about whether or not learning has occurred. **Motor performance** is the demonstration of a skill or set of skills. In contrast to motor learning, motor performance is not permanent, as it is contingent upon other factors. While one may have learned how to perform a jump shot in basketball, the success of the jump shot will differ based on the changing environment. Further, the individual's fitness level, fatigue, stress, and other factors impact performance. In contrast to motor learning, motor performance can be observed.

KNOWLEDGE OF PERFORMANCE AND KNOWLEDGE OF RESULTS

Knowledge of performance is the quality of a performance. It is often felt by the learner while executing the movement or observed while watching the movement. These feelings or observations help to identify either errors that need correction or actions that need to be replicated to promote consistent performance, a process known as **descriptive feedback**. For example, the hand positions and release of a basketball during a free throw can be observed. If the hand position and

16

release of the basketball are to the left, the ball will likely go in that direction. This observation of performance would warrant a change in technique or positioning to improve performance. The feedback given to correct the error in performance is **prescriptive feedback.** In contrast, the **knowledge of results**, or terminal feedback, is the outcome feedback that occurs after a skill has been performed. An example of the knowledge of results is evident during a free throw shot in basketball or a penalty kick in soccer where the outcome is that the ball either goes in or out. When only outcome feedback (knowledge of results) is given, there is little improvement of motor skills. Conversely, knowledge of performance feedback appears more impactful for improving motor skill acquisition and performance.

SKILL TRANSFER

The three types of skill transfer are positive, negative, and zero. **Positive transfer** is when a previously learned skill benefits the performance of another skill. An example of positive transfer may include performing a forehand in racquetball after learning a forehand in tennis. **Negative transfer** is when a previously learned skill impedes the performance of another skill. An example of negative transfer is someone's knowledge of how to properly swing a baseball bat impeding their ability to learn how to properly swing a golf club. **Zero transfer** is when a previously learned skill has no impact on the learning of a future skill. The skills are usually unrelated (though not always). For example, dribbling in basketball has little to no impact on dribbling in soccer. However, positive transfer is often evident during invasion games (team sports that involve two teams with the goal of scoring an object into a goal) such as these because the offensive and defensive concepts and strategies in basketball and soccer are the same.

THEORY OF DELIBERATE PRACTICE

"Practice makes perfect" is a common phrase often used in physical education. This concept is included in the five tenets of **deliberate practice** described here.

1. Skills must be developed through practice, even among those with natural ability. While it is often assumed that some students have "natural talent," practice is still necessary for improvement and permanency.
2. The frequency of practice and the opportunities to respond must be high for students to master a skill.
3. Short duration and high quality practice tends to yield better results, so variety in activities is beneficial. This also keeps students on task.
4. Goals or objectives must be established to give students focus and to aid in assessment.
5. Direct, early feedback is given to both prevent errors and redirect students towards the goal.

PROVIDING FEEDBACK FOR MOTOR SKILLS

Feedback is the information that teachers provide to students to improve motor skills. Types of feedback include general, specific, positive, negative, and constructive. **General** feedback is vague and not focused on the skill performance. It includes statements like "good job" and "nice shot." **Specific** or descriptive feedback is explicit and focuses on the skill action. An example of specific feedback is, "You demonstrated early preparation of your racket by moving it behind you before striking the ball." **Positive** feedback is praise and focuses on what is correct, while **negative** feedback focuses on what is wrong. Both positive and negative feedback can be either general or specific. **Constructive** feedback gives specific details on what the student is doing incorrectly and explicit details on how to improve. An example of constructive feedback is, "You are standing up too straight during your golf swing. You need to keep your knees bent as you make contact with the ball." Students often perceive constructive feedback as negative, therefore, the three-step **sandwich method** of providing feedback is recommended:

1. **Positive specific feedback** is given on what the student is doing well.
2. **Specific constructive feedback** is given on what is wrong and why or how it impedes success.
3. **Positive specific feedback** completes the feedback loop by giving explicit cues on how to correctly perform the skill.

TYPES OF FEEDBACK

When giving student feedback, multiple approaches should be employed, including verbal (e.g., talking), visual (demonstration, images, video), and kinesthetic (student practice). As students move kinesthetically in physical education, it is often recommended to use the **tell-show-do** method to ensure that verbal (tell), visual (show), and kinesthetic (do) types of feedback are reinforced to optimize student learning. This approach is further enhanced by providing video feedback, a type of visual feedback that has shown to have a significant impact on student learning. Similar to other types of feedback, video feedback works best when accompanied by verbal and visual cues, and must be used consistently to have the greatest impact.

Perceptual-Motor Development

FLEISHMAN'S PERCEPTUAL-MOTOR ABILITIES AND PHYSICAL PROFICIENCY ABILITIES

Fleishman's taxonomy of motor abilities consists of perceptual-motor abilities and physical proficiency abilities. **Perceptual-motor abilities** are the sensory motor aspects of how the body interprets and responds to the environment. These perceptual-motor abilities include reaction time, rate control, aiming, manual and finger dexterity, control precision, and arm-hand steadiness. In contrast, Fleishman's **physical proficiency abilities** include both skill-related and health-related fitness components or the physiologic aspects of motor ability. The abilities are less dependent on the environment. Health-related examples of physical proficiency abilities include muscular strength, muscular endurance, flexibility, and cardiovascular endurance. Skill-related examples include coordination, power, speed, and balance. Both motor ability categories influence skill development and motor performance. Optimal performance is increased when both are utilized, which can be developed and refined through practice and training. Further, the rates of development and improvement depend on one's abilities, which are determined by biological and physiological influences.

PERCEPTUAL-MOTOR DEVELOPMENT

Perceptual-motor skills are needed to perform the fundamental movement skills. While perceptual motor abilities are genetic, they are developed according to stage of development and through practice. Perceptual-motor development is impacted or enhanced by auditory, visual, and kinesthetic discrimination. **Auditory discrimination** is the ability to differentiate between sounds (e.g., loud or soft, the sound of a cow versus the sound a dog). **Visual discrimination** allows students to differentiate between images (people, sizes, shapes, colors, objects). **Kinesthetic discrimination** is the ability to detect small changes in muscle movement, which involves large gross motor movements. The ability to discriminate in all of these areas will foster perceptual-motor development, whereas the inability in one or more of these areas of discrimination will make it more difficult to develop perceptual-motor skills.

VISION AND COORDINATION

Vision is a perceptual ability that aids in balance and coordination, as the information received through the eyes is transmitted to the muscles and the inner ear, which informs or detects movement and a movement response. As such, vision helps with equilibrium, which then helps during physical activities. Performing an activity such as standing or walking with the eyes closed illustrates the impact that vision has on coordination, as the ability to see the environment reduces the difficulty of movement. Vision training helps with other perceptual-motor skills, including eye tracking, movement precision, reaction time, peripheral vision, improved hand-eye coordination, and improved visual discrimination.

HEARING AND PERCEPTUAL MOTOR DEVELOPMENT

Similar to vision, the ability to hear also impacts perceptual-motor skills, including reaction time, as the sound alerts or prepares the body for the response (e.g., hearing a ball thrown outside the peripheral view). Activities that start with sound (e.g., verbal command, whistle, bell, horn) require auditory senses to transmit information to the brain, which informs movement. Hearing impairments slow down perceptual motor response. Using audition to improve perceptual-motor skills often combines verbal cues in unison with tactile learning, or learning through touch, especially for fine motor activities (e.g., catching a ball after hearing "hands out in front" or "get ready").

RELATIONSHIP BETWEEN AWARENESS AND PERFORMANCE

The kinesthetic system (sensory) involves proprioception and joints, muscles, and tendons, as well as receptors of the skin, ears, and eyes. It is largely responsible for body awareness and spatial awareness. Exposure to activities that involve gross motor movements combined with multiple sensory experiences (touch, sound, sight) enhances perceptual-motor performances. Perceptual-motor performances include an awareness of the body's position when stationary (e.g., upright, seated) and during movement (e.g., hands out front when falling forward to prevent injury), which requires balance. This is also developed through a variety of kinesthetic experiences.

Factors Affecting Motor Development and Performance

CONSTRAINTS AND MOTOR PERFORMANCE

Constraints are boundaries that limit or promote movement options. **Individual constraints** have two sub-categories: 1) structural constraints, which include physical body structures (e.g., height, weight, gender), and 2) functional constraints, which include psychological (e.g., arousal) and cognitive (e.g., IQ) conditions. **Task constraints** include movement goals, game rules, and equipment used in movement and games. Examples of task constraints include ball size (e.g., women's vs men's basketball size) and game rules (e.g., regulation or modified rules). Adjusting ball size can make the task easier or more difficult. **Environmental constraints** include external factors and also have two sub-categories: 1) **physical environment**, which includes the space (e.g., indoor or outdoor), lights, temperature, and weather, and 2) **sociocultural environment**, which includes social and cultural aspects that impact physical activity engagement and may include gender (e.g., beliefs that girls should not be engaged in physical activity or develop muscular bodies), race, ethnicity, religion, and social class.

ALBERT BANDURA'S SOCIAL LEARNING THEORY

Social or observational learning theory acknowledges that one's behavior influences others and vice versa. Three elements of social learning theory are **modeling** (watching others), **reinforcement** (rewarding or penalizing), and **social comparison** (the evaluation of skills to the model or a peer). For example, demonstrations, which include learning through observation or the ability to follow a model, are social learning theory methods used in physical education settings. The downside of this theory is that teachers are unable to control all observational learning, since students can learn or observe motor skills outside of class. To ensure effectiveness of observational learning, Bandura suggests a four-step process:

1. **Attention:** students must focus instructional or skill cues
2. **Retention:** students need to remember the demonstrated model (reinforced by skill cues and mental imagery)
3. **Motor reproduction:** students must practice or try to replicate the demonstration
4. **Motivation:** the teacher needs to motivate students to increase their desire to imitate the performance. Reinforcement is often used at this stage.

By including these steps, students are better able to achieve both the psychomotor and cognitive aspects of motor skill acquisition.

IMPACT OF EMOTIONAL DEVELOPMENT ON MOTOR PERFORMANCE

The ability to control and recognize emotions (e.g., anger, happiness) impacts motor performance. **Emotional self-regulation** is the control of emotions that starts to develop during infancy and becomes more refined by the age of six. **Emotional knowledge** is the awareness of emotions in other people. **Emotional development** is important because students need to manage emotions in order to focus on instruction. Physical activities that foster positive emotions contribute to positive self-esteem. **Self-esteem** is how one feels about themselves. Positive self-esteem can lead to **competence motivation**, which is the desire to continue to engage in physical activities even when difficult. **Self-efficacy** is the belief in one's ability to perform motor skills. Experiences that foster negative emotions can result in low competence motivation, low self-efficacy, and even disengagement or non-participation in physical activities. As such, increasing student successes in physical education classes fosters the development of competence motivation and self-efficacy.

PSYCHOLOGICAL STIMULATION AND PERFORMANCE

Arousal is the activation of physiological and psychological responses that vary in intensity from resting to extreme happiness. **Anxiety** is a collection of negative feelings that include fear, worry, and nervousness. A person in a state of anxiety is in a state of arousal, but a person in a state of arousal may or may not be in a state of anxiety. As arousal increases, motor performance tends to increase. According to the Yerkes-Dodson **inverted-U hypothesis**, however, after arousal exceeds the performer's highest level of arousal, performance tends to regress. Some individuals are able to perform well in high-arousal situations, which is dependent on skill level and experience. Those who are predisposed to **trait anxiety**, or anxiety in non-threatening environments, don't do well in high-arousal environments. **State anxiety,** on the other hand, is a temporary state of anxiety and is only triggered in certain situations (e.g., experienced when serving a volleyball in front of others but not when serving alone). Those with high trait anxiety, however, tend to have high state anxiety in high-pressure situations when compared to those with low trait anxiety.

EVALUATING MOTOR SKILLS

Techniques used to evaluate motor skills include observation and comparison to the model or skill cues. Video analysis software (e.g., Coach's Eye) is also effective, as students' skills are performed and recorded, then replayed simultaneously with the model performance or skill cues, which is used to evaluate strong and weak performance areas. Self-assessments, in which the student checks their performance according to the model or cues, can also be used. Pre-assessment and post-assessments of skills is another way to evaluate improvement in motor skills. Tracking student performance over time also provides information on the consistency or stability of a performance and evaluates whether students are able to transfer skills or adapt to other situations.

DETECTING ERRORS IN MOTOR PERFORMANCE

Techniques used to detect errors in motor performance include familiarizing students with the appropriate skill tasks. Using videos tends to work best, as they can be replayed. Students should practice skills, observe their performance, and compare it to the desired outcome (self-assessment and reflection). During this strategy, students should be encouraged to identify and solve their own skill problem and follow it with practice. Attentional focus cues would accompany the video analysis of the skills so that students can develop an understanding and vocabulary for error detection. This technique helps students pay attention to relevant information and begin to detect and correct errors independently.

PROVIDING CORRECTIVE FEEDBACK

Research shows that the best approach to providing effective **error-based** or **corrective feedback** is to surround the error-based feedback with positive feedback, which is widely known as the sandwich method. The focus should be on the desired outcome rather than the error. Therefore, providing skill cues to direct students to the appropriate movement pattern should be given. For example, if a student does not pivot the back foot during the overhand throw, the cue might be "squish the bug" for younger students or "pivot the back foot" for older students—both cues tell the students what to do rather than focus on what they are doing incorrectly.

DELIVERING EFFECTIVE FEEDBACK

To provide effective feedback, the developmental stage or level of the student must be considered. After consideration of the student's level, the activity (or sport), and the feedback schedule, frequency, timing, and precision should all be considered. The interests and motivations of students are also important. For example, a beginner is more likely to respond well to error correction feedback to help improve the action or skill, while this type of feedback would be ineffective for an advanced student because they are able to self-detect and correct their own errors. For

unmotivated or disinterested students, feedback that focuses on the performance of correct actions or skills is more beneficial because this type of feedback fosters engagement in the activity. The amount and precision of feedback varies according to student level, where more feedback is generally given to beginners and tapers off as students progress to higher levels. Feedback should also be vague during the beginner stage and become more precise as students improve.

Elements and Characteristics of Movement

LOCOMOTOR MOVEMENT

Locomotor movements are fundamental movement skills that allow an individual to move from one place to another. There are eight locomotor movements: walking, skipping, jumping, hopping, leaping, sliding, galloping, and running. Children perform most locomotor movements naturally, however, they are developed through play and practice. Most children are proficient in the locomotor movements by age eight. Learning these skills helps students learn how and where the body moves and aids in movement efficiency. Locomotor movements are used to teach movement concepts, including **pathways** (e.g., straight, zigzag), **directions** (e.g., forward, backward), and **time** and **speed** (e.g., fast and slow).

NON-LOCOMOTOR MOVEMENT

Non-locomotor skills are fundamental movements that consist of moving without traveling. Bending, twisting, curling, stretching, reaching, pulling, turning, and swaying are types of non-locomotor movements. **Movement concepts** often taught with non-locomotor movements include personal space, levels (e.g., low, medium, high), directions (e.g., clockwise and counterclockwise), and relationships with the body (e.g., shape formation like round, narrow, twisted, symmetrical, and asymmetrical). In addition to bending and twisting, **skill themes** that complement non-locomotor movements include balancing, jumping and landing, and transferring weight. As students become proficient in non-locomotor skills, they combine them with locomotor and **manipulative skills** to develop mature patterns of movement (e.g., run while jumping; walk while twisting, shuffling, or sliding; and stretching to catch a ball).

RHYTHMIC ACTIVITIES

Rhythmic activity is the combination of body movements and music or sounds. Common rhythmic activities in physical education include creative movement, dance, and gymnastics. **Creative movements** use the body (with or without sound) to communicate. Creative movement is the cornerstone for dance and gymnastics. Creative movements or creative rhythms are designed to give students the freedom of expression to move to their own beat without the pressures of formalized dance or gymnastics (e.g., staying on beat to music, performing steps correctly, performing a routine). By design, there are no mistakes when students move creatively, which helps foster **self-efficacy**, or the belief in one's ability to perform motor skills.

GENERAL SPACE AND PERSONAL SPACE

The two types of space in spatial awareness are general space and personal space. **General space** is the space that does not belong to anyone and is used for students to travel during activities. It is the area in gymnasiums and athletic fields where students have plenty of room to move freely without touching someone or something. **Personal space** belongs to the individual—no one should invade another person's personal space. Personal space is private and is often described as an "arms-length" distance. It is recommended that personal space is taught first because this concept can be taught using non-locomotor movements (bending, twisting, marching in place), which gives students time to focus on and develop awareness of how their bodies move without distraction or interference.

KICKING AND DRIBBLING

Kicking and dribbling are **manipulative skills** because the learner manipulates a ball or a piece of equipment. Manipulative skills are more difficult to grasp because they are used alongside locomotor and non-locomotor movements. Kicking is the act of striking an object, such as a ball, with one foot. Kicking is used in games and sports like soccer, kickball, football, and three-ball kick

baseball. Foot dribbling, which is small, rapid kicking used to advance the ball forward, which occurs in soccer and speedball. Hand dribbling, which uses the hands to advance the ball forward, is evident in basketball and team handball. When manipulative skills are developed, students are likely to be more engaged in physical activities and sports that use these skills.

MATURE MOTOR PATTERNS FOR JUMPING AND LANDING

Jumping is one of the eight locomotor movements. During the jump, the body becomes airborne after pushing off of a surface with two feet and then returns to the surface with a two-foot landing. The two basic jumps include the vertical jump and the horizontal jump (broad jump). A mature horizontal jumping pattern is when the learner bends the knees, swings the arms back, and then swings the arms forward in unison with the jump. These actions help the jumper propel forward. Bent knees and the arm swing are the same for the vertical jump, however, the jumper's arms swing upward instead of forward. These actions help the jumper propel upward. The **landing** in both jumps require soft or bent knees to absorb the force of the ground and protect the knees. Learning the basic jumps helps with positive transfer of jumps used in sports and other physical activities. Jump patterns and techniques vary among sports and sometimes are actually hops (one-foot take off) like in the long jump, triple jump, and high jump sporting events. Other types of jumps include jumping jacks and tuck jumps. Jumps are also present in jump rope, basketball, volleyball, baseball, diving, and jumps that are performed on a trampoline.

OVERHAND THROW

The **overhand throw** is a manipulative skill that involves propelling an object (usually a ball) with one hand above the shoulder. There are generally three phases to the overhand throw: the preparation phase, the execution phase, and the follow-through. In the **preparation phase**, the non-throwing side faces the target and the arm is back with a high elbow. The action of bringing the arm back with the elbow leading is often referred to as the **wind-up phase**. During the **execution phase**, a step is taken with the opposite foot as the elbow leads the arm forward. During this phase, the trunk of the body rotates internally towards the target. The final phase of the overhand throw is when the arm **follows through** diagonally across the body. A one-handed overhand throw is used in several sports, including baseball, softball, basketball, football, and team handball.

STRIKING SKILLS

Striking with an implement is a manipulative skill where an object (e.g., ball) is struck with another object (e.g., racket, paddle, baseball bat, golf club). The implement becomes an extension of the user's body. Striking with implements is taught during the latter part of elementary school as hand-eye coordination and visual tracking are needed to produce mature motor patterns. Further, there are two objects that students have to focus on: the implement and the ball. This increases the complexity of the skill. To prepare students to strike with an implement, striking with body parts (e.g., hands) followed by rackets and paddles is the recommended progression. Longer implements (baseball bat, golf club) increase the difficulty of the skill and should be taught last. There are a variety of physical activities that involve striking with an implement, including golf, baseball, tennis, pickleball, badminton, cricket, and racquetball.

Promoting Student Motor Development

USING ANIMAL WALKS TO AID IN THE DEVELOPMENT OF MOVEMENT SKILLS

Animal walks are fun, simple activities that help students develop gross motor skill movements (locomotor and non-locomotor). Animal walks help students gain understanding of body awareness, body control, spatial awareness, effort, directions, and levels as only the body is needed to accomplish them. Animal walks also allow students to use their imaginations by drawing on previous animal movement knowledge and experiences. Teachers can also check for movement concept understandings by how students respond to animal cues. Examples of animal walk cues include "walk like a sloth," to illustrate the concept of slow movement; "move like a cheetah," to illustrate the concept of fast movement; "show me how an elephant moves," which illustrates a large shape and slow speed; and "slide like a snake," which illustrates a low level and curved pathway. Students also develop strength ("crawl like a bear"), cardiovascular fitness ("run like a fox"), and improve flexibility ("stretch like a dog") from engaging in animal walks, which are needed for more complex skills (chasing, fleeing).

PROMOTING STUDENTS' DEVELOPMENT OF MANIPULATIVE SKILLS

Manipulative activities require the interaction of gross motor and fine motor skills. Strategies used to build manipulative skills include using a variety of manipulable objects. For example, when teaching catching and throwing, different sizes, shapes, and textures of throwing objects should be used with varied distances, targets, and speeds. Performing manipulative skills without locomotor movements before adding locomotor movements also aids in the development of manipulative skills and provides a foundation for game-play actions. An example of this would be to have students start by playing a stationary passing game, then follow that with a game that requires students to run three steps before passing.

CHASING, FLEEING, AND DODGING GAMES

Students should be introduced to chasing, fleeing, and dodging skills after they have demonstrated proficiency in the locomotor movements. Students should also have an understanding of spatial awareness, as chasing, fleeing, and dodging are more complex due to combination movements that often include manipulative skills. It is ideal to teach these activities outdoors to give students a lot of space for safety. Clear boundaries also help facilitate these skills. Tag games are often used to develop chasing, fleeing, and dodging skills where there are one or more chasers, while others are fleeing (running) and dodging (bending or ducking) to avoid getting tagged by the chaser. These movements further promote and enhance the movement concepts of **effort** (speed), **relationships** (with others), and **space** (movement with others within boundaries), which are the skills needed to participate in manipulative games (e.g., basketball, soccer, tennis). As such, these are the foundational elements of defensive and offensive strategies.

USING PARTNER ACTIVITIES TO TEACH LOCOMOTOR AND NON-LOCOMOTOR MOVEMENTS

Strategies used to teach locomotor and non-locomotor movements during partner activities include mirroring, matching, and leading and following. **Mirroring** is when partners are positioned face-to-face and one partner copies the other, **matching** is when partners are positioned side-by-side and one partner copies the other, and **leading and following** is when one partner leads and the other follows. Traveling while mirroring, matching, and leading and following are other strategies used to teach locomotor and non-locomotor movements in pairs. It can be beneficial to have students who are proficient in the movements lead first in order to help the developing students learn the mature movement patterns.

REFINEMENT OF MANIPULATIVE SKILLS

Developmentally appropriate techniques that can aid in the **refinement of manipulative skills** include demonstrations, written and verbal cues, feedback (peer, self, teacher), and video analysis. To further aid in the refinement of manipulative skills, multiple objects with various shapes, textures, and sizes should be used, as well as combination fine and gross motor activities. Student choice and gradual progressions (easy to difficult tasks) increase student motivation to participate in skill development activities. There should also be several opportunities for students to practice, or opportunities to respond, in order to refine skills, which requires an adequate amount of equipment (2-1 ratio). Station practice can be used to facilitate the refinement of skills in isolation at various learning stages, and small-sided games allow students to put skills into practice.

REFINEMENT AND INTEGRATION OF RHYTHMIC ACTIVITIES

Teacher-led movements aid in the refinement and integration of rhythmic activities. This technique allows students to follow the movements of the teacher. Students can also create their own movement patterns or routines by incorporating the movement concepts and integrating locomotor, non-locomotor, and manipulative skills. For example, students might be given 6 to 12 criteria that include the fundamental movement skills and movement concepts. These may include tasks such as four locomotor movements, two rolls, two body shapes, two levels, four balances with different bases of support, and ending on two feet. This example includes both locomotor and non-locomotor movements and several movement concepts, but may also include equipment like balance beams, balls, and ribbons. For students struggling in any of the respective skills, **modifications** or **remediations** should be used. For example, if a student is unable to perform a forward roll, a cheese mat may be useful to give the student more force to turn around the axis of rotation while providing more cushion than regular mats. A student might also use a beanbag between the chin and chest to keep the ball-shaped position needed for the forward roll, which makes it easier to rotate. For students who excel in the forward roll, they should be given additional challenges or **extensions**, like performing a dive roll or multiple rolls in succession.

LOCOMOTOR SKILL INTEGRATION AND REFINEMENT

Using **movement concepts** (spatial awareness, effort, relationships) along with locomotor movements will aid in skill integration and refinement. Adding movement concept tasks helps move students from the basic locomotor movements to more mature movement patterns that are used in games, sports, and other physical activities. Examples of movement concept tasks include walk fast, walk slow, walk on your tip toes, walk on the low beam, walk on the high beam, walk in a circle, walk in a zigzag pattern, walk clockwise, walk counterclockwise; jump high, jump low, jump over, jump alone, jump with a partner; crawl under, crawl in a circle; hop on top, hop over. Another technique is to combine locomotor and non-locomotor movements. For example, run to the cone, touch your toes, leap and hold, jump and turn. Participation in **small-sided and tag games** also aid in the refinement of locomotor skills by giving students optimal opportunities to practice skills. Students are also challenged to transfer movements performed in isolation to performing the skills with obstacles, defenders, boundaries, and rules. Game play criteria requires students to integrate locomotor and non-locomotor movements and movement concepts independently, which fosters thinking and decision-making.

REFINEMENT AND INTEGRATION OF NON-LOCOMOTOR SKILLS

Incorporating the movement concepts (spatial awareness, effort, relationships) will aid in the refinement of non-locomotor movements. Movement concepts help students move from the basic non-locomotor movements to more mature movement patterns that are used in dance, gymnastics, and other physical activities. Examples of non-locomotor movements and (movement concept)

27

tasks include bend one leg, bend two legs, bend one arm, bend your fingers, bend your head up and down (relationship with the body, personal space, and levels); balance on one or multiple body parts; balance on your tip toes; balance in a squat position; twist right, and twist left (relationships with the body and objects, direction, levels). Another technique is to combine non-locomotor movements, which helps with skill integration. For example, balance on one foot while bending the support or non-support leg, or raise and extend (levels and balance) one arm and the opposite leg forward (direction).

COMBINATION MOVEMENT PATTERNS

The overhand throw is a multi-action skill that combines non-locomotor actions with a manipulative skill. Without a ball, all of the movements in the overhand throw are non-locomotor (e.g., non-traveling position, with bending and extending the arm, twisting the torso, and pivoting the foot). The rear or throwing foot pivots simultaneously as the arm, hips, and trunk rotate towards the target. Body weight is evenly distributed on both feet before throwing actions start. The lead foot lifting prior to taking a step forward causes the body to lean slightly sideways, which transfers the thrower's body weight to the rear foot and the body is balanced momentarily on one foot. As the lead foot takes a step and lands, the balance and weight transfer to the lead foot until the follow-through motion is completed.

BALANCE AND WEIGHT TRANSFER DURING THE FORWARD ROLL

The forward roll combines non-locomotor and traveling skills. Movement concepts involved in the forward roll include shape formation (C-shape), balancing on different bases of support and weight transfer (hands, feet, back), and effort (speed). Students should be competent in basic weight transfer tasks before performing the forward roll. Students can practice weight transfer tasks that include foot to foot, from the feet to the hands, and in rocking motions. These actions can progress to being performed on or with equipment or being held (balancing) longer. Rolls that are generally taught before the forward roll include sideways (log and pencil rolls) and the forward shoulder roll. Before teaching the forward roll, students should be strong enough in the arms to support their bodies to reduce the risk of neck and back injuries. Cues to help students perform the forward roll include: 1) squat or crouch down in a C-shape, 2) chin to chest, 3) hips up, 4) push-off hands and feet, 5) body tight, 6) roll onto feet.

AGILITY AND BALANCE

Agility is the ability to move quickly in various directions while maintaining control. Agility is evident in most physical activities and sports. An example of agility is running or shuffling quickly in a zigzag shape, which is a common skill pattern performed in basketball and soccer. Agility is also evident during invasion games when players quickly transition from offense to defense. Agility requires coordination, speed, and balance. **Balance** is what keeps the body stable and upright, which helps keep the body in control. Balance is often highlighted in dance and gymnastics. However, agility is also evident in these activities when performers quickly change directions during sequences.

COMMON COMBINATION STEPS AND SEQUENCING USED IN LINE DANCES

Line dances are dances that can be performed in large groups without a partner, and include locomotor and non-locomotor movements. Basic line dance steps include steps forward, backward, clockwise, counterclockwise, diagonally (three steps and tap), right and left (step touch), or sideways (step-together-step). The grapevine, shuffle, rock steps, taps, and half-turns and quarter-turns are also frequently used. The music used for most line dances is a 4/4 beat, which is a medium to fast tempo. Steps are counted to a 4/4 beat, which usually ends with a tap before changing directions.

An example of a basic step sequence is:

1-4 counts/beats	Walk/step forward and tap
5-8 counts/beats	Walk/step forward and tap
9-12 counts/beats	Grapevine right
13-16 beats	Grapevine left
Repeat	

VERBAL CUEING

Verbal cues reinforce desired movement outcomes and help students perform and improve movement skills. **Verbal cues** are action verbs that should be just a few words or less, usually three or four words, as students are better able to focus their attention and remember short phrases.

Example cues for the overhand throw:

Cue	Desired skill outcome
Squash the bug	Reminds students to pivot as they conduct overhand throw
Pick up the telephone	Wind up phase for the overhand throw
Buckle your seatbelt	Follow-through diagonally across the body

Verbal cues are more effective when coupled with demonstrations and written or visual cues.

KINESTHETIC FEEDBACK

Kinesthetic feedback utilizes proprioception to relay messages from muscles, tendons, and joints to the spinal cord to respond to movement commands. Intrinsic feedback or the knowledge of performance are other terms used for kinesthetic feedback. Kinesthetic feedback allows the performer to feel the movement, which helps skilled performers correct errors. Performers can only correct feedback for slow movements, which occurs at subconscious and conscious levels. When movements are slow, smooth, and continuous, like walking on a balance beam, they are subconsciously compared to previous motor patterns, which aids in the refinement of the skill or routine. At the conscious level, the movements are slow, jerky, or both slow and jerky, like when performing a squat. As such, the kinesthetic feedback is conscious and coupled with visual feedback. Therefore, if one squat was ill-performed, the performer has time to correct the errors before performing another squat. Kinesthetic feedback can be improved through practice and refined by also providing visual feedback (pictures, video) and verbal cues to help with the execution.

VIDEO ANALYSIS FOR FEEDBACK

Video recordings have shown to be more beneficial than other types of feedback because students can watch a demonstration or see their actions and movements, especially when slowed down. Videos can also be replayed. When students are able to view their own performance, it provides instant feedback on the quality or knowledge of performance (technique, skill execution), which other visual aids cannot do. Further, students often believe that they are performing a skill correctly until they view their performance. Video analysis is often considered the gold standard when giving feedback, but to increase effectiveness, it should be used consistently and be paired with verbal feedback. Teachers can also post video demonstrations and analysis online for students for ongoing review to further develop skill competencies.

Movement Concepts and Biomechanical Principles

MOVEMENT CONCEPT OF FLOW

Flow is the contrast between smooth and jerky movements, and the contrast between free and bound movements. **Smooth** movements are fluid, and cues often used to convey this concept are "glide," "melt," and "ooze." In contrast, **jerky** movements are rigid, and cues used to describe this include "rough" and "bouncy." Another type of smooth movement is **free**, in which the movements appear as if the movement is controlling the body rather than the body controlling the movement. An example of free movement is a dancer or an ice skater who spins effortlessly, or someone running downhill without the ability to stop. These movements tend to be fast, which reduces the amount of control the performer has over their movements. In contrast, **bound** movements are always voluntary and controlled and appear tense or stiff at times, like when lifting a heavy object.

BIOMECHANICAL PRINCIPLES INVOLVED IN THE LEAP

Biomechanical principles that are evident during the leap include **power** and **force.** The movement concept categories that are evident are **spatial awareness** (moving through general space), **effort** (force of the leap), and **relationships** with the body and surface. **Power** is strength multiplied by speed (strength × speed), which is generated by the amount of leg force (effort) used during the push-off phase of the leap. The **center of mass** is the equal distribution of the body's weight, which is illustrated during the airborne and landing phases of the leap. Children need to be aware of the relationship of their bodies in-flight and at a medium or high level (spatial awareness).

MOVEMENT CONCEPTS OF TIME AND FORCE

Effort is the movement concept category that includes time, force, and flow. **Time** is either fast or slow, which is the speed, beat, or pace in movement. Fast and slow are often illustrated through dance movements to different music tempos. Distance events like cross country or 100-meter runs and the timing of actions when striking a pitched ball are also evidence of time in physical activity and sports. Changes in time are elicited when the teacher provides opportunities for students to increase (acceleration) and decrease (deceleration) speed at different rates. Force is either strong or light. **Force** is evident in every physical activity because skeletal muscle force is required to move the body. However, the appropriate amount of force to use when performing a certain task (e.g., striking a pitched ball) is learned through practice. Example cues of force are: "stomp hard when you walk," or "walk like a feather" to illustrate and contrast strong and light forces.

SPATIAL AWARENESS AND THE MOVEMENT CONCEPT OF SPATIAL DIRECTIONS

Direction is one movement concept under **spatial awareness** (where the body moves). There are several **directions** or routes the body can take that include traveling forwards and backwards; clockwise and counterclockwise; right and left; up and down, and diagonally. **Spatial directions** are often grouped and taught in pairs (e.g., forwards and backwards) for better conceptual understanding. Proficiency in the directions helps build a strong foundation for combining movement patterns that occur during rhythmic activities and team sport transitions (offense to defense), which often require agility or the quick change in direction.

MOVEMENT CONCEPT OF RELATIONSHIPS WITH OBJECTS

Similar to directions, **relationships with objects** are often grouped in pairs and include on and off, under and over, behind and through. Relationships with objects are taught before relationships with people because there is more predictability with objects. Objects used in physical education include balls, balloons, scarves, cones, ropes, hula hoop boundaries, goals, discs, and targets. These skills are taught alongside locomotor (e.g., walk behind your ball) and non-locomotor (e.g., stand behind your ball) movements. Activities that involve objects allow for fine and gross motor

developments that are needed in more complex manipulative activities and games (soccer, basketball).

BIOMECHANICAL PRINCIPLES IN SPORTS AND PHYSICAL ACTIVITIES

Exercise biomechanics and **sport biomechanics** involve the study of forces (internal and external) that impact human movement during physical activity and sports with the goal to improve performance. To help improve performance, biomechanics focuses on improvements in technique, equipment, training, injury prevention, and rehabilitation. Common units of measure used in biomechanics include length (how far or long), time (how much time it takes to complete a task), and mass and inertia (weight and resistance of a body or a piece of equipment), all of which can promote or impede performance.

BUOYANCY AND DRAG IN SWIMMING

Buoyancy is the ability to float in water or air. **Drag** is the amount of resistance that occurs in the air, water, and the body that can negatively impact one's buoyancy. **Body type,** or the amount of muscle mass and fat mass in the body, is critical for buoyancy. For example, fat mass floats more easily than muscle mass, therefore, students with more muscle mass and little fat will have a more difficult time staying afloat and an easier time sinking than students with less muscle mass and more fat mass. To compensate for drag from the water and body, swim techniques are designed to keep the body afloat, including arm strokes, leg kicks, body position, and breathing techniques. Staying in a **streamlined**, or straight, position and synchronizing breathing with strokes also helps one stay afloat. Relaxing muscles and not fully filling the lungs with air also aids in buoyancy and reduces drag.

PHYSICAL LAWS IN MOVEMENT

Newton's first law of motion is the **law of inertia**, which states that the objects or the body will continue to move or remain unmoved until met with an unbalanced force. The **moment of inertia** is the difficulty in getting a body or object to rotate around an axis. The goal is to reduce the moment of inertia. During the forward roll, the performer pushes off, or applies **force**, with the hands and feet, which moves the body forward and increases **angular velocity,** or the increase in speed around an axis (or the angle turned through per second). The **moment of inertia** will depend on the position, size, and speed of the performer to determine how easy or difficult it will be to roll. Making the body small and compact, with the chin tucked in, and pushing off with great force makes it easier to roll forward because this increases the **angular momentum**, or the **angular velocity** multiplied by the **moment of inertia**. The rolling motion will continue until met with greater force (law of inertia) of the feet or body landing on the floor or mat.

ROLE OF GRAVITY IN BALANCE AND STABILITY

Gravity is an external force that attracts a body or object towards the earth's center and is commonly referred to as the gravitational pull. **Balance** is the ability to stay in an upright position or maintain equilibrium and an equal distribution of body weight on all sides. **Stability** is the body's ability to regain balance after displacement. Stability is impacted by the size of the base of support, weight of the object, and the height of the center of gravity. Since the body is dynamic, its center of gravity can change. As such, the body is able to accomplish stability by changing stances and body positions during movement activities. For example, while surfing, the surfer (body weight) has to bend the legs and extend the arms (a change in body position) with a wide stance (a change in stance) on a surfboard to maintain stability and prevent from falling.

FORCE PROJECTION AND ABSORPTION

Absorption is the body's ability to absorb or reduce the kinetic energy of an object by applying negative force (e.g., catching a ball). The force is absorbed in the muscles, which helps protect the body (bones). Another example of absorption is when landing from a jump. However, the distance or height of the jump can impact the amount of force that can be absorbed, and if too great (e.g., jumping from a 10-story building or into an empty swimming pool), injury and potential death can occur. For some activities, the body is unable to safely absorb kinetic energy, therefore, additional absorption is created. For example, sand is added to the long and triple jump pit, and a mat is used for high jump landing, which are safety measures used to prevent injury.

BIOMECHANICAL PRINCIPLES IN THE OVERHAND THROW

Biomechanical principles used during the wind-up, release, and follow-through phases of the overhand throw include force, torque, acceleration, and the angle of release. **Force** is mass multiplied by acceleration ($F = m \times a$), or the amount of push or pull of an object or body. **Torque** is the force used during twisting actions that often cause rotation. Torque is evident at the shoulder joint during the wind-up phase or external rotation. Torque is also evident during the twisting action or internal rotation of the abdominal trunk during the follow-through phase. **Acceleration** is an increase in speed and **deceleration** is a decrease in speed. Acceleration occurs during the release of the ball, which is often called the speed of release. The **angle of release** is also evident, which is the point that the ball is released at the shoulder joint.

BIOMECHANICAL ERRORS FOR AN OVERTHROWN BALL

An overthrown ball is often the result of throwing too hard (applying too much force), the angle of release being too large, performing little to no follow-through, or a combination of these errors. To correct the overthrown ball, right-hand students should release the ball at the 2 o'clock position as if facing a clock on the wall, and 10 o'clock for left-hand students to adjust the angle and the timing of the release. "Buckle the seat belt" is a cue that can be used for students to follow through diagonally across the body of the throwing arm, or at the 7 o'clock position for right-hand throwers and 5 o'clock for left-hand throwers. The follow-through helps with speed, but also keeps the ball in line with the target.

BIOMECHANICAL ERRORS IN A FREE THROW

A missed free throw can be the result of the shooter lacking upper body strength or leg strength, thus the force applied is not enough for the ball to reach the rim. There may not be enough flexion in the knees to aid in more power. The shooter may be shooting from the palm of the hands rather than rolling the ball upward and across the hand. The student might also be shooting upward instead of up and outward. If maturation is the problem, the student can try to shoot the ball underhanded between the legs (aka the "granny shot"), as more power will be generated, thereby giving the ball more lift force. If maturation is not the problem, the student can be cued to "bend the knees," "bend and jump," or "bend and extend" for more power. Releasing the ball between 50 and 60 degrees may also help the student achieve the goal.

BIOMECHANICAL PRINCIPLES IN THE FOREHAND IN TENNIS

The biomechanical principle most evident in the tennis forehand is torque. **Torque** is the twisting force shown in the external and internal rotation during the racket preparation phase of reaching back (external rotation) to the contact and follow-through phases (internal rotation). **Force** is also evident when the racket makes contact with the ball, which is also under the movement concept **effort.** The striking of the ball sends or projects the ball forward (**projectile motion**). The **timing** of the strike is also a movement concept under the effort category. **Spatial awareness** is evident as the player needs to position themselves to make contact with the ball, and the player illustrates relationships with the self (body awareness); the racket and ball (objects); and, if playing against an opponent, the relationship with another. The player may further illustrate spatial awareness by the direction, pathways, and levels based on the angle of the stroke and desired placement of the ball.

SPATIAL CONCEPT OF PATHWAYS

Pathways is a movement concept under the space and spatial awareness (where the body moves) movement concept category. There are three pathways or patterns the body can create when traveling:

- straight, meaning to walk in a straight line
- curved, or moving in a C-shaped or bent pattern or motion
- zigzag, or moving in a Z-shaped or alternating diagonal pattern or motion

These movement concepts are taught alongside locomotor, non-locomotor, and other movement concepts (e.g., speed, directions, levels). To help students conceptualize and apply pathways, pictures of pathways should accompany the definitions, cues, and phrases used. Associating pathways with previously known information like animals, letters, and gym floor lines also aids in understanding. For example, "walk in a circle" conceptualizes a curved shape, whereas "travel in a 'Z' shape and repeat" would help students understand a zigzag shape.

SPATIAL CONCEPT OF LEVELS

Levels are a movement concept under the space and spatial awareness (where the body moves) movement concept category. The body can move at three levels: low, or below the knees (crawling on the ground); medium, or between the knees and shoulders (walking); and high, or above the shoulders (walking on tiptoes). This movement concept is taught alongside non-locomotor movements first, then progresses with locomotor and other movement concepts (e.g., pathways and direction). To help students conceptualize and apply the concept of levels, pictures of examples of the three levels should accompany the definition, cues, and phrases used. Associating the levels with previously known information like animals or the other concepts aid in understanding. For example, "stretch your hands high towards the sky" conceptualizes a high level, while "lie down on your back like a mat" illustrates a low level.

QUALITATIVE BIOMECHANICAL ANALYSIS

Qualitative biomechanical analyses are commonly used by physical education teachers and coaches. There are generally four steps in a qualitative biomechanical analysis that are used to improve movement skills:

1. Develop a description of the best technique and decide on the desired movement to be observed.
2. Observe the student's performance to determine how the student performs.
3. Compare the student's performance to the desired movement and identify and assess errors.
4. Provide feedback and inform the student with skill cues and other information to correct the errors.

BIOMECHANICAL PRINCIPLES NEEDED TO MAINTAIN BALANCE

The key biomechanical principles involved in **balance** are the stance, base of support, and the center of gravity. The **base of support** is the area below a person that involves each point of contact or the parts of the body that are in contact with the surface. For example, when standing (stance), the base of support is the area where the feet are in contact. In a push-up position (stance), the base of support is the area where the hands and feet are in contact. A narrow base of support (e.g., standing on tiptoes) raises the center of gravity and reduces the area of support, thus limiting stability or balance. Adjustments (leaning forward or backward) are made during different activities (forces) to prevent falling. A wide base of support with bent knees is the ideal position for balance as the center of gravity is lowered, thus aiding in stability and the prevention of falling.

IMPROVING BODY MECHANICS FOR SAFE AND EFFICIENT MOVEMENT

Injury prevention, rehabilitation techniques, and equipment are improvement areas of focus under the study of biomechanics. Sporting injury prevention techniques identified through biomechanics research include bending the knees on landings during gymnastics and adapting the tennis backhand technique to include a neutral wrist position that reduces tennis elbow (overuse). An advance in equipment includes running shoes that provide more cushion to absorb more force. Teachers and coaches also demonstrate an understanding of these principles by taking measures such as requiring the use of mats when students practice tumbling skills and the wearing of shin guards during soccer.

MOVEMENT CONCEPTS AND CREATIVE MOVEMENT

Movement concepts help students take simple movements (locomotor and non-locomotor) and make them more dynamic and interesting to create an aesthetic appeal. The movement concepts give students additional guidance on how and where the body can move. For example, walking in a zigzag pathway allows for more dimension of the movement than walking in a straight line. Forming different shapes (V-shape, X-shape, round shape) while combining locomotor and non-locomotor movements also helps with the aesthetics of movement. Further aiding in the aesthetics of creative movements are the concepts of fast, slow, high, medium, low, jerky, and soft. These concepts help students get comfortable with and refine the fundamental movement skills necessary for dance.

RUNNING PATTERNS IN TEAM SPORTS

In team sports, running patterns are forward and straight and forward and zigzag. Running or jogging backwards may occur during transition play (offense to defense and vice versa). At times, a runner's path may be curved into a clockwise or counterclockwise direction when a player maneuvers to receive a pass or to avoid a defender. Running tends to be fast, but may slow down to a jog or walk. There are also a lot of start and stop patterns (e.g., run-stop-run, run-walk-run, run-jog-run), so runs are intermittent. Runs often change directions quickly, which illustrates agility skills used in these sports.

THROWING PATTERNS IN BASKETBALL AND TEAM HANDBALL

While both basketball and team handball are invasion games that use throwing (or passing) to advance a ball down a court or field, the throwing actions used in each game differ. In basketball, most throws are two-handed chest, bounce, or overhead passes. Sometimes players use one hand to bounce or chest pass, but this technique reduces the power of the pass and is often discouraged. Although a one-handed overhand pass can be used to advance the ball far down the length of the court, it is seldom used. In basketball and team handball, a player has the option to shoot, dribble, pass, fake, or pivot after receiving the ball. In team handball, one-hand overhand throws are most common, however, players sometimes use underhand throws. One-hand bounce passes, chest, and baseball passes are also used. Unlike basketball, which uses jump shots and layups to score, the overhand throw is used to score in team handball against a goalie. The scoring differences are due to the position, size, and height of the goals in each respective sport.

Copyright © Mometrix Media. You have been licensed one copy of this document for personal use only. Any other reproduction or redistribution is strictly prohibited. All rights reserved.
This content is provided for test preparation purposes only and does not imply an endorsement by Mometrix of any particular political, scientific, or religious point of view.

JUMPING PATTERNS USED IN SPORTS AND PHYSICAL ACTIVITIES

Jumping occurs in volleyball, basketball, and jumping rope. It is also central to the high jump, long jump, and triple jump in track and field. Most jumps are vertical, including jump shots and rebounds in basketball, blocking and spiking in volleyball, and while jumping a rope, which consists of an up-and-down motion. Horizontal jumps, however, occur during the standing broad jump, long jump, and triple jump, where the body is propelled forward during the jump. Although the long and triple jumps have a one-foot take-off and two-foot landing, they are still considered jumps. Similar to the track and field jumps, the layup shot in basketball has a one-foot take off and two-foot landing pattern.

Jumping is both an offensive and defensive skill. It can be used to score points in basketball (jump shot) and volleyball (spike). Jumps are also used to prevent opponents from scoring and to gain or maintain possession of the ball (e.g., blocked shot, spike, rebound). Some jumps have a runup or step approach like a layup or spike, while others do not (e.g., jumping rope).

KICKING PATTERNS USED IN SPORTS

Kicking is a manipulative skill that involves striking a ball, object, or body with the foot. Kicking is evident in soccer, kickball, and football. The basic kicking pattern consists of using the top of the foot (shoelaces) to strike behind the ball. Making contact in the center of the ball keeps it on the ground, while contact below the ball propels it in the air. Like throwing, there is a follow-through motion in kicking, however, the kicking follow-through is upward and forward. The hop-step taken by the support, or non-kicking, leg and leaning forward slightly help with power. The placement of the support foot also determines the direction. For example, if the support toes are pointing left, the ball will go in that direction. Soccer skills also include foot dribbling or rapid kicks back and forth between the feet to advance the ball forward. The insides and outsides of the feet are used to dribble in soccer. Punting is a type of kick done for height and distance and is used in soccer and football. The punt consists of kicking a dropped ball and making contact at a 45-degree angle. A step-hop pattern is also used for punting, although the stride is longer.

Individual, Dual, and Team Sports and Activities

CONDITIONING PROGRAMS AND SKILL PROGRESSION TECHNIQUES

Conditioning is the process of getting the body prepared for the physical demands of physical activity and exercise. Conditioning practices are designed to increase health-and skill-related fitness. A general conditioning program consists of a warm-up, health-related movements, skill-related training, and a cooldown with stretching. The intensity of conditioning sessions should gradually progress to reduce the risk of injury or overtraining. This gradual increase is call **progressive overload**, where the intensity of the exercise or activity is above the normal limits. Skill progressions are also used to teach sports, where the easiest form of the skill is introduced and gradually gets more difficult. Skill progressions start at the beginner stage and progressively increase to the advanced stage. A skill progression example for kicking the ball in soccer would be to kick a non-moving ball before kicking a ball in motion or with a partner. In softball, one would strike a ball off of a tee before striking a pitched ball. Each skill builds on the previous skill.

RULES AND SAFETY PRACTICES IN INDIVIDUAL AND DUAL SPORTS

Individual and dual sports often include handheld equipment (tennis racket, golf club) that can increase the risk of accidental injury if not used carefully. Students need to look to make sure that people or objects are not in their personal space or striking distance so that they do not hit someone or something. Cones or poly spots are items that can be used to space and mark off waiting and playing areas. Spacing and positioning away from target areas is also crucial during target activities (archery, darts). A proper warm-up should be conducted, and the proper shoes should be worn to reduce injury (ankle strain or sprain). All safety rules must be explained, and consequences for safety violations must be enforced.

DEFENSIVE STRATEGIES IN INVASION GAMES

Defensive strategies used during invasion games include reducing open space, shuffle steps, drop steps, and fast transitions. Strategies used to reduce open space include staying close to the opponent when they are near the goal. The body should be positioned on the goal side to make it more difficult for the opponent to score. The player should also begin with a large angle for passing and gradually decrease it, executing a technique known as closing the passing lanes. Footwork is also important to help the defender travel faster. Shuffle steps are used because they are quick and crossing the feet over one another slows down lateral movement. Drop steps towards the pass are also used to try to intercept or steal the ball. The defensive player should also leave upon the release of the opponent's pass to increase the likelihood of stealing the ball or forcing a turnover.

OFFENSIVE STRATEGIES IN INVASION GAMES

Invasion games are team sports where the objective of the game is to advance an object (ball, puck, Frisbee) down a field or court to score a point into the opponent's goal. While the specific skill actions differ, offensive movements and strategies are similar. Common offensive strategies used are passing, getting open, or creating space, which are used to advance the ball forward and maintain position in order to attack the opponents' goal. Passing strategies include ball or body fakes, or body feigns, to slow down the opponent. Passes should also be quick to avoid getting trapped or defended. In order to receive a pass, players should get open or create space. To create space, sharp movements, or cuts, are made that may include L-cuts and V-cuts to keep steady motion to avoid the defense stealing the ball. Movement in these letter formations help draw the defense away or in the wrong direction. Body fakes and feigns are also effective because they slow down the opposition by confusing the opponent on the direction of the player. To aid with maintaining possession, screens or picks should be used, which is when a teammate uses their body to block an opponent. All of these strategies aid in the goal of attacking or scoring a goal.

36

EQUIPMENT IN NET AND WALL SPORTS

Net sports have a net that divides the court in half and include striking an object like a ball (volleyball) or shuttlecock (badminton). Some net sports also use rackets (tennis). Wall sports use a ball that is hit off a wall, and some also include rackets (racquetball, squash). Standards (portable poles) are often used to set up volleyball and badminton nets, although some gyms are equipped with built-in standards that lift and lower from the floor. Some schools have outdoor courts, but sports typically played outside can also be played inside gymnasiums. Nets are sometimes interchanged. For example, if volleyball or tennis nets are unavailable, badminton nets might be used and vice versa. Sometimes play occurs without nets or with net substitutes, such as PVC pipes arranged between two cones to represent the height of the net. If court lines are not available, floor tape and cones can be used to establish boundaries.

EQUIPMENT IN COMBATIVE ACTIVITIES

Combative activities include fencing, wrestling, and martial arts. Cardio-kickboxing is a type of combative activity that derived from martial arts. Rather than kicking, punching, or fighting an individual, air punches and kicks are used to improve and maintain health-related and skill-related fitness. Equipment, including punching gloves, mitts, bags, and shin guards, can be used. If equipment is limited, station work can be employed or movements can be done without equipment. For example, while one student uses gloves to punch a punching bag, another student can air punch. Students can switch roles after the allotted time so that all have an opportunity to use the equipment. Equipment should be cleaned after each use or session to avoid passing germs. Fencing is an extracurricular activity that involves a sword or weapon (foil, epee, and saber), a face mask, and a head-to-toe uniform or outfit to protect the body. Wrestling is also an extracurricular activity that involves a thick, large mat, and players wear a singlet and male players wear a groin cup.

RULES FOR PARTICIPANTS AND SPECTATORS

Rules are important to maintain order and promote good classroom management, which helps keep participants, classmates, and spectators safe. Game rules outline the objectives of the game; player positions; movements allowed; boundaries; and fouls or consequences for infractions, like game ejection after committing a flagrant foul. Game rules also govern the expected attire, including clothing, jewelry, and the type of shoe. For example, athletic clothes and shoes are expected to be worn during sporting events and at fitness or workout centers. These expectations are also evident in many physical education programs. Class or gym rules also foster a safe and positive learning environment. Students should be taught the rules and routinely reminded of them. Rules should also be posted for students, players, and spectators. Coaches also have expectations of following the rules and can suffer consequences as well. For example, when coaches exhibit negative behaviors (e.g., yelling at the officials, throwing things, standing when required to sit, or coaching on the court or field), consequences of these violations include team or technical fouls (basketball), yellow and red cards (volleyball and soccer), and ejections from the game (basketball, volleyball, soccer).

DISCIPLINE IN SPORTS

Discipline in sports is the adherence to the game rules and the expectations of the coach or teacher. Discipline also involves actions or practice used to improve skill and fitness. Some players and students have great self-discipline and follow all of the rules and the training involved in sport participation. However, most of the discipline relies on the teacher or coach to enforce consequences for undisciplined behaviors. Physical punishment (e.g., running laps, push-ups) is a form of discipline sometimes used in sports, however, this type of consequence is discouraged. Other types of consequences include the temporary or permanent removal of the activity or a reduction in playing opportunities.

ETIQUETTE IN SPORTS

Etiquette refers to the unwritten rules of conduct that participants and spectators are expected to adhere to. Etiquette helps to promote safety, fair play, and values. **Sportsmanship** is a term associated with sports etiquette, which includes following the rules, "playing hard but fair," accepting the officials' decisions, shaking the opponents' hands after play, and refraining from outbursts and the taunting of players. Wishing the opponent "good luck" and losing without anger are also examples of sportsmanship, as the enjoyment of the game supersedes the outcome. Sports etiquette also includes remaining silent during a free throw, volleyball or tennis serve, and before the start of a track or swim event.

TEAMWORK IN SPORTS

Teamwork is the collective effort of a group to reach a common goal. In dual and team sports, teammates work together to score or win a game. The level of teamwork is dependent on the players, the coach, leadership (e.g., captains and managers), the size of the team, and the amount of time a team has been together. For example, teams of two have fewer distractions and attitudes to manage than teams of six, 11, or 25. Teams that have been together a long time tend to have better social cohesion (the degree to which groups get along) than newly formed groups. Further, the more things that players have in common (skill, age), the more likely a team is to work together. Task cohesion also helps establish teamwork, as the desire to win is so important that the team is more likely to cooperate with each other.

APPROPRIATE PARTICIPANT AND SPECTATOR BEHAVIOR IN SPORTS

Participants are expected to follow the rules of the sport, accept the coaches and referees' decisions, and engage in fair play. In team sports, spectators are expected to make noise and to cheer for their team except during penalty shots or kicks. There are exceptions, such as the fact that spectators tend to make noise during basketball free throws. Spectators are expected to be quiet during golf strokes, tennis and volleyball serves, and at the start of track and swim events. Spectators are also expected to refrain from jeers and profanity.

DIFFERENCES IN ETIQUETTE BETWEEN SINGLE, DUAL, AND TEAM SPORTS

Etiquette differences between single, dual, and team sports are noise level, attire, and warm-up procedures. In team sports, crowd participation is encouraged, therefore there is a high level of noise during game play. In contrast, in individual and dual sports, crowd participation is not encouraged during game play, therefore, the noise level is much lower. The attire also varies. For example, a collared polo shirt is expected to be worn while playing golf, but jerseys are worn in team sports. Jewelry is not worn during team sports, but may be worn during individual and dual sports. Warm-ups also differ. For example, in team sports, opponents tend to have separate warm-up sessions, but in tennis, the opponents warm up with each other (warm-up strokes and practice serves are done collaboratively).

ELEMENTS OF SUCCESSFUL PERFORMANCE IN INDIVIDUAL SPORTS

Self-efficacy is belief in one's ability to perform motor skills. Building a performer's self-efficacy positively impacts performance. According to Bandura, self-efficacy can be enhanced through performance accomplishments, vicarious experiences, persuasion, and physiological state. Goal setting also aids in improving self-efficacy. **Performance accomplishments** include the individual reflecting on previous and current performances to set goals on the desired performance. **Vicarious experience** is learning by observing others complete the desired task (modeling). **Persuasion** is a strategy used to encourage the individual, but the individual must respect and value the person (coach, teacher) who is doing the persuading for it to be effective. Last, the physiological state is dependent on the individual's arousal levels and their ability to focus on important tasks. Therefore, for a successful performance, the individual needs to be able to focus on important factors and ignore meaningless information (selective attention) to improve performance outcomes. These elements are also effective in dual and team sports, although there are more variables that affect performance to consider (e.g., teammates).

ELEMENTS OF SUCCESSFUL PERFORMANCE IN DUAL AND TEAM SPORTS

Successful performance in dual and team sports is enhanced with team cohesion, established team roles, and goal setting, which fosters cooperation. Team cohesion is when all members of the group or team have the same goal (to win), which has shown to positively impact team performance. Cooperation can be developed by having identified roles (captains, positions) and acknowledgement of the benefits of informal roles. Also aiding in cooperation is sharing individual goals, formulating group goals, and including everyone in the decision-making process. Training should also be fun but challenging, which contributes to an athlete's performance and satisfaction. Collectively, these factors are the elements of successful performance in dual and team sports.

IMPROVING STUDENTS' PERFORMANCE IN INDIVIDUAL SPORTS

Modeling, mental practice, and physical practice are strategies used to improve students' performance in individual sports. **Modeling** is observing the desired performance skill(s) with the goal of replicating the movements. This can be done by observing a teammate, coach, teacher, or by watching a video demonstration. **Mental practice**, also referred to as mental imagery and mental rehearsal, is visualizing or thinking about the performance or skills to be executed. Mental practice is more effective when used in conjunction with **physical practice**, or performance of the skills.

IMPROVING STUDENTS' PERFORMANCE IN TEAM SPORTS

Practice helps students improve performance in team sports. There are several practice types, including variable practice, massed practice, distributed practice, blocked practice, and serial practice. While all of these types of practices can benefit students' performance in team sports, variable practice has shown most effective. **Variable practice** is performing the same skill in a changing or dynamic environment as it would occur in a game setting. For example, when practicing receiving a pass in soccer, basketball, or flag football, the coach would create different angles and distances for receiving the pass, as the environment is constantly changing. As such, students are better able to respond to the dynamic situations that occur during game play, thus improving performance.

DEVELOPING TEAMWORK

Strategies that help improve teamwork include program structure, communication, goal setting, and shared responsibilities. The **structure of the program** (practices and games) is designed by the coach and includes team organization (time, day, and location of practices; rules; positions; playing time). **Input** (communication) from all members in the group on goal setting (individual and team), **shared responsibilities** (everyone sets up and breaks down the equipment), and team building activities are additional strategies that improve teamwork. Team building activities include trust falls, high-ropes courses, tug-of-war, the human knot, and spending time together in non-sporting activities, which are often done before sports practices begin.

IMPROVING SKILL COMBINATIONS

Part practice is a strategy used to improve skill combinations that are low in organization but high in complexity. **Part practice** is the process of breaking down each segment of the skill before combining the whole movement. For example, the overhand volleyball serve has several parts: the stance, toss, footwork, contact, and follow-through. When using a part practice approach, each part of the serve would be taught in isolation. Each element would build on another before combining all of the elements to perform the serve. Small-sided games also help improve skill combinations, as the combination of isolation skills are put into practice and the opportunities to respond are increased. For example, in a two vs. two game of basketball, players have more opportunities to practice combination skills like dribbling and shooting, dribbling and passing, or shooting and rebounding.

SELECTING SPORTS ACTIVITIES THAT PROMOTE PERFORMANCE

The selection of developmentally appropriate sports activities helps promote performance. The national and statewide physical education standards and physical education curricula are organized by scope and sequence. **Scope and sequence** are a gradual building of concepts and skills that consider the development rather than the age of students. Once skills or concepts are learned, they continue to be promoted, thus refining performance. For example, when striking with an implement, starting with a short-hand implement is introduced before a long-hand implement due to the increase in difficulty. As students learn these skills, the skills are revisited and performed in small-sided or real game play to promote skill refinement, which in turn promotes performance.

SIMPLIFICATION TO PROMOTE PERFORMANCE IN SPORT ACTIVITIES

Simplification is a method used to break down skills to promote performance. An example of simplification for the overhand volleyball serve would be to use a larger or lighter ball such as a beach ball, move closer to the net, or slow down the pace of the serve to allow more time to perform the serve. As students become proficient with the simplified versions, modifications would be gradually eliminated. Simplifying game rules also helps promote performance. For example, during a volleyball rally, a simplified rule may be to allow the ball to hit the floor one time before making a play to help students work on footwork and reaction time needed to make contact with the ball. This simplification slows down the pace of the game to promote passing skills without a lot of interruptions.

ADAPTATIONS AND MODIFICATIONS TO PROMOTE PERFORMANCE IN SPORTS

Adaptations and **modifications** are things that make tasks easier to promote performance. In net activities like tennis, badminton, and volleyball, adaptations and modifications that can be used include lowering the net. In volleyball, the rules can be modified to allow the ball to bounce once on the floor during play to give students more time and opportunities to respond. In tennis, the ball can similarly be allowed to bounce twice. During target activities (archery, throwing), there can be various target distances to accommodate all student levels and abilities. In team sports, the number of players can increase or decrease. Multiple balls can also be used to give more opportunities to respond, and boundaries can be eliminated in both individual and team sports to promote continuous play.

TACTICAL GAMES APPROACH

The **tactical games approach** is a strategy used to teach team sports. The goal is to develop the cognitive aspects of team sports that includes skills, decision-making, and strategies, thus fostering understanding. There is an intentional focus on developing intrinsic motivation. Rather than the direct teaching of skills in isolation that eventually lead up to game play, the tactical games approach uses a whole-part-whole method in which students play the game first after an objective has been presented ("Today, we will focus on how to get open"). The teacher observes student behaviors to determine areas of growth. However, feedback is given in the form of questions (inquiry-based) to the group to help guide the students in solving problems. For example, the teacher might state, "I noticed that Team A had a difficult time getting open. What are some things we can do to get open?" With the teacher's guidance, students brainstorm and share techniques, then implement them during the next game play session. Game play is paused for a debrief session to discuss if and how the objective was met. Students then practice the identified problem(s) and return to play to work on implementing concepts, skills, or strategies in the game that were discussed during the debriefing session.

SPECIFICITY IN PRACTICE

Practice specificity is the practice of skills and movements as they appear in a game rather than in isolation. Practice specificity is often accomplished through small-sided games. For example, in basketball where a game consists of five vs. five, a small-sided game may consist of two vs. two or three vs. three. Instead of 11 vs. 11 in soccer, there may be three vs. three or five vs. five games. A three vs. three game of keep-away could also be used to teach passing and movement skills used in a real game, as the dynamic movements in the skills mimic game play. The inclusion of a referee or line judge also provides a game-like situation where calls, fouls, and other infractions are being made.

Performance Activities and Non-traditional Recreational Activities

JAZZ AND MODERN DANCE

Jazz and modern dance are social dances that require good posture and body alignment, as this is the foundation used in dance. These dances involve constant changes between neutral movements (static or isometric movements that are held for a period of time such as in a stretch) and dynamic movements (active, controlled movements through a full range of motion).

Basic dance skills used in most dance forms include locomotor and non-locomotor movements:

- Bending (non-locomotor)
- Stretching (non-locomotor)
- Rising (non-locomotor)
- Sliding (locomotor)
- Jumping, or leaping (locomotor)
- Darting (locomotor)
- Turning (non-locomotor)

While the steps in jazz and modern dance are similar, as both consist of free and creative movements, jazz dance has faster tempos and more elaborate movements than modern dance, and may include ballet and hip-hop movements. Modern dance tends to include several dance forms, but the movements are more connected to or guided by the music.

DANCE SEQUENCES IN FOLK DANCE AND SQUARE DANCE

Folk dance is a dance form that is the expression of cultural traditions and customs. Folk dances tell stories about a particular group of people, and are part of rituals and ceremonies like weddings, births, funerals, holidays, and social events. Folk dances also express the trials and tribulations marking certain time periods or eras. Sequences and steps used in folk dance include the basic dance steps, but they are performed in accordance to the beat of the music. Folk dances are often performed by several couples (pairs) at one time. Steps include step close, step-cross-step (grapevine), step point, step hop, slide steps, and step swing, and the steps repeat along with the music. While some folk dances may be ethnic dances, **ethnic dances** are associated with or originate from a specific ethnic group's culture (African, Asian, European). **Square dance** has explicit dance moves that are verbally called out (by a caller) along with music. Square dance is performed with four couples, called a set, who are numbered 1, 2, 3, and 4. Couples 1 and 3 are the head couples and face each other, and couples 2 and 4 face each other. Square dances start by bowing or honoring your partner and corner. Some movements are performed as a group, including grand marches. Other movements involve changing partners, such as swing your corner, or steps, including forward and back, do-si-dos, promenades, and circling left or right.

CONDITIONING PROGRAMS FOR DANCE

Conditioning for dance is similar to other forms of physical activity and sport, and should include exercises that address the health-related fitness components. For building cardiovascular endurance and stamina, aerobic dance is effective because it continuously engages large muscle movements needed for dance. Dance also requires muscular strength, muscular endurance, and flexibility, and so a dance conditioning program should incorporate activities that involve muscle contraction and muscle relaxation. Core strength (abdominals and back) is essential for good posture and body alignment is needed for dance. Depending on the goals and needs of the dancer, cardiovascular activities should be done three to five days a week, strength training two or three days a week, and flexibility training four to six days a week.

SAFETY PRACTICES WHEN TEACHING DANCE

Safety considerations in dance include posture and body alignment training; a warm-up (to prepare the body for more vigorous activity); dancing on non-slip floors; having students wear the appropriate footwear; providing water breaks before, during, and after dancing; using damage-free equipment; and a cooldown (to return the body back to normal). Other safety considerations include maintaining adequate spacing so that students do not bump into each other, having the instructor positioned to where all students can be seen, or performing dance in a space that has mirrors for multiple angles of visibility.

EQUIPMENT USED IN DANCE

One of the most common types of equipment used in dance is a sound system or device to play music and speakers or amplifier to project the music. Metronomes can also be used to help keep students on beat. Drums, other percussion tools, and musical instruments can be used to create sounds that accompany dance. A microphone aids in voice projection that can be heard while the music is playing. A wireless microphone allows the teacher to move around during instruction. Dances that involve jumps, leaps, and tumbling may be done on mats. Although not required, dance studios or gyms with mirrors provide a visual of the performer and during teacher-led instruction, allowing for all to be seen. Circus arts such as aerial dances require a high level of expertise, as dancers perform while suspended in the air.

WALKING, JOGGING, AND HIKING

Walking, jogging, and hiking are recreational activities that can be done over a lifespan. These cardiovascular activities are non-competitive, and most people are able to participate with little or no equipment. To improve fitness, these activities should be done several days a week and get progressively more challenging. Increasing the frequency (how often), time (duration), or intensity (effort and speed) of an activity, along with setting goals, can help aid in improving outcomes. For example, a beginner may start with walking for 10 minutes and gradually increase the time by 5-10 minutes every two weeks. To increase the intensity, they might walk faster or hike. One may also start with a 20-minute walk and incorporate intermittent bouts of jogging in between (interval training), which also increases the intensity. Accountability measures also help with improving fitness that involve walking, jogging, and hiking, like the use of pedometers or activity trackers to track or monitor step count, calories burned, distance covered, and elevation (for hiking, walking, or jogging upwards).

ORIENTEERING

Orienteering is an outdoor adventure activity designed to teach students how to use maps and a compass by following routes and finding checkpoints. Each checkpoint has a score, with higher point values for increased difficulty (rough terrain, longer distances). Orienteering involves physical activity (running), and students have to learn how to pace themselves (walk, jog, or run without getting fatigued or "running out of gas"). Maps should be in paper format and a handheld compass is used. Teamwork and decision-making are also involved and can be designed for cooperative and competitive engagement. To help build students' skills with maps and compasses, partners or teams can be given short routes. Students can also create their own maps to use throughout the unit. Because an efficient use of time is critical in orienteering, students must know how to pace themselves. Distance by pace is a common technique used to help students establish a proper pace. Set up practice courses of 100 feet and have students count the number of times one foot (right or left) touches the ground. The number of times the foot touches the ground should be divided by 100, or the course length, to get a pace count. Varying the terrain by distance (e.g., a half-mile to one or two miles) can also help students work efficiently, which is called distance by terrain.

43

In descriptive orienteering, maps are not used. In lieu of maps, bearing (the degrees between map points), distance, and descriptive clues are given to help complete the routes.

SWIMMING SAFETY

Water safety guidelines should be taught before swimming skills. Water safety includes the following:

- Never swim alone
- Jump in water feetfirst
- Avoid attempting to save someone from drowning if untrained
- Do not run on pool decks
- Wear life jackets on boats
- Avoid playing breath-holding games
- Wear proper swim attire

Introductory swimming skills should be taught first and include pool entry and exit, blowing bubbles, opening eyes under water, floating, treading water, and motions or land demonstrations of the swim stroke. The front crawl or freestyle stroke is generally taught first, using the part method because it is a multi-limb activity that includes arm strokes, kicks with the legs and feet, and breathing.

As such, skills are broken down. Examples of skill progression include:

- Floating, both on the front and the back
- Treading water
- Breathing (blowing bubbles from the mouth and nose, alternating breathing)
- Alternating arm action (on land, standing in water, and with flotation device)
- Kicking action (holding onto pool wall and with kickboard)
- Front crawl or freestyle practice – putting the skills together

PERIODIZATION IN SPORTS CONDITIONING

Periodization is a structured training program used by athletes that is broken down into three phases.

1. Phase 1 is the **transition** or **post-season stage**, when athletes are tired and take time off to recover from the season for about three or four weeks. To maintain fitness during this stage, athletes continue to work out, however, they engage in cross-training activities that differ from their regular sports training.
2. Phase 2 is the **preparation** or **pre-season stage.** This is a stage, lasting three to six months, where athletes prepare for competition. There are two sub-phases:
   a. The **general preparatory** phase, where the focus is on fitness
   b. The **specific preparatory** phase, where training is specific to the skills and techniques needed for the sport.
3. Phase 3 of periodization is the **competition phase,** where the athlete maintains fitness and works on sports skills and techniques that enhance competitive play.

BOWLING

Bowling is a recreational activity that involves rolling a ball down a lane with the goal of knocking down 10 pins. It is also a manipulative activity. While bowling pins can be set up in the gym or outside on the ground to help students learn, bowling is generally played at a bowling alley. The bowling ball has three holes, two in the middle for the middle and ring finger and one to the side for the thumb. The **grip** (ball hold) of the bowling ball can cause stress on the forearms, so forearm exercises can be used to strengthen this area. An underhand motion is used to roll the ball using a delivery (approach and release) of one to five steps. The one-step delivery is taught before the other deliveries in progressive order, as it is easier. Students should aim for the pins using an imaginary line from the delivery to the targeted pins. Markers are on the floors at bowling alleys to help guide bowlers. A skills progression example is: stationary, two-hand ball roll; stationary, one-hand ball roll; one-step delivery; and so on. The distance of the pins can also be progressed by starting the pins closer and gradually increasing the distance until they reach regulation distance (60 feet). Lane width can be adjusted as well, from wider to narrower, until reaching regulation bowling width (42 inches).

IMPORTANCE OF RULES AND SAFETY PRACTICES IN VARIOUS RECREATIONAL ACTIVITIES

In swimming and other aquatic activities, rules are important because people can drown quickly in bodies of water. Pool rules also help keep patrons and participants safe (e.g., prohibiting running to avoid slipping and falling, avoiding swimming in extremely cold water to prevent hypothermia). For road activities (cycling, in-line skating) wearing a helmet protects the skull from subsequent injuries (and possibly death) should an accident occur. Individuals engaging in road activities should follow all traffic rules to prevent accidents. Appropriate attire helps protect the body from the elements (e.g., light and loose clothing during the heat, and wick-away layers during the cold). Drinking fluids helps prevent dehydration. For hiking, following hiking trails monitored by park rangers, competence in using a map and compass, and hiking with others are important safety measures that prevent one from getting lost. Sharing the hiking itinerary with someone not hiking is a safety measure that can be used in case one does get lost or injured on the trail. Proper hiking gear (boots, socks, and clothing) prevents slippage and weather-related issues (e.g., sunburn, wind, precipitation). It is also best to stay visible and move to the right so faster hikers can progress. Carrying a cell phone, when possible, is another safety measure to use when hiking.

DISCIPLINE IN VARIOUS RECREATIONAL PURSUITS

To engage in recreational activities, self-discipline is required, especially when no officials, leaders, teachers, or coaches are monitoring practice, training, or safety. Discipline requires that the individual follow the rules of play and engagement along with consistent fitness and skill training that have shown to lead to successful outcomes in recreational activities. Discipline fosters the motivation to train, practice, study the activity, and observe behaviors that will improve performance or outcomes of consistent performance (e.g., cardiovascular fitness). Focusing on the outcome or creating measurable goals and accountability measures (tracking progress, fitness testing, planning) helps instill discipline.

GENERAL SPORTS ETIQUETTE

General sports etiquette practices include:

- Listen to the coach
- Know the game rules
- Put forth effort
- Respect all participants
- Discuss disagreements, don't yell
- Be fair (keep score, admit fouls and infractions, make the right call)
- Do not use profanity
- Be a gracious winner and loser (e.g., no bragging after a win and no sulking after a loss)
- Shake hands at the end of a game or match

- Help teammates and opponents if they fall or injure themselves
- Provide words of encouragement to teammates
- Thank the coach after games and practices

SAFETY PRACTICES AND CONSIDERATIONS IN RECREATIONAL ACTIVITIES

Safety practices reduce or eliminate injury or traumatic experiences that may occur when walking, jogging, or running outdoors. Safety considerations include wearing proper athletic shoes to support the feet and ankles. Clothes that do not restrict movement should be worn. Running with a buddy or in high-visibility areas is recommended to avoid potential harm. Wearing sunscreen and hats can prevent or limit sun damage and lower skin cancer risks. In extreme heat, the coolest part of the day should be chosen to engage in activities. Drinking fluids (water) before, during, and after activity keeps the body hydrated and reduces the risks of dehydration, which can lead to heat exhaustion and heat stroke. More fluids are needed in hotter temperatures. When cold, layering clothes and wearing wicking materials keeps the body warm and dry, which prevents hypothermia.

SUPERVISING STUDENTS IN RECREATIONAL PURSUITS

Issues and procedures to consider when supervising students in recreational pursuits include students changing clothes, locker room or change room duties, hygiene, classroom management of large or multiple classes, equipment, taking attendance, and safety. To promote a safe environment, the national physical education recommendations for teacher-student ratio is 1-25 for elementary; 1-30 for middle school, and 1-35 for high school. For class sizes larger than this, a request should be put in for a teacher's aide. Routines (roll call, or attendance; warm-up; squad lines, teams, or groups) will aid in classroom management, but consistency should be employed. Further, positive reinforcement should be used to encourage favorable behaviors, and consequences should be issued for not adhering to routines. If students change clothes, it is important to adhere to all local and state guidelines to ensure that students are safe but have an appropriate level of privacy. As such, a time limit should be allotted, and if a locker room is used, there should be adult supervision to help students move quickly and prevent theft or bullying. Student hygiene can be problematic because students might not shower after physical activity. Providing adequate time and a private space to shower are ways to address this issue.

INSTRUCTIONAL TRANSITIONS

Issues with instructional transitions involve time and students finishing early. To help expedite transitions, transitions should be planned and written out ahead of time. Clear, quick, and concise start and stop signals ("Go," or a single whistle blow) help speed up transitions. Students who complete activities early can continue and rotate to the next station and repeat until the cue to stop has been given. This transition strategy keeps students engaged. Timing activities instead of giving a repetition prompt can also help manage transitions. For example, students might engage in the activity for two minutes until they are cued to stop instead of completing 10 jumping jacks or kicks, as students will finish at varying times.

EQUIPMENT MANAGEMENT PRACTICES

The lack of equipment, cost, transportation, storage, distribution, cleaning, and repairing are common equipment issues that impact physical education programs. Procedures to help with transporting equipment include setting up or organizing equipment in the space one or two days prior to the lesson. Equipment transition time and distribution procedures can also be built into the lesson. Students can help set up, distribute, and break down equipment by groups, teams, or partners. Students can also be assigned or taught to wipe down equipment after each use. If there is not enough equipment to teach an activity or unit, equipment can be made or modified, or multiple activities can go on simultaneously to give students opportunity to engage in the activities regardless of equipment availability. Requesting funding for equipment from a PTA or PTO can also be considered. Storage facilities should be easy to access and secure, and old or damaged equipment should be discarded and replaced when possible. Keeping an inventory to avoid repeat orders should aid in maximizing equipment budgets. Assessing what students want can also aid in utilizing equipment.

LOGISTICS REGARDING FACILITIES, SPACE, STAFF, AND TECHNOLOGY

Physical education facilities and teaching spaces are often shared by other classes. Classes also tend to be large and understaffed with limited technology. Team planning should occur to determine who will teach, what will be taught, and where (in the gym or outside field) the class will occur. Team teaching might also be employed for large classes so that one teacher is leading instruction while the other is monitoring student behavior. To accommodate technology needs, professional development with instruction technology (IT) personnel should be requested to discuss the desired technology uses (videography, LCP projector). When recording students, parental permission needs to be granted. Physical education teaching spaces are often interrupted for school assemblies and other non-PE curriculum activities. To reduce the number of interruptions, a yearly teaching plan with a calendar should be made, compared to the school's calendar, and shared with school leadership to avoid scheduling conflicts.

Copyright © Mometrix Media. You have been licensed one copy of this document for personal use only. Any other reproduction or redistribution is strictly prohibited. All rights reserved. This content is provided for test preparation purposes only and does not imply an endorsement by Mometrix of any particular political, scientific, or religious point of view.

Selecting, Adapting, and Modifying Activities

SELECTING AND MODIFYING ACTIVITIES BASED ON STUDENT CHARACTERISTICS

Students are diverse and vary in abilities and learning styles. It is important to use a variety of teaching methods to increase effectiveness. Asking students their preferred methods of learning might assist with student engagement and learning. Observations and assessment of abilities should help with the differentiation of instruction. From observation and student data, **modifications** (aka adaptations) should also be used to accommodate diverse learners by making tasks easier or more challenging. For example, allowing students to walk during activities that require a jog, or increasing the speed for students who find jogging too easy. Another modification example is to allow novice students to strike a ball from a stationary tee instead of a pitched ball, whereas a student on the baseball team might practice striking a ball from a pitching machine. The teacher can also incorporate students' personal goals into activities throughout the unit or academic year.

SELECTION OF ACTIVITIES AND GAMES BASED ON INSTRUCTIONAL GOALS

Instructional goals are dependent on national, state, and district standards. Content standards help guide the instructional framework, thus they set the objectives or instructional goals. There are three objective domains:

- psychomotor
- cognitive
- affective

The psychomotor domain is where most PE objectives are derived, as the focus is on the motor development of skills (throwing, kicking). The cognitive domain is the knowledge and understanding component that should align to the psychomotor domain (explaining or identifying the cues for throwing or kicking). The affective domain focuses on values, feelings, and attitudes (assisting with cleanup or helping a classmate perform a skill).

SELECTING, ADAPTING, AND MODIFYING ACTIVITIES BASED ON A RANGE OF SKILL LEVELS

Differentiation is tailoring education to meet each student's needs. During times when individualized instruction is impossible (large class sizes, little instructional time), teachers can create a variety of learning opportunities and experiences to help meet objectives. For example, a teacher can set up beginner, intermediate, and advanced activities that students can choose from. Students may be in all three groups depending on the skill(s). To ensure that all students are able to work on each skill, the class can be divided into groups that rotate through the type of activity. The difficulty level for practicing can be self-targeted by the student.

Basketball examples:

Skills	Beginner	Intermediate	Advanced
Dribbling	Stationary dribble	Walk and dribble	Run and dribble
Jump shots	5-foot jump shot	10-foot jump shot	15-foot jump shot
Applied practice	Two vs. two	Three vs. three	Five vs. five

In this situation, students would cycle through three stations. When they go to the jump-shot station, students can pick the distance that they think they need to practice to appropriately meet their current skill level. Coaches standing nearby can help students make a better choice if they pick a target that is too easy or too hard for them. This style of variation allows for both differentiation of skill type and adequate variety for each student's skill level.

SELECTING, ADAPTING, AND MODIFYING ACTIVITIES AND GAMES BASED ON EXCEPTIONAL NEEDS

There are students already competent in the motor skill objectives planned, while others are still developing or may have a disability. **Extensions** are a type of modification that makes tasks more challenging for students with high ability or who are competent in the tasks. For example, a student on the volleyball team may work on jump serves or target serving rather than the underhand and overhand serves during the service unit. These students can also peer-teach to demonstrate their understanding of the skills and movement concepts. There are also simplified versions (**remediations**) of the skill for students who need more time and direction to grasp the tasks or concepts. There are also students who need additional supports or adaptations that include playing basketball in a wheelchair or using a ramp to assist a wheelchair-bound student in bowling. Modifications or adaptations can be task specific (e.g., use a two-handed, underhand basketball free throw for students who have not developed their upper-body strength), equipment specific (e.g., lower or raise the net in volleyball, or use different size balls), or boundary, or space, specific (e.g., increase or decrease boundaries).

Major Body Systems and Physical Activity

MUSCULOSKELETAL SYSTEM AND PHYSICAL ACTIVITY

The musculoskeletal system is a combination of the muscular and skeletal systems that is comprised of muscles, bones, and joints. The skeletal system includes bones, cartilage, ligaments, and joints, and provides the body with protection, support, and movement. There are several types of joint movements, but the most common used during physical activity are synovial joints, which are moveable joints. There are three types of muscles (smooth, cardiac, skeletal) that make up the muscular system. However, skeletal muscle (voluntary movement) is responsible for mobility and movement via muscular contraction. Muscles are attached to bones and cause them to move, which changes the angle of the joint (increases, decreases, rotates, extends). These components work in unison for movement to occur, thus they are the components responsible for physical activity. Repetitive and consistent use of the musculoskeletal system has a positive impact on fitness, which translates to better health.

CIRCULATORY AND RESPIRATORY SYSTEMS AND PHYSICAL ACTIVITY

The circulatory system is responsible for blood transport around the body through blood vessels to the heart and lungs. The respiratory system is primarily contained in the lungs and is responsible for oxygen transport and excreting carbon dioxide from the body during physical activity, which is also known as gas exchange. During exercise, respiration increases to accommodate the oxygen demands of the muscles, and circulation also increases to bring more blood to the working muscles. During respiration, oxygenated air is inhaled through the nose or mouth and travels through the windpipe (trachea), to the bronchial tubes, and then to the lungs. The alveoli in the lungs are where gas exchange occurs (deoxygenated blood for oxygenated blood) and carbon dioxide (waste product) is exhaled.

DIGESTIVE AND EXCRETORY SYSTEMS AND PHYSICAL ACTIVITY

The digestive and excretory systems work in unison. The digestive system is responsible for converting food into energy and transporting nutrients to the body via blood and other tissues. The excretory system is responsible for removing waste, including blood, from the body. The digestive tract includes the mouth, esophagus, stomach, and the small and large intestines and is responsible for excreting urine and feces. During physical activity, the excretory system rids the body of water through sweat and the lungs of carbon dioxide through exhalations. Physical activity strengthens the digestive track, which makes it easier to remove waste.

IMMUNE, ENDOCRINE, NERVOUS, AND INTEGUMENTARY SYSTEM AND PHYSICAL ACTIVITY

Engaging in regular physical activity helps boost **immunity** by increasing white blood cells, which help fight off disease. Getting a cold or the flu also become less likely as the body flushes bacteria from the lungs more efficiently. The **endocrine system** is comprised of the pituitary gland (increases bone and muscle mass), thyroid (regulates heart rate, blood pressure, and body temperature; also increases alertness), adrenal gland (aids in anti-inflammatory response and helps regulate hydration), and the pancreas (helps transport glucose to the working muscles). It also regulates insulin, a process that is improved by physical activity. The **integumentary system** is the function of the skin, which is the point where sweat is released, therefore aiding in thermoregulation. As the body heats up during physical activity, the body releases water (in the form of sweat) to cool off and maintain homeostasis. When the body gets too cold, the skin contracts to retain heat. During physical activity, the **sympathetic nervous system** responds and is responsible for the increase in heart rate. As physical activity diminishes or slows down, the **parasympathetic nervous system** slows down respiration and heart rate.

Cardiovascular Endurance and Aerobic Activities

ACUTE RESPONSES TO AEROBIC EXERCISE

Acute responses when performing aerobic exercise include an increase in ventilation, cardiac output, heart rate, and stroke volume. However, after longer durations of continuous aerobic exercise, cardiac output occurs at a constant rate. Blood flow is also redistributed during aerobic exercise because during rest, about 83 percent of the blood is distributed between the muscles, liver, kidneys, and brain. During aerobic exercise, 84 percent of the blood is redistributed towards the working muscles. This is able to occur because **vasodilation**, or the widening of the of blood vessels, allows for greater blood flow to the muscles.

DIFFERENTIAL PHYSIOLOGICAL RESPONSES TO AEROBIC ACTIVITY

At rest, aerobically conditioned or trained individuals will have lower blood pressure, lower resting heart rate, greater stroke volume, and slightly lower resting cardiac output than an untrained individual. During sub-maximum exercise, the trained individual will have a lower heart rate, higher stroke volume, and lower cardiac output than the untrained individual. During maximum exercise, the trained and untrained individual will have about the same maximum heart rate. The trained individual, however, will have a higher stroke volume and cardiac output. To train aerobically, one can gradually increase the distance, intensity (moving faster or adding power), and frequency of aerobic activity for improvement. Interval training, in which one would engage in short bouts of high-intensity activity, followed by short bouts of rest or lower intensity activity, is also effective.

EXERCISES THAT PROMOTE AEROBIC CONDITIONING

Exercises that promote aerobic conditioning include running, jogging, swimming, walking, biking, aerobic dance, jumping jacks, and jumping rope performed continuously for at least 20 to 30 minutes. However, high-intensity interval training has also shown effective in promoting aerobic conditioning. **High-intensity interval training (HIIT)** is a combination of high-intensity aerobic and muscular fitness activities performed in short bouts followed by a short rest period. **Tabata** is a type of HIIT training with a work interval of 20 seconds followed by a rest interval of 10 seconds. Repeating these intervals for four minutes has shown to be as effective as a 60-minute aerobic session. A general rule for aerobic interval training is the rest time should be half the work time. Other HIIT work-rest intervals include 30/15, 40/20, and 60/30 seconds.

METABOLISM AND AEROBIC CONDITIONING

Metabolism is the process of breaking down foods and converting them to energy (carbohydrates, fats, proteins) that is needed to sustain life. Carbohydrates are the primary source of energy, followed by fats, which are the back-up system once carbohydrate stores (glucose and glycogen) are depleted. After the glucose (carbohydrates) and glycogen (stored glucose) stores are used during aerobic activity, fat stores become the fuel source needed to continue aerobic activity because it is long lasting. This process is called **fat oxidation,** which is a metabolic process that helps create the energy. Monounsaturated and polyunsaturated (plant-based fats, liquid at room temperature) fats are easier to break down than saturated fats (mostly animal fats, solid at room temperature) due to the slower metabolic and oxidation processes of saturated fats. This is the reason that limiting saturated fats is recommended, especially among those who want to lose weight or avoid adding additional weight. To burn fat in an effort to lose weight, aerobic activity needs to occur long enough or at high-intensity levels to reach the stored fat in the adipocytes (fat cells).

CARDIOVASCULAR RECOMMENDATIONS FOR ELEMENTARY-AGED CHILDREN

It is recommended that elementary students between the ages of five and 12 engage in cardiovascular activities 5 to 7 days a week in sessions of 15 minutes or more several times throughout the day to an accumulated 60 minutes. Activities should vary and students should engage in low (stretching, yoga), moderate (walking), and vigorous (biking, jumping rope, games that involve running or chasing) physical activities. Continuous activity and working towards a specific heart rate goal are discouraged, as the goal at these ages is to encourage and promote physical activity.

CARDIOVASCULAR RECOMMENDATIONS FOR SECONDARY SCHOOL-AGED CHILDREN

Moderate and vigorous cardiovascular activities are recommended for secondary-aged students (aged 11-18 years) three to seven days a week in bouts of 20-60 minutes. Middle school-aged students are not expected to have target heart-rate goals, but are encouraged to use rate of perceived exertion scales to monitor effort and intensity. This is also the stage where target heart concepts are introduced. High school students are encouraged to work at 60-90 percent of their target heart rate because the goal is not only to promote physical activity, but to teach students how to plan for exercise as adults. Activities should vary and may include participation in individual, dual, and team sports; speed walking; jogging; dancing; swimming; skating; cycling; and mowing grass.

CONTINUOUS TRAINING

Continuous training is also known as steady state training because the same activity is performed at long durations or several minutes without rest (e.g., jogging, swimming, walking). Although continuous training is not encouraged for students in elementary school, continuous activities that range from three to five minutes with rest is appropriate for the primary years (grades K-2) or unfit students, 10-minute bouts are appropriate for upper elementary (grades 3-5), and 20-minute and longer sessions are appropriate for middle and high school students. A gradual increase in intensity should occur for all groups, and students should be able to take rest and water breaks when they need to. There should also be a gradual decrease in intensity.

FARTLEK TRAINING

Fartlek training, also known as "speed play," is a type of interval training that consists of performing aerobic and locomotor movements over natural or rough terrain at varied intervals. For example, if students are running on a cross-country trail or on grass, the teacher or student may randomly decide when to run hard and when to slow down to a jog and walk. This differs from the traditional interval training that has a set work-rest ratio (20 seconds of work followed by 10 seconds of rest). It is a method used in lieu of continuous training that helps students increase aerobic capacity, maintain a steady pace, increase speed, and develop mental toughness. It is appropriate for older elementary-aged students (grades 3-5) and middle and high school-aged students. All locomotor movements are used during Fartlek sessions in elementary school, and the teacher generally controls the intensity and pace. In secondary school, students are expected to control their intensity and pace based on fitness goals, and the locomotor movements consist of running, jogging, or walking.

USING HEART RATES TO PACE ACTIVITY

Instead of working at a particular pace, **heart rate training** involves changing intensities based on heart rate. A heart rate monitor is used throughout the activity to ensure that the desired heart rate zone is maintained. For example, if the goal is to work between 70 to 80 percent of the maximum heart rate, the exerciser would slow down their speed when the heart rate exceeds 80 percent, and increase their speed when the heart rate drops below 70 percent. This is a fair training method to use among students because heart rate is unique to the individual. Drastic or abnormal increases in heart rate can indicate an illness, such as a cold or fever, or a potential for sudden cardiac death. Therefore, heart rate training can also alert the performer of a problem to slow down, stop, or seek medical attention.

HEART RATE MONITORING METHODS

Heart rate is used to monitor intensity levels during aerobic activities. Methods used to assess heart rate include manually taking the pulse rate or heart rate and using devices that monitor heart rate. Manual heart rate methods include measuring the pulse at the wrist (radial artery) or the neck (carotid artery), which can be done by placing two fingers (first and middle fingers) at the artery locations and calculating the beats per minute, either by counting for 10 seconds and multiplying the pulse count by six, 15 seconds multiplied by four, 20 seconds multiplied by three, 30 seconds multiplied by two, or for 60 seconds. In every instance, the calculation equates to the number of beats in one minute. Ten seconds is preferred after engaging in physical activity or exercise because it is fast and accurate. A 60-second count is preferred to determine the resting heart rate. Elementary students should monitor heart rate by placing their right hand over the heart. To help elementary students understand the concept of intensity, various activities can be set up with pictures and words to convey low ("move like a turtle"), medium (brisk walking), and high-intensity (running) activities.

TALK TEST AND RATE OF PERCEIVED EXERTION

The talk test and rate of perceived exertion scales are easy alternatives to measuring heart rate that are used to establish exercise intensity. If one can talk but not sing during an activity, then the intensity level is appropriate; if one can sing, then the intensity is too low; and if one cannot talk or sing, then the intensity is too high. Rate of perceived exertion (RPE) scales are estimates of how one feels while engaging in aerobic activities. RPEs use a rating scale from 0 (extremely easy) to 10 (extremely hard). There are RPE scales designed for children and adults, and the most common are the OMNI and Borg scales.

Rating	Difficulty	Indicator
0	Rest	No effort
2	Easy	Very minimal effort, walking, able to talk and do other things.
4	Moderate	Not too hard. Activity can be done for extended time, and should still be able to talk while performing activity.
6	Hard	Able to sustain for some time, but pushing the cardiorespiratory limit, meaning they won't be able to talk while performing or sustain for long periods of time.
8	Very hard	Not quite full effort, but nearing that level of intensity. Unable to talk or do anything else while performing. Not sustainable for more than a few minutes at the most.
10	Maximum	Short bursts only. When finished, will be breathing very hard and unable to talk until they catch their breath.

TRACKING DURATION AND DISTANCE OF AEROBIC ACTIVITIES

Techniques used to measure the duration of aerobic activities are timetable devices that include watches, activity trackers, stopwatches, cell phone timers, and clocks. Techniques used to measure distance include performing aerobic activities in marked areas (e.g., standard track at 400 meters per lap, swimming pool at 50-100 meters per length) or built-in capabilities (e.g., treadmill, stationary bike, elliptical trainer). For aerobic activities that do not have standard measures or equipment (e.g., aerobic dance, walking or running on the street or unmarked area), a pedometer or accelerometer can be used. The purpose of monitoring the duration and distance is to track progress. For instance, at the start of an exercise program, a brisk 20-minute walk may be difficult, but with consistency and time, the brisk 20-minute walk will likely get easier as the body has adapted to the physical stress. Therefore, one will need to either walk longer or increase the pace (jog) to experience similar physiological responses (e.g., increase in heart rate).

MAXIMUM HEART RATE AND TARGET HEART RATE ZONE

Maximum heart rate (MHR) is the maximum number of beats the heart pumps per minute and is dependent on age. The formula for computing MHR is 220 minus the subject's age, so the MHR for a 15-year-old is 205 beats per minute (bpm). The **target heart rate zone (THRZ)** is a percentage of the MHR and has a range of low-intensity and high-intensity that is generally between 60 and 90 percent. As the model below demonstrates, the THRZ for a 15-year-old is 123 bpm to184.5 bpm (formula below).

	Moderate intensity	High intensity
Base number	220	220
Age	-15 years old	-15 years old
Difference	205	205
Intensity	× 0.60 (60 percent)	× 0.90 (90 percent)
THRZ	123 bpm	184.5 bpm

Beginners and unfit individuals should work at the 60 to 70 percent range of their THRZ and gradually increase over time. Fit individuals should work at the 80 to 85 percent range of their THRZ, athletes or those with high levels of fitness should aim for 90 percent, and some elite athletes can aim for 95 percent. However, working at this intensity for long periods can be dangerous, so interval training is recommended when working at high intensities.

KARVONEN METHOD FOR CALCULATING TARGET HEART RATE ZONE

The Karvonen method (aka maximum heart rate reserve) for calculating the target heart rate is one of the preferred methods because it takes fitness as measured by resting heart rate (RHR) into account. It is often used as the method for training. The preferred target heart rate under the Karvonen method is 60 to 75 percent because working at higher rates can produce lactic acid via anaerobic systems, thus causing fatigue. Using an individual's resting heart rate ensures that the correct intensity is used for adaptations to occur.

A worked example of the Karvonen formula illustrates the differences between a 15-year-old with a resting heart rate of 72 bpm and a 15-year-old with a resting heart rate of 60 bpm.

Age 15 with 72 BPM RHR		Age 15 with 60 BPM RHR	
60 Percent	**90 Percent**	**60 Percent**	**90 Percent**
$220 - 15 = 205$	$220 - 15 = 205$	$220 - 15 = 205$	$220 - 15 = 205$
$205 - 72 = 133$	$205 - 72 = 133$	$205 - 60 = 145$	$205 - 60 = 145$
$133 \times 0.60 = 79.8$	$133 \times 0.90 = 119.7$	$145 \times 0.60 = 87.0$	$145 \times 0.90 = 130.5$
$79.8 + 72 = 151.8$	$119.7 + 72 = 191.7$	$87 + 60 = 147$	$130.5 + 60 = 190.5$

USING RESTING AND EXERCISE HEART RATES TO ASSESS CARDIO-RESPIRATORY FITNESS

Tracking resting heart rate and exercise heart rates over time can aid in determining cardiovascular fitness progress and physiological adaptations. With consistent cardiorespiratory training, the resting heart rate should slow down. The exercise heart rate should also slow down at similar work rates done previously. The exerciser would use heart rate data to determine if and what changes need to be made. For example, at the start of a fitness program, the resting heart rate is 85 bpm. If there has been no change after six weeks of training, then the individual either needs to increase the exercise time, frequency, intensity, type, or a combination of those variables. The participant may also want to get a physical examination to ensure that there are no underlying conditions (e.g., high blood pressure, illness).

RECOVERY HEART RATE AND CARDIOVASCULAR FITNESS

Recovery heart rate is the time it takes for the heart to return to normal after engaging in cardiorespiratory activities. As the body becomes more conditioned by adapting to the physiological stresses of engaging aerobic activity, the heart will return to normal faster than someone who is not conditioned. A common recovery heart rate assessment is the three-minute step test, which is also used to predict VO2 max. The **Queen's College step test** is commonly used where a continuous step cadence (up, up, down, down) on a 41 centimeter (16.142 inches) high box or bench at a rate of 88 bpm for females and 96 bpm for males for three minutes. After three minutes has elapsed, a 15-second pulse should be taken and multiplied by four to equate 60 seconds, which corresponds to recovery heart rate and VO2 max estimates. Ranges to aim for are 128-156 bpm for females and 120-144 bpm for males. Students can track their recovery heart rates over time to see if they decrease.

HEALTH RISKS WHEN ENGAGING IN CARDIOVASCULAR ACTIVITIES IN THE HEAT

Engaging in cardiovascular activities in the heat increases the risks of dehydration, heat cramps, heat exhaustion, and heat stroke. **Dehydration** (aka hypohydration) is the when the body does not have enough fluids to maintain the body's processes. **Heat cramps** are painful spasms in the muscles due to fatigue or sodium lost via sweat. **Heat exhaustion** is the result of the increase of a negative balance of water resulting from dehydration, and heat stroke is the result of dehydration and thermoregulation failure (the ability to sweat). These conditions can cause **hyperthermia** (overheated body with thermoregulation failure) and lead to death. To prevent these heat and endurance-related conditions, it is best to hydrate before, during, and after activity, and take more frequent water and rest breaks. Engaging in activity during the coolest part of the day and lowering the intensity and time of activity can also reduce risk. Light-colored clothing is recommended because light colors reflect more wavelengths of light and therefore absorb less heat. Exercising in the shade and wearing a hat with a visor is also recommended.

RISK REDUCTION AND CARDIOVASCULAR TRAINING

A risk reduction technique to consider when preparing for cardiovascular endurance training is to have a physical examination from a licensed medical professional (e.g., doctor, nurse) to ensure that there are no underlying health conditions that can be exacerbated by physical activity. Another risk reduction technique is to complete the Physical Activity Readiness Questionnaire (PAR-Q), which asks questions used to determine if one is prepared to engage in physical activity. This survey consists of yes and no questions, and if one or more yeses are checked, a visit to the doctor for medical clearance is typically recommended. Once activity starts, conducting a warm-up, a gradual increase in intensity, wearing a heart rate monitor, and performing a cooldown after activity are risk reduction techniques.

HEALTH RISKS WHEN ENGAGING IN CARDIOVASCULAR ACTIVITIES IN THE COLD

Engaging in cardiovascular activities in the cold increases the risks of skin and body temperature dropping, thus creating heat loss that can lead to hypothermia. Another potential health concern is the increased possibility of inducing an asthma attack for those who suffer from exercise-induced asthma. Conducting cardiovascular activities in cold water exacerbates the effects of the cold and can increase the risk of tachycardia (abnormal resting heart rate) and hyperventilation (higher-than-normal respiration rate), both of which are cold shock responses. A rapid drop in skin temperature (jumping into a cold body of water) increases cold shock responses. When swimming in cold water, vasoconstriction (when the blood vessels narrow) and blood flow to the muscles are reduced, which makes movement stiff and more difficult. **Frostnip** (superficial skin tissues freeze) and **frostbite** (cooling and freezing of cells) are other cold-related concerns. To reduce risk, insulated, breathable clothing that draws sweat away from the body is recommended. When performing activities on dry land, layering clothes and removing layers as the body warms up is recommended. A longer warm-up should also be employed.

ALTITUDE AND CARDIOVASCULAR EXERCISE

Most physical activities are performed at sea level, or zero feet of altitude. Altitude training is training at least 7,874 feet above sea level (2,400 meters). There are three main physiological changes that occur when altitude training: 1) red blood cell count increases, allowing increases in the oxygen-transport change, which increases blood flow to the working muscles, which helps the body move more efficiently, 2) breathing rate increases, which reduces the amount of carbon dioxide, thus reducing fatigue, and 3) there is an increase in myoglobin, which is a temporary substance that acts as oxygen when oxygen delivery is compromised (e.g., during long, strenuous activities). These physiological changes, due to acclimatization from training at a different altitude, have a positive effect on cardiovascular performance when returning to sea level.

CARBOHYDRATE LOADING

Carbohydrates consist of sugars and starches that are the body's primary source of energy (aka fuel). Carbohydrates are broken down into glucose (sugar) to be used for energy. Any overage of carbohydrates (glucose) is stored in the muscles as glycogen, which is easy energy to recruit during cardiovascular endurance activities. Therefore, the purpose of carbohydrate (pasta, potatoes, rice) loading before endurance activities is to provide sustained energy for longer periods of time without accessing fat storage, which takes longer to recruit. Carbohydrate loading has shown effective for longer-duration cardiovascular events, such as 90 minutes of running and other long-duration cardiovascular activities. The negative side to carbohydrate loading is the athlete or performer may increase body weight because more water is retained to adequately store the extra glycogen. Carbohydrate loading is not recommended for most activities because shorter activities do not last long enough for the body to need to metabolize more carbohydrates, so the extra calories will actually work against a person who is trying to lose weight through shorter activities.

TREADMILLS AND STATIONARY BIKES

Treadmills promote options for walking, jogging, or running without the need for space. Treadmills are great when it rains or is too hot or cold for outdoor exercise, as they replicate or are specific to the motions that are performed outdoors. Treadmills also allow for inclines and declines to train different parts of the muscle used when walking, jogging, or running. The speed and resistance can also be adjusted. Stationary bikes work in a similar fashion but for biking. The downside of using treadmills and stationary bikes is they are not performed on the same terrain as when performing outside, but are still effective in improving cardiovascular fitness.

MODIFICATIONS FOR CARDIOVASCULAR ENDURANCE ACTIVITIES

Modifications for cardiovascular activities can make the activity easier, more challenging, or less impactful. For example, modifications for jogging include brisk or power walking (lowers the intensity and reduces the impact on the knees), running (increases the intensity), or a combination of all three (interval training). All modalities can increase cardiovascular endurance. However, in order to meet similar cardiovascular outcomes as jogging, one would need to engage in walking longer. Modifications for swimming include using a flotation device to stay buoyant to work on arm strokes and kicks, performing the doggy paddle, and water aerobics. One could also hold onto the wall of the pool and practice kicking and breathing. Endurance and interval sports activities can be used in lieu of traditional exercise activities or programs. They can also be used to cross-train and give the body a break from normal routines.

Muscular Strength and Endurance

ABDOMINAL STRENGTH

Muscles in the abdomen are part of the **core muscles**, which also includes muscles in the back, which work in agonist and antagonist pairings. Often referred to as the abdominals, or abs, these muscles aid in stability and posture. A strong core helps with other exercises. The abdominals should be engaged (contracted, pulling the navel towards the back) during abdominal activities. Exercises to work the abs include curl-ups, plank holds, and variations of these exercises. When performing curl-ups and sit-ups, exhalation should occur in the up position when the muscles contract (the work phase). Inhalation should occur when lowering to the down position when the abs relax. To keep contraction throughout the exercise, the head and shoulder blades should be slightly off the surface on the down phase. Bending the neck should be avoided to prevent neck pain. Holding the arms across the chest is a safer option. Plank holds are an isometric exercise that is measured by time (seconds or minutes). Planks also engage the muscles of the back (erector spinae), the deltoids, and the glutes. Ab exercises are usually done at two to three sets until fatigue or a predetermined rep count. Abs are generally trained three or four days a week, and are usually incorporated into a complete workout program. However, they are also indirectly trained as they act as synergistic stabilizers during other exercises.

LOWER BACK STRENGTH

The **lower back** is used for most activities, as it provides stability. Exercise recommendations for the lower back include plank holds, Superman's exercise, pelvic tilts, bridges (glute raises), reverse curls, deadlifts, leaning back, leg lifts, low rows, stretching (cat and cow, lying on back alternating knees to the chest), and windshield wiper with knees. However, it is important to note that lower back injuries are common, so care should be taken to protect it. When lifting items off the floor, the knees should be used to lift and the hips and glutes should be kept back, rather than bending over and lifting with the back. Lower back exercises should be done in a slow and controlled motion. Inhalation occurs during the contraction portion and exhalation occurs during the relaxation portion. For isometric exercises, inhalation and exhalation are maintained throughout the hold (e.g., plank). Lower back exercises should be trained three to four days a week, although lower back stretches can still be performed daily.

UPPER BODY AND TRUNK STRENGTH

The **upper body** includes the arms, chest, back, and shoulders. Along with the abdominals, these body parts comprise the **trunk** (body parts above the waist and below the neck). Muscles in these areas should be trained two to three times a week, with at least one rest day between sessions. Types of exercises, the associated muscles, and common exercises are indicated below.

Major Group	Muscle	Recommended Exercises
Arms	Biceps	Dumbbell curls, barbell curls, hammer curls, cable curls, preacher curls
	Triceps	Seated dips, dips, tricep kickbacks (extensions), overhead extensions
Chest	Pectorals (major and minor)	Push-ups, bench press, cable crossovers
Back	Latissimus dorsi and rhomboids	Lat pull downs, seated row, bent row, one-arm row
	Erector spinae	Reverse curls, Superman's exercise, deadlifts
	Trapezius muscles	Shrugs, shoulder blade squeezes

Major Group	Muscle	Recommended Exercises
Shoulders	Deltoids	Front/lateral/rear deltoid raises, shoulder press – dumbbells, barbells.

Many of the exercises for these muscle groups are also performed on exercise equipment, which tends to be a safe option because machines have more support than free weight exercises.

LEG STRENGTH AND ENDURANCE

To train muscles in the legs for strength, high weight and low reps (3 to 5, 6 to 8, or 8 to 10) should be employed. For endurance, low weight and high reps (10 to 12, 12 to15, or 15 to 20) should be employed. Sets generally range from one to five, depending on the goal(s). One to three sets are often conducted for endurance and three to five sets are often done for strength. Shorter rest times between sets are taken for endurance, and longer rest times between sets for strength. Alternating workouts between strength and endurance allows for focus on each health-related fitness component.

Common exercises that work the muscles in the legs include:

- **Quadriceps**: Squats, lunges, leg extensions
- **Hamstrings**: Deadlifts, hamstring curls
- **Soleus/gastrocnemius**: heel/toe/calf raises (double or single-leg), seated calf raises.

Flexibility and Posture

PROMOTING GOOD POSTURE AND FLEXIBILITY IN THE HIPS, ANKLES, AND KNEES

Hip flexors are the muscles that, with proper flexibility, make it possible to bring the knees upwards and towards the body (chest). The hip flexors also help with good posture because they aid in spinal stabilization. Sitting for long periods can reduce flexibility, while engaging in certain physical activities (dance, soccer, cycling) can improve it. To increase flexibility in the hip flexors or alleviate "tight hips," hip flexor stretches should be conducted using the hip hinge motion (leading with the glutes moving backwards while the chest leads the forward bending motion) to prevent lower back injury.

Mobility in the ankles work in unison with the hip flexors to maintain posture. As the body stands from a seated position (chair) or bends, the hips hinge while the ankles dorsiflex (toes toward the body). Exercises that help build strength and flexibility in the ankles include alternating between dorsiflexion and plantar flexion (toes pointing downward), ankle rotations, hopping side-to-side on one foot, and balancing on one foot while the other one swings forward and back, then switching sides.

The knees also aid in good posture. To maintain good posture when standing, the knees should be soft (slightly bent), the feet should be placed shoulder-distance apart, the arms should be relaxed and hanging, and the body should stand straight and tall with the shoulders back. During exercises, the knees should also be soft, and locking the knee joint should be avoided. When performing squats and lunges, the knees should be aligned or behind the toes. To protect the knees, avoid hanging them over the toes.

PROMOTING GOOD POSTURE AND FLEXIBILITY IN THE LOWER BACK AND TRUNK

Lower back stretches that promote good posture and flexibility include child's pose, cobra, upward facing dog, supine twist, and lying on the back and bringing the knees to the chest. Trunk exercises that aid in good posture and flexibility include back extensions, spinal twist, crunches, crunches with a twist, and wood chops. Trunk stretches for flexibility include upper trunk rotations, trunk flexion rotation, standing and seated lateral trunk stretch, seated trunk rotation stretch, and dolphin stretch. For the chest and upper back parts of the trunk, reaching (stretching the arms) back aids in posture by keeping the chest lifted, shoulders back, and back upright. This is a counter-balance stretch because the shoulders and posture can be compromised (shoulders rounded forward, curve in the upper back) when the muscles on the anterior side are stronger than the posterior muscles.

PROMOTING GOOD POSTURE AND FLEXIBILITY FOR THE SHOULDERS AND NECK

Shoulder exercises that promote good posture and flexibility include reaching the arms back, reverse plank, threading the needle, dolphin, eagle arms, sphinx, and alternating shoulder stretch (hands touching behind the back in opposition). The following exercises are used to increase strength and flexibility in the neck, which also aids in good posture. Neck exercises include tilting the head forward (chin towards the chest), bending or tilting the head towards the left and right (side to side), and rotating the head to the right and left. These stretches should be held for 5 to 10 seconds and repeated up to five times each. Bending or tilting the head back is not recommended.

RESISTANCE TRAINING TO PROMOTE FLEXIBILITY

Weight and resistance training increase the range of motion, thus increasing flexibility. Research shows that heavy weight training is more effective for increasing flexibility than static stretching. As such, during weight training, especially when performing exercises through a full range of motion (push-ups, squats, pull-ups, deadlifts), there is no need to stretch because stretching occurs while building strength. During exercises, the core should be engaged, the chest should be lifted, the knees should be slightly bent, and the pelvis and spine should be in a neutral position. Foam rollers (compressed tubes) are also effective in improving flexibility since they can apply pressure that is able to penetrate deep inside the muscle tissue, which aids in muscle lengthening.

Evaluating Strength, Endurance, and Flexibility

EVALUATING MUSCULAR STRENGTH

The steps used to conduct a one-repetition max (1RM) test are listed below.

Pectoral strength measured by the bench press:

1. Warm-up the area evaluated: light-weight bench press for two to five sets
2. Use two or three spotters
3. Select a heavy weight within the limits of the student
4. The student will bench press the amount of weight as many times as possible. If they can bench press one time in good form without assistance, then that is the 1RM. If they can bench press the selected weight more than one time, they should stop, add more weight, and repeat three to five minutes later. This would continue until the 1RM is achieved.

A safer method to use is the estimated 1RM. Two methods of estimated 1RM are below.

1. Use an estimated 1RM table to determine what the 1RM would likely be. For example, students select a weight that they can lift for six repetitions but cannot lift for more than 10 repetitions (chart dependent). If a student performed eight reps at eight pounds, they would use the estimated 1RM table corresponding chart and would find that their estimated 1RM would be 10 pounds.
2. Another method is to use the 1RM estimated max formula: (weight lifted × 0.03 × repetitions) + weight lifted = estimated 1RM max. Using the example of a student performing eight reps at eight pounds: (8 reps × 0.03 × 8 pounds) + 8 lbs = 9.92 pounds, which rounds up to 10 pounds.

EVALUATING ENDURANCE

There are two types of **endurance**: muscular endurance and cardiovascular endurance. At times, they work together, like when jogging or swimming—although these activities require muscular and cardiovascular movements, they are classified as aerobic because they use large amounts of oxygen. The amount of time engaged in the activity is how both are measured. For example, timing how long one can engage in continuous movement and tracking trends helps to determine improvement. When participating in locomotor endurance activities, tracking distance is another method used to evaluate endurance. For example, if someone jogs for 30 minutes a day, they can track the distance covered in the amount of time. If the distance increases, the data would suggest they are getting faster and the heart, lungs, and muscles are working more efficiently. Common cardiovascular endurance assessments include the 1-mile run, multi-stage progressive runs, 12-minute runs, and three-minute step tests. Common muscular endurance (and strength) tests are the curl-up test, push-up test, and plank hold. The amount of reps completed over a certain amount of time (e.g., two minutes) is another method of evaluation. Muscular endurance activities performed in isolation are classified as anaerobic because little to no oxygen is required to engage in the activity.

EVALUATING FLEXIBILITY

Flexibility is often evaluated by length or a decrease in joint angle. For example, the sit-and-reach is a test commonly used in physical education programs to measure lower back and hamstring flexibility. The test is usually performed on a box to protect the back, but can also be performed on the floor. In a seated position with the legs extended forward, the goal is to reach towards the feet as far as possible with slight tension but without pain. A tape measure on the floor or ruler on the

62

box measures the distance or the length of the stretch. The back saver sit-and-reach is conducted with one leg at a time (while the other is bent upward). A tape measure is not required, as reaching an area on the body also provides information on progress. For example, one may only be able to reach their shins, but with practice can eventually reach their toes or go beyond their toes, indicating improvement.

Safe and Appropriate Activity for Improving Fitness

ACTIVITIES FOR IMPROVING MUSCULAR STRENGTH

Muscular strength can improve with and without equipment. Body weight exercises are generally introduced first because they are safer than exercises that use equipment. Body weight exercises also allow students to become familiar with what the body can do (e.g., body awareness). Some body weight exercises that help build strength are push-ups, curl-ups, planks, squats, lunges, and several variations of these exercises. Exercise tubes, resistance bands, and stability balls also improve strength because they add a little more resistance than body weight training alone. For faster strength gains, kettlebells, medicine balls, and dumbbells can be used. These types of equipment allow the body to complete exercises that mimic regular movements. Weight lifting machines (e.g., hamstring curl, leg press, lat pulldown) allow for heavy weight to be lifted, but restricts some natural movements, which makes it a safe option. Over time with consistency, exercises should get easier as the body adapts, and the load (weight) will need to either increase or more repetitions will be required to see further progress. It usually takes between four to six weeks for adaptations to occur. If the intensity remains the same, the body may plateau, which means there will be no more improvement gains.

ACTIVITIES FOR IMPROVING ENDURANCE AND INDICATORS OF IMPROVEMENT

The cardiorespiratory system needs to be challenged at least three days a week for 20-60 minutes for endurance to improve, increase, or maintain cardiovascular fitness. With consistency, the body adapts to the exercises and becomes more efficient and capable of meeting the cardiovascular demands on the body. Activities that help improve endurance include jumping rope, walking, jogging, running, swimming, aerobic dance, HIIT training, road and stationary biking, elliptical trainers, rowing, and high-repetition muscular fitness activities. Indicators of improvement include lower resting and working heart rates, faster recovery heart rate, longer durations, and a decrease in fatigue response. The activities will also get easier to do over time. Using a variety of these activities (aka cross-training) will prevent a plateau effect by putting different challenges across all body systems (e.g., musculoskeletal, circulatory, respiratory).

ACTIVITIES TO IMPROVE FLEXIBILITY AND POSTURE

A warm-up lasting five to 10 minutes is recommended prior to engaging in flexibility and posture activities. Selecting activities depends on the goal. Range of motion (ROM) exercises can be done every day to increase flexibility. ROM exercises are static holds (e.g., touching the toes, grabbing one foot, spinal twist) where the position or posture is maintained for 20 to 60 seconds. **Proprioceptive neuromuscular facilitation (PNF)** stretching, which is comprised of static holds with a person or object applying pressure to help deepen the stretch, has been shown to be most effective for increasing flexibility. These stretches should be used in intervals of stretch-relax-stretch. Static and PNF stretches are good for physical therapy (rehab for an injury) and are often done at the end of a workout. Static stretching is also preferred for students in elementary school as they learn body awareness. Dynamic stretches are introduced in middle school. Dynamic stretching is often used in warm-ups because it increases blood flow while stretching in positions and movements similar to the workout or sport. In this way, dynamic stretches prepare the body for the specific work.

PROGRESSIVE-PARTNER-RESISTANCE EXERCISES

Partner exercises allow for greater isolation of the muscle than when performing exercises alone. These exercises are also good for students who are too small to use exercise machines. Ideally, partners should be the same height, weight, and ability level (e.g., strength, flexibility). Communication is essential to prevent injury, therefore, the student performing the exercises needs

64

to inform or cue the partner with how much pressure should be applied. The partner that is assisting should provide feedback on technique and form to ensure safe, correct movements. Equipment that can aid in partner-resistance exercises include exercise tubes, bands, and towels.

PRINCIPLES, SAFETY PRACTICES, AND EQUIPMENT FOR WEIGHT TRAINING

When engaging in weight training, weight selection should take into account the concept of progressive overload (start with a light weight and gradually increase) to prevent injury. A warm-up should also be conducted to prevent the risks of injury. Warm-ups usually consist of performing the same activities with little to no weight and is commonly referred to as a "warm-up set." For example, when conducting the biceps curl, a warm-up set might consist of 20 reps at five pounds before performing the biceps curl at the desired weight of 20 pounds at 10 reps for three sets. General principles include training the same muscle group at least two days a week; high weights with low reps for strength and size; low weights with high reps for endurance; rest between sets (30 seconds to three minutes), taking longer rests for size and shorter rests for endurance; and including at least one rest day between weight training workouts for the targeted body part or muscle group. Below are two **splits**, or weight training workout schedules. Depending on the segmentation and muscle groups to exercise, splits can come in hundreds of different variations.

Sunday	Monday	Tuesday	Wednesday	Thursday	Friday	Saturday
Legs	Arms, shoulders	Chest, back	Legs	Rest	Arms, shoulders	Chest, back

Sunday	Monday	Tuesday	Wednesday	Thursday	Friday	Saturday
Legs, arms	Chest, back	Shoulders, core	Rest	Legs, arms	Chest, back	Shoulders, core

PRINCIPLES, SAFETY PRACTICES, AND EQUIPMENT FOR CIRCUIT TRAINING

Circuit training is a combination of cardiovascular and non-cardiovascular activities performed at stations for a certain number of minutes or repetitions. Circuit training exercises may only include body weight exercises, free weights, resistance equipment (bands, suspension trainers), or a combination. In addition to the normal exercise safety (e.g., warm-up, cooldown, hydration), there are additional safety concerns that must be considered for young children (elementary school-aged). During physical activity and exercise, teachers should be aware that young children's bodies are less able to thermoregulate due to a lower sweat response than adults, therefore children may overheat faster than adults. As such, young children should be given more frequent rest and water breaks (before, during, and after activity). Their breathing capacity is also lower than older children and adults, which can cause them to hyperventilate, so the intensity should be moderate, not high.

DETERMINE APPROPRIATE INTENSITY OF TRAINING

Appropriate measures used to determine cardiovascular endurance training include training in one's target heart rate zone. The target heart rate zone is a percentage (60 to 90 percent) of an individual's maximum heart rate. Once the target heart rate has been computed, it can be monitored by taking the pulse or by wearing a heart rate monitoring device. The goal is to stay within the 60 to 90 percent range; beginners should stay in the 60 to 70 percent range and gradually advance to the 85 to 90 percent range. The talk test is another way to determine intensity: if the subject is able to talk, but not able to sing during the activity, then they are working at an appropriate intensity. If they are unable to talk, then the intensity is too high, and if they are able to sing, then the intensity is too low. For muscular fitness activities, gauging how one feels during the activities is a method used to determine the intensity of exercises. Whether training for strength or endurance, the last few reps in each set should be challenging but doable. When the last few reps are easy, it is an indication that the weight or rep count needs to increase, thus increasing the intensity.

APPROPRIATE DURATION OF TRAINING

The duration of training is dependent on the goal. For example, if the goal is to complete a 5-kilometer (3.1 miles) race, a gradual increase in distance should occur until the 5-kilometer goal is met. Running or swimming slightly over 5 kilometers can help train the body so that the stress response during the 5-kilometer run is easier. On the other hand, if someone is training for a marathon (42.185 kilometers, or 26.22 miles), multiple longer runs leading up to the marathon are recommended. Given the distance of a marathon, however, it is not recommended to train at or beyond the marathon distance. A few 20-mile runs are a general recommendation when training for a marathon. These recommendations are based on the principle of specificity. If one is training at shorter distances (e.g., 100-meter run), the duration should be short and explosive with repeated trials or attempts. It would be inappropriate to train in short bouts for activities that take a long time to complete and vice versa.

APPROPRIATE FREQUENCY OF TRAINING

The frequency of training depends on goals, fitness level, and the time available to train. For beginners, a training program consisting of two to three days a week at low-intensity activity is recommended. For intermediates, frequency recommendations are three to four days a week of moderate activities. For advanced exercisers, four to seven days a week of vigorous activities. A gradual increase over time has shown the most effective in exercise adherence. For weight training, it is generally recommended to perform two or three sets of each exercise (e.g., push-ups in three sets of 10) two to three days a week. More sets are recommended for those who are focused on size, and the frequency of workouts could be once a week because it will take longer for the body to recover and repair after heavy loads.

SAFETY, EFFECTIVENESS, AND CONTRAINDICATIONS OF THE TYPES OF TRAINING THAT PROMOTE STRENGTH

Safe and effective training that promotes strength in children and adolescents includes body weight training and lifting weights. It is a myth that children should not engage in strength training as it was once thought doing so would stunt their growth. Research shows that elementary-aged children benefit from strength training activities, however, the activities should vary to reduce the risk of injury and prevent overtraining. Since children and youth's bones (epiphyseal plate, or growth plate) are still developing, a slow progression should occur. Non-strength activities should be included (e.g., those that improve cardiovascular performance and flexibility). Specialization in training should not occur until later adolescence (e.g., high school-aged). Although multi-joint activities have shown safe for young children, proper form and technique that include slow and controlled movements are a must, as these types of exercises can put additional stress on the shoulder joint and lower back. To ensure safety, and in addition to progressive overload, the teacher should be trained, students should be taught about the benefits and risks, a warm-up should be conducted, frequent water breaks should be given, and rest days or non-strength activities should follow strength-training days. **Contraindications** or risky movements to avoid include jerky movements, locking of the joints, hyperextension, and fast and uncontrolled movements.

SAFETY AND EFFECTIVENESS IN ENDURANCE TRAINING

Most endurance activities (walking, jogging, running) conducted during physical education are appropriate for K-12 students, however, because of developmental stage, modifications should be made. For example, elementary-aged children should engage in bouts of endurance activities not to exceed 15 minutes at a time, while middle and high school students can engage in longer durations (20 minutes or longer). HIIT training can be used across grade levels, but it is only recommended for students who are moderately fit and should be avoided by students who are not. Swimming activities are effective, although specialized training among personnel is required and a certified lifeguard should be on duty during instruction. Students need to be proficient in floating and swimming or need flotation devices that keep non-swimmers buoyant. Endurance machines are also effective, but are unsafe for elementary-aged students due to size and developmental stage.

SAFETY AND EFFECTIVENESS IN STRETCHING

Static stretching and yoga poses are effective in promoting flexibility and enhancing posture. A warm-up should be conducted prior to stretching to reduce the risk of injury. To be effective, stretching should occur at least two days a week and be held for 10 to 60 seconds to the point of tension (not pain), followed by relaxation and repeat. There should be a gradual increase (progressive overload) in the amount of time the stretch is held. Regular breathing should occur, and during exhalation is the time to try to go deeper or reach farther (in small increments) in the stretch. No more than four stretches per muscle group at three sets each are recommended. Static stretching is recommended for elementary-aged children because it is more controlled and they are still learning how to move the body. Furthermore, dynamic stretching (with movement) can increase injury in young children because they can easily overstretch. Caution should also be used among older populations because static stretching can restrict blood flow and increase blood pressure, as the majority of blood is pooled to the area being stretched. Athletes and students in secondary school tend to warm-up using dynamic stretches, which are mobility exercises that mimic sporting movements and prepare the body for more intense motion specific to the activity.

Diet and Nutrition

MACRONUTRIENTS

Macronutrients (large amounts) include carbohydrates, proteins, and fats. Macronutrients are energy-yielding nutrients because they provide the body with energy to fuel exercise and physical activity. Water is not an energy-yielding macronutrient, but it does it help transport the energy-yielding nutrients. Water is the most essential nutrient because the body cannot survive without it. Carbohydrates (sugars and starches) are the primary source of energy, followed by fats and proteins. Fiber is a substrate of carbohydrates and comes from plant-based foods (vegetables, fruits, and grains). Fiber is either soluble (digestible) or insoluble (indigestible). Carbohydrates are either simple and easy to break down (table sugar, fruits) or complex (pasta and bread), which are more filling and supply longer energy than simple sugars. Fats supply long lasting energy after energy from carbohydrates (glucose, glycogen) have been used. Fats are either saturated (semi-solid at room temperature) or unsaturated (liquid at room temperature). Unsaturated fats are better for health. Protein's main role is muscle building and repair. Proteins are found in animal products like meats and eggs. There are also plant-based proteins, including beans, legumes, and soybeans (tofu). Proteins are made up of 20 amino acids, 11 of which are non-essential as the body can produce them, while the remaining nine are essential and can only be obtained through food.

Micronutrients

Vitamins and minerals are micronutrients (small amounts) and are responsible for growth, development, and maintaining the body's processes. Vitamins have two categories: 1) fat soluble (vitamins A, D, E, and K) and 2) water soluble (vitamins B, C, and all others). Having an overabundance of fat-soluble vitamins can be toxic. However, vitamin D deficiency is a concern in the United States, especially among people of color. Vitamin D helps with calcium absorption and is responsible for bone, skin, and immune health, and serves as a protective factor against cancer and other health conditions. Sources of vitamin D include dairy, salmon, and other fatty fish. Sources of vitamin A include carrots, sweet potatoes, spinach and liver. Vitamin E sources include almonds, sunflower seeds, and peanuts. Sources of vitamin K include broccoli, brussels sprouts, and spinach. Minerals also have two categories:

- Macro (calcium, potassium, sodium)
- Micro, or trace minerals (copper, fluoride, iron)

Ingesting too many minerals can lead to life-threatening conditions (e.g., too much sodium can lead to hypertension), so one should follow the recommended daily allowances based on age, gender, pregnancy status, and illnesses or predisposed conditions. Minerals are found in meats, fruits, vegetables, nuts, dairy, and fortified foods (cereals).

BASIC PRINCIPLES OF WEIGHT MANAGEMENT

The energy balance equation shown below is a simplified formula to describe weight management. Energy in is the amount of **calories** (unit of energy or unit of measure for fuel) consumed from foods and substances, and energy out is the amount of calories burned from movement or physical activity.

Energy in = Energy out = No change in weight
Energy in > Energy out = Weight gain
Energy in < Energy out = Weight loss

Physical activity patterns impact the equation. For example, individuals who engage in more physical activity will need more calories as fuel. In contrast, sedentary individuals will need fewer calories because inactivity consumes calories at a much slower rate. For individuals who want to gain weight, the energy in would need to exceed the energy out. Those who want to lose weight would need to burn more calories than they consume.

DIET AND EXERCISE PATTERNS

Generally, it is recommended that 45 to 65 percent of our diet comes from carbohydrates, which is the primary source of energy. Complex carbohydrates (vegetables and grains such as sweet potatoes and brown rice) are preferred over simple carbohydrates (fruits, desserts, sugar, fructose) because they take longer to break down, thereby providing longer bouts of energy. 20 to 35 percent of a person's diet should come from fats. Unsaturated fats (oils that are liquid at room temperature, includes plant-based oils like olive oil and canola oil) are preferred over saturated fats (solid or semi-solid at room temperature such as animal fats, lard, and butter) because too much saturated fat increases the risks of heart disease and obesity. Saturated fat should account for less than 10 percent of total fat intake. 12 to 20 percent should come from proteins, which are made up of 20 amino acids (building blocks of proteins), 11 of which are non-essential (the body can produce) and the remaining nine of which are essential (obtained from the diet foods consumed). The ranges take into account the needs and patterns of the exerciser and include the type of the activity. For example, someone who wants to increase muscle mass should take in more protein, while someone who wants to train for endurance may increase or consume more carbohydrates. In addition to physical activity, calorie intake and the way the body burns fuel is also dependent on genetics, gender, age, and body size and structure. There are online calculators that can provide an estimate of what is needed based on these factors.

BASIC NUTRITION PRINCIPLES

The basic nutrition principles include getting food from multiple food groups for a balanced diet. The five food groups include:

1. Dairy or dairy alternatives (e.g., milk, cheese, yogurt, soy) – should be low or reduced fat
2. Proteins – fish, poultry, lean meats, eggs, tofu, nuts, beans, legumes, seeds
3. Vegetables, including beans and legumes
4. Fruit
5. Grains – rice, bread, cereal, pasta, noodles

Intake of foods from the food groups ensures that the body is getting essential nutrients for the body's processes (systems). Low consumption of fat and moderate consumption of sodium and sugars are recommended because consuming too much of these can lead to obesity, obesity-related illness, high blood pressure, high cholesterol, and type 2 diabetes.

BODY MASS INDEX

Body mass index (BMI) is the most widely used measure of body composition. It is the relationship between weight and height squared. The BMI formula is: weight (kg)/height (m²), and is used to determine or predict the body fat of an individual.

BMI Categories
Underweight $\leq$ 18.5 Normal weight = 18.5 to 24.9 Overweight = 25 to 29.9 Obese $\geq$ 30

BMI is the most commonly used body composition measure because it is easy to calculate and non-invasive. However, there are several limitations. BMI is an indirect measure of body fatness because it does not measure the amount of fat in the body. There are also race, ethnicity, gender, and structural differences (mesomorph, ectomorph, and endomorph) to consider. **Ectomorphs** tend to be extremely thin and have a difficult time gaining weight. However, these individuals can also be "skinny fat" and have more fat on the body than appearances suggest. **Endomorphs** tend to be short and stout and have large bones, which can elevate or positively skew BMI. While these individuals carry larger amounts of fat, they are able to build muscle. **Mesomorphs** have athletic builds, tend to be lean, and have large muscle mass, but may register as obese even when they actually have low levels of body fat.

SKINFOLDS AND WAIST CIRCUMFERENCE FOR MEASURING BODY FAT PERCENTAGE

Skinfolds are a common measure of body fat percentage which involves pinching certain areas (e.g., biceps, triceps, subscapular, suprailiac, chest, abdomen, thigh) on the body using a skinfold caliper. This method is accurate and inexpensive, but involves touching the skin. The three-site and seven-site skinfolds are commonly used and vary by gender and age. The sum score (measured in millimeters) of the sites corresponds to a body fat percentage. Waist circumference is another measure of body composition and health risks as abdominal fat poses greater threats to good health. Although there are race, ethnicity, age, gender, and body structure differences in appropriate body fat percentages and waist circumference, general guidelines suggest to keep these low and small on respective criteria.

Waist circumference is another measure of body composition, which is also easy and accurate to measure and involves taking a spring-loaded tape measure above the iliac crest to measure the circumference of the waist. Too much fat around the abdominal area increases the risk of metabolic conditions. It is recommended that women maintain a waist circumference less than 35 inches and men should aim for less than 39 inches to minimize health risks.

DIET AND EXERCISE PLANS FOR WEIGHT MANAGEMENT

A combination of physical activity, low-fat, and high-fiber diets aid in maintaining a healthy body composition. Physical activities should include cardiovascular, muscular-strength, and muscular-endurance exercises conducted most days of the week. Cardiovascular activities help burn fat during the activity, and muscular-fitness activities help burn calories during and up to one to three days after. Diets that include consuming vegetables tend to have a positive effect on body composition because these foods are low in calories but are nutrient dense (vitamins, minerals, fiber). Eating lean proteins also aids in maintaining a healthy body composition. Limiting sweets, high-fat foods, and alcohol will help maintain a healthy body composition because these contain large amounts of sugar, fat, and empty calories.

CALORIC APPROACH TO WEIGHT MANAGEMENT

Counting calories is a strategy used to help maintain a healthy body composition. To do this, one needs to calculate their basal metabolic rate to determine their caloric needs. The **basal metabolic rate (BMR)** is the number of calories needed to keep functioning at rest. To compute BMR, height, weight, gender, and age are needed. A revised version of Harrison Benedict's BMR formula is below.

Male: (88.4 + 13.4 × weight in kilograms) + (4.8 × height in centimeters)– (5.68 × age)

Female: (447.6 + 9.25 × weight in kilograms) + (3.10 × height in centimeters)– (4.33 × age)

Once BMR is established, calories consumed would be counted not to exceed the BMR if the desired body composition is met. For weight loss, either fewer calories or more physical activity is recommended for desired body composition. For weight gain, more calories (ideally from lean proteins) or heavy muscular fitness activities are recommended.

Effects of Various Factors on Health and Fitness

REST AND NUTRITION

Resting the body is essential for peak physical performance and good health. Rest includes taking a break (a day off) from training and getting adequate amounts of sleep. Rest allows the body to recover and rebuild from the physical stress put on the body. When the body and muscles are well-rested, performance tends to be more efficient, whereas little to no rest can impede progress. Nutrition is also important for physical performance and good health because poor nutrition (high fat, high sodium, no fiber) negatively impacts growth, energy, exercise recovery, and a healthy body weight. Good nutrition (vegetables, grains, lean protein, low fat) provides energy and allows for greater demands on the body.

ALCOHOL AND TOBACCO

Consuming alcohol and tobacco can negatively impact physical performance and health. Alcohol contains empty calories (7 calories per 1 gram of alcohol) and no nutritional value, which can cause unwanted weight gain. Alcohol is metabolized before carbohydrates and fat, which disrupts weight-loss goals. Alcohol is a depressant drug that slows down the central nervous system, so movement responses (e.g., reaction time) are slower. Alcohol also lowers inhibitions and impairs judgment, and when working out, an injury may occur. Excessive alcohol consumption can lead to cirrhosis of the liver (scarring) and alcoholism (addiction). Nicotine is the addictive substance that is found in tobacco products. Smoking tobacco increases the risk of cardiovascular disease (hypertension, stroke) and makes it more difficult to breathe, especially during physical activity since blood flow is restricted due to the narrowing of blood vessels. Chewing tobacco increases the risks of tooth loss and throat and mouth cancers. When people stop smoking and drinking, many of the ill effects diminish over time.

HEREDITY

Heredity (genetic characteristics) impacts physical performance and is the foundation of one's health. For example, abilities (power, reaction time, muscle fibers) are hereditary, and some have more ability than others. While all can improve, improvement will only go as far as one's genetic abilities. The same is true for health, as some people are predisposed or have a higher risk of poor health if conditions and illness run in their family. For example, if a parent has hypertension or diabetes, the offspring are at greater risks. Physical activity and nutrition can help mitigate negative heredity aspects.

PERSONAL HEALTH RISK FACTOR ASSESSMENTS

Health risk assessments (HRA) are commonly used to evaluate personal health risk. HRAs contain a battery of questions to help determine areas of health risk. HRA questionnaires tend to ask the age, gender, race, ethnicity, history of depression, physical activity, emotional health, social activities, pain, seatbelt usage, tiredness, injuries, smoking, alcohol consumption, and other questions that pertain to health. Based on the results of the questionnaire, physicians may administer a corresponding health assessment. Today, however, there are also online versions of HRAs that can help one evaluate their own health and make changes according to the results. Another option is to get an annual physical with blood work to receive an annual report on cholesterol, lipid, blood glucose, red and white blood cell profiles, and a host of other factors that can be determined by blood tests. Results provide information on how to maintain or improve health and reduce health-risk factors.

Healthy Choices and Behaviors

SELF-DETERMINATION IN MAKING HEALTHY CHOICES

As children transition from childhood to adulthood, they need to be capable of making healthy choices for themselves. In early childhood, nutrition, sleep, hygiene, and fitness are almost solely in the hands of parents. As children age and make more decisions for themselves, they can vary the amount and types of food they eat, time they sleep, and what types of activities they participate in. Usually by middle school or high school, students have enough decision-making power over their own lives that they are really controlling their own fitness and health. It is essential to provide students with the knowledge of what types of choices there are to make and how their choices affect them in the short term and in the long term. For instance, students may not consider how sleep habits affect them, but may decide to make better choices if they realize that sleep deprivation has powerful effects on one's mood, weight management, and stress level. Self-monitoring strategies, such as a health journal or calorie-tracking applications, may be helpful in encouraging students to increase their own self-awareness and pick good goals for themselves.

PATTERNS IN HEALTH CHOICES

Habits are when a behavior choice becomes repeated enough that those choices become the default way of acting. As good habits are formed, the choice involved becomes less difficult to make, as it becomes the natural pattern. Many healthy choices are difficult to make because they require effort or sacrificing something, such as time or instant gratification. Most health choices involve short-term sacrifices to achieve a long-term result, such as losing weight from skipping snacks or candy bars every day. The ultimate result is usually very rewarding, but requires considerable effort in the short-term. Key elements to successful habit-forming is to make sure that the goal is visible and that the behavior is consistently repeated. For example, if a student wants to lose weight by skipping sugary snacks, it is best not to cheat on the diet and occasionally have a candy bar. Cheating on the diet would undercut the development of a desired good habit. The goal also must be visible. If a student cannot see progress from their efforts, then they will not feel rewarded by their hard work and will struggle to maintain it. In this situation, it should be encouraged that the student keeps records of their initial weight or size and track the changes over time to see how well their behavior choices are affecting their outcomes.

MAINTAINING A HEALTHY WEIGHT

Choices that aid in maintaining a healthy weight include engaging in regular physical activity rather than sitting, taking stand-up breaks or moving every hour instead of sitting for very long periods throughout the day, choosing a low-fat diet over a high-fat diet, and eating baked foods instead of fried foods. Taking the stairs instead of the elevator or parking the car far away from a destination rather than close can increase physical activity, which burns calories and helps with weight management. Choosing to have at least three vegetables a day instead of none will increase fiber and nutrients, which also aid in weight regulation. Choosing to eat sweets in moderation (once a week instead of seven days a week) and adhering to serving size recommendations (rather than all-you-can-eat consumption), or eating smaller portions, further support healthy weight maintenance.

Effects of Stress and Stress Management

STRESS AND ITS EFFECTS ON THE BODY.

Stress is the body's response to the demands placed on it. Stress can be either physical or psychological (mental, emotional), and it can be either positive (eustress) or negative (distress). The stress response is usually fight (confront and deal with the stress) or flight (run away or avoid the stress). Chronic stress can have damaging mental and physical effects on the body, including high blood pressure, obesity, diabetes, heart disease, heart attack, stroke, anxiety, body aches, insomnia, irritability, fatigue, chest pain, sadness, depression, and a sense of being overwhelmed.

TECHNIQUES FOR MANAGING STRESS

Techniques or strategies that help manage stress include getting adequate sleep (8 to 10 hours per day), meditation, daily physical activity, deep breathing, yoga, tai chi, laughter, and mindfulness (awareness of behaviors and responses). Progressive relaxation (alternating between tensing and contracting muscles or releasing and relaxing muscles), guided imagery, and visualization also help to manage stress. Connecting with friends and family, engaging in hobbies, listening to music, and reading a book have proven effective in managing stress. Talking to a trusted friend or a therapist is another way to help manage stress. Avoiding illicit drugs, non-prescribed prescription drugs, excessive alcohol, and excessive caffeine also helps reduce the effects of stress because such substances exacerbate the effects of stress. Too much screen time (TV, computer, video games) can also increase the effects of stress.

BENEFITS OF STRESS MANAGEMENT

Physiological benefits of stress management include increased blood flow, an ache-free body, less muscle tension, lower resting and exercise heart rate, lowered blood pressure, lowered sweat response when confronted with stress, increased concentration, lowered release of stress hormones (e.g., cortisol), and improved mood. Psychological benefits of stress management include improved mood, positive self-esteem, enhanced quality of life, positive thoughts, increased confidence in handling stressful events, lowered stress response, and reduced risk of anxiety and depression. A combination of both physiological and psychological benefits can lead to overall better health.

Common Misconceptions in Health and Fitness

COMMON MISCONCEPTIONS REGARDING PHYSICAL ACTIVITY, EXERCISE, AND HEALTH

A common misconception is that exercise and physical activity can ward off the ill-effects of a poor diet or poor nutrition. While physical activity and exercise can burn additional calories from high caloric diets, the negative effects of diets that are high in fat and sugar remain. Another misconception is that lifting weights (barbells, dumbbells, medicine balls) is the only way to get stronger, as one can also get strong by using bodyweight. This misconception is linked to the belief that a gym is needed for exercise, even though exercise can be done at home or outdoors. There are also gender misconceptions that include the belief that girls should not participate in strength training and boys should not participate in cardiovascular activities. Both types of activities are beneficial for all gender groups. The belief that one has to exercise for long bouts of time to be effective is also erroneous because research shows that health benefits can result from short bouts of intense activities that last for as little as seven minutes.

COMMON MISCONCEPTIONS ABOUT BODY SIZE AND PHYSICAL ACTIVITY, HEALTH, EXERCISE, AND DIET

Two common misconceptions about body size in relation to physical activity, health, exercise, and diet are that 1) a large body size or thick frame is unfit and unhealthy and 2) a small body size or thin frame is fit and healthy. In reality, it is difficult to assess fitness and determine health simply by looking at someone. A large person can be fit, healthy, and lean, whereas a thin person can be unfit, unhealthy, and overfat. It depends on the behavior and genetics of an individual. For example, a large body or a person classified as overweight can engage in regular physical activity and eat a healthy diet and have a better fitness level and metabolic profile than a sedentary (inactive) thin person who eats poorly. A fitness assessment and medical exam (e.g., blood work) are required to determine fitness, fatness, and health. These misconceptions are attributed to the war on both childhood and adult obesity, which is responsible for weight loss misconceptions, such as the effects of fad diets. Fad diets are temporary programs that usually involve the extreme restriction of one or more food groups (no carbs, no fat, one meal a day) and are designed for fast weight loss. This short-term solution is not sustaining and once the fad diet stops, the lost weight is regained, and sometimes more weight is gained than prior to starting the fad diet.

EDUCATING STUDENTS ON HEALTH, PHYSICAL ACTIVITY, EXERCISE, DIET MISCONCEPTIONS, AND FAULTY PRACTICES

Teaching students about nutrition and the functions of nutrients at rest and during physical activity is a strategy for combating diet **misconceptions**. Using simulations and videos that accompany the misconceptions has also shown effective. Conducting **mini-research projects** by evaluating fad diets and weight loss products gives students practical opportunities to see the effects of health and fitness misconceptions. Students can also learn how to calculate their caloric needs and shop for foods (online or in-person) that promote optimal functioning, rather than the foods and calories needed for fad diets. Illustrations of the harmful effects of certain behaviors, foods, and practices are also helpful. Students should also learn how to read food labels and ingredients lists. Contraindicated exercises and joint movements and their harmful effects should also be taught (e.g., a lat pull behind the neck can damage the neck, shoulders, and back) because the risks of some exercises supersede the benefits.

Evaluating Health and Fitness Products and Services

QUACKERY AND FALSE INFORMATION IN HEALTH

Quackery is exaggerated, non-scientific claims (testimonials) about the benefits or effectiveness of a product. Quackery is used to sell quick-fix solutions to health and fitness problems. Quackery products tend to use actors to sell the items or testimonials from individuals who had atypical results. The adage "it's too good to be true" is a common and accurate response to quackery. Strategies used to avoid quackery and evaluate health and fitness products include reading labels and ingredients and researching where the content originates. Health and fitness products should originate from or be supported by scientific evidence or medical experts. The Food and Drug Administration (FDA) is the evaluating agency for food, drugs, medical devices, and other substances to ensure that products are safe for Americans to consume or use. Only FDA-approved items have gone through rigorous scientific evaluation that includes thousands of trials before dissemination to the public. Some FDA products require a doctor's prescription (controlled) and some are over-the-counter (e.g., aspirin, ibuprofen). The FDA further ensures safety by continual tracking of effectiveness and side effects, and will remove substances and devices from the public if the risks outweigh the benefits. Many over-the-counter health and fitness substances are neither FDA approved nor supported by scientific research.

EVALUATING INFORMATION RELATED TO HEALTH AND FITNESS PROGRAMS

One strategy to use to evaluate health and related fitness programs is to determine the reputation of the source. For example, programs developed by health and fitness agencies that are accredited to grant certifications are more reputable than programs that are not because they have experts from diverse fields engaged in research on the most effective practices and go through a rigorous process to become accredited. Agencies with strong health and fitness programs include the American College of Sports Medicine, the American Council on Exercise, the National Academy of Sports Medicine, and the National Strength and Conditioning Association, although there are others. Nutrition programs should also be endorsed by reputable agencies, and nutrition plans should only be prescribed by licensed nutritionists or dietitians.

EVALUATING HEALTH AND FITNESS FACILITIES AND SERVICES

Visiting several health and fitness facilities is one strategy used for evaluation to determine the best option. Things to consider during visits include evaluations of facility size; equipment, including the type, age, safety, and maintenance; the location; dates of operation; parking; the distance to travel; fitness class offerings and schedule; day care options; costs; cleanliness; showering and changing facilities; members (coed, same-sex, age, general fitness, body building, power lifting); and personnel. Personal trainers and group fitness instructors should be certified by reputable agencies and certified in first aid, CPR (cardiopulmonary resuscitation), and AED (automated external defibrillation). A serviced AED and fire extinguisher should be visible, and emergency plans posted or available.

Legal and Ethical Responsibilities

CONFIDENTIALITY ISSUES IN PHYSICAL EDUCATION

There are certain legal and ethical considerations in regards to keeping student confidentiality. Any information shared in meetings about students, including students with individualized education plans (IEP) and medical or health conditions, should be kept confidential. When students share confidential information with a teacher, the teacher must weigh the risk involved and report any information a student tells them that may cause physical harm to the student or another person. For example, if a student is homicidal or suicidal, the teacher must report this immediately to the counselor and an administrator. If a student shares that they are harming themselves (e.g., cutting), this too must be shared with the counselor. However, the teacher should both encourage the student to tell the counselor themselves and inform the student of their intentions. Teachers must adhere to any school and district policies and also to local and state laws. If the student discusses a sexuality issue (gay, lesbian, transgender), pregnancy, or relationship status in confidence, while not illegal, disclosing this type of information may eliminate student trust and could possibly pose physical or psychological harm to the student, depending on the environment.

SUPERVISION, LIABILITY, AND NEGLECT

Providing a safe environment is a top priority for teachers. To keep the environment safe, adequate supervision is essential. The teacher should position themselves where they can see all students and be aware of unsafe behaviors. The teacher should also be first to arrive in the teaching space, and should put rules in place if students arrive first. For instance, students should not touch any equipment or engage in physical activity until the teacher arrives and provides instructions. The teacher should check the equipment for damage, and review and post safety rules. Teachers should be aware of their students' strengths and limitations to ensure that activities are safe and appropriate. Accidents and injury are more frequent in physical education settings than other subject areas, thus prevention is critical so that teachers are less likely to be held liable or deemed negligent. **Liability** is a violation of responsibilities (aka duty) usually attributed to negligence. **Negligence** is misconduct that includes failure to create a safe environment that eliminates or reduces the risk of harm. For example, if students are playing soccer without using shin guards and a student gets injured (fractured shin), that would be considered negligence and the teacher could be held liable.

LEGAL AND ETHICAL ISSUES AND RESPONSIBILITIES IN REGARDS TO THE STANDARDS OF CARE

It is the responsibility of school personnel, including the teacher, to ensure that the teaching environment is safe and that standards of care procedures are in place. It is expected that teachers identify or foresee risks and take actions to eliminate or minimize those risks. Teachers should be aware of all legal liability policies, as they are expected to provide a reasonable standard of care according to their professional expertise. Lawsuits may occur if standards of care were not provided, in which negligence would have to be proven. **Malfeasance** is a type of negligence when a teacher engages in misconduct by committing an unlawful act. For instance, a teacher may give a student two negative discipline choices (corporal punishment or run a mile) after misbehaving, but because both choices can cause physical harm, emotional harm, or both, the teacher is liable. **Misfeasance** is the type of negligence where the teacher adheres to proper protocols, but implements them inappropriately (improperly spotting a student during the bench press). **Nonfeasance** is when a teacher fails to act (aka act of omission). For example, if the teacher knows how to spot a student performing the bench press but does not do so, they can be held liable if an injury occurs.

ABUSE AND EXPLOITATION

Abuse is the misuse of another person or treating another person with cruelty. **Exploitation** is using someone unfairly for personal gain. It is against the law to abuse and exploit children. Examples of abuse include physical (e.g., hitting, spanking), verbal (profanity, derogatory words), mental or emotional (humiliation, sarcasm, name calling), and sexual abuse (touching students inappropriately). Physical activity should not be used as punishment (e.g., 10 push-ups for misbehaving) because doing so is considered physical abuse. If it is suspected that a student is experiencing abuse (bruises, broken bones, unexplained injuries, inappropriate contact), the teacher should make record of it and notify the school counselor or psychologist immediately. An example of exploitation would be having students do the teacher's work for free (e.g., supervising students, locker room duty).

TEACHER RESPONSIBILITIES IN RELATION TO STUDENT RIGHTS

Other **student rights** include free speech, the right to wear certain clothing and hairstyles, immigration status, speaking English as a second language (ESL), and the freedom from racial, ethnic, and religious discrimination. At times, schools have policies that are discriminatory (no dreadlocks or long hair allowed, English proficiency required for entry), or illegal practices (asking for students' social media and cell phone information) that infringe on freedom of speech and expression, with the latter infringing upon privacy laws—all of which can cause lawsuits. Teachers have the responsibility to ensure that the environment is **safe and equitable** to meet all students' needs. For instance, a female Muslim student should be allowed to wear a head covering (hijab) at school and in physical education, since the prevention of this would be a violation of the student's religious freedom. Schools and teachers are required by law to provide assistance to students who are not proficient in English. Teachers should also not engage in racist behaviors (treating students negatively based on race or ethnicity).

SEX AND GENDER DISCRIMINATION LAWS (TITLE IX)

Title IX is a federal law enacted in 1972 to end sex and gender discrimination in education and athletics, as girls had less physical education time, less equipment, and fewer sporting opportunities than boys. Prior to Title IX, physical education classes were segregated by gender. After Title IX was enacted, physical education classes became coeducational (coed) with a few exceptions. Title IX was later expanded to protect other groups, including individuals who identify as LGBTQ. Teachers need to make sure that they balance privacy and protection while also maintaining accountability and safety for themselves and other students. For instance, if the only alternative location for a student to change clothes is unsupervised, then the teacher will have to conduct a risk-benefit analysis on the steps to take.

INCLUSION LAWS AND GUIDELINES FOR STUDENTS WITH DISABILITIES

The Individuals with Disabilities Education Act (IDEA) is a federally sanctioned law that ensures a quality educational experience for students with disabilities. Teachers should ensure that accommodations are implemented to meet the needs of students with disabilities. Disabilities can be mental, physical, or both. In physical education settings, adapted physical education (APE) focuses on students with disabilities. To make sure that the learning environment is inclusive, teachers must design instruction to serve all students. As with students without disabilities, teachers should plan intently on helping the students with disabilities to be successful or able to meet the outcomes with modifications and adaptations.

PRIVACY LAWS INVOLVING MEDICAL AND PERSONAL INFORMATION

Privacy laws are mandated by the federal government. States can also have independent privacy laws, but they cannot deviate from the federal mandates. The Federal Education Records and Privacy Act (FERPA) indicates that any school receiving federal funding cannot share student records or any other identifiable information without consent (permission) of the student or parent of a minor. This includes individual education plans (IEPs), health and medical issues, and other personal information about the student. However, IEPs and some health issues (such as attention deficit disorder, or ADD, and attention deficit hyperactivity disorder, or ADHD), may be shared with teachers of the student to best meet the student's needs. Students also have the right to see their records or personal school files. Photos and videos of students should not be shared or posted without student or parent permission and consent. Students, however, only have moderate levels of privacy in situations where supervision is still required to ensure student safety and minimize bullying risk, such as in locker rooms.

Management, Motivation, and Communication

Student Motivation and Lifelong Physical Fitness

MOTIVATING STUDENTS TO PARTICIPATE IN LIFELONG PHYSICAL ACTIVITY

Teachers who role model or engage in physical activity have shown to motivate students to engage in physical activity for life. Students who are skilled or proficient in the fundamental movement patterns are also more likely to engage in physical activities as adults. Positive feedback with explicit acknowledgement of effort and improvement is another effective strategy that encourages regular physical activity. Furthermore, activities that promote self-efficacy and autonomy, which are better achieved with student goal-setting, also helps foster physical activity engagement. Students who have knowledge of the benefits of physical activity and the consequences of not engaging in physical activity further fosters motivation to engage in physical activity over the lifespan.

EFFECTS OF SELF-ASSESSMENT AND PROGRESS TRACKING ON STUDENT MOTIVATION

Self-assessment aids in motivating students to participate in lifelong physical activity as it allows students to evaluate their own performance. From the assessment, students evaluate and reflect on their performance and will either continue, revise, or update goals. As students revisit goals and create a plan to achieve those goals, they will track progress over time to determine growth or the lack thereof. Ongoing self-assessment and reflection allows students to take ownership and responsibility in their performance and develop a plan suitable for their needs. These activities help develop intrinsic motivation, which has shown more effective than extrinsic motivation in promoting lifelong physical activity.

SELF-EFFICACY

Self-efficacy is belief in one's ability to perform motor skills. The development of self-efficacy leads to self-motivation and is strongly associated with engaging in physical activity over the lifespan. There are four circumstances that have shown to increase self-efficacy listed below.

1. Past performance: previous experience of accomplishment or success in a performance task or skill (success in one sport increases the self-efficacy of learning a new sport)
2. Observing others (vicarious learning): watching someone else perform the task or exhibit the skill, which fosters confidence to attempt and perform the task or develop the ("If they can do it, so can I")
3. Verbal persuasion: encouragement from a teacher, parent, or peer ("You can do it!")
4. Physiological cues: kinesthetic responses to the environment (body position or sensory awareness, which is enhanced through repetition and practice)

Classroom and Resource Management

ORGANIZING TIME, LOCATION, AND EQUIPMENT

Planning ahead and providing clear and concise instructions will reduce classroom management and behavioral issues. A schedule of teaching space should be known long before the semester begins. Once the location has been determined, the dimensions of the space and knowledge of the type, amount, and location of equipment should also be known. If there are other teachers on staff, communication on teaching rotations and activities should be discussed to avoid conflicts and time wasting. Establishing routines from student entry and exit, attendance, warm-up, equipment distribution, and equipment cleanup helps students move quickly without losing instructional time or allowing time for students to get off task. A strategy for entrance and attendance is to have students walk to assigned squad lines and conduct an active warm-up while attendance is taken. The teacher can take attendance or assign a squad line leader. Squad lines make it easy to see who is absent. Another management strategy is to have students conduct an instant activity (IA) as soon as they enter the gym or field that can be posted for students to read upon entry. Attendance should be taken during the IA, which allows students to immediately engage and reduces time for off-task behaviors. This IA can also serve as a warm-up or an opportunity to pre-assess or post-assess students' skill levels and performance.

ALLOCATING TIME, LOCATION, AND EQUIPMENT

Every minute of instructional time should be accounted for. All tasks and activities, including transitions, should have an allotted time when lesson planning (e.g., three minutes, five minutes). The equipment should be out and ready for easy retrieval (e.g., on the sidelines, in the corners of the teaching space). If outside, a backup plan (go to the gym, multi-purpose room, classroom) should be in place in case of inclement or unsafe weather (e.g., rain, heat, cold). Students should be trained and assigned roles to help put equipment away. This saves time and promotes personal responsibility and teamwork, which will minimize disruptions in the future. When sharing teaching space, communication and planning are extremely important because conflicts are likely to occur when there is a communication breakdown. Teachers who teach at the same time, in the same place, and use the same equipment should meet before the school year to map out activities, equipment usage (setting up and breaking down), teaching space (one-half or one-third of the court or field), rules, routines, duties, and protocols (e.g., locker room, attendance, and warm-up procedures) to optimize the learning experience. Some teachers elect to team teach, where one teacher leads while the other helps facilitate. This is often done so teachers can teach to their strengths and to reduce management issues.

CLASSROOM MANAGEMENT APPROACHES

Large class sizes, minimal space, and lack of equipment are limitations of taking attendance, physical activities, and managing time. Large classes require more time to move and take attendance, and they require extra safety measures in cramped spaces. Squad lines (students arranged in rows or lines of 5 to 10, forming a box shape) are more effective than instant activities for large groups because students are more contained, which reduces the risk of injury. Large class sizes, minimal space, and the lack of equipment do not give students the opportunity to engage in all of the same activities at the same time. For example, a common approach is to have half of the class in the center of the court or field engaging in activities, while the other half are doing activities on the sidelines. While this approach increases safety, it does not allow students to fully engage in the learning objectives and decreases practice time for refinement and improvement. Large class sizes also make it more difficult for the teacher to see all students and provide appropriate feedback.

Review Video: <u>Classroom Management - Rhythms of Teaching</u>
Visit mometrix.com/academy and enter code: 809399

Maintaining a Positive Learning Climate

GENDER DIVERSE CLASSES

To avoid gender favoritism and gender disparities in physical education, teachers should expect all students to engage in the activities and work towards the performance goals. Teachers should create coeducational activities and incorporate student preferences into the curriculum and activities. All students should be included in gender stereotypic games activities (e.g., boys engaging in dance and gymnastics and girls engaging in team sports like football). Teachers should not use or allow stereotypic language like, "You throw like a girl." The teacher should also monitor time given to all groups to ensure equal time is given and that one group does not dominate another. The teacher can also reflect on their behaviors to make sure that they are not responding to one gender group over another.

MIXED-ABILITY CLASSES

A cooperative environment helps foster inclusion in mixed ability classes. Depending on the objective, groups can contain students of mixed abilities, but sometimes students with the same abilities need to be grouped. For example, novice learners may need to be grouped together to focus on skill levels because grouping these novices with more skilled students may intimidate and discourage them from participation. The skilled students may get frustrated as beginner skills and activities below their more advanced skill level become boring and causes them to go off task. However, sometimes mixed groupings may be beneficial when peer coaching or teaching is practiced and advanced students work with beginners, since there is evidence that students learn best from peers.

DIFFERENT CULTURAL BACKGROUNDS

Strategies that promote a healthy social climate for students of various cultural backgrounds include offering diverse curricula, activities, and teaching approaches that include all student groups. If English is a second or additional language for students, cues and assignments should also include the student's first language. Respect and understanding of other cultures should be the standard, and derogatory language and behaviors should not be tolerated. The teacher should explore cultural practices, differences in discipline, and physical activity expectations. For instance, in some cultures, it is disrespectful to look teachers or authority figures in the eyes. In other cultures, and in some religions, physical activity is discouraged. In these instances, asking questions about cultural and physical activity expectations and conveying the facts (not opinions) about the benefits of physical activity and social engagement in American culture should be shared with students and parents. Additionally, some cultures and religions do not allow for bare skin to be exposed, so students should not be penalized if these factors prevent them from changing out of their clothing and into the school PE uniform.

Developing Positive Interpersonal Skills in Physical Education

DEVELOPING CONFIDENCE THROUGH PHYSICAL ACTIVITIES

Games and sports promote the development of confidence through leadership in both the various roles involved and accomplishing a goal. For example, in team sports, everyone has a role and a responsibility that helps the team work towards a goal. Games and sports also involve competition, which provides opportunities to develop competence, which has shown to increase motivation and confidence. Successful students, players, and teams tend to have greater confidence than unsuccessful students, players, and teams. Therefore, the learning environment should be challenging yet attainable to help build confidence. Dance helps promote confidence as students are able to move freely without judgment or competition. In dances that involve steps, learning or mastery of these dances helps build confidence through accomplishing the task of learning the dance steps.

FAIRNESS AND RESPECT FOR DIVERSITY

Games and sports are governed by rules that involve fair play. Fair play has to be taught and includes personal responsibility, showing respect to self and others, giving full effort, and being helpful. Diversity is promoted through games and sports as teams and opponents tend to include different types of individuals (gender, race, ethnicity, ability, learning styles), and sport and games allow for interactions across groups that can aid in a better understanding of similarities and differences. A respect for diversity can also be developed and promoted through dance as individuals have the opportunity to engage in freedom of expression. In PE curricula, dances from around the world and from different cultures are taught (the Virginia reel, polka, African dance, folk dances, square dance), exposing children to other people's cultures and fostering inclusion, diversity, and respect for others.

CONFLICT RESOLUTION SKILLS

Outdoor pursuits help develop conflict resolutions skills by having students engage in challenging tasks like high ropes courses and partner or group activities like trust falls. Partner and group activities require frequent communication to problem solve or accomplish a task. Dual and team sports are also avenues that promote conflict resolution skills, as communication is needed for the team's success. It is customary for a player to apologize when they make an error. Players also communicate how to strategize against an opponent, which is an example of solving a problem. For example, when a teammate keeps losing to his or her opponent, the team will need to communicate with each other to either switch roles, provide assistance, or utilize a different defensive strategy to solve the problem.

TURN TAKING AND TEAMWORK

Games and sports require cooperation and collaboration, thus the promotion of teamwork. Teamwork is shown through working together to score a point, playing defense and offense, and communicating to accomplish these tasks. Taking turns is evident in games and sports when players have to substitute in and out of a game. In softball and baseball, batters have to wait for their turn. Taking turns is also evident in group games like jumping rope, where the jumpers have to wait for the person in front to complete their jump before entering. The rope turners also take turns. Students or players on the sidelines also demonstrate teamwork by cheering and encouraging other active students or players.

TREATING OPPONENTS WITH RESPECT AND LEADERSHIP SKILLS

Sport and game etiquette are promoted and teach how players should treat their opponents. For example, if a player from the opposing team falls, a respectful act would be to assist the opponent with getting up. During a sport, it is common to take a knee out of respect when a player gets injured. This knee position is held until the player gets up or is taken off of the field or court. Calling personal fouls and apologizing if one causes harm are other examples of treating opponents with respect that are developed and promoted through games and sports. Wishing the opposition good luck before the game and shaking hands at the end of play are other examples of how to treat opponents with respect. Opportunities for leadership are promoted in roles including team captain and positions played. For example, in basketball, the point guard is usually responsible for bringing the ball up the court and calling the offense, making this player the leader in this capacity. Other players also have a role and lead in their respective positions.

EXAMPLES OF LEADERSHIP, TAKING TURNS, AND LOYALTY IN OUTDOOR ACTIVITIES

Examples of teamwork, taking turns, and loyalty are evident in outdoor activities. For instance, rock climbing activities in physical education require a climber and three to four belayers (anchors who support the climber). The belayers work and communicate as one unit and provide safety (loyalty) and leadership for the climber. The belayers also provide encouragement to help the climber reach the top of the climb, which illustrates leadership. If the belayers are not focused while supporting the climber, injury can occur. Climbers and belayers change roles, which illustrates taking turns. In partner or couples' dances (foxtrot, tango, salsa), there is a leader and follower, which gives students opportunities to engage in leadership. These roles are usually switched, which illustrates taking turns in the leader and follower roles. The climber in rock climbing and the follower in dance have to trust that the belayers and leader know what they are doing, and consistency in performance helps students demonstrate loyalty.

Promoting Self-Management Skills

PROMOTING SELF-MANAGEMENT SKILLS

Self-assessment (evaluating performance) and **self-monitoring** (observation of self) are used to help students reflect on and evaluate their own performance by identifying strengths, weaknesses, and the learning process. These self-monitoring methods are self-regulation strategies or self-management skills that help students take ownership of their learning. Self-management skills include the ability to identify successes and failures and to create goals for improvement, which promotes intrinsic motivation to engage in physical activity. Of these strategies, goal setting is considered the most important because students are choosing their own specific focus and outcome. As such, goals should be specific and measurable, which helps students determine the next steps for practice, remediation, or growth.

STUDENT RESPONSIBILITY AND SELF-CONTROL

Assigning roles to students helps them develop responsible behaviors and self-control. Common roles in physical education include line or squad line leader, exercise or warm-up leader, equipment manager, and attendance taker. Behavioral rules and expectations help promote self-control. A common behavioral method used in physical education is Don Hellison's teaching personal and social responsibility (TPSR) model, which aims to teach personal and social responsibility. The TPSR model has five levels listed below.

1. Respect for others' rights and feelings (manage temper, work towards peaceful conflict resolution)
2. Effort: practice and learn persistence and intrinsic motivation, take on challenges
3. Self-direction: goal-setting, refraining from peer pressure
4. Helping others
5. Behaviors are carried over outside of the gym: the goal of having values learned in class transfer to other environments (e.g., home, playground)

These behaviors can be the focus during an individual lesson, unit, or every lesson. However, students are often taught each level and evaluate where they were on a particular day or lesson. It is recommended that this model is embedded with other instructional models because stand-alone use is not effective for behavior change.

HELLISON'S TEACHING PERSONAL AND SOCIAL RESPONSIBILITY (TPSR) MODEL

Hellison's **Teaching Personal and Social Responsibility** (TPSR) model seeks to promote students' ability to take responsibility for their actions in the physical education classroom and carry that responsibility into the students' lives. This model, therefore, is useful in helping to develop students' ability to **manage success** and **failure** well. The elements of the TPSR model apply to both success and failure. Students who may care too much about winning or losing may lose their temper when losing, and therefore may need to work on improving their **respect** for others' rights and feelings. Other students may not care enough about success and may not put in the necessary **effort** to perform well. Alternatively, a student who succeeds in sports on talent may have a poor attitude about their abilities and not respect other students who are not as skilled. Another consequence might be that a talented student may not put forth the effort required to further develop their skills. The **self-direction** stage may be a good focal point for a student who remains unchallenged without specific goals. Helping the student to **self-evaluate** and target particular skills may help to keep the student motivated and able to grow more efficiently. Ultimately, the goals of TPSR are skills well suited to learning through physical education, but apply to the whole life of a student.

STUDENTS' GOAL-SETTING ABILITIES

To help students develop goal-setting abilities, they must be taught that goals should be specific and measurable. An example should be given, such as, "I can hit the target 6 out of 10 times." Students should be told to create a moderately challenging goal. A goal that is too easy lacks challenge, and a goal that is too difficult can create frustration. Students should also be encouraged to set short-term and long-term goals. When students set their own goals, they gain a sense of accomplishment and personal satisfaction, which fosters intrinsic motivation and competence.

PROBLEM-SOLVING SKILLS

Teachers can help students analyze and problem-solve through guided discovery and cooperative learning. **Guided discovery** is when the teacher structures the environment to where students can figure out or solve the problem on their own. Using this method, the teacher asks students questions to help "guide" them to accomplish predetermined tasks. This has also been called a **problem-solving approach.** Rather than having one right answer, there are usually several options to complete the tasks. For example, a task may be to get from one obstacle to another without walking. Students would then analyze the obstacles, make a decision on what they think is the best method, and attempt the tasks. If the students are successful, they have solved the problem. To further aid in analyzing and problem-solving, the teacher may follow up and ask if there is another way to complete the task, at which time students would have to continue with their analysis and attempt to solve the problem another way.

DECISION-MAKING SKILLS

Tactical learning approaches help students with decision-making skills used in individual, dual, and team sports. In sports, every move made or action performed is a decision. Practicing sports skills during modified game play (e.g., the tactical approach) allows students opportunities to consistently make decisions. Depending on the outcome of the decision, students will either continue or do something different. For example, if a student conducted a fake before kicking the ball into the goal, he or she may try to do the same thing the next time. However, if the fake was unsuccessful and the ball got stolen, the student will likely make another choice. If a student continues to make the same error, the teacher may have to ask questions to help the student do something different. Experiencing the tactics helps students develop an inventory of things to do and what decision to make according to the environment.

Planning, Instruction, and Student Assessment

Principles and Benefits of a Physically Active Lifestyle

CARDIOVASCULAR ENDURANCE

Cardiovascular endurance is one of five health-related fitness components. Cardiovascular activities involve engaging in continuous gross motor movements that work the heart and lungs. Cardiovascular activities include walking, jogging, swimming, cycling, hiking, and aerobic dance. It is recommended that youth engage in at least 60 minutes of cardiovascular activities three to six days a week. Adults should engage in at least 30-minute exercises five days a week, or 150 to 225 minutes per week. Cardiovascular outcomes are enhanced with muscular fitness and flexibility training because they have a synergistic effect (work together in unison).

BENEFITS OF LIVING A PHYSICALLY ACTIVE LIFESTYLE

The benefits of living a physically active lifestyle include lowering the risk of diabetes, heart attack, and heart disease, which are the foremost killers in the United States. Blood pressure and blood cholesterol are also lowered. Further, bones and muscles are strengthened, which lowers the risks of falling or developing osteoporosis. Physical activity increases metabolism, helps maintain a healthy body weight, and helps improve immunity needed to fight off infections, including some cancers. Physical activity also improves mood, reduces stress, increases energy, improves sleep, and has shown to improve academic outcomes.

CIRCUIT TRAINING

Circuit training is a great way to introduce students to multiple types of exercises. Circuit training is a fitness activity made up of 6 to 10 stations that are used to improve the health-related fitness components (cardiovascular endurance, muscular strength and endurance, flexibility, body composition) and skill-related fitness components (agility, speed, power). Students participate in each activity for a designated time or number of repetitions before rotating to the next exercise. Circuit training tends to be enjoyable because it is non-competitive, provides variety, and allows students to work at their own pace. Music usually accompanies circuit training, which has shown to positively impact student intensity and engagement.

LEARNING OPPORTUNITIES THAT PROMOTE PARTICIPATION IN PHYSICAL ACTIVITIES

Learning opportunities that promote participation and enjoyment of physical fitness activities include engaging in a variety of activities and developing individualized programs that include personal goal setting, feedback, encouragement, enthusiasm, and role modeling. Variety in activities reduces boredom and allows students to engage in activities they will find enjoyable. Individualized programs with personal goals give students ownership of want they want to work on or improve, which increases the likelihood of participation. Encouragement and providing feedback with a positive attitude foster positive feelings among students, which in turn can elicit student buy-in. Students are also more likely to engage in physical activity if the teacher also engages in physical activity.

PHYSIOLOGICAL ADAPTATIONS IN RESPONSE TO REGULAR PHYSICAL ACTIVITY

Physiological adaptations that occur from regularly engaging in cardiovascular physical activity include increased perspiration, stronger and more elastic smooth muscles, decreased heart rate,

88

and an increase in both the size and strength of the heart, which increases blood flow and volume. Oxygen transfer (gas exchange) becomes more efficient due to an increase in alveoli and capillaries in the lungs, which aids in an increase in VO2 max or aerobic capacity. There is also an increase of nutrients and glucose to the muscles performing the work. Exercise recovery also improves as it becomes easier to remove lactic acid. Slow twitch fibers (responsible for slow continuous movements) become more efficient as they are easier to recruit by regularly engaging in cardiovascular physical activity. These adaptations aid in lowering the risks of hypokinetic diseases and obesity-related conditions (e.g., diabetes, heart disease, metabolic syndrome).

HEALTH BENEFITS OF REGULARLY PHYSICAL ACTIVITY

Engaging in **regular physical activity** increases life expectancy, improves mood, reduces the risk of some cancers, lowers blood pressure, aids in weight loss, and helps maintain a healthy body composition. Physical activity strengthens bones, which lowers the risk of developing osteoporosis, improves mobility and flexibility, and reduces the risk of falling. Regular physical activity has shown to improve mental alertness, judgement, learning, and relieve some symptoms of depression. Heart rate is also lowered by engaging in regular physical activity, and the risk of heart disease goes down. Blood glucose and insulin are also regulated, and diabetes and other metabolic conditions can be managed by engaging in regular physical activity.

HYPOKINETIC DISEASES AND METABOLIC SYNDROME

Hypokinetic diseases result from inactivity or living a sedentary lifestyle. Hypokinetic diseases include heart disease, obesity, diabetes, and stroke. **Metabolic syndrome** is a collection of diseases or risk factors, including high blood glucose, high blood pressure, excessive fat around the waist, and high cholesterol, which increases the risk of heart attack, stroke, and diabetes. Hypokinetic diseases and metabolic syndrome are often referred to as lifestyle diseases or conditions because most can be prevented by engaging in regular physical activity, eating a healthy diet, avoiding or limiting certain foods (sodium, fried foods) and substances (smoking tobacco and excessive alcohol intake). Engaging in regular physical activity lowers these risks.

Components of Health-Related Fitness

MUSCULAR STRENGTH AND MUSCULAR ENDURANCE

Muscular strength is the amount of force (push, pull, lift) exerted by the muscles, as shown in lifting weights and performing push-ups. **Muscular endurance** is the ability for the muscles to work continuously or repeatedly without excessive fatigue. Muscular endurance is measured through assessments such as the curl-up test. Although these are two separate health-related fitness components, improvement in one will improve the other. For example, if the fitness goal is to increase size and strength in the quadriceps, training would include lifting heavy loads at low rep counts. Muscular endurance would also improve, but endurance would be gained at a slower rate than size and strength. To train for muscular endurance in quadriceps, the load would be lighter and the rep count higher. Again, the quadriceps will get stronger, but would not likely increase in size due to the low weight and high rep count.

CARDIOVASCULAR ENDURANCE

Cardiovascular endurance is the ability to engage in continuous physical activity that increases the heart rate and sweat response. Cardiovascular activities use the heart and lungs, which become more efficient with regular engagement. Engaging in cardiovascular activities lowers the risk of heart disease (coronary artery disease, high cholesterol, heart attack), hypertension, obesity, and metabolic conditions such as type 2 diabetes. Cardiovascular activities also improve mood as endorphins ("happy hormones") are released. Blood also flows more freely, which increases oxygen levels, thus making it easier to breathe. The benefits of cardiovascular activities increase as the frequency and time increases.

BODY COMPOSITION AND FLEXIBILITY

Body composition is the measure of muscle, bone, and fat in the body. It is commonly associated with a measure of body fatness (e.g., body mass index, body fat percentage). Maintaining a healthy body composition reduces the risks of obesity and obesity-related conditions. Engaging in muscular and cardiovascular fitness activities along with good nutrition help with the maintenance of a healthy body composition. **Flexibility** is the range of motion at the joint. The lengthening or stretching of muscles helps increase flexibility, which helps increase mobility. Flexibility is often overlooked, but it should be developed just as the cardiovascular and muscular fitness components are. Flexibility contributes to more efficient mechanical movements in these health-related fitness components. In addition to increasing mobility, flexibility helps with posture, body awareness, reduces muscle soreness after engaging in other vigorous activities, and reduces the risk of debilitating back pain. Deep stretching along with deep breathing (e.g., yoga) has also shown to also improve mental health and wellbeing. A lack of flexibility increases the risk of poor health, including pain, stiffness, and difficulty performing daily tasks.

FITT PRINCIPLE

The **FITT** acronym stands for frequency, intensity, time, and type. It is a simple guide to fitness training principles deemed appropriate for children and sedentary adults. **Frequency** is how often one engages in physical activity or exercise. **Intensity** is the difficulty or challenge of the activities (heart rate, load and weight, reps). **Time** is the duration or how long one engages in physical activity per session (20 minutes, 60 minutes). **Type** is the kind of activities chosen (weight training, cardiovascular activities, yoga). When using the FITT principle, favorable physiological outcomes can occur, as engaging in a variety of physical activity several days a week has shown to promote good health.

Warm-Up and Cooldown in Exercise

Conducting a **warm-up** before engaging in exercise prepares the body for more vigorous activity and may reduce the risk of injury. Warm-ups generally consist of bouts of low-intensity activities and dynamic movements, lasting 5 to 10 minutes, to increase blood flow to the muscles and heart. The warm-up should reflect or be specific to the activities that will be performed. A cooldown also consists of low-intensity activities and helps return the body back to pre-exercise or normal conditions to restore the body's homeostasis (equilibrium, or bringing heart rate and other systems back to normal). The **cooldown** is the gradual slowing down of the more vigorous exercise session. Stretching may or may not be involved in the cooldown, although stretching during the cooldown, when the muscles are still warm, is best. To increase flexibility, static stretching (holding the stretch for several seconds) is preferred during the cooldown as well.

Overload and Progression in Exercise

Overload is performing more work than is normal or putting stress on the body's systems, either of which can produce physiological adaptations. For example, if one mile of walking is the normal activity done throughout the day, then to increase cardiovascular fitness, one would have to walk more than one mile a day or adapt the routine to include jogging or running, either of which would put more stress on the body than what is normal, thus increasing the intensity. **Progression** (aka progressive overload) is the gradual increase in overload to reduce the risk of injury and to prevent overtraining or overuse, which can demotivate individuals to continue in an exercise program.

Fitness Goals and Planning

SMART GOAL-SETTING METHOD

The **SMART** goal-setting method is designed to help individuals create goals, track progress, and have accountability measures. When setting fitness or exercise goals, they should be specific, measurable, achievable, relevant, and timely. For example, a weight loss goal for someone who is 10 pounds overweight might be to lose five pounds (specific, attainable, and measurable) in 12 weeks (attainable within in the time frame). Based on this goal, the person would design a physical activity program that complements the goal and take an inventory of foods that negate this outcome. A pre-assessment and post-assessment of weight would be taken on a scale (measurable) to determine if the goal was met. They could also measure their weight once a week to track progress over time, especially if the goal is met sooner. If the goal is met before the timeline, a new goal would be created.

DESIGNING EFFECTIVE HEALTH AND FITNESS PLANS

In order to reap the rewards or experience of the physiological adaptations that occur as a result of engaging in physical activity and exercise, the activities must be performed with **regularity**, or consistency. The activities should also be performed with **specificity**, which is achieved by participating in activities that address the desired outcomes. For example, if the goal is to increase muscular strength, then the activities should involve lifting weights (resistance training) at least two to three times a week. For cardiovascular goals, one should engage in cardiovascular activities for 150 minutes a week. To increase flexibility, one should engage in stretching activities at least twice a week. The principle of **individuality** is also important, as it is recognized that fitness training is personal and a host of factors influence engagement and outcome goals (sport, baseline fitness levels). Factors to consider under the principal of individuality include genetics (gender, muscle fiber type), body type and size, fitness levels, personal preferences, personal goals, and different abilities in reaching fitness goals. Given the understanding that students are individuals with different needs, students should have the opportunity to use the FITT principle and teacher's guidance to develop their own goals and the activities that they want to engage in.

SELECTING AND EVALUATING PHYSICAL ACTIVITIES

Creating SMART goals is the first step that should be taken before selecting activities. Once goals are set, activities should be chosen based on enjoyment and proficiency in the skills needed to perform the activities. For example, playing a game of basketball or soccer can also meet cardiovascular goals instead of traditional cardiovascular activities like running or swimming. Monitoring heart rate (e.g., working in the target heart rate zone) is one way to evaluate the intensity and the effectiveness of training, as the resting heart rate lowers as fitness improves. When initially selecting weight training activities, light weight(s) should be used to ensure proper form and reduce the risk of injury. If the weight is too easy, gradually increase weights until the last few reps in a set are challenging. Lifting at a percentage of a one-repetition max (1RM), the maximum amount of weight that can be lifted one time with excellent form, or a predicted 1RM can be used to select an appropriate weight. Although a 1RM can be used to evaluate strength gains, they are discouraged unless the teacher and students have advanced training and understanding. Reflection journals and workout logs also help evaluate progress.

Self-Assessment of Health and Fitness

ACTIVITY TRACKERS

Activity trackers are devices that record step count, distance traveled, minutes engaged in activity, calories burned, and heart rate. **Pedometers** are activity trackers worn around the waist or wrist that track step count and distance traveled. **Accelerometers** measure acceleration, and most also track step count or distance traveled. **Heart rate monitors** measure heart rate or the intensity of activity through heart rate. Some activity trackers measure all of the above, including body position, and some are waterproof and can be used for aquatic activities. Students may not only be challenged and motivated by activity trackers, but they may even have fun using them. Activity trackers also provide instant and continuous feedback that can help students monitor their engagement and make decisions on the frequency, intensity, and duration of their physical activity, which holds them accountable. Heart rate data is specific to the user, which creates potential for a fair environment where students can work in their own target heart rate zones. Data is also objective, which reduces teacher bias in assessments.

JOURNALS AND FITNESS LOGS

Maintaining **journals** and **fitness logs** are writing activities that help students make connections to concepts and apply them. Journals require students to reflect on skills, performance, fitness, and feelings. Journals can also be used for students to respond to questions regarding the relationships between FITT and behaviors to fitness outcomes. Students can also describe how they felt during the exercise ("The workout was easy, so I need to increase my weight," or "I was exhausted and did not complete the exercises because I had little sleep."), which further aids in their understanding of the interrelated components of health and physical activity. Fitness logs record or document activity over time. Students can log minutes engaged in activity (10 minutes on the treadmill), sets, repetitions, and weight (two sets of 12 reps at eight pounds), and types of activity engaged in (weight training, swimming). Logs also provide students with a visual of progress, which can be adjusted as goals are met.

SELF-ASSESSMENT

Self-assessments help students track their progress, which helps them develop competence in creating their own fitness programs. Self-assessments may include fitness tests (e.g., number of push-ups completed in a certain time frame to evaluate upper body strength or measure endurance) that students can conduct on their own. Self-assessments may also be performance-based (e.g., the quality of the push-up: hands below shoulders, arms extended, 90-degree angle, body flat). The latter is most important because it helps students gain an understanding of the movements before focusing on fitness outcomes. Self-assessments also remove stress, demotivation, and the unhealthy competition that is often associated with group fitness testing and assessments.

Identifying and Addressing Various Student Needs

IDENTIFYING AND MEETING ALL STUDENTS NEEDS

Assessments are used to determine if students have met, not met, or are making progress towards their objectives. The teacher needs to make sure that assessments both measure the objective and are specific. For example, a general objective is being able to perform the overhand throw; however, the elements of the overhand throw (e.g., wind-up phase, follow-through) are what should be assessed. For instance, if there are five elements or critical skill cues that make up a skill, the student would need to meet four or five of the cues to meet or exceed the objective. A student who can perform two or three of the critical skill cues may indicate that they are making progress towards meeting the objective, but performing only one or none of the cues would indicate that the student is not meeting the objectives. Based on how the student is performing, corrective feedback would be given to help the student meet the objective. If a student is already proficient with all five cues, the teacher should provide instruction to make the task more challenging (e.g., run, throw, and hit the target) to keep the student progressing and to reduce boredom and off-task behaviors.

ROLE OF STUDENT CHOICE IN PHYSICAL EDUCATION

Student choice is another way to differentiate and provide equitable instruction. **Equity** is defined as providing equal opportunity, sometimes through modification, whereas **equality** is treating everyone the same regardless of individual needs. While these terms are often used interchangeably, equity is the goal during instruction because not everyone has the same needs. For example, giving each student a basketball to shoot at a 10-foot basketball goal is equality, but equity is lowering the goal for students who are much shorter than their peers (e.g., four feet tall when other peers are five feet tall and taller), which makes the distance proportional to height. Student choice has shown to motivate students to engage in physical activity settings. By offering choice, students can select activities based on their strengths. Allowing student choice also reduces embarrassment for students who are unable to perform the desired outcome. Student choice also allows students to select activities that they are comfortable with and take greater challenges if desired. During choice activities, the teacher should provide progressive activities from the beginner stage to the advanced stage as students become more proficient or comfortable moving through the tasks.

EQUITABLE INSTRUCTION PRACTICES

Teaching practices that contribute to equitable instruction include taking an inventory of student's needs through assessment and asking students questions. Tracking teacher and student behaviors can also aid in equitable instruction to determine if there are unconscious biases. For example, a teacher might call on or help boys more than girls in a class, may discipline one ethnic group harsher than another, or give more attention to athletes than non-athletes. Tracking teacher behaviors allows for the teacher to reflect and make changes to instruction. **Reflection** is when the teacher has an opportunity to think about the lesson(s) and determine what went well and what needs improvement. When a teacher makes a change that benefits all students, equitable instruction can be achieved.

Designing and Implementing Instruction

SAFETY CONSIDERATIONS FOR DESIGNING AND IMPLEMENTING INSTRUCTION

Safety practices to consider when designing and implementing instruction include a warm-up and stretching before physical activity engagement. The equipment used should be damage-free and spaced where students can move about freely. **Protective equipment** should be used to prevent injury (e.g., shin guards, helmets, weather-appropriate clothing). When instruction is outside in the heat and sun, protective clothing, hats, and sunscreen should be encouraged, and water should be easily accessible. Students should be informed of precautions to take when engaging in road activities (walking, jogging, cycling, skating). The teacher should watch for **overexertion** and students who have a **medical condition** (e.g., asthma). An **emergency plan** should be in place and teachers should be certified in first aid and CPR or have knowledge of actions to take for common injuries in physical education. Teachers should also know when to call 911 and who will make the call in the event of an emergency.

MOTIVATION CONSIDERATIONS FOR DESIGN AND INSTRUCTION

Teachers can create an environment where all students can succeed, which helps build student confidence in the ability to complete more difficult tasks. This is known as **self-efficacy**, which fosters intrinsic motivation. Teachers should provide positive feedback, allow for student choice, and have students set goals. The teacher can also set up the environment where students are encouraged and allowed to make mistakes by allowing multiple non-accessed opportunities to practice or engage in the activities. The teacher can design healthy competitive activities (e.g., no one is eliminated, ability group for fair and equal teams, don't take score) as some students do not enjoy competitive activities, which can demotivate students. If available, the teacher can also recommend that higher performing or competitive students enroll in sport-specific or competitive physical education courses. The teacher can give rewards (e.g., student choice, stickers, pencils), which has shown effective, although these should be used with caution because they can negatively impact intrinsic motivation, especially when not related to learning. The teacher should design lessons that allow for social interaction and provide students with a rationale (objectives) for tasks to aid motivation.

STUDENT PROGRESS AND PHYSICAL EDUCATION

Instructional strategies that aid in ensuring students' progress includes high expectations, providing adequate learning time to engage in activities, giving students maximum opportunities to respond, providing students with cues and corrective feedback (e.g., "Look up," "Keep your eyes on the ball," "Use a wider stance"), differentiation in instruction (written, oral, physical, video), and accommodating students' learning styles (verbal and auditory, visual, and kinesthetic instruction). Assessments also ensure students' progress (self, peer, formative, homework, quizzes), which should vary and appropriately address the objectives. Students can be motivated by incorporating curriculum that is developmentally appropriate (larger size equipment for students in the primary grades) and encourages student social responsibility and social skills (putting equipment away, team work). A safe, equitable, inclusive, and cooperative environment have all shown to help students improve.

VARYING INSTRUCTIONAL APPROACHES

There are various approaches and accompanying models used in physical education, including skill development (skill themes approach), team sports (sport education model, tactical games), and physical fitness and health-related fitness education. The skill themes approach is primarily used in elementary school and focuses on building the fundamental movement skills used in individual and dual sports. There are two common approaches when teaching team sports. The **sport education**

95

model is where students not only play the sport, but are also responsible for leadership roles, including coaching, refereeing, keeping score, calculating statistics, managing equipment, and other roles specific to the sport which foster team cohesion and leadership. This model provides students with details involved in all aspects involved in sports rather than focusing only on skills and game play. In contrast, the **tactical games approach** is designed to promote cognitive connections with the physical aspects of play and focuses heavily on building students' decision-making skills. Fitness education models are designed for students to engage in health-related fitness to prevent disease and increase the quality of life. Fitness curriculums are generally introduced during middle school with increased focus during high school.

MOVEMENT EDUCATION FRAMEWORK

Movement education is the foundation of physical education programs and is where the direct physical application of psychomotor, cognitive, and affective domains derived, as well as the movement concepts of spatial awareness, effort, and relationships of the body. Movement education is another approach used often in elementary physical education programs and is most evident in creative movement, dance, and gymnastics curriculums. Movement education is not common in secondary schools because middle school physical education involves team sports and high school focuses on health-related fitness. However, movement concepts are evident in other models. When adopting a movement education approach, it is understood that students must have an understanding of how, what, why, and where the body moves and be able to demonstrate the fundamental movement skills in order to progress to more complex movements (manipulatives, games, and movement skills used in individual, dual, and team sports). A criticism of movement education is that it lacks structure as students are guided through activities to come to their own conclusions, but this criticism fails to recognize that student creativity is one of the strengths of movement education.

MATERIALS AND TECHNOLOGIES

There are many materials and technology tools that help students meet objectives and address their needs. A common tech tool is the heart rate monitor, which assesses the intensity of cardiovascular activities to ensure that students are working within their target heart rate zone. Heart rate monitors also add a safety element, as students can monitor when they are above their target heart rate zone and slow down activity accordingly. The pedometer is another technological tool that helps students track step count and meet activity or step count objectives. Other effective technologies include slideshows and videos of concepts and skills, which provide students with visual tools that support verbal instruction. Recording students on a device (iPad, smartphone) can provide students with visual feedback of their performance, and corrective feedback can be given for improvement. Written assignments (e.g., worksheets) and journals are materials that can be used to assess student learning and understanding. Posters or boards with objectives and cues can aid as reminders for students of the focus of the lesson.

Physical Education Models

TACTICAL GAMES APPROACH

The **tactical games approach** is a teaching model used to teach team sports. The goal is to develop the cognitive aspects of team sports that include skills, decision-making, and strategies, thus fostering understanding. There is an intentional focus on developing intrinsic motivation, which has shown to increase metacognition (the knowledge of how someone knows something). Rather than the direct teaching of skills in isolation that eventually lead to game play, the tactical games approach uses a whole-part-whole method where students play the game after an objective (how to get open) has been presented. The teacher observes student behaviors to determine areas of growth. However, feedback is given in the form of questions (inquiry-based) to the group to help guide the students in solving problems. For example, the teacher might state, "I noticed that Team A had a difficult time getting open. What are some things we can do to get open?" With the teacher's guidance, students brainstorm and share techniques, then implement during the next gameplay session. Gameplay is paused for a debrief session to discuss if and how the objective was met. Students then practice the identified problems and return to play to work on implementing concepts, skills, and strategies discussed during the debriefing session.

COOPERATIVE LEARNING

Cooperative learning is a teaching approach used in physical education settings. **Cooperative learning** is a student-centered, non-competitive approach that develops tasks around group work or through collaboration. Cooperative learning complements the affective domain that includes values, feelings, and sportsmanship. The fostering of collaboration (teamwork) is a strength of this approach because it requires students to work together to meet goals. This is one of many approaches that can be used to teach team sports (e.g., basketball, lacrosse), as group members share a common goal and work together to accomplish it. Using this approach alone may limit the amount of motor skill development needed to perform the skills necessary for team sports, as the learning environment is designed so students can solve problems rather than listen to the teacher explicitly provide the information.

SKILL THEMES APPROACH

The **skill themes approach** is an elementary physical education framework that aids in the development of the fundamental movement skills (locomotor, non-locomotor, and manipulative) with an overarching goal to ensure that students are proficient or competent in these areas. There are four characteristics that underpin the skill themes approach:

1. Competence in the fundamental movement skills, where students are able to perform locomotor, non-locomotor, and manipulative skills
2. Providing ample student experiences to perform and develop these skills is important, as more opportunities to practice increases skill competency
3. Scope and sequence (progression) ensures that developmentally appropriate movements start from easy movements to progressively more challenging, complex movements. This is done because the more successes students have, the more likely they will continue to engage in physical activities. The scope and sequence characteristic focuses on stage of development rather than the age or the grade of the students
4. Instructional alignment is intentional instruction that includes objectives and assessments. Teachers explicitly plan for students to learn the fundamental movement skills by setting goals (objectives), providing activities that support the objectives, and administering ongoing assessments (formative) and cumulative final assessments (summative) to ensure students are competent in the skills or have reached mastery.

Modifying and Adapting Activities for All Students

ACADEMIC LEARNING TIME IN PHYSICAL EDUCATION

Academic learning time in physical education (ALT-PE) is a strategy used to create an equitable learning environment. ALT-PE is an observation and evaluation tool in which the teacher can analyze instructional time, student activity time in games, time off-task, learning and practice time, opportunities to respond, and equipment usage opportunities. Analysis can occur for a few students, the entire class, or an analysis of teacher behaviors to determine what is transpiring in class and to make any necessary changes. For example, the teacher may identify that a student or some students never get possession of the ball during a three vs. three basketball game. From this data, the teacher can modify the rules to require all players to touch or have possession of the ball at least three times before scoring or other parameters to ensure equal opportunity. The teacher may also observe an imbalance in teams by numbers or abilities and can modify the rules, change team rosters, or provide extra equipment to level the playing field.

DEVELOPMENTALLY APPROPRIATE MODIFICATIONS

Game rules, equipment, and activities should be **modifiable** to ensure that all students participate, learn, and succeed. For example, beginners may be allowed to travel with a basketball when learning how to dribble as stop-and-go action limits the opportunity to practice and learn. The teacher can also use basketballs of different sizes to accommodate varying hand sizes or use balls that include the correct hand and finger-pad placements (palm print) to help guide the students with proper technique. **Developmentally appropriate game modifications** include limiting the number of rules, skills, and strategies to help build competence before more difficult tasks. Increasing the amount of balls used in team sports also creates more equity in skill development. For example, using three to five soccer balls of different colors during game play, whether with the same or different criteria for each ball (dribbling, passing, etc.), allows for more students to get involved. Targets and goals can also be positioned closer, farther, higher, wider, or narrower to accommodate various abilities.

ADAPTATIONS TO ACTIVITIES

Adaptations that promote equity in opportunities for students to participate, learn, and succeed include using lighter weight equipment, making goals wider and larger (for students having difficulty) or shorter and narrower (for students who need more challenge as they are proficient with the normal goals), decreasing target distances (for students unable to reach the target), allowing peers to assist students who may have physical challenges (e.g., wheelchair-bound), and including more frequent rest or water breaks (for unfit or obese students). Other adaptations include how objects are manipulated to ensure equitable activity. For example, some students may be able to kick a moving ball, while others may need to kick a stationary ball or drop kick a ball. A lighter ball can also be used for students with less muscular strength (e.g., a student with muscular dystrophy or muscular atrophy). Adaptations should be student specific. For example, if one or two students need an adaptation, the entire group should not be required to engage in the adaptation, as it may not meet their needs and could possibly impede the progress of others, which can increase off-task behaviors.

Providing Appropriate and Effective Feedback

PROVIDING POSITIVE FEEDBACK

Positive feedback increases student motivation and performance. Specific positive feedback is more effective than general feedback. For example, "Good job" is general feedback that does not inform the student of what went well or what was good about the performance. A more effective example is, "Good job, I like that you kept moving during the entire aerobic session. Next time, try to march in place with high knees rather than walk in place with low knees to increase your heart rate and reach your target heart rate zone. By increasing the intensity, you will increase your cardiovascular endurance, which leads to a healthy heart and better overall health." In this example, the teacher provides positive feedback on something they are doing well and provides an explicit suggestion on how to improve in this area along with its own rationale. Not all students will need corrective or improvement feedback, however, feedback is necessary to increase the challenge for students who meet or exceed the objective.

VERBAL AND NONVERBAL TEACHING CUES

Verbal and nonverbal teaching cues help with student performance. Verbal cues are descriptive words or phrases that help students perform a skill or task. Verbal cues should be short and brief (no longer than three to four words) for ease in delivery and student retention. Cues that are too long are difficult to remember and may confuse students and impede progress. Common verbal cues include "follow-through" (overhand thrown), "squish the bug" (pivot), "t-shape" (forming a "T" with the body), and "move like an airplane" (locomotor movement and speed). Teachers can make up cues designed for the student population, region, or based on the school's mascot (e.g., "Tiger high-five"). To cue (lead) a group fitness or aerobics session, verbal cues should be given in advance to give students time to respond, as there is a brief delay while the brain processes the verbal information. Nonverbal teaching cues include hand gestures (pointing in a direction, as when leading a group fitness or aerobic dance session), moving the head and eyes in different directions, facial expressions (smiling at a correct behavior or frowning when a student does something inappropriate), and thumbs up, down, and sideways can be used for cues and to provide behavioral or performative feedback. Written cues (nonverbal) posted around the gym or teaching space that support the verbal cues students refer to when needed are useful to reinforce the concepts and address the various learning styles.

Assessment in Physical Education

TYPES OF FORMAL ASSESSMENTS

Assessment	Advantages	Disadvantages	When to use
Observational checklists	Fast and easy (Y/N)	Non-descriptive	During large class sizes; can be used as pre-tests or post-tests.
Performance assessments	Descriptive and student-specific; allows the teacher to evaluate if students are able to put skills and concepts into practice.	Can take up a lot of time; without recording and reviewing, the teacher can miss performances.	During game or activity play; when assessing one or two concepts (e.g., getting open, shooting).
Fitness tests	Fitness tests assess health-related and skill-related fitness; fitness tests are often easy to administer; fitness tests have a competitive element, which is great for high-performing, competitive students.	Fitness tests can take up a lot of instructional time; some students may get embarrassed, especially if they are unfit, overweight, or non-competitive students; fitness tests have a competitive element, which has shown to demotivate some students; shown ineffective when not connected to learning and fitness principles	To measure fitness before, during, and after instruction, practice, or training to evaluate growth and deficits and to adjust programming.

INFORMAL ASSESSMENTS

Assessment	Advantages	Disadvantages	When to use
Journals	Students can reflect and see their growth over time; there are no right or wrong answers; students can write in journals at home; students take ownership of their learning.	Writing time can take away from physical activity time; journals can be difficult to mark or assess.	At the end of each class or unit, or assigned for homework.
Peer coaching	Increases student learning opportunities, as this requires explaining, correcting, or identifying correct and incorrect performances; after students are trained, assessment time can decrease; promotes social interaction; all students get to lead (coach) and follow (receive coaching).	Reliant on students who may provide inaccurate information or do not fully understand; can take up instructional time as students have to be taught how to use and what to look for; some students may give improper feedback (e.g., higher or lower marks because of friendship status.)	Large class sizes; limited space where half the class is performing while the other half is coaching; when focusing on the affective domain.

SELECTING, CONSTRUCTING, ADAPTING, AND IMPLEMENTING ASSESSMENTS

Standards, objectives, students' needs, class size, facilities, and equipment should all be used to select, construct, adapt, and implement assessments in physical education. Pre-assessments should occur at the beginning of a new lesson, unit, or concept to determine the ability and needs of the students, which should consist of the objectives or the desired outcome by the end of the lesson. For example, if the goal is to have students engage in 10 or 20 minutes of continuous aerobic activity, then the pre-assessment would consist of asking students to perform cardiovascular activities (jogging, team sports, step aerobics) to the best of their ability for as long as they can. Some students will complete this objective, while others may tire before the time expires. Based on these data points, the teacher will construct or design cardiovascular activities that help students reach the goal. Progress can be tracked over time. Longer rest breaks are an adaptation to accommodate students with low ability, while shorter rest breaks would accommodate students with high ability. While the cardiovascular activities should vary in class for improvement, the activity used for the assessment should be practiced regularly and used as the post-assessment.

Technology in Fitness Assessment

HEART RATE MONITORS AND PEDOMETERS FOR MONITORING ACTIVITY LEVELS

Technological devices used in physical education to assess progress in fitness and performance include pedometers and heart rate monitors. These devices help the teacher and students track and analyze performance to include step count (pedometers), intensity, and duration (heart rate monitors). For example, 10,000 steps a day is a good goal to ensure that moderate levels of physical activity are achieved. Teachers and students can track and examine daily, weekly, or monthly step count to determine if students have improved, regressed, or maintained their level of activity. Steps achieved during class can also be used, and pedometers can be worn during most physical activities, not just walking or running. Tracking heart rate also aids in determining student progress in cardiovascular fitness, as engaging in consistent cardiovascular activities usually leads to lower resting heart rates. Heart rate monitors can also track when students are working too hard or not hard enough.

ACTIVITY TRACKERS, FITNESS APPLICATIONS, AND WEBSITES FOR TRACKING ACTIVITIES

In addition to heart rate monitors and pedometers, other activity trackers are found on fitness and computer applications (apps) via smartphones, tablets, devices worn on the wrist, and website platforms. When using website platforms, students can enter the types, duration, and frequency of activities that they engage in. Recommendations are given based on anthropometric measures (height, weight), gender, age, activity levels, and fitness goals. Many platforms allow for the entry of nutrition intake, which further aid in activity recommendations. Activity trackers worn around the wrist or carried on a cell phone have accelerometers which, in addition to tracking step count, measure speed and distance traveled. Many activity trackers also have the ability to measure heart rate. There are also weight training apps where students can enter the amount of weight lifted, reps, and sets. As with cardiovascular tracking, the amount of reps, sets, or weight lifted should increase over time.

INTERPRETING PERFORMANCE DATA

Cardiovascular data analysis and interpretation includes tracking resting and exercise heart rates (HR) over time, as both provide insight on health risks and improvement and should decrease over time with participation in frequent cardiovascular activities. A normal resting HR is between 60 and 90 beats per minute (bpm). Individuals who engage in regular physical activity may have resting heart rates lower than 60 bpm. For instance, if a student starts with a resting heart rate of 90 bpm, with consistent training, the resting heart rate should decrease. A resting HR over 90 bpm is considered high. Students over 90 bpm should be referred to a physician. Muscular fitness data analysis and interpretation includes tracking the amount of weight lifted and the number of repetitions over time. The weight and reps should increase, which illustrates growth and improvement. For example, if a student went from lifting 3 sets of 8 pounds at 10 repetitions at the beginning of the semester to lifting 3 sets of 15 pounds at 10 repetitions, that indicates an improvement in strength. However, going from lifting 3 sets of 8 pounds at 10 repetitions to lifting 3 sets of 8 pounds at 20 repetitions indicates an improvement in muscular endurance, and the student will likely need to increase the weight for greater improvement and challenge.

FITNESS FEEDBACK AND RECOMMENDATIONS FOR STUDENTS

Fitness feedback is often given in the form of a recommendation or suggestion. For all types of feedback, it is helpful to start with a positive comment on what the student is doing well. For example, "I love that you are trying this out!" Next, state the issue: "I noticed that you are just below your target heart rate zone." Instead of giving the student the answer(s), ask students questions that can help guide them to an appropriate answer while also checking for understanding: "What can you do to increase your exercise heart rate?" Pause for student response(s). If they are accurate, support and commend their response. The teacher can also make a few suggestions: "Try to engage or move your arms," or "Incorporate high-impact movements and take larger steps." Students who do not challenge themselves or who have not grasped fitness concepts may be encouraged to choose a heavier weight (intensity), conduct more repetitions (duration), engage in physical activity an additional day or two each week (frequency), or find an activity they enjoy (sport, hiking).

Cultural Influences on Student Physical Activity

EFFECTS OF PEER PRESSURE AND MEDIA MESSAGES

The media has a strong influence on children and adolescents and can positively or negatively impact students' attitudes regarding engagement in physical activity. The same is true for pressure from peers, which is especially strong during adolescence. Media messages and images tend to focus on thinness and unhealthy methods to achieve it, including extreme calorie restriction and extreme exercising. Awareness of these factors have improved and include positive messages from the National Football League (NFL) to "Play 60," which encourages children to engage in 60 minutes of physical activity every day. Positive and negative peer pressure also impact student attitudes and engagement in physical activity. For example, peers who value and appreciate physical activity can sometimes convince friends to engage in physical activity. In contrast, peers who do not value and appreciate physical activity can undermine positive messages given by the teacher and influence classmates not to engage.

EFFECTS OF CULTURAL INFLUENCES

Culture, family background, and community all influence student attitudes on physical activity engagement. For example, if a student is in a family that does not value physical activity, they may adopt those same beliefs and vice versa. Sometimes families do value physical activity, but they may not have the privilege of leisure time to engage in physical activity because they may work long hours, have an additional job (or jobs), or have childcare responsibilities. Some families and communities are unaware of the benefits of physical activity. Furthermore, there are some cultures and religions that are not keen on physical activity, especially for girls and women, which will influence students' attitudes and engagement in physical activity. To combat some of the negative messages surrounding physical activity that some students may receive at home, share the benefits of physical activity with parents by inviting them to school events, creating family fun activity nights or weekends, or sending emails or newsletters with tips for improving health and exercise to keep them informed and engaged. It may possibly change their negative perceptions of physical activity engagement.

GENDER EXPECTATIONS IN PHYSICAL EDUCATION

Title IX, introduced in 1972, provides equal access to physical activity and sports to female students. Prior to its introduction, girls were more culturally discouraged from engaging in vigorous physical activities which were considered less feminine. Instead, females who wanted to participate in athletics usually only had options in activities such as dance and gymnastics and were steered away from team sports. While more female students participate in sports today, there are still differences in cultural expectations for males and females. Females tend to have lower expectations to participate in competitive athletics, whereas males are generally expected to participate as a rite of passage into manhood. This distinction can act as a cultural gender stereotype that leads to unhealthy habits or tends to exclude students who want to participate in sports or force students to engage in activities to a higher degree than is reasonable to expect.

EFFECTS OF BODY IMAGE EXPECTATIONS

Body image and skill level both have a powerful impact on student attitudes and engagement in physical activity. Students who are highly skilled tend to enjoy physical education and physical activity, whereas low-skilled students have less enjoyment. Negative concepts of body image also impact attitudes and engagement in physical activity. When students do not feel good about their bodies, they are less likely to engage in physical activity due to a fear of being judged for their appearance. This fear is common among obese students. Alternatively, students may suffer from anorexia nervosa, an eating and mental disorder where one starves themselves because of an

irrational fear of gaining weight, and may engage in extreme and unhealthy levels of physical activity.

Physical Education and the General Curriculum

RELATIONSHIP BETWEEN PHYSICAL EDUCATION AND THE GENERAL CURRICULUM

The **integrated physical education model** incorporates other subject areas to aid in the understanding of concepts in a real-world setting and their application. Also known as **interdisciplinary learning** or an **interdisciplinary teaching model**, physical education is inherently aligned to other subject areas. For example, physical education teachers use and teach the principles of physics and biomechanics when teaching throwing, jumping skills, and most other physical activities. History is also taught in physical education when students learn about physical activity, sports, dance, and gymnastics history during the physical components of these activities. Robin J. Fogarty asserts that physical education is the leading field of integration and has identified the following four integration methods:

- Sequenced integration, where two or more subject areas focus on one topic
- Shared integration, or the overlap of subject areas
- Webbed integration, the use of themes to guide instruction
- Threaded integration, which combines cognitive and social domains in every subject area

PHYSICAL EDUCATION CONCEPTS ACROSS THE CURRICULUM

Physical education teachers often collaborate with teachers in other subjects to determine the best approaches to meet students' needs. Sometimes physical education teachers are required to integrate by school districts or personnel. For example, some schools have DEAR (Drop Everything and Read) programs to help foster literacy and reading comprehension. Physical education teachers can select books that are related to physical education but are categorized under another subject area. Some schools choose a book or movie to integrate across all subjects and grade levels. For example, Harry Potter, the popular book and movie series, has been used in schools to teach literacy, history, math, science, art, choir, and physical education. In fact, a physical education teacher implemented the game of Quidditch from Harry Potter into his classes in response to a school's interdisciplinary approach to Harry Potter. Quidditch has become a competitive, sanctioned sport played in many physical education programs and on several college campuses.

INTEGRATING PHYSICAL EDUCATION CONCEPTS IN OTHER SUBJECT AREAS

Physical education teachers can take the initiative and contact teachers in other disciplines to explore ways to incorporate physical education in other subject areas. For example, English language arts teachers can use physical education objectives to teach nouns and verb tenses. Math teachers can have students compute and analyze sports data or use sports and physical activity examples in word problems. Science teachers can incorporate exercise physiology for human physiology concepts or sporting examples to use in biomechanics. History teachers can incorporate the history of sports and physical activity, especially during events like the Olympics.

Safety and Risk-Management

GENERAL SAFETY RULES AND CONSIDERATIONS

Teachers should be competent in what they teach. Teachers can invite a visiting instructor (another PE teacher or coach) to help teach a unit where the teacher is untrained (e.g., swimming, gymnastics). Teachers should ensure that they are able to adequately supervise all students. Physical education teachers are usually required to hold first aid, CPR, and automated external defibrillation (AED) certifications. Teachers should inform students of the rules and any hazards or risks. Rules should be revisited regularly and posted in high-visibility areas (gym walls, locker rooms, high-risk areas). Dangerous areas should be roped or coned off. Lesson plans should be written to include safety guidelines in language that a substitute teacher (non-PE teacher) can understand. Students should be required to wear appropriate and safe athletic attire. Students wearing unsafe clothing (e.g., high-heeled shoes) should not engage in physical activity. Court and field surfaces should be inspected for dust and spills (slippage), glass and other sharp objects, and rocks. Ensure students have frequent breaks when engaging in moderate to vigorous activities and when exercising in the heat.

RISK MANAGEMENT PLANS

A risk management plan is designed to prevent, minimize, or prepare for any problems (e.g., injury). Risk management plans in physical education include being trained and certified in first aid and cardiopulmonary resuscitation (CPR), eliminating hazards (e.g., sharp objects), and being aware of any medical conditions (e.g., asthma). Teachers should maintain an equipment safety checklist to identify broken equipment. Emergency phone numbers should be posted and easy to locate. Schools often have risk management flowcharts that should be reviewed and posted. Fire and intruder drills help prepare students on safe routes to take and places (rooms) to go to in the event of an emergency. Safeguards should be put in place for high-risk physical activities (e.g., mats for gymnastics, additional spotters, trained personnel).

EMERGENCY PLANS

A school-wide emergency plan is often developed in advance and should be on file in writing. Furthermore, students and teachers should be aware of the basic procedures of the plan. Most emergency plans include emergency exits, routes, and phone numbers (911, principal, school and district numbers, school resource officer). The telephone numbers of parents should be easily retrievable. First aid kits and ice should be available and replenished after each use. Student health records (medical conditions, allergies) should be up-to-date. Student medications (e.g., inhaler, insulin) should be listed with administration guidelines, properly stored (some require refrigeration), and easily accessible to students in need. Teachers are usually trained in administering certain medications (e.g., EpiPen for allergies).

PROTOCOLS FOR INJURIES IN CLASS

In the event of an injury, the teacher should follow the emergency care plan. After an assessment of the injury, the teacher should ensure that the student is in a safe location. If the injury is minor (e.g., open cut from a student's fingernails), the teacher should administer first aid (clean the wound and put on a bandage). Gloves should be worn before touching any blood or bodily fluids and hands should be washed both before and after treatment. If there is an illness that requires over-the-counter (OTC) medication (e.g., high temperature or fever), the student should be sent to the school nurse or other personnel, who will usually call the parents for permission to administer OTC medication. Sometimes parents give permission for students to take OTC at the beginning of the school year. For major injuries (e.g., broken limb), the teacher should make a phone call to the emergency system (e.g., 911 or school required number) and a call to the parents. An injury report should be provided for minor and major injuries and kept on file. The injury report should provide an accurate description of the injury; the cause, time, location, and treatment of the injury; and a list of any witnesses. The teacher should also notify the principal and school nurse of the injuries and give them a copy of the report.

PHYSICAL DANGERS ASSOCIATED WITH PHYSICAL ACTIVITIES

There are inherent risks associated with physical activities. Potential risks include injuries such as overstretching the muscles, overexertion, and muscle sprains, strains, and spasms. Trips and falls due to shoe laces, equipment, and other objects may occur, which can cause cuts, scrapes, bruises, fractures, and broken limbs. Students may also slip or fall on exercise equipment (e.g., treadmills) or get their fingers smashed by a weight room apparatus. Fingers can also get jammed when catching sports balls (e.g., basketball). Students also acquire bruises and nose bleeds after getting struck by an object or a classmate, and collisions may occur during game play. There is also cardiovascular risk that includes cardiac arrest. Proper supervision, however, can reduce or eliminate many risks.

ENVIRONMENTAL RISKS INHERENT IN PHYSICAL ACTIVITIES

Environmental risks that are inherent when engaging in physical activities include the weather (rain, sleet, snow), the temperature (too hot, too cold), and road-related issues (gravel, slick roads). In hot environments, risks include hyperthermia (overheating), which can lead to heat exhaustion and heat stroke. It is easy to lose fluids and become dehydrated when engaging in physical activities in the heat. In cold environments, risks include hypothermia (low body temperature) and risks of frostbite. Traffic and pedestrians can also be potential hazards when engaging in physical activity outdoors, including bumping into others or getting hit by an automobile. Precipitation (rain, sleet, snow) can increase the risks of slipping, and can speed up cold-related conditions. Other risks include tripping on uneven pavement or stepping on glass, which can lead to physical injuries. Precautions to take against environmental risks include checking the weather forecast, wearing protective clothing appropriate for the weather, having an emergency plan, using the buddy system by never engaging in physical activity alone, finding alternative routes when visibility is low (fog) or concentration is high (too much traffic, too many people in the area), and hydrating before, during, and after activity. Teachers will need to use their judgement. For example, physical activity can occur outdoors with a small amount of precipitation (rain drizzle), but engaging in physical activity when lightning is present requires a safe, indoor shelter.

LIABILITY IN PHYSICAL EDUCATION

Liability is an obligation or the responsibility to perform the duties required in a job. Liability in the legal aspect is a failure to perform the duties as a result of negligence. **Negligence** is a breach of duty that increases the risk of harm. Actions that increase a teacher's liability or acts of negligence in physical education include having students participate on broken or defective equipment, failure to cover or protect sharp objects, and failure to report an injury. Other acts of negligence include the failure to block off unsafe areas, not providing students with rest and water breaks, and failure to incorporate a warm-up. Failure to maintain first aid, CPR, and AED training is another potential liability. Failure to supervise students, review and post safety rules, and form an awareness of students' strengths and limitations are also potential liabilities. Teachers could also be held liable if they allow or ignore student misconduct that can lead to injury.

DISCLOSING RISKS

Students and families should be informed that the benefits of engagement in physical activity outweigh the risks associated with physical activity. Obtaining informed consent will ensure that parents are aware of the risk. Requiring liability waivers will also provide some legal protection should an injury occur. Students should be informed of the risks through lecture, video, practical labs, or simulations. Risks and safety guidelines should be posted in the teaching and learning space (e.g., risks of weight training equipment or risks of not using a spotter) and reviewed with students regularly.

ROUTINE INSPECTIONS OF EQUIPMENT

Equipment that is not in use should be stored and secured. Routine inspections of equipment include checking for loose screws and making sure sharp or blunt edges are removed or covered with protective padding. Professional-grade equipment often used in school weight rooms and fitness centers should have scheduled maintenance in addition to the daily checks of equipment. Students should be informed of gym etiquette rules, which include wiping down equipment after use to keep it clean and reduce germ transmission and returning equipment to its proper location to prevent injury. When students perform tasks such as these, the teacher should inspect to ensure safety guidelines were followed. Any broken or malfunctioning equipment should be roped off and have an "out of service" sign. The floor and field should be routinely inspected for damage, objects, glass, and uneven surfaces to minimize injury risks and liabilities.

RISK CONSIDERATIONS FOR AGE, SIZE, MATURITY, AND SKILL

Because students develop at different rates, the developmental stage (maturity and size) of students should inform teaching and instruction, rather than age. For instance, a boy in grade six might be six feet tall (early maturation in physical size means the boy's skeletal age is greater than chronological age), while another boy in the same class is four feet tall (late maturation, meaning his skeletal age is less than his chronological age). To minimize injury risks and liabilities, early-maturing students should be paired with other early-maturing students, as the larger and stronger student might inadvertently hurt the smaller student. In addition to the physical advantage that the early-maturing student has, the imbalance can also cause psychological harm to the less-developed student. Students should also be matched by skill and cognitive development (maturity) to minimize risks and liabilities, including safe engagement, as the four-foot-tall student might have a higher skill level and greater cognitive abilities than the six-foot-tall student, which would again be an unfair pairing and could pose psychological harm to the student with lower cognitive abilities. Equipment should also be developmentally appropriate and scaled to the sizes for diverse learners (e.g., the early-maturing student may need larger pieces of equipment).

MATCHING PLAYERS TO MINIMIZE RISK

Matching players based on skill level minimizes risks and liabilities. For instance, higher-skilled players tend to engage in more advanced and aggressive play because they are faster and stronger (more muscle and bone) than lower-skilled players. A mismatch in skill can lead to bullying from players with more skill or an increase in accidents as novice players may make errors that put them or others at risk for injuries. As such, the teacher could be held liable for not foreseeing potential risks of the mismatched skill levels or the recognition that students vary in skill development. For example, a novice player may be unaware of certain infractions (fouls, pushing, and the types of physical contact that are acceptable and unacceptable) that could put other players at risk.

CONFLICT RESOLUTION

There are generally three types of behavior evident in conflict situations: the **cooperator** (gets along with everyone), the **appeaser** (pleaser and conflict avoider), and the **dominator** (conflict starter, bully). Bullying and fights increase the risk of harm, which increases potential liabilities, so teachers should teach and model conflict resolution strategies as a prevention measure. Strategies shown effective in conflict resolution include stopping aggressive behaviors immediately, collecting information to establish the cause of the conflict, collaborating with students on possible solutions, incorporating the solutions that the students agree on, implementing a plan, and debriefing with the students to determine the plan's effectiveness. Using these steps both teaches and empowers students to solve their own conflicts. However, if the plan does not work, the teacher can step in to modify. This approach also helps the teacher refrain from taking sides or choosing a solution, which does not encourage students to think about their actions.

FIRST AID AND INJURY PREVENTION

The purpose of **first aid** is to provide immediate care to an injured person to reduce further injury or deterioration and sometimes even to prolong life or prevent death. The person administering first aid should ensure a safe environment and keep both the victim and bystanders calm. If an ambulance is required, the person in charge will have to call the authorities if they are alone, or should have someone else call if others are present. Prevention techniques for cuts and scrapes include tying shoelaces and removing objects to prevent tripping. Wearing long pants and sleeves can minimize risks to prevent burns, and hot items that are not in use should be turned off and removed from areas where students might touch them accidentally. Inspecting and repairing hardwood flooring and other wooden objects can reduce the risks of splinters, fractures, muscle sprains and strains, and dislocated joints.

MODIFICATIONS TO IMPROVE SAFETY

- **Equipment**: cover hard objects and equipment with padding (e.g., volleyball standards and polls) to avoid painful collisions.
- **Environment**: sweep floors before class, make sure that students have their shoelaces tied to prevent slips and falls, review and post the rules to remind students to avoid dangerous areas and to abstain from dangerous behaviors (e.g., tumbling off of the mat, tripping a classmate), have sunscreen available and encourage students to wear hats or visors when outdoors to prevent sun or heat-related conditions, have an emergency plan on file to expedite care when needed, and ensure that first aid and CPR trainings and certifications are current.
- **Activity-related**: ensure students engage in a warm-up and cooldown to prevent muscle-related injuries, allow students to get water to prevent dehydration, allow for appropriate breaks to avoid overexertion.

RICE PROCEDURE

RICE is a first aid treatment best used for sprains, strains, and muscle aches. RICE stands for **rest** (stop use), **ice** (wrapped in protective coating or an ice pack), **compression** (gentle pressure, usually with an elastic bandage to the injured area), and **elevation** (to move blood away from the affected area to reduce swelling). RICE reduces swelling, inflammation, and pain, that could otherwise prolong healing time. **NSAIDs** are non-steroidal anti-inflammatory drugs that include pain and inflammation reducers like ibuprofen and naproxen sodium. NSAIDs are often used in conjunction with RICE to also reduce inflammation, pain, and speed up recovery time. Acetaminophen is a common over-the-counter (OTC) drug which is also used to reduce pain, but because it does not reduce inflammation, it is not an NSAID. NSAIDs and acetaminophen also reduce fever.

CPR PROCEDURE AND EMERGENCY RESPONSE

Check, call, and care are emergency steps to take in the event that a victim is unconscious. **Check**: Shout and tap the victim's shoulder and ask if they are ok. If there is no response, the next step is to check for consciousness (check for breathing, pulse). **Call**: After this initial assessment, a call should be made to 911 that includes the symptoms. If another person is present and able, it is best to have them call 911, rather than the person attending to the victim. For example, the person checking the victim would point to a bystander and instruct them to call 911 and describe the victim's ailment to the first responders. **Care**: If the victim has a pulse but is not breathing, someone trained and certified in CPR should provide two rescue breaths to see if air goes in (e.g., chest rises) or if there is a blockage causing the victim to choke. They should then look, listen, and feel for breathing and a pulse. A protective mask is recommended to reduce transmission of any illnesses or infections. If there is still no breathing, rescue breaths should occur for two minutes before checking again. If there is no pulse, 30 CPR compressions should be administered, followed by two rescue breaths. This process should be repeated for two minutes (about five cycles) or until the victim is breathing and has pulse, until an AED or emergency care arrives, or when the person administering CPR is too tired to perform it effectively.

Collaboration, Reflection, and Technology

Goals, Trends, and Philosophies of Physical Education Programs

PURPOSE OF PHYSICAL EDUCATION PROGRAMS

The main purpose of physical education programs is to ensure that students are physically literate. According to the Society of Health and Physical Educators of America (SHAPE), **physical literacy** is "the ability to move with competence and confidence in a wide variety of physical activities in multiple environments that benefit the healthy development of the whole person." With the goal of physical literacy, physical education programs are designed to promote physical activity over the lifespan. To do this, quality physical education programs ensure that students are engaged in psychomotor (movement), cognitive (thinking), and affective (social and emotional) domains, thus influencing the development of the whole person.

ROLE OF THE SOCIETY OF HEALTH AND PHYSICAL EDUCATORS OF AMERICA (SHAPE)

SHAPE America is the oldest and largest physical education professional organization in the United States. SHAPE is the national governing body of physical education, and each state and US territory has a SHAPE (aka AAHPERD) equivalent (e.g., Texas Association for Health, Physical Education, Recreation and Dance, or TAHPERD). There are five SHAPE districts which combine states and territories by region. For example, TAHPERD is in the Southern District along with 12 other states. SHAPE America sets the national physical education standards and learning outcomes; however, each state can decide whether to adopt SHAPE standards, devise their own, or use a combination of SHAPE and state-level standards. For example, Texas has its own standards called the Texas Essential Knowledge and Skills (TEKS). SHAPE America and state-level organizations require membership, but both advocate for physical education, disseminate best teaching practice information, provide professional development, and manage state and national policies—usually for free. They also hold annual conferences where teachers and experts hold teaching workshops and training.

STATE-LEVEL PHYSICAL EDUCATION PROGRAMS

Physical education programs in each state and U.S. territory are governed by state-level law and policy. These laws and policies include setting physical education requirements that concern the format (in-class or online), amount, and frequency of physical education; the time allocated for physical education; and fitness testing, teacher certification requirements, and class size. These are usually minimums or recommendations that school districts should aim to achieve. For example, the state of Texas requires that students in elementary school engage in structured physical activity for at least 135 minutes every week, and at least 30 minutes a day for students in middle school. High school students must earn 1.0 physical education credit, but each school district determines the implementation. The state also decides on waivers, exemptions (Texas does not allow for waivers and exemptions), and activities that can be substituted for physical education (e.g., athletic sports team participation, JROTC, dance teams).

LOCAL SCHOOL DISTRICT PHYSICAL EDUCATION PROGRAMS

While the state sets physical education standards and determines the number of minutes students should be actively engaged in elementary and middle schools, schools have flexibility in the structure of the physical education program. For instance, schools are responsible for scheduling, teaching models and modalities, class size, and curriculum approaches. For example, the state of Texas requires a maximum of 45:1 student-teacher ratio in physical education, however, districts

112

and schools may choose to endorse SHAPE America's 25:1 student-teacher ratio for elementary grades, 30:1 for middle school grades, and 35:1 for high school grades. Some states do not require physical education teacher certification for school districts, but most public school districts require a degree in physical education and physical education teacher certification. Private and parochial schools are governed independently and do not have to adhere to district policies.

TRENDS IN PHYSICAL EDUCATION

Due to an increase in childhood obesity related to poor dietary habits and sedentary lifestyles, many physical education programs have shifted to health-related fitness curriculums instead of team sport curriculums in efforts to prevent obesity. Fitness and physical activity have also shown to improve brain functioning and learning. This is especially true in high school, when students are preparing for adulthood and making independent choices. Many schools now have fitness centers and weight rooms to meet the needs of this trend. Alongside fitness is the use of technology to monitor fitness, including heart rate monitors, pedometers, and activity trackers. Another trend is the focus on social and emotional learning (SEL) due to increased mental health concerns of youth and the understanding that physical education and physical activity can aid in reducing and managing mental health risks. As a result, there has been an increase in yoga and mindfulness in physical education programs.

COMMON ISSUES IN PHYSICAL EDUCATION

Common issues that affect physical education programs are financial cuts, large class sizes, little or reduced instructional time, and the lack of value in its role of educating and developing the whole child. Other issues include the lack of equipment or teaching space and frequent, unexpected teaching interruptions (e.g., the gym is needed for an assembly). Assessment and grading are also topics of debate in physical education programs, as some believe students should get an A grade for participation while others believe that students should meet learning outcomes. Fitness testing has been and continues to be an issue in physical education, especially when used for a grade. While fitness testing can be a good assessment tool and provide educational and motivational opportunities, fitness testing takes time and may embarrass some students. Other issues with fitness testing are that students are often unaware of the rationale or that they are not working on the fitness measures throughout the year.

BEHAVIORISM, COGNITIVISM, AND CONSTRUCTIVISM PHILOSOPHIES

Behaviorism takes on a repetitive approach. Teachers who engage in behaviorist practices focus on repetition of the ideal movement, or gold standard. The goal is to have students repeat tasks until they achieve mastery. This approach is best used for students who need more direction, as it could demotivate high-performing students. Cognitivism was developed out of disagreement with behaviorism, as the cognitive domain is not addressed. The beliefs that underpin **cognitivism** are that students will be unable to master movement without an understanding of the movement, therefore, emphasis needs to include both cognitive and psychomotor domains. As such, information processing must occur in the brain before movement can occur. **Constructivism** evolved out of cognitivism and is evident in physical education programs as constructivists believe in getting students actively involved during the learning process. For example, students who engage in and learn the history of dance will better understand movement concepts. Constructivism includes the psychomotor, cognitive, and affective domains and takes on an interdisciplinary approach. As such, students learn the skills for a game (e.g., lacrosse), the rules, the history, and the values of the game.

HUMANISM PHILOSOPHY

Constructivism underpins **humanism**, which focuses on the affective and cognitive domains, takes a student-centered and holistic approach, and was derived out of criticisms of behaviorism and cognitivism. Teachers who operate from a humanist framework believe in the facilitation of learning by creating optimal learning environments. These teachers provide constant encouragement and positive feedback with the aim to help students grow at their own pace and in their own time. These teachers also focus on the good (effort, persistence) of students rather than the bad (use of profane language, pushing or shoving), and try to foster the positive aspects of students. Abraham Maslow and Carl Rogers were well-known humanists who created Maslow's hierarchy of needs, which posits that when the basic needs are met (physiological, safety, belongingness, and esteem), self-fulfillment, or self-actualization, can be achieved.

CHARACTERISTICS OF EFFECTIVE PHYSICAL EDUCATION PROGRAMS

An effective physical education program is student-centered and attempts to balance short-term goals with lifelong health and fitness. The ultimate outcome of a physical education program is to help students fully develop their motor skills, to inform them about health and fitness principles, and help them to develop the skills to make good decisions for themselves as they transition to adulthood. The use of high expectations and standards-based instruction helps to keep students in a mode of progress toward particular goals that are generally developmentally appropriate. Instruction needs to be appropriate to the developmental needs and skill level of students. This means that classes should be appropriately sized to set specific enough goals to be effective for the class. Instruction should be rich and engaging, with adequate equipment and resources, and plenty of opportunity for extracurricular activities that will help with achieving health and fitness outcomes. With younger children, goals should be focused on developing motor skills and coordination, and as they age, they should be given more decision-making opportunity to help students take their health into their own hands as they progress from children to adults.

PURPOSE OF ASSESSMENT AND ITS ROLE IN EFFECTIVE PHYSICAL EDUCATION PROGRAMMING

The purposes of assessment are to determine or measure student learning and to identify strengths and deficiencies or areas of weakness. Assessment results should inform the teacher (as well as students and parents) on the next steps for improvement or growth. Psychomotor, cognitive, and affective assessments are included in effective physical education programs. The teacher should be clear in the expectations, and criteria should be communicated to students prior to assessments. The teacher should also engage in appropriate uses of physical activity and fitness assessment tools. For example, when assessing fitness, results should only be shared with students and parents, not posted on walls for all to see. Assessments should be ongoing (formative) and allow for students to self-assess and engage in monitoring their activities before a final (summative) assessment is given. There should also be adequate opportunities to respond in order to foster growth and learning.

PRESIDENTIAL YOUTH FITNESS PROGRAM

The Presidential Youth Fitness Program (PYFP) is the national fitness test program designed by the United States government. The PYFP adopted FitnessGram testing protocols for its fitness assessments. FitnessGram is a battery of fitness tests designed for students aged 8-17 that measures the five health-related fitness components. These assessments are designed to assess a student's fitness to inform the teacher, student, and parents of fitness levels, strengths, areas of growth, and potential health risks. Fitness outcomes should also inform teachers how to proceed with the physical education program to ensure that meaningful fitness activities and concepts are

114

embedded in the physical education program to help students gain knowledge and understanding of fitness principles to engage in for a lifetime. Fitness assessments should be conducted at regular intervals (e.g., every two, four, and six weeks) to monitor progress and the effectiveness of fitness programming, as these are components that reinforce effective physical education practices.

SHAPE AMERICA'S HEALTH MOVES MINDS

SHAPE America's Health Moves Minds is a national service-learning program that promotes the benefits of physical activity and mindfulness on overall health with a particular focus on mental health, including anxiety (extreme and exhaustive worry that affects mental and physical health) and clinical depression (mood disorder with chronic feelings of sadness). Childhood stress, anxiety, and depression are on the rise, and this program recognizes the relationship of physical activity and health. The program supports and reinforces the physical literacy concept of developing the whole child, which includes the mental, physical, emotional, and social wellbeing of students. Health Moves Minds lesson plans have been created for teachers to implement in K-12 health and physical education programs.

Evaluating the Effectiveness of the Physical Education Program

EVALUATING EFFECTIVENESS OF THE PHYSICAL EDUCATION PROGRAM

One technique used to evaluate the effectiveness of the physical education program through data collection is to track students' progress over time. For example, sets, weights, and reps of a student can be tracked to determine if strength or endurance have improved, regressed, or remained the same. The teacher and student can devise a plan (increase weight, sets, reps) to accommodate each scenario. Heart rate data can also be tracked randomly (monitor one class to see if students are working in their target heart rate) or over time to track trends in fitness. For example, taking the resting heart at the beginning, during, and at the end of the semester will inform the teacher and student of intensity levels and allow them to make adjustments accordingly. Taking heart rate over time will also determine the effectiveness of the program, as the resting and exercise heart rate should stay the same or decrease. Students' oral and written responses to quizzes and tests also provide data on what is known, what is unknown, and what needs to be re-taught.

REFLECTING ON TEACHING PRACTICES TO SHAPE FUTURE INSTRUCTION

Reflective teaching helps teachers make decisions that are instructionally and developmentally appropriate. Reflective teachers take inventory (in the form of data) of their own behaviors and of students' strengths, abilities, attitudes, and deficiencies. For example, if the teacher is taking too long to give instructions, he or she can work on giving concise instruction or different delivery methods (e.g., posted on the wall, slideshow, verbal instructions). If students are waiting too long, the teacher may need to increase the number of stations, distribute more pieces of equipment, or reduce group sizes. If students have difficulty performing a task, the teacher should provide modifications to help the students achieve the goals. For example, if students' balls consistently hit the net during serves (tennis or volleyball), the teacher can lower the net, provide cues (toss the ball higher, make contact here), or move students closer to the net.

REFLECTING ON STUDENT ASSESSMENT DATA TO SHAPE FUTURE INSTRUCTION

Student assessment data helps the teacher determine if class activities are aligned with assessments. Assessment data also informs the teacher if assessments are too easy, just right, or too difficult. For example, if the majority of students are unable to meet the objective, then the assessment is either too difficult, inappropriate, or the activities that the teacher designed did not correspond to the assessment. Based on these data points, the teacher can reteach using different methods and activities, provide students with more time to engage in the activities, focus on different skill cues, and create a new assessment that is aligned to the activities taught. If all of the students meet the objective, then the teacher may be extremely effective or administering an assessment that is too easy. In this situation, the teacher can add challenge to help students continuously improve and to increase motivation.

Advocating for Physical Education

ADVOCATING FOR PHYSICAL EDUCATION

The Every Student Succeeds Act (ESSA) recognizes that health and physical education are integral parts of developing the whole child. Teachers can advocate for schools and communities by applying for state and federal support (funding) to provide quality programming in schools, including school improvement and teacher effectiveness. SHAPE America also has advocacy toolkits for physical education that includes participating in legislation events that have an impact on physical education policies and practices. Fundraising for program needs is another way to advocate for quality physical education programming. Inviting parents, school leaders, and decision-making personnel to observe physical classes is another way to advocate physical education within the community.

OPPORTUNITIES AND RESOURCES FOR PHYSICAL ACTIVITY IN THE SCHOOL COMMUNITY

Additional opportunities for physical health in schools includes after-school physical activity programs, intramural and athletic teams, recess, and physical activity breaks. Some schools have fitness centers, weight rooms, swimming pools, tennis courts, and athletic fields that are open to parents and the greater school community. Information newsletters, flyers, and emails can be created and distributed to notify recipients of opportunities, as well as any specials or discounts. Making PA announcements and networking with the PTA, PTO, and PTSO (parent-teacher association, parent-teacher organization, and parent-teacher-student organization) to organize presentations for parents and the community can also help communicate this information. Teachers can also take students on field trips to local fitness centers, rock climbing walls, and other facilities that offer physical activity opportunities.

PHYSICAL ACTIVITY OPPORTUNITIES AND RESOURCES IN THE COMMUNITY

Local parks, Frisbee and disc golf parks, recreation centers, hiking trails, golf courses, fitness centers, roller skating rinks, bowling, biking, skateboard parks, and swimming pools are additional opportunities for individuals to engage in physical activities. There are also physical activity meet-up groups that are free or have minimal costs (e.g., walking and running groups, tennis groups) where people can build community with others who enjoy similar activities. Most parks have walking or biking trails, and many have playground and exercise equipment. Recreation centers tend to offer team sporting activities (basketball, soccer, volleyball), swimming, group fitness classes, weight rooms, rock climbing, racquetball, and recreational games (shuffleboard, croquet).

Health Education as a Discipline

Health-Related Decision Making

ASPECTS OF DECISION-MAKING TO CONSIDER FOR INSTRUCTING ADOLESCENTS

The life stage of **adolescence** brings greater pressures on teenagers to solve more difficult problems and make harder decisions about matters like risk behaviors, sexuality, school involvement, and career choices. Thus, **decision-making** during adolescence can powerfully affect adult futures. Awareness of the possible impacts of their decisions informs teen motivation to learn effective **decision-making skills**. Such skills incorporate identifying available options and their potential consequences, evaluating the relative desirability or undesirability of each consequence, estimating each consequence's probability, and using a "decision rule" to choose among options. Decision-making models (e.g., Wilson & Kirby, 1984) require the skills of defining a necessary decision, gathering information for self-education and thinking of alternatives, considering options and choosing one, making a plan to execute the decision, and evaluating the decision and its results. Such models enable planned, goal-directed decision-making. Researchers have noted both cognitive elements of decision-making, and other aspects beyond cognition, as important in **adolescent risk-taking**.

RESEARCH-BASED CONCLUSIONS ABOUT HOW ADOLESCENTS MAKE DECISIONS

Various studies have identified variables that determine how prepared each individual adolescent is to make **effective decisions**, including intelligence, age, gender, race or ethnicity, social class, temperament, family dynamics and structure, cultural and social environment, and religiosity. Additionally, adolescent perceptions of and attitudes toward risk, perspectives regarding time, and compliance and conformity relative to parents and peers influence decision making abilities. Both contextual and developmental variables affect how teens ascribe subjective value to consequences, and how they use information, for decision-making. The **teen dilemma** is a need to make critical decisions having lifelong consequences, yet lacking ample life experience to inform those decisions. Studies have found positive results from **intervention programs** to improve adolescent decision-making skills, including decreased antisocial, socially disordered, and self-destructive behavior and increased prosocial, positive behavior; reduced tobacco use; more responsible sexual behavior in parenting and pregnant teens; higher school retention levels; and greater economic self-sufficiency. Some researchers consider decision-making ability to be one component of risk behavior. They emphasize assessing teen decision-making and planning skills for identifying intervention need areas, and teaching future orientation for considering long-term as well as short-term consequences and goals. Transferring acquired cognitive decision-making skills effectively requires opportunities for practicing real-life decision-making.

ASSERTIVENESS

Assertiveness can be defined as expressing our personal rights, feelings, needs and wants honestly, directly, clearly, and appropriately, and insisting that others recognize these, while still always respecting the beliefs, thoughts, and feelings of other people. While not being **assertive** may ultimately be a result of having low self-esteem, **non-assertiveness** may be functionally defined as using **inefficient communication skills**. Assertiveness, in contrast, is viewed as a balanced response in that it is neither aggressive nor passive. Some people confuse assertiveness with aggression. However, aggressiveness is not balanced in that it involves such behaviors as telling people to do things instead of asking them; ignoring others; being inconsiderate of others' feelings; unnecessarily rushing others; verbally insulting, blaming, or attacking others; or being pushy in

118

general. Aggression discourages assertive responses and invites passivity or mutual aggression. Passive responses include saying "yes" when wanting to say "no"; agreeing outwardly when disagreeing inwardly; deferring one's wishes to others'; and not communicating or asserting one's feelings, thoughts, needs, or wants—often motivated by needing to please others and be liked. Passivity avoids and cedes responsibility and decision-making to others.

ASSERTIVE COMMUNICATION

In **empathic assertion**, first acknowledge how the other person feels, then express what you need. For example, "I understand you are having trouble working together, but we need to finish this by Friday. Let's make a plan together." When needs are not met after repeated requests, **escalating assertion** involves increasing firmness, including informing others of consequences for continued noncompliance. Requesting more time is an assertiveness technique to use when caught off-guard, need to compose your thoughts, don't know what you want yet, or are too emotional to respond immediately. Changing verbs can make responses more assertive: substitute "won't" for "can't," "need" for "want," "I choose to" for "I have to," and "could" for "should." Another technique is the "broken record": when someone tries alternately to intimidate, bully, force, wheedle, cajole, beg, or bribe you to do something you cannot, repeat the same "no" message, e.g., "I cannot take on any more work right now." Whether the other person says "I'll pay you for helping me," "This is seriously important," "I'll be in big trouble if you don't help," "Please do a personal favor", etc., repeating the message will eventually make the point clear. This should not be used to manipulate others, but to protect yourself from exploitation.

CHARACTER EDUCATION

Academic underachievement, failure in school, antisocial behaviors, aggressive behaviors, drug use, premature sexual activity, and criminal activities are all social problems among students that researchers have found can be prevented by high-quality, comprehensive **character education programs**. Even though such programs are designed for the purpose of promoting young people's development of good character and their overall positive development, they are also found to be just as effective for preventing specific negative behaviors as other, more specific programs designed specially to prevent those behaviors. Character education not only **reduces youth risk** for engaging in detrimental behaviors, it also has positive effects of helping students develop **proactive attitudes and skills**, personally and socially, that enable their living productive, satisfying lives and participating in society as effective, active citizens. Researchers think this may make effective character education programs more cost-effective in terms of policy to augment learning—as well as promote prosocial behaviors and prevent problems—than implementing numbers of separate specific school-based behavioral prevention programs.

DEFINITIONS OF CHARACTER AND CHARACTER EDUCATION

While some people recognize following rules, avoiding criminal acts, completing school, and becoming productively employed as criteria for having character, experts say these are not enough. They define **character** as encompassing a wider range of attitudes, motivations, skills, and behaviors. These include wanting to do one's best; caring about others' welfare; being committed to contributing to the community and society; critical thinking and moral reasoning skills; emotional intelligence and interpersonal skills enabling effective interactions in various situations; and responsibility, honesty, and confronting injustice by defending moral principles. Experts interpret these qualities to mean character equals a person's realizing positive intellectual, emotional, social, and ethical development to be the best person s/he can be. They also point out that good character is not only personal, but also social, e.g., supporting respect, equality, and justice for all people as part of democratic living. This sometimes includes breaking rules predicated on conscience rather than constant conformation to the status quo. **Character education** is defined as purposefully using all aspects of school—e.g., curriculum content, instructional processes, disciplinary management, co-curricular activity management, relationship quality, and the full learning environment's ethos—to create learning environments enabling all students' optimal character development.

COMPREHENSIVE APPROACH TO CHARACTER EDUCATION

The Character Education Partnership (CEP), has identified the following 11 general principles (Lickona, Schaps, and Lewis, 2003) that serve to articulate **character education** in terms of a comprehensive approach.

- Comprehensively defining character as encompassing thought, emotion, and behavior.
- Applying a proactive, intentional, effective, comprehensive approach.
- Furthering core ethical values as the foundations of good character.
- Establishing caring learning communities in schools.
- Cultivating internal student motivation to be good persons and to learn.
- Giving opportunities for students to act morally.
- Engaging school personnel as professional members of moral learning communities.
- Supplying students with a challenging, relevant curriculum that assists all of them in succeeding.
- Cultivating long-term support for character education and shared moral leadership.
- Engaging students' families and members of the community as partners in character education.
- Informing the endeavor of character education by evaluating the character of the students, employees, and the school itself.

HEALTH-RELATED DECISION-MAKING SKILLS NEEDED TO MAKE POSITIVE HEALTH CHOICES

Individuals need a number of health-related decision-making skills to make positive health choices and to express health information and concepts. Education to improve **health-related decision making** should begin in elementary school so students entering high school have a good base and understand when assistance is needed, what healthy and unhealthy options are, and what outcomes may result from poor choices. The high school student should have the knowledge to understand health information and the skills to identify barriers (such as peer pressure) to good decision making, to understand when to use a problem-solving approach, to justify reaching a decision in collaboration with others or independently, to recognize alternative solutions to health-related problems/issues, to defend the choices they make, and to assess the outcomes of their decisions. Students can participate in role-playing and problem-solving exercises to improve these skills.

INFLUENCES ON HEALTH DECISIONS AND BEHAVIORS

Many factors influence health decisions and behaviors, including the following:

- **Beliefs**: Beliefs about health are often culture-bound and may influence behavior. Some cultures, for example, believe that illness is a punishment or it means that life is out of balance, whereas others believe in karma. Some cultures believe that it is shameful to have a mental disorder and may deny problems or refuse treatment.
- **Knowledge**: People are often better able to make decisions if they are armed with factual knowledge and can use critical thinking skills. Lack of knowledge may lead to confusion about the best health decisions and reliance on anecdotal advice.

- **Attitudes**: Despite knowledge, some people (especially adolescents) may feel that they are invincible and that problems that arise for others, such as from drinking alcohol, will not occur with themselves. Some may have difficulty accepting cause-and-effect relationships, and some may feel resentful of those in authority, such as parents, and purposefully make poor decisions.
- **Peers**: Friends and other peers often have a profound influence on health decisions and behaviors because of the strong desire to be accepted. This influence can be negative or positive, depending on the relationship.
- **Family**: The influence that parents or caregivers have varies according to the relationship. If the relationship is poor, then the influence may be minimal. Older siblings often exert a strong influence, either negative or positive, on younger siblings who look up to the older sibling and try to emulate that person.
- **Role models**: People that adolescents look up to—often sports figures, actors, or singers—may have some influence on behaviors, sometimes in ways that are negative, but positive role models who are actually in the person's life, such as a teacher, can have a more direct positive influence if the adolescent sees the person as a model for success.

SEEKING ADVICE AND GUIDANCE IN MAKING DECISIONS ABOUT PERSONAL HEALTH

Adolescents are often unprepared to make decisions about personal health because of a lack of knowledge and experience. They may be uncertain about decisions or unaware of resources and may need **assistance**. If their relationships with their family members are positive, then those family members can provide valuable **guidance** because they know the individual well and may understand the implications of health decisions. However, they may also be biased toward certain decisions. Healthcare professionals may provide the best advice, especially if the adolescent is concerned about confidentiality. The healthcare professional has the expertise to know what options are available and whether referral is needed, and the adolescent may feel more comfortable asking him or her for help. For example, an adolescent may want to use birth control but is unwilling to or afraid to ask family members.

TEACHING RESPONSIBLE DECISION-MAKING TO STUDENTS

A health educator teaching a responsible decision-making model to middle and high school students can begin with an overhead projection and student worksheets with term definitions. They discuss definitions with students: **empowerment** is feeling control over one's decisions and behavior, resulting in inspiration. Teachers tell students they must take responsibility for their decisions to achieve empowerment; decision-making styles determine responsibility. They explain that teens with **inactive decision-making styles** cannot or do not make choices; they lack control, accountability, and the ensuing self-confidence and empowerment. They explain that teens with **reactive decision-making styles** let others make decisions for them; needing others to like them and being easily influenced by others also impede self-confidence and empowerment. They then identify **proactive decision-making styles** as those involving analyzing a necessary decision, identifying and evaluating potential actions, choosing one action, and taking responsibility for the consequences of taking that action. Teachers can then introduce students to a model for **responsible decision-making** as a guide for making proactive decisions.

A model for responsible decision-making is meant to make sure that student decisions result in actions that show good character; that follow guidelines which parents, guardians or other responsible adults have established for them; that demonstrate self-respect and respect for others;

and that protect safety, obey the laws, and promote health. A health educator can teach students in grades 6-12 the following seven steps included in a **responsible decision-making model**:

1. Describe the situation requiring you to make a decision.
2. List all of the decisions you could potentially make.
3. Share this list of potential decisions with an adult you trust.
4. Evaluate what the consequences of each of the decisions could be.
5. Determine which of the potential decisions you identified is the most appropriate and responsible one.
6. Take action on the decision that you have chosen.
7. Evaluate the outcomes of the decision that you have made.

When instructing middle and high school students, a health educator can help them define **peer pressure** as the influences that individuals exert on others of similar status or age to engage in certain behaviors or decisions. S/he can explain that peer pressure may be positive or negative. The class can then discuss **resistance skills**, defined as skills enabling individuals to leave situations or say no to actions. A model for using resistance skills includes the following steps:

1. The student says "no" in an assertive manner to individual(s) attempting to exert peer pressure.
2. The student tells the other(s) his/her reasons for saying no.
3. The student uses nonverbal communication that matches his/her verbal communication—e.g., eye contact, facial expressions, body postures, and gestures consistent with what s/he is saying.
4. The student avoids getting into situations with peers that will involve pressure from them to make detrimental decisions.
5. The student resists peer pressure to engage in illegal actions.
6. The student works to exert influences on his/her peers to make responsible decisions.

ELEMENTS THAT INFLUENCE ADOLESCENT DECISION-MAKING

Adolescent decision-making is influenced by both **external variables**, like relationships with parents and friends; and **internal variables**, like personal self-concept and locus of control. Teen decision-making is influenced by **motivational variables**, e.g., personal values, beliefs, attitudes, goals, and emotional states. **Developmental variables** including cognitive (intellectual) development, affective (emotional) development, and social development are additional influences. Coping ability also affects decision-making ability. Because critical decisions that teens make occur in changing social contexts, they must develop abilities for evaluating decisions and adjusting and adapting them as needed. Due to society's constraints, teens must learn to identify and cope with options that are relatively more and less available to them. They must learn to apply different decision-making styles to different decision types, like career decisions as opposed to stressful or emotionally sensitive circumstances. Educators can advise teens that any single decision may be viewed as a series of choices rather than a one-time occurrence. Teens do not decide in isolation; decisions are influenced by feedback. Because current decisions influence future ones, decision-making sets precedents. Decision-making is not a linear process but a complex one; as teenagers mature and gain experience, their decision-making skills develop.

RESISTING PRESSURE FROM OTHERS

Children and teens often have more life experience being cared for, controlled, and told what to do, and relatively less experience being on their own, making independent choices, and taking initiative. Adults should tell them that being **pressured** is not good for them and is not right. Many children and teens (and even adults) have difficulty resisting pressure. **Motivations** include because they want to be liked, don't want to alienate friends, are afraid others will reject them, do not want others to make fun of them, do not want to hurt other people's feelings, are afraid others will perceive refusal as rejection, are not sure what they actually want, or do not know how to extricate themselves from the situation. Children and teens must know they have the right to say no, not to give any reason, and to walk away from any situation involving pressure. Some brief tips to support **resisting pressure** and **refusing** include standing up straight, making eye contact with the other person, stating one's feelings clearly, not making excuses, and standing up for oneself.

REFUSAL STRATEGIES FOR CHILDREN AND ADOLESCENTS

Children and teens (and adults as well) can find it hard to **resist pressure** that other people exert on them through their words. It is normal for most of us not to want to hurt other people's feelings or feel responsible for bad feelings in others. However, children and teens especially must be reminded how important it is for them to stand up for themselves in order to prevent others from verbally pressuring them into doing unsafe or unwanted things. Some strategies recommended by experts to help young people refuse to use alcohol, or to do other things that they know are not in their best interests and that they do not wish to do, include the "Dos and Don'ts." **Dos**: do say no assertively. Do abstain from drinking alcohol. Do propose some alternate activity. Do stand up for others being pressured who do not want to drink. Do walk away from the situation. Do look for something else to do with other friends. **Don'ts**: don't go to a party without being prepared to resist alcohol use. Don't be afraid to say "no." Don't mumble. Don't say "no" in an overly aggressive way. Don't behave like a "know-it-all" when refusing.

Health-Related Goal Setting

TEACHING RESPONSIBLE DECISION-MAKING TO STUDENTS

QUESTIONS STUDENTS CAN ASK THEMSELVES IN THE FOURTH STEP FOR EVALUATING THE POTENTIAL CONSEQUENCES

The steps in the **responsible decision-making model** are describing the situation wherein they need to make a decision, listing the decisions they could potentially make, sharing their list with a parent or other responsible adult, evaluating each decision's potential consequences, deciding which decision is the most suitable and responsible, acting on the chosen decision, and evaluating the outcomes of that decision. When evaluating **potential consequences** of each decision, students can ask themselves the following six questions:

- Will making this decision lead to taking actions that are lawful or legal?
- Will making this decision lead to taking actions protecting my and others' safety?
- Will making this decision lead to taking actions that agree with the guidelines and advice that my parents and other responsible adults have given me?
- Will making this decision lead to taking actions that demonstrate my respect for myself and for other people?
- Will making this decision lead to taking actions that are demonstrations of good character?

STEPS RELATED TO THE RESPONSIBLE DECISION-MAKING MODEL IN THE EVENT OF AN INCORRECT OR POOR DECISION

As they learn to make decisions responsibly, students are bound to make mistakes as with all new learning. Teens may experience anxiety over responsibility for poor decisions with unwelcome consequences. Paralyzed by doubt and indecision, they may avoid taking responsibility and action. In the same way that many teens fear being judged, rejected, disliked, or even viewed as different, they also fear **doing the wrong thing**. In addition to peer pressure and desiring acceptance, fear of misusing new responsibilities can motivate inaction to avoid unintentionally doing harm and experiencing guilt. Health educators can offer four steps to take after a bad or otherwise **wrong decision**:

1. Admit it; take responsibility, not trying to hide the mistake, blame others, or make excuses.
2. Immediately consider things done based on the decision; avoid perpetuating actions misguided by a wrong choice.
3. Parents and guardians are responsible for decision-making guidance: inform them of the decision and discuss corrective actions.
4. Apologizing is not always adequate: make restitution for any harm, damage, or loss by paying, replacing something, volunteering time, and/or similar appropriate effort as applies.

STEPS FOR STUDENTS TO TAKE FOR SETTING HEALTH GOALS FOR THEMSELVES

1. Students write long-term and short-term **health goals** in brief sentences starting with "I will..." Educators may suggest potential goals. **Long-term goals** can require a month, year, or even lifetime to attain and may be broken down to more achievable **short-term goals**. For example, a student's long-term goal could be "I will run a mile daily," with the preceding short-term goal being "I will run a quarter-mile daily."
2. Make **action plans**, i.e., detailed descriptions of steps for attaining goals, and have teachers review them for realism. Some teachers and students may establish health behavior contracts as action plans.

3. Identify potential **obstacles** to realizing the action plan. Prioritize these; brainstorm how to address high-priority ones.
4. Establish **timelines** with specific dates for reaching health goals. Consider whether these are realistic in light of other responsibilities.
5. Use a chart, graph, journal, or diary to **track progress**. Keeping records makes goals and progress concrete, supporting accountability.
6. Develop a **support system**. List people to give advice and encouragement, join a support group, form a club, and/or enlist friends. Avoid people who could sabotage health goals.
7. If needed, **revise** timelines and/or action plans, allowing additional time and/or requesting help.
8. Give yourself healthy **rewards** for meeting health goals.

Environmental Health

EPA SOURCE FOR REDUCING, REUSING, AND RECYCLING TO HELP THE ENVIRONMENT

The **US Environmental Protection Agency** (EPA) website offers information on how to reduce, reuse, and donate products to protect the environment and save natural resources and money; how to donate and recycle used electronics; how to compost and reduce wasted food; how to reduce, reuse, and recycle at home, school, work, in the community, and on the go on its wastes website; resources for educators and students including publications, games, and activities; and information on the basics, benefits, and how-to of recycling. **Recycling** reduces waste going to incinerators and landfills; conserves water, wood, minerals and other natural resources; saves energy; reduces greenhouse gas emissions involved in world climate change; sustains the environment for posterity; and creates new, well-paid jobs in American manufacturing and recycling industries. Recycling steps are:

- collection and processing
- manufacturing
- purchasing products made from recycled materials

Recycled product contents include: aluminum cans, car bumpers, carpeting, cereal boxes, comic books, egg cartons, glass containers, laundry detergent bottles, motor oil, nails, newspapers, paper towels, steel products, and garbage bags. EPA also provides instructions on recycling paper, batteries, plastics including plastic ID codes, glass, oil, household hazardous waste, tires, compact fluorescent light bulbs, etc.

HISTORICAL AND REGULATORY INFORMATION REGARDING POLLUTION PROBLEMS IN THE UNITED STATES

Air and water **pollution** and growing hazardous waste disposal problems in America came to government attention in the 1970s. The Environmental Protection Agency (EPA) developed standards, regulations, and enforced laws emphasizing "end-of-pipe" solutions, measurably improving environmental quality. In the 1980s, better detection methods and subtler, diffuser pollution sources raised awareness of the longevity and ubiquity of American waste problems. Realizing global environmental issues and difficulty controlling pollution sources prompted reorientation of America's pollution approach to prevention. The 1990 **Pollution Prevention Act** declares Congress's national policy of preventing and reducing pollution, environmentally safe recycling of non-preventable pollution, treatment of non-preventable and non-recyclable pollution, and environmentally safe disposal and release only as a last resort. It identifies America's annually producing millions of tons of pollution, and spending tens of billions of dollars to control it; industry's significant opportunities for decreasing and preventing pollution at its sources by cost-efficiently changing raw materials use, production, and operations to protect the environment, worker safety and health, and save costs for liability, pollution control, and raw materials; existing laws and industrial resources' emphasizing treatment and disposal, not source reduction; businesses' requiring technical assistance and information to adopt source reduction measures; and the EPA as implementing it.

CONSERVING ENERGY FOR SUSTAINABLE LIVING AND PREVENTION OF SEVERE GLOBAL DISRUPTIONS FROM GREENHOUSE GAS EMISSIONS

In 2009, America produced one-fifth of the world's CO_2 emissions, approximately 6 billion metric tons annually—7 billion projected by 2030. **Buildings** produce the most, 38 percent from private homes, shopping malls, warehouses, and offices, primarily from using electricity; average new American houses are 45 percent larger than 30 years ago. Walmart, maintaining thousands of buildings, has significantly conserved energy by using natural light in shopping areas, radiant floors, high-efficiency refrigeration, evaporative cooling units, etc.; one pilot supercenter consumed 45 percent less power than comparable stores. Oak Ridge National Laboratory researchers say 200 million tons of CO_2 could be reduced annually through smart design and retrofitting, but find this unlikely without financial incentives, appliance standards, and new building codes. For example, commercial building owners are unmotivated because tenants pay power bills. Development increases traveling distance, making **transportation** the second-biggest source. **Industry** is third. Dow saved \$7 billion from 1995-2009 by reducing energy intensity, reducing CO_2 emissions 20 percent; DuPont and 3M have also profited through energy-efficiency. Other developed nations surpass America with solar and wind power, bicycling, fuel-efficient cars, and carbon-neutral houses. Experts advocate developing CO_2-burial and elimination technologies, slowing deforestation, and replacing fossil fuels with renewable energy faster to reduce global emissions 80-100 percent by 2050.

CAUSES AND EFFECTS OF ENVIRONMENTAL PROBLEMS

AIR POLLUTION

Air pollution is primarily caused by the use of fossil fuels, such as oil, gas, natural gas, and coal; these fuels release carbon monoxide, hydrocarbons, and other pollutants into the atmosphere when they are burned. **Motor vehicles** are the primary polluters, but industrial emissions from factories and manufacturing plants also are implicated because many depend on fossil fuels as well, and some release various chemicals used in or resulting from the manufacturing process. Air pollution can also result from **agricultural chemicals** (such as crop spraying) and **household chemicals** (such as fumigants). Air pollution can reduce visibility in some cases, but it may also be invisible, so people may be unaware that the air is polluted. Air pollution is considered to be one of the causes of **global warming**. Air pollution can also have a serious impact on **health** by impairing lung function and resulting in an increased incidence of cancer and respiratory diseases, such as asthma and chronic obstructive pulmonary disease.

WATER POLLUTION

Water pollution occurs when pollutants flow into surface water sources, such as rivers, lakes, reservoirs, and oceans. Contamination of **surface water** can result from sewage, oil spills, industrial wastes, and chemical runoffs (fertilizers, weed killers). In areas with air pollution, surface water may become contaminated through atmospheric deposition (rain, snow). **Drinking water**, even from clean water sources, can become contaminated through erosion of lead pipes or lead solder used with other types of pipes that are part of the delivery system. **Groundwater** can also become polluted as pollutants, such as noxious chemicals from fertilizers and weed killers, are leached through the ground and enter underground water. Water pollution not only kills fish and wildlife, but it can harm wetlands and coral reefs. Water pollution has been implicated in waterborne diseases (such as typhoid fever), neurological impairment, and cancer. Children exposed to polluted water may suffer developmental disorders and intellectual disabilities.

HAZARDOUS WASTE

Hazardous waste is waste that poses a threat to the health of individuals or to the environment. The Environmental Protection Agency (EPA) classifies hazardous wastes according to the following characteristics:

- **Ignitable**: Liquids and nonliquids that can ignite and cause fires.
- **Corrosive**: Based on pH or the ability to corrode steel.

- **Reactive**: Wastes that are unstable, may react with water, or result in toxic gases. They may also explode.
- **Toxic**: Wastes that are harmful if ingested or absorbed.

Wastes may also be classified as **listed wastes**. These include wastes from manufacturing and industrial processes. **Hazardous wastes** are often produced in manufacturing, nuclear power plants (nuclear wastes), and healthcare facilities (needles, materials contaminated with body fluids). **Nuclear wastes** are classified as mixed waste because they contain a radioactive component as well as a hazardous component. Hazardous wastes can result in disease (such as from needle punctures), injury (from fire and explosions), and death (from toxic exposure, disease).

Noise Pollution and Overcrowding

Noise pollution is increasingly a problem in the urban environment where individuals are almost constantly surrounded by transportation noises, people, alarms, sirens, dogs barking, and everyday noise from walking, eating, and interacting. Noise is often an issue in the work environment because of the equipment used, especially in manufacturing. **Noise pollution** may also result from inadequate urban planning, social events, and construction. The results of noise pollution can be hearing impairment (especially if exposed to high decibels), stress, fatigue, insomnia, and high blood pressure. Animals exposed to noise pollution may become aggressive, disoriented, or hard of hearing. Wildlife that use mating calls or echolocation may not reproduce or migrate. **Overcrowding,** too many people in a space, is often associated with noise pollution and can occur in individual homes, such as with four or five families sharing one apartment, or in an urban area, such as when a large population is impacted by a severe housing shortage. Overcrowding can result in disease epidemics, mental health problems, and academic problems.

Strategies for Reducing Environmental Hazards and Promoting Health
Water Purification and Emission Control

Water purification is the process that removes contaminants, such as biological matter, chemicals, gases, and debris, from water in order to make it safe for drinking or other purposes. Boiling water does not always remove all contaminants—nor does the use of activated charcoal filters. **Drinking water** is typically not made sterile, whereas water for **medical purposes** should be sterile. Steps to purification include pumping the water from the source, screening to remove debris, pH adjustment, coagulation/flocculation, sedimentation, filtering, and disinfection.

Emission control is the system used to reduce emissions that result in air pollution from both mobile sources (such as motor vehicles) and point sources (power plants, manufacturing plants). **Toxic emission pollutants** include carbon monoxide, hydrocarbons, sulfur oxide, organic compounds, nitrogen dioxide, smoke, and soot. Emissions are regulated by the EPA as well as some state regulation agencies. Motor vehicles use catalytic converters to convert carbon monoxide, hydrocarbons, and nitrous oxide to harmless gases.

Waste Management

Waste management is the process by which waste products are collected, transported, and disposed of or recycled. **Municipal waste management** usually involves weekly collection with separate containers sometimes provided for garden waste, recyclables, and garbage, although garbage is mixed by the consumer and then separated at a facility in some waste management plants. Waste management is regulated by the EPA through the **Resource Conservation and Recovery Act**, which regulates the handling and disposal of hazardous and nonhazardous waste. Because **hazardous waste** can result in disease, injury, or death, special handling is required. Hazardous waste cannot be disposed of with regular trash or in drains or the sewer system. In schools, chemistry labs often have hazardous wastes to dispose of, such as corrosive liquids, heavy-metal solutions, and organic solvents. The art department and the school nurse may also have hazardous wastes, such as used paints, pigments, dyes, needles, and dressings contaminated with body fluids.

IMPROVING COMMUNITY AND ENVIRONMENTAL HEALTH

Individuals can contribute to improving community and environmental health through the following actions:

- **Advocacy**: This include identifying public health problems within the community and/or environment, researching the problems and possible solutions, and taking steps to educate the public and those in positions of power to help reduce or eliminate the problems by influencing political and social policy. A primary goal of advocacy is to increase public awareness in order to generate support for change.
- **Volunteerism**: This involves providing services in the community without financial gain or coercion, such as volunteering to clean up the environment or volunteering in a local hospital or school. Many nonprofit agencies and governmental agencies welcome volunteers or have volunteer programs. Volunteerism is a required part of service learning for students in some areas, but students can often be mobilized to volunteer for causes that interest them, and an educator can provide a good role model through volunteerism.

Health-Related Information

HEALTH EQUITY TERMS AND ISSUES RELATED TO US DEMOGRAPHIC DISPARITIES

The **Healthy People 2020** government initiative informs its focus on eliminating health disparities, attaining health equity, and improving American health with these 2008 US Census Bureau statistics: over 100 million people, approximately 33 percent, belonged to racial or ethnic minorities. Of these, 154 million, i.e., 51 percent, were women. Another 36 million, around 12 percent, not living in nursing homes or other residential care facilities, had disabilities. Yet another 70.5 million, or 23 percent, were estimated to live in rural areas; 233.5 million, or 77 percent, lived in urban areas. HealthyPeople.gov also cites 2002 data that four percent of the American population 18-44 years old was estimated to identify as gay, lesbian, bisexual, or transgender. The initiative defines **health disparity** as a specific health difference associated with environmental, economic, and/or social disadvantages. In the past, endeavors toward health equity and away from disparities mainly concentrated on healthcare services and illnesses or diseases. But current Healthy People 2020 experts point out that good health does not equal absence of illness. They define **individual and population health determinants** as interrelationships among genetics, biology, physical environment, socioeconomic status, individual behavior, literacy levels, discrimination, racism, legislative policies, health, and health services.

FACTORS THAT INFLUENCE AMERICAN HEALTH AND FEDERAL HEALTH INITIATIVES

All American citizens experience numerous **influences on their health status**. These include whether the following **factors** are available, and whether people have access to them: unpolluted air and clean water; safe, adequate housing; reliable, affordable public transportation; nutritious food; high-quality educations; health insurance coverage; and culturally sensitive healthcare providers. The Healthy People federal initiative (www.HealthyPeople.gov) has historically set goals focusing on changing **health disparities** over the past 20 years. In the Healthy People 2000 program, the goal was to decrease health disparities for American citizens. The Healthy People 2010 program augmented its goal to eliminate health disparities rather than just decrease them. The Healthy People 2020 program additionally extended the goal, not only to eliminate health disparities, but also to establish **health equity** and improve all Americans' health. This initiative plans, from 2014-2024, to track the rates of diseases, mortality, chronic conditions, behaviors, and other factors relative to race, ethnicity, gender, sexual identity, sexual orientation, disability status, special healthcare needs, urban and rural geographic locations, and other demographic factors. Through such research, the Healthy People staff members hope to achieve their health equity and improvement goals.

RESOURCES FOR COORDINATED SCHOOL HEALTH APPROACHES

Basic information on **coordinated school health approaches** include: "School Health 101 Packets" from the National School Boards Association; *Guidelines for a Coordinated Approach to School Health: Addressing the Physical, Social, and Emotional Health Needs of the School Community* from the Connecticut State Department of Education; *Guidelines for Coordinating School Health Programs* from the Maine Departments of Education and Health and Human Services; the Comprehensive Health Education Network (CHEN) listserv, a mailing list of national, state, and local school health professionals; a PDF, "Building a Healthier Future through School Health Programs" from the CDC's *Promising Practices in Chronic Disease Prevention and Control;* and an "at a glance" webpage, "School Health Programs: Improving the Health of Our Nation's Youth." All of these are on the CDC website's page of Coordinated School Health Publications and Resources. This page also offers links and PDF documents on the relationship between school and student health and academic achievement. For school health assessment and planning, it includes links to the School Health Index (SHI) Self-

Assessment and Planning Guide, and to Curriculum Analysis Tools for Health Education and Physical Education.

RESOURCES FOR COLLABORATION AND PARTNERSHIP, EVALUATION, AND PARENT AND FAMILY INVOLVEMENT

The Centers for Disease Control and Prevention (CDC) website's page on Coordinated School Health Publications and Resources includes links to PDF documents on **collaboration and partnership**, including a primer for professionals serving children and youth and a guide to community-school health councils, a link to the National Association of Chronic Disease Directors page about how health departments function and how schools can partner with them, and a link to the American Cancer Society's PDF on community-school health councils. Regarding **evaluation** of coordinated school health approaches, the CDC website includes a page, "Evaluations of Innovative Programs," including an overview of its Division of Adolescent and School Health's (DASH) assistance with evaluating programs, a list of links to applied evaluation projects, information on eligibility, characteristics of initiatives subject to applied evaluations, and a contact link for the CDC Evaluation Research Team. Regarding **parent and family involvement**, CDC's web page on Coordinated School Health Publications and Resources offers a PDF, *Parent Engagement: Strategies for Involving Parents in School Health.*

RESOURCES PERTAINING TO POLICY, PROFESSIONAL ASSOCIATIONS, AND PROMISING PRACTICES

Addressing **policy** related to coordinated school health approaches, the Centers for Disease Control and Prevention (CDC) website page of Coordinated School Health Publications and Resources includes download links to PDF documents of an Executive Summary; *A CDC Review of School Laws and Policies Concerning Child and Adolescent Health;* and a link to the National Association of State Boards of Education resource, the State School Health Policy Database, which includes compiled laws and policies from all 50 states covering over 40 school health subjects, e.g., school health councils, school health coordinators, and coordination. This page offers external links to these **professional associations**: American Association for Health Education; Academy of Nutrition and Dietetics; School Nutrition Association; National Association for Sport and Physical Education (NASPE); National Association of School Nurses; American School Counselor Association; National Association of School Psychologists; School Social Work Association of America; and the Health Educator, School Health Coordinators, and Mental Health Professionals Sections of the American School Health Association. Under "**Promising Practices**," this page includes links to National Association of County and City Health Officials, "Building Healthier Schools"; National School Boards Association's database of successful school district health policies and practices; and partnership program and school nutrition success stories.

EFFECTIVE COMMUNICATION WITH STUDENTS, PARENTS, AND THE COMMUNITY

Forming and sustaining partnerships depend on **effective communication** among schools, students, parents, and community. Also, schools are responsible for assisting parents in understanding learning language. School health educators should consider whether and how they communicate student progress to parents in relevant, positive ways; whether and how they clarify what teachers and parents must discuss; whether they have established a language of learning that teachers and parents share for exploring student learning successes, challenges, and development; how schools can collaborate with parents and communities to develop shared educational expectations; how parents with language barriers and/or busy work schedules communicate with the school; and how the school communicates with business and industry partners. Possible **strategies** include: home-school liaisons to teach parents educational language, current classroom characteristics, and how to talk with teachers and children about school experiences. Parent/community and parent-teacher meetings, newsletters, websites, web conferencing, emails, text messages, and assemblies are communication channels and tools to utilize. School-year transition calendars highlighting specific times and activities critical to parent and community engagement can also help. Educators should know and share how to access information in diverse forms and languages. Sharing consistent and ongoing high expectations of students and professional teacher development in communicating with parents are additional strategies.

There are several things that school health educators should consider for open, genuine **consultative communication**. They should encourage honest, open dialogues. To empower parents for effective consulting participation, their schools should offer support and training to build parental leadership capacities. When schools make informal and/or formal decisions, policy reviews and new policies regarding curriculum, assessment, and reporting, they should invite interested community members to consult. They can apply strategies such as flexible consulting with a representative cross-section of students, parents, and community members, rather than only those who are most assertive; make sure they broadly disseminate information in a variety of formats about opportunities to consult; offer opportunities for skill development and/or training to teachers and parents; develop solutions to aid teachers in balancing issues of workloads and time to facilitate their engagement in decision-making consultation; and encourage students to participate in decision-making processes and participate actively in the school council and/or parent and citizen groups.

INDICATIONS OF EFFECTIVE COMMUNICATION

Effective communication achieving strong engagement is indicated when educators acknowledge **parents** as their children's first educators; engage them as partners in children's learning; and encourage their close, sincere interest in the school's work. Educators communicate information to parents about current student learning status, progress over time, and how they can support their further learning. Language used by students, parents, and school personnel in both informal and formal settings reflects caring, respectful relationships. Schools have established continuing, regular methods for determining what parents require for engaging with their children's learning. Parents are able to identify the school's primary expectations for student attendance, homework, and behavior. Teachers and administrators applying diverse communication styles appropriately to parental availability, work conditions, cultural backgrounds, etc., also indicates effective communication, which produces strong engagement. Another indication is that school administrators and teachers connect with every student's parents regularly. Additionally, a school that has mechanisms established for building relationships with pertinent community members indicates effective communication for strong engagement.

FERPA

"FERPA" stands for the **Family Educational Rights and Privacy Act**. According to the US Departments of Health and Human Services and of Education (2008), any educational agency or institution that receives federal funding under any program administered by the Department of Education is subject to FERPA regulations protecting the privacy of **student educational records**. This federal funding specification includes all public school districts and schools, as well as most public and private post-secondary schools, including medical and other professional schools. Elementary and secondary religious and private schools not receiving such funding are not subject to FERPA. "Education records" refers to records directly related to a student, and maintained by an educational institution, agency, or a party acting on its behalf. These include elementary and secondary student health records, immunization records, and records kept by public school nurses. Special education student records kept by public schools, including records of services these students receive under the Individuals with Disabilities Education Act (IDEA), are also included in the FERPA definition of "education records."

HIPAA

HIPAA is the **Health Insurance Portability and Accountability Act** (1996). Among its purposes are to protect the security and privacy of individually identifiable health information and improve the effectiveness and efficiency of the healthcare system by setting national requirements and standards for electronic healthcare transactions. Provisions related to these purposes issued by the US Department of Health and Human Services are called **HIPAA Administrative Simplification Rules**, including a **Privacy Rule**. "Covered entities" subject to these rules include health insurance plans; healthcare clearinghouses; and healthcare providers, e.g., doctors, dentists, other practitioners, hospitals, other medical and health service providers, and any other organizations or persons that provide, are paid for, or bill for healthcare in their normal courses of business, and electronically transmit health information associated with covered transactions. HIPAA's Privacy Rule requires covered entities to protect the privacy of individuals' health records and other information by limiting disclosure without patient permission; and ensures patient rights to examine, get copies, and request corrections of their health records. Schools providing student healthcare with related electronic transactions are "covered entities." However, when school health records are defined as "education records" or "treatment records" under FERPA, they are not subject to the HIPAA Privacy Rule.

MANDATED REPORTING OF CHILD MALTREATMENT

According to the US Department of Health and Human Services Administration on Children, Youth and Families (ACYF) Child Welfare Information Gateway, Children's Bureau (www.childwelfare.gov), as of 2012, 48 states, D.C., American Samoa, Guam, the Northern Mariana Islands, Puerto Rico, and the Virgin Islands designate professions legally required to **report child maltreatment**. These mandated reporters typically are often in contact with children. Such professionals include teachers, principals, administrators, and other school employees; physicians, nurses, and other healthcare employees; social workers; therapists, counselors, psychologists, psychiatrists, and other mental health professionals; child care providers; coroners and medical examiners; and law enforcement officers. Additional professions often mandated to report include clergy in 27 states and Guam; probation and parole officers in 17 states; substance abuse counselors in 14 states; commercial film processors in 12 states, Guam, and Puerto Rico; directors, employees, and volunteers at camps and day camps, youth and recreation centers and other places providing organized activities for children in 11 states; court-appointed special advocates in 10 states; domestic violence workers in seven states and D.C.; humane and animal control officers in seven states and D.C.; and faculty, administrators, other employees and volunteers at public and private colleges, universities, and technical and vocational schools in four states.

Health-Related Products and the Services-Informed Consumer

PREVALENCE OF HEALTH QUACKERY IN ADVERTISING

Advertising has long promised results "too good to be true," such as instant miracle cures for cancer, "smart" drugs ensuring longevity, or things that "magically" make arthritis pain "disappear." **Quackery** is the activity of selling unproven remedies. While quacks have existed for many years, today they have more venues than ever before—in addition to word of mouth, newspapers, magazines, and direct mail, TV and radio have been added, and then the Internet. Not only do websites abound selling a variety of health scams, but most of us are also familiar with seeing ads all over our computer screens as we view our email or surf the web. According to government research, the majority of **healthcare scam** victims are above age 65; fraudsters target vulnerable older people. Unproven remedies not only waste consumers' money, they can also prevent them from getting genuine, effective medical treatment. Some, beyond being useless, can be harmful. They also offer false hope, preying on people's pain and fear. Two of the most common fraudulent remedy categories advertised are for arthritis relief and anti-aging claims.

ACCESS TO HEALTHCARE

Access to quality, comprehensive healthcare is critical to increasing health and life quality for all. **Healthcare access** involves three steps:

- acquiring healthcare system entry
- accessing locations providing needed services
- finding providers that patients can communicate with and trust.

Healthcare access has impacts on overall physical, mental, and social health; disease and disability prevention; health condition identification and treatment; life quality; life expectancy; and preventable deaths. **Impacts** on individuals and society are caused by healthcare access disparities; access limitations impede individuals' abilities to realize their full potentials, diminishing their quality of life. **Service obstacles** include lack of insurance coverage, lack of available services and providers, and expenses; the consequences of these obstacles include lack of preventive services, delayed care, unmet health needs, and hospitalizations which could have been avoided. People without health insurance coverage are less likely to get healthcare, more likely to have poor health status, and more likely to die sooner.

According to the Healthy People 2020 initiative (www.HealthyPeople.gov), an important factor in healthcare access is **primary care providers (PCPs)** as ongoing, regular, usual healthcare sources. PCPs are significant for good patient-provider relationships and communication, higher patient trust, and greater probabilities of receiving needed care. Preventive services include primary prevention, like detecting early symptoms and signs to prevent illness; and secondary prevention, such as identifying illness earlier when more treatable. **Emergency medical services (EMS)** constitute another crucial healthcare area, including basic and advanced life support. In recent years, complicated emergency care system problems have developed. HealthyPeople.gov identifies all citizens' access to pre-hospital, rapid-response EMS as an important population health improvement goal. Time waiting in ERs and provider offices, and time between identification and receipt of tests and treatments, are measures of **healthcare system timeliness**. Delays increase patient attrition, decrease patient satisfaction, and cause clinically significant care delays. More non-emergency patients attending ERs, and fewer total ERs, cause delays. Fewer PCPs and medical students interested in primary care are workforce concerns. Emerging issues include meeting needs for many more newly-insured Americans; measuring and increasing access to safe, quality preventive, emergency, long-term, and palliative services; and decreasing disparities and measuring access for elders and minorities.

ELECTRONIC PERSONAL HEALTH RECORDS

Electronic personal health records eliminate problems with paper records like disorganization, losing and misplacing individual papers, and not having papers available when needed. Unlike hospital, physician practice, or health insurance company electronic medical records, **personal health records** are accessible to **patients**. Though electronic adoption has been slow relative to technological capability, more physician practices, hospitals, and insurance companies are providing records accessible over the Internet via computer, tablet, and smartphone. According to the Mayo Clinic (2014), patients should add information including their PCP name and phone number; drug and other allergies; current medications and dosages; chronic health conditions, e.g., hypertension; major surgeries and their dates; any advance directives or living will; immunization history; and family history. They may also want to include prevention activities, e.g., blood pressure, cholesterol levels, dietary and exercise habits, screening test results; and health goals, e.g., losing weight or smoking cessation. Benefits are not only organization, but emergency life-saving; health assessment and tracking; doctor visit preparation; health management between doctor visits; and timely scheduling of wellness, prevention and screening services, vaccinations, and appointments.

MOBILE HEALTHCARE AND MEDICAL APPLICATIONS

The mobile applications industry estimates that by 2015, 500 million people in the world will be using healthcare apps on their smartphones; and by 2018, half of all smartphone and tablet users, who number over 3.4 billion, will have downloaded **mobile health apps**. Consumers, patients, and healthcare professionals are included among these users. The US Food and Drug Administration (FDA), which oversees safety and effectiveness in medical devices, includes mobile medical apps among those devices, and encourages mobile medical app development that will give consumers and healthcare professionals valuable health information and improve healthcare. Consumers can use mobile apps like **MyFitnessPal** to monitor and manage how many calories they eat and burn to manage their own wellness. The National Institutes of Health provides **LactMed**, an app that gives nursing mothers information about how various medications affect their breast milk and their nursing infants. Healthcare professionals can use apps like **Radiation Emergency Medical Management (REMM)**, which offers guidance for diagnosis and treatment of radiation injuries. Other mobile medical apps can diagnose heart arrhythmias or cancer. And some can serve as command centers for insulin-dependent diabetes patients' glucose meter use and measurements.

STUDENT ACCESS TO VALID HEALTHCARE INFORMATION, PRODUCTS, AND SERVICES

Students should first identify health information, products, and services they need, contacting healthcare providers for information and product recommendations; then find identified information, services, and products. Students researching reports on health topics can find free, reliable **information** from websites including CDC, American Heart Association, American Cancer Society, American Medical Association, and American Association for Health Education; print and online medical journals, public libraries; professional health organization-produced TV programs and videos; school counselors; and healthcare professionals. They can obtain **health products** from healthcare providers, pharmacies, and supermarkets; and parental help accessing prescription and over-the-counter medications. To evaluate information, students should consider source reliability, qualifications of information providers, information's currency, reputable healthcare professional evaluations, whether information's purpose is to inform or sell, whether it educates or only appeals to emotions, how to acquire additional information, and whether claims are realistic. Before paying for products or services, they should consider whether they need them; understand how to use

135

them and what they do; if they are safe, high-quality, and worth their price; consumer agency reviews; and what to do if dissatisfied. The Food and Drug Administration (FDA), Federal Trade Commission (FTC), Consumer Product Safety Commission (CPSC), and US Postal Service for mail-order products and services can help with complaints.

COMMUNITY HEALTH SERVICES OFFERED BY THE AMERICAN RED CROSS

The American Red Cross is a national nonprofit health agency with many local community chapters. It offers **training** in swimming safety for lifeguards, physical education teachers, and others; in first aid techniques, cardiopulmonary resuscitation (CPR), automated external defibrillator (AED) use, how to control bleeding, what to do in the event of seizures, what to do if someone is choking, and other training for dealing with emergencies until medical personnel arrive. Training is also provided to prepare individuals who want to become instructors in American Red Cross first aid, CPR, and AED courses. The Red Cross also offers Babysitter's Training to teach 11-15-year-olds the confidence and skills they need for safely and responsibly caring for infants and children. The training includes caregiving skills like feeding, diapering, playtime, and bedtime routines; and how to address illnesses, household accidents, injuries, and other child emergencies.

COMMUNITY HEALTH CENTERS

The US Department of Health and Human Services (HHS) supports community-based health centers nationwide through its **Health Resources and Services Administration (HRSA)**. These centers are patient-directed organizations designed to serve populations with limited healthcare access. They provide quality, comprehensive, and culturally competent primary healthcare services to vulnerable populations and medically underserved communities. HRSA defines **medically underserved** populations and areas as having insufficient primary care providers, high poverty rates, high infant mortality rates, and/or large elderly populations. It defines **Health Professional Shortage Areas** as geographical (service areas and counties), demographic (low-income populations), or institutional (federally qualified health centers and other public facilities or comprehensive health centers) having shortages of primary medical, dental, or mental health care providers. Health centers serve such high-need communities; are governed by community boards, with 51 percent or more being patients representing the population served; provide comprehensive primary healthcare and support services (translation, transportation, education, etc.) promoting healthcare access; and provide services to all patients, adjusting fees based on ability to pay. Public and private non-profit health centers meeting Medicare and Medicaid criteria are grant-supported, non-grant-supported, identified by HRSA and Medicare and Medicaid-certified, or outpatient health facilities and programs run by tribal organizations under the Indian Self-Determination Act or Indian Health Care Improvement Act.

MASS MEDIA CAMPAIGNS FOR PROMOTING HEALTH MESSAGES

Mass media campaigns can deliver health-promoting messages to large numbers of people. By raising their awareness and communicating educational information through social media, they can enforce positive health behaviors to achieve large-scale **positive health changes**. Messages can be communicated in **print and digital media**. Another avenue is **radio**, found more cost-effective than TV by health organizations because it not only costs less, but moreover it reaches people at work and in cars as well as at home. Also, research in America found radio listeners surprisingly accurate in their memories of broadcast details months later. This retention supports radio's educational potential. In other countries, particularly developing ones, TV and electricity are unavailable in rural villages; however, battery-operated radios are common. Public health, rural development, health education, nutritional education, family planning, and awareness of correct breastfeeding practices have been promoted respectively in Swaziland, India, Nicaragua, the Philippines, and Trinidad and Tobago. **Puppet shows** appeal to younger students and can introduce hygiene, nutrition, and other health topics. Puppetry is an important cultural tradition in Cambodia, and is often used to teach critical health concepts to all ages. UNAIDS advocates mass media TV and radio campaigns for AIDS awareness, education, and destigmatization.

SELECTING APPROPRIATE HEALTHCARE PROVIDERS

The strategy that the individual will use for **selecting appropriate healthcare providers and treatment** may depend on the type of insurance coverage that the individual has. If, for example, the person is covered by Medicaid, then the first concern is whether or not the healthcare provider accepts Medicaid patients. If the individual is in an HMO or PPO, then the individual may need to discuss his or her needs with a primary care physician, who can make referrals. Many specialists require referrals from primary care physicians before they will see a patient, so that's often the best place to begin. Additionally, most individuals aren't adept at diagnosing their own problems and are unsure of what type of healthcare provider to see. The individual can also search online to find out information, such as credentials and experience, about potential healthcare providers, including websites that rank healthcare providers.

OPTIMIZING HEALTH INSURANCE BENEFITS

The first step in optimizing health insurance benefits is to have a clear understanding of the **insurance plan** and what it does and does not cover as well as the **frequency** of which certain procedures, such as laboratory tests, can be done. For example, some tests, such as the Hgb A1c, which monitors diabetes, may be covered only every three months, whereas others may be covered once every 30 days. If the insurance plan provides a network of healthcare providers, it is more cost-effective to seek care from those in the network because the plan will not likely cover the full cost of out-of-network providers. The individual should be aware of preauthorization requirements, such as those for expensive procedures or surgery, and should verify that healthcare providers have received preauthorization before providing care. Once the deductible for the year is met, the individual should plan to see all other necessary healthcare providers before the end of that year so they are covered by the deductible.

PATIENT'S BILL OF RIGHTS

A patient's bill of rights in relation to what should be expected from a healthcare organization is outlined in the standards of The Joint Commission and the National Committee for Quality Assurance. **Rights** include the following:

- Respect for the patient, including personal dignity and psychosocial, spiritual, and cultural considerations.
- Response to needs related to access to pain control.
- Ability to make decisions about care, including informed consent, advance directives, and-end of-life care.
- Procedure for registering complaints or grievances.
- Protection of confidentiality and privacy.
- Freedom from abuse or neglect.
- Protection during research and information related to ethical issues of research.
- Appraisal of outcomes, including unexpected outcomes.
- Information about the organization, services, and practitioners.
- Appeal procedures for decisions regarding benefits and quality of care.
- Organizational code of ethical behavior.
- Procedures for donating and procuring organs/tissue.

COMPARISON SHOPPING SKILLS FOR HEALTHCARE PRODUCTS

The price for healthcare products may vary widely, so the consumer should practice comparison shopping.

- **Telephone**: The individual can make a list of needed healthcare products, including medications, and then call local pharmacies, including big box stores such as Costco and Sam's Club, and ask for prices.
- **Newspapers**: Specials on healthcare products may be printed in weekly flyers for drugstores and other stores.
- **Comparison shop**: The individual may check prices and availability in a variety of stores, including Wal-Mart, Target, and dollar stores, which often carry some healthcare products even if they don't have a pharmacy.
- **Internet**: Online comparison shopping is relatively easy, and the individual can often find products that are less expensive than in local stores. Internet sites that offer free shipping are often a better value because shipping costs can be high, and some states require that items be taxed as well.

INTERPRETATION OF SIGNS AND SYMBOLS

Sign/Symbol	Interpretation
	Flame: Includes flammable materials and gases and those that are self-heating or self-reactive.
	Corrosion: Includes substances that can cause skin burns, metal corrosion, and eye damage.
	Health hazard: Includes carcinogens, toxic substances, and respiratory irritants.
	Poison: Includes materials, gases, or substances that are extremely toxic and may result in death or severe illness.

Sign/Symbol	Interpretation
	Irritant: Includes material, gases, or substances that are irritants to skin, eyes, and/or respiratory tract, acutely toxic, or have a narcotic effect.
	Biohazard: Includes biological substances, such as body fluids, that pose a threat to humans. Appears on sharps containers that hold contaminated needles.

FOOD PRODUCT LABELS

The FDA, under the Federal Food, Drug, and Cosmetic Act, regulates **product labeling**. Labels on food products contain information specific to the product, but the same type of information is contained for all food products:

- **Serving size, servings per container, and calories**: The calories are based on the serving size, so if there are three servings and the calorie count is 150, then the entire product has 450 calories. The calorie count also indicates the number of calories derived from fat.
- **Nutrients**: This includes the amount of fat, carbohydrates, and protein per serving as well as cholesterol, sodium, sugar, and fiber. The amounts are indicated in grams or milligrams but also as a percentage of the daily recommended value. Grams of dietary fiber can be subtracted from the total carbohydrate grams because fiber is carbohydrate that is not digested.
- **Vitamins and minerals**: These are listed as a percentage of daily recommended value per serving.
- **Footnote**: This explains how the percentages displayed are based on a 2,000-calorie diet.

TYPES AND CHARACTERISTICS OF HEALTH INSURANCE

Types and characteristics of health insurance:

- **HMO** - With health maintenance organizations (HMOs), a primary care provider (PCP) coordinates care and referrals to a network of healthcare providers. The individual has little choice and requires a referral from the PCP to see a specialist. Plans may provide preventive care, but they may also require copayments and deductible.
- **PPO** - With a preferred provider organization (PPO), an individual can choose to see any healthcare provider, including specialists, in a network of healthcare providers. The individual is not usually required to select a PCP but may have to pay copayments and a deductible, depending on the plan. Individuals can usually see healthcare providers outside of the network, but reimbursement is typically lower, so the individual may have to pay part of the costs.
- **EPO** - The exclusive provider organization (EPO) is similar to the PPO in that the individual can see any physician within a network except that the individual does not have the option of seeing a healthcare provider outside of the network except in emergency situations.

- **POS** - The point of service plan (POS) is a combined HMO and PPO. The individual has a PCP within a network, and the PCP makes referrals, but the individual can see out-of-network healthcare providers; however, the individual must pay part of the cost for out-of-network providers.
- **HDHP** - The high-deductible health plan (HDHP) may be an HMO, PPO, or EPO, but it is characterized by a high deductible before the insurance begins to reimburse for care. People with low income often select this option to avoid catastrophic costs, but they may end up with large bills for healthcare services.

SOURCES OF HEALTH-RELATED INFORMATION

Source	Characteristics of the source of health-related information
Libraries	Research librarians are available to assist the user to find valid print/electronic information.
Health practitioners	Health practitioners, especially nurses and doctors, are excellent resources for information about disease, treatments, and preventive measures.
Computerized databases	Databases that provide access to valid medical articles in journals and health publications include Cochrane Library, CINAHL Plus (Cumulative Index of Nursing and Allied Health Literature), ClinicalTrials.gov, Drugs@FDA, MedlinePlus, Medline/PubMed, Merck Manual of Diagnosis and Therapy, Online Mendelian Inheritance in Man (OMIM), PDR.net (Physicians' Desk Reference), and PubMed.
Print media	Many magazines and newspapers have health-related information, but the most valid are medical journals, such as the *American Journal of Medicine,* because popular media are often only reporting on articles in these journals or giving anecdotal reports.
Electronic media	Social media, such as Facebook, Twitter, and numerous websites, have health-related information that may or may not be valid because anyone can write anything online whether it is true or not, so this type of information should always be verified with a valid source.

EVALUATING DIFFERENT SOURCES OF HEALTH INFORMATION

Strategies for evaluating different sources of health information include the following:

- **Consider the source**: Medical journals, medical databases, government sources, and medical experts (physicians, nurses) provide the most valid information. Information in the popular press or social media sites, including Wikipedia, should always be verified by searching more valid sources.
- **Check authors' credentials**: It's important to verify authors' expertise by doing an Internet search to confirm the authors' credentials and experience. Researchers and medical experts are often cited numerous times.
- **Do a second search**: Determine if others have written similar information that verifies the findings in the first.

- **Ask a reference librarian**: If unsure about validity, a reference librarian can help to verify whether or not the source is valid.
- **Consider the type of research and the data**: Consider how the authors reached their conclusions and determine whether the conclusions appear to be supported by the data.

ROLES OF GOVERNMENTAL AND NONGOVERNMENTAL AGENCIES IN PROVIDING RELIABLE HEALTH INFORMATION

The National Institutes of Health (NIH) is the primary health-related **U.S. governmental agency** that is involved in health research and health education. The NIH supports numerous individual institutes, including the National Cancer Institute, National Eye Institute, National Institute on Aging, National Institute on Alcohol Abuse and Alcoholism, National Institute on Drug Abuse, and National Institute of Mental Health. The Centers for Disease Control and Prevention (CDC), another governmental agency, provides current information on numerous topics including health conditions, healthy living, travelers' health, and emergency preparedness. The government sponsors numerous prevention centers. **Nongovernmental professional organizations**, such as the American Medical Association, and numerous prevention centers, such as the Child Abuse Prevention Center, carry out or support independent research and publish the results of this research. The Prevention Research Centers are 26 academic research centers in public institutions, such as medical schools, that carry out preventive research and influence public health policy.

STAYING INFORMED ABOUT MEDICAL AND HEALTH-RELATED ADVANCES

Strategies for staying informed about medical and health-related advances include the following:

- Subscribe to free **health-related electronic newsletters**: Johns Hopkins Medicine (Your Health), Cleveland Clinic newsletters (Health Essentials, Children's Health Essentials, Center for Integrative Medicine, Speaking of Women's Health, The Beating Edge, The Competitive Edge), Medpage Today, and Healthbeat (Harvard).
- Subscribe to **print newsletters**: *NIH News in Health* (a PDF version is available), *Global Health Matters* (NIH Fogarty International Center).
- Review newspaper and popular press **health-related articles**: Survey articles for topics of interest including new information about diseases and treatment to research further.
- Use **TV and radio**: Watch or listen to health-related news and shows for current information.
- Use **electronic sources**: Routinely check government sites, such as CDC.gov and NIH.gov, and private organization sites, such as the American Heart Association, for new information. *ScienceDaily* provides summaries of medical research findings, including information about original sources.
- Attend **lectures/presentations**: Local hospitals often provide consumer education about disease and health matters.

EFFECTIVE USE OF TECHNOLOGY IN ACCESSING ACCURATE HEALTH INFORMATION
DATABASES AND BOOLEAN SEARCH

Accessing accurate health information requires comprehensive evaluation of current (≤5 years) and/or historical information. Most literature research begins with an Internet search of **databases**, which provide listings of books, journals, and other materials on specific topics. Databases vary in content, and many contain only a reference listing with or without an abstract, so once the listing is obtained, the researcher must do a further search (publisher, library, etc.) to locate the material. Some databases require a subscription, but access is often available through educational or healthcare institutions. In order to search effectively, the researcher should begin by writing a brief explanation of the research to help identify possible keywords and synonyms to use as **Boolean search** words:

- Truncations: "Finan*" provides all words that begin with those letters, such as "finance," "financial" and "financed."
- Wildcards: "m?n" or "m*n" provides "man" and "men."
- Boolean logic (AND, OR, NOT):
- Wound OR infect* OR ulcer
- Wound OR ulcer AND povidone-iodine
- Wound AND povidone-iodine NOT antibiotic NOT antimicrobial.

NIH HEALTH INFORMATION WEBSITE AND THE HEALTHFINDER WEBSITE

The National Institutes of Health (NIH) maintains the **Health Information website** (nih.gov/health-information) that provides a searchable database and links to other sites with health information. The home page contains links to common topics of interest, such as breast cancer, diabetes, and Zika. Additionally, the site provides a link to health information lines (lists of telephone numbers individuals can call for information about numerous topics, including disease and alcohol and drug abuse). The site also contains information about clinical trials, guides to talking to a doctor, science education, community resources, and an A to Z health search.

Healthfinder (healthfinder.gov, U.S. Department of Health and Human Services) contains a directory of healthcare services (doctors, dentists, other healthcare providers) so individuals can locate a healthcare provider in their community. The site also contains a health topics index (A to Z), free health content that can be loaded onto websites or printed, health news, and information about national health observances and healthcare reform.

MEDPAGE TODAY AND SCIENCEDAILY

MedPage Today is a free daily online newsletter that provides the latest news in the field of medicine with summaries of research articles as well as articles about public health, health policy, and legislation. Additionally, *MedPage Today* provides searches in 30 specialty areas, such as pediatrics and HIV/AIDS. *MedPage Today* also has a video information center.

ScienceDaily is an online source of information about the latest science news, including topics related to health, technology, the environment, society, and quirky (unusual) research. The home page has a list of top science news and the latest science-related headlines and a search option. For example, a search of "high school health education" yielded 20,400 results, but the search results can be organized by relevance or date. The articles are summaries of research articles and contain a citation for the original journal article in case the individual wants to research further.

School Health Education Program and Role of Educator

IMPLEMENTING A COMPREHENSIVE SCHOOL HEALTH EDUCATION PLAN

According to the Education Development Center, district and school actions for strengthening curriculum planning and development includes raising community awareness and support of **comprehensive school health education**. While **planning curriculum**, assess student health cultures, strengths, needs, and interests. Form collaborations for developing plans to fund, develop, select, implement, and evaluate comprehensive health education curriculum. Regularly review and modify school policy and enforcement methods. For **implementing curriculum** more easily, furnishing enough implementation support is recommended. Also, create a system for assuring professional development, distribution of materials, and student assessment. Give each grade level a minimum of 50 hours of health education. Incorporate information technologies in health education curriculum. Support collaborative curriculum planning and team-building among health education and other subject teachers. Apply varied techniques promoting family engagement. For assuring adequate teacher preparation, choose qualified, academically prepared teachers able to apply active instructional and authentic assessment methods. Supply implementing teachers, administrators, staff, and board members with continuing incentives and professional development opportunities. Furnish continuing technical support and booster follow-up sessions. For **assessing health education**, incorporate process evaluation procedures in curriculum implementation plans, and assess student skills and knowledge in grades 4, 8, and 11.

COMPONENTS OF A COORDINATED SCHOOL HEALTH PROGRAM

- **Family and community involvement**: schools should partner with families and individual and group members of the community to make the best use of all available expertise and resources for child, youth, and family's healthy development.
- **Comprehensive school health education**: to motivate and help students decrease risk behaviors and improve their health, educators should design classroom instruction to tailor teaching to every developmental and age level; further health attitudes, knowledge, and skills; and cover the physical, cognitive, affective, and social domains of health.
- **Physical education (PE)**: designed to develop cognitive, affective, and social skills as well as physical fitness and basic movement and sport skills, PE should promote lifelong physical activity through sequential, planned instruction.
- **School health services**: to promote student health, prevent and detect injuries and health problems, and assure proper student care, schools should provide education, preventive services, referral, management of chronic and acute health conditions, and emergency care.
- **School nutrition services**: to optimize every student's lifelong health potential and education, these should be designed to integrate environments that promote all students' healthy eating habits; nutritional education; and appealing, affordable, nutritious meals.
- **Counseling, psychological, and social services**: to enable healthy behavior and positive learning, improve healthful development, and prevent and solve problems, these should include activities that concentrate on individual, family, and group cognitive, affective, behavioral, and social needs.
- **Healthy school environment**: learning environments should be designed to furnish safety through their physical plans, and settings that support and encourage learning through healthy physical, emotional, and social school climates.
- **Health promotion for school personnel**: schools should provide fitness activities, education, and assessment for their faculty and staff members. These services should be designed for preserving and enhancing the well-being and health of school employees who influence students as role models.

EXTRACURRICULAR ACTIVITIES FOR STUDENTS IN COMMUNITIES AND SCHOOLS

If students cannot find **extracurricular activities** that interest them within schools, they can look at community centers, volunteer for local businesses or nonprofit organizations, or participate in service programs through Youth in Action and similar organizations. Within schools, athletically inclined students can join school tennis, gymnastics, track, volleyball, weightlifting, baseball, basketball, or other teams; participate in student government; school radio stations; school newspapers; yearbooks; 4-H clubs; debate teams; choirs or glee clubs; jazz bands; environmental, computer, math, French or other language clubs; Business Professionals of America; Future Teachers of America; Students Against Destructive Decisions; Jewish, Latino, other ethnic or cultural clubs; and others. Benefits include making new friends; exploring creative, social, political, and physical interests with like-minded others; eliminating social barriers, e.g., volunteering to integrate disabled and non-disabled youth through sports, games, and other activities; enhancing college and employment applications; furthering job goals, e.g., language club activities for teaching languages and bilingual jobs. Students should consider available time, abilities, skills, interests; trying new things; roles to try; whether activities have physical, fee, grade, and/or age requirements. Feeling overextended after joining an activity is a signal to quit, permanently or temporarily.

SELECTION AND ORGANIZATION OF EDUCATIONAL MATERIALS

Selection and organization of education materials begins with review of the course outline, which may include state-mandated topics or approaches (such as with sex education), to ensure that materials support this outline. Materials are also organized according to the outline. Methods of selection include the following:

- **Networking**: Talking to other health educators to determine what effective materials they have found or developed.
- **State and national conference book/materials exhibits**: Examining textbooks and materials that are on display to determine if they meet needs and requesting free samples, attending product demonstrations, and talking to sales representatives.
- **Sales representatives**: Discussing products with traveling sales representatives at the school. Sales representatives often have promotional materials and free samples as well as information about materials used in various school districts.
- **Online publishers and materials vendors**: Table of contents for books and brief previews are often available as well as order forms for free samples and descriptions of supporting materials and manipulatives.

ROLE OF TEACHERS WITHIN COORDINATED SCHOOL HEALTH EDUCATION PROGRAM

The teacher's role in a coordinated school health education program requires active collaboration with other educators and support staff as well as with families and community agencies. The teachers must review classroom materials to determine those that need revision. Teachers must work together with others to develop curriculum and lesson plans that reflect health issues across the curriculum. In preparation, teachers who are not health educators may need to educate themselves about health issues. The health educator must serve as an **advocate** for health education as well as school health policies, such as those regarding safety measures, staff wellness programs, violence, nutrition, and sex education. The educator must also take an active role in **implementation** of new policies and programs, serving as a resource person for those who need guidance to participate effectively in the coordinated school health program.

PLANNING AND IMPLEMENTING A SCHOOL HEALTH EDUCATION PROGRAM

A school health education plan usually involves planning that covers at least five years into the future, so it's important to look at the current situation as well as to make estimates based on the best evidence about the future. Procedures for planning and implementing a school health education program include the following:

- **Prepare** for planning and implementation, including time needed, staff, and resources.
- Carry out **assessments**, including researching evidence-based practices as well as conducting local and student surveys and reviewing local data during the planning process so that credible data support proposals.
- Use the **School Health Index** (CDC) to assess current programs and policies.
- Develop a **plan** that has the input of all stakeholders and that is based on evidence-based findings.
- **Communicate** with others regarding progress during the planning and implementation phases.
- Implement the plan beginning with **pilot studies** or small tests of change, if possible, before full implementation.
- Establish measurable **goals** and monitor **progress** during implementation.
- Make **modifications** as indicated during implementation.

INVOLVING OTHERS

Involving others in planning, implementing, and supporting a school health education program is critical to the success of the program, but it does not occur without a plan to encourage involvement. Strategies may include the following:

- Gain **administrative support** by outlining benefits to the school and students and the cost-effectiveness of a better school health program because the administrator can serve as an advocate to the school board, which controls funding that is necessary to implement a health education program.
- Involve all **faculty and support staff** in the planning process.
- Promote a **school health advisory council** to assist with health planning and development and implementation of policies. This council should include family members, representatives of community agencies, healthcare professionals, and interested parties.
- Communicate openly with all **stakeholders** as well as the **media** in order to ensure that the public and stakeholders are informed.

PARENTS/GUARDIANS AND THE NEEDS AND INTERESTS OF LOCAL CULTURE

Parents/Guardians and the needs and interests of local culture must be considered as part of the development of a school health education program. Strategies to include these stakeholders include the following:

- Review **demographics**, such as age and ethnicity, of the students as well as the members of the community to obtain a complete picture of the student body.
- **Survey** the local cultures about issues of interest to ensure that their values are respected and incorporated into the planning process.
- Use **focus groups** within the different cultural groups in the community to explore specific issues.
- Establish a **family/community advisory committee** that includes key members of the community as well as family members.

- Provide information to family members during **student-teacher conferences**, using this opportunity to recruit family members to take active roles in planning and to provide input. Engage students in recruiting family members as well.

EVALUATION

Evaluation is essential to development of a robust school health education program, but evaluation can be costly and time consuming, so planning for evaluation must be included in all phases of program planning. There are three basic types of evaluation that are carried out on school health programs:

- **Monitoring**: This is an ongoing process that involves observation and assessment of some outcomes. Monitoring may also include satisfaction surveys and assessment of implementation in terms of the timeline.
- **Formal evaluation**: This requires collection of data on all applicable student and program outcomes and analysis of the data, including processes such as incident reports, visits to the nurse, behavioral problems, attendance, family involvement, and suicide clusters.
- **Applied research**: This requires planning an experimental design and carrying out research, such as research comparing two different teaching approaches for the same health information, and analysis of the data.

Professional Foundations of Health Education

CONTINUING EDUCATION

NCHEC

One resource for continuing education knowledge and credits is the **National Commission for Health Education Credentialing (NCHEC), Inc.**, accredited by the National Commission for Certifying Agencies (NCCA). NCHEC offers workshops, seminars, and conferences in various health education topics, e.g., lung summits sponsored by the American Lung Association; conferences on annual public health, annual mental health and aging, and breastfeeding; seminars and workshops on teen contraceptive counseling approaches, age-related dementia, creating aging-friendly communities, trauma, and addiction; nutritional training, medical school tobacco treatment specialist trainings, wellness and health coaching workshops and certification courses, family planning health worker courses, asthma educator certification courses; and programs on Medicare, diabetes, women's gender-specific treatment, technology use integrating sexual and reproductive health with primary care, behavioral healthcare in the criminal justice system, worksite wellness certification and health promotion, nonprofit finance, project management, etc. Health educators can also take self-study courses for wellness coaching certification training and information about physical activity, nutrition, weight control, injury prevention, skin assessment, wound care, suicide prevention, grief, mental health, PTSD, substance abuse, addiction recovery, peer education, teen health risk behaviors, weight control, trauma, prevention, health equity, program evaluation, qualitative research, social media, etc. from diverse sponsors, for certification, knowledge, and credits.

SOPHE

The **Society for Public Health Education** (SOPHE) is a national nonprofit organization dedicated to providing **continuing education** for health and education professionals. It includes an affiliate membership program with local chapters. SOPHE is designated by the National Commission for Health Education Credentialing (NCHEC) as a multiple event provider of Continuing Education Contact Hours (CECH). SOPHE is approved by the National Board of Public Health Examiners as a provider of renewal credits for the Certificate in Public Health. SOPHE is one of the largest continuing education providers for Certified Health Education Specialists (CHES). Health educators can take advantage of continuing education opportunities SOPHE offers, including attending local chapter events; attending the SOPHE Annual Meeting; pursuing eLearning including taking online courses, Journal Self-Study Tests, playing back meeting webcasts, marketing and promotion videos, archived webinars, and streaming live webinars; publishing and/or reviewing manuscripts in SOPHE Journals; and participating in Journal and Meeting Calls for research. Health educators can create accounts and profiles at SOPHE's updated Center for Online Resources and Education (CORE), log in, and earn CE credits via courses and other activities.

PROFESSIONAL DEVELOPMENT OPPORTUNITIES FOR HEALTH EDUCATORS

Resources offering health educators **PD opportunities** include National Education Association's (NEA) Educational Support Professionals (ESP) PD; US Centers for Disease Control and Prevention's (CDC) Division of Scientific Education and Professional Development (DSEPD); ShapeAmerica.org, aka American Association for Health, Physical Education, Recreation, and Dance (AAHPERD); American Public Health Association (APHA)'s Center for PD, Public Health Systems and Partnerships; and health and education departments of many state and private universities and colleges. Shape America offers a webinar series covering topics including Adapted Physical Education (APE); APE for autism; sport coaching; Common Core State Standards (CCSS); Early Childhood Education (ECE); PE e-learning, etc.; a Researcher's Toolkit; a Distinguished Lecture

Series; and workshops on fitness, PE, and the Presidential Youth Fitness Program (PYFP). The CDC Learning Connection includes thousands of public health learning products and continuing education (CE) courses, many free, through CDC TRAIN; online educational resources; Quick-Learn Lessons for mobile devices; and links to Facebook and Twitter posts on public health topics. NEA offers its ESP National PD Conference; Leaders for Tomorrow program; and trainings in results-oriented job descriptions, crisis action plans, leadership, air quality action plans, collective action, mentoring, and school community team-building.

OHDSI

An interdisciplinary collaborative initiative among disciplines including biomedical sciences, physics, informatics, epidemiology, computer science, and statistics; and multiple stakeholders including healthcare providers, academics, medical product manufacturers, payers, and government agencies is the **Observational Health Data Sciences and Informatics Program (OHDSI)**. Its purpose is to use large-scale analytics to demonstrate the value of **observational health data**. With its coordinating center headquartered at Columbia University, OHDSI has developed an international network of observational health databases and researchers. In 2014, at the EDM (Electronic Data Methods) Forum in San Francisco, OHDSI released Achilles, its first open-source software application. OHDSI has produced a two-minute YouTube video to welcome new participants, and has published a paper in the Drug Safety periodical. Those who can benefit from participating in the OHDSI community include: scientists exploring large-scale data methodologies; clinical researchers using OHDSI's network for answering clinical questions; members of organizations that have healthcare data, for more effectively using their data; members of healthcare systems, for improving the efficiency and quality of healthcare using OHDSI's tools; and software designers and developers, for contributing to projects to enhance patient health.

The Observational Health Data Sciences and Informatics Program (OHDSI) includes participation from multiple disciplines and stakeholders. Participants are developing **open-source software tools** to analyze, characterize, and evaluate health data; medical product safety; healthcare quality; comparative effectiveness; and for predictive patient-level modeling. They are also developing an **international data network** to use large-scale analytical methods for extracting evidence from observational health data. OHDSI's Columbia University center will house open-source summary statistics to share throughout the network, enabling all stakeholders to learn from real-world evidence. OHDSI aims to evaluate the reliability of the evidence it produces by systematically assessing observational analysis methods performance. This collaboration holds weekly webinar teleconferences where members present current research including proposals, works in progress, and final products for collaboration, feedback, and review. At these meetings they also review funding and publication opportunities and topics of shared interest. OHDSI has formed specific workgroups for design and implementation of the Observational Medical Outcomes Partnership Common Data Model, version 5 (OMOP CDMv5) specifications and vocabulary standard; data characterization; patient-level prediction; population-level estimation; the knowledge base; a phenotype library; and visualization/communications.

VALID, RELIABLE ONLINE DATABASES

The US Department of Health and Human Services (HHS) includes the National Institutes of Health (NIH). The NIH offers a number of **public databases** that users can search for valid, reliable **health-related data**. These databases include: NIH RePORTER, the database of RePORT (Research Portfolio Online Reporting Tools); NIDB (NeuroInformatics DataBase) Resources; the NCBI (National Center for Biotechnology Information) Literature Databases; PubMed Central; PubMed Medline; Research.gov; Community of Science (COS); Science.gov; World Wide Science; and ClinicalTrials.gov. The Centers for Disease Control and Prevention (CDC) have interactive database systems on their website for these topics: birth defects and developmental disabilities; child and adolescent health; chronic disease; crosscutting; diabetes; disabilities; environmental health; global health; health risk behavior; HIV, STIs, and viral hepatitis; infectious disease; influenza; injury; maternal and child health; occupational safety and health; oral health; and population. The World Health Organization (WHO) has an online database of survey information from health and human rights organizations, established through collaboration with the Harvard School of Public Health's Program for International Health and Human Rights. WHO also offers an online library catalogue, WHOLIS, for searching WHO's printed publications collection from 1948 to the present, historical medicine and public health monographs, and international health literature.

YRBSS DATABASE

The YRBSS is the (National) **Youth Risk Behavior Surveillance System** used in the National Youth Risk Behavior Survey conducted by the Centers for Disease Control and Prevention (CDC). Data from this survey are available online in ASCII and Access® file formats for download and use. The YRBSS website also offers SPSS® and SAS® programs for converting ASCII data into datasets compatible with SPSS® and SAS® use. Users can access YRBS national high school data files from 1991-2013 online, including user's manuals for each year. Every year of data has its own format library. The website includes instructions for using the data files in the different formats, plus methodology of the YRBSS; a review of analysis software; best practices and guidance for combining YRBS data from multiple years, for conducting trend analyses of the data, and interpreting trend data; for groups to conduct their own YRBS surveys; and frequently asked questions (FAQs).

SHAPEAMERICA RESOURCES AND AMA DATABASE LICENSING AND DATA ACCESSING PROCEDURES

The **American Alliance for Health, Physical Education, Recreation, and Dance** (AAHPERD.org), aka **ShapeAmerica**, offers databases and other resources, including: a database with regularly updated information about available research and program grants from the NASPE (National Association for Sport and Physical Education); a database where research fellows can enter and update their information; a database of grassroots contacts, through its Legislative Action Center Tutorial PDF; and its Library/Shared Files Exchange for lesson plans, assessment tools, etc. from which educators can access, contribute, and share. The AMA has offered healthcare community access to its Physician Masterfile for over 60 years to benefit the medical industry and public good. Today, **Database Licensees** contract with the **AMA** to arrange access to a variety of databases containing health-related research activities and marketing services. Medical schools, hospitals, pharmaceutical manufacturers, medical supply and equipment companies, consultants, insurance companies, market research firms, and commercial organizations all use the AMA Masterfile. The AMA reviews data requests from Database Licensees daily to monitor licensing agreement compliance. Physicians can restrict their prescription information from pharmaceutical sales representatives, and request no contact and no release restrictions to their AMA Physician Masterfile records.

CSHP

A **coordinated school health program** (CSHP) should include comprehensive health education (K–12); health services; psychological and socials services; safety initiatives/safe environment; physical education; nutritional services; and partnerships with local public health staff, parents, and state and community agencies and organizations. The purpose of the CSHP is to recognize that **academic success** and **physical and emotional health** are linked and that all components must be integrated and work together for the benefit of the students' health and well-being as well as health promotion for the staff. The CSHP helps to focus attention on behaviors that have a negative impact on students' health and achievement, such as risk-taking behaviors. Some of the goals of this program include better attendance, improved academic outcomes, fewer dropouts, fewer behavior problems (including bullying/violence), better nutrition, increased physical activity, and increased participation by family, educational staff, and other members of the community.

HEALTHY PEOPLE 2020

Healthy People 2020, enacted in 2010 and released by the U.S. Department of Health & Human Services, is a 10-year guide to national public health practice and objectives. *Healthy People 2020* is based on previous initiatives, including *Healthy People 1990, 2000,* and *2010. Healthy People 2020* is particularly relevant to the health educator because many funding sources are tied to these objectives and educational materials are developed in support of them. Additionally, one section specifically addresses **adolescent health** with the goal of improving the "development, health, safety, and well-being of adolescents and young adults." This section addresses public health and social problems (such as unintended pregnancies), environmental influences on behavior and outcomes, and emerging issues. *Healthy People 2020* can be used to guide the focus of instruction because it includes a framework for health promotion and disease prevention and measurable objectives, such as increasing the proportion of students who graduate with a regular diploma after four years of high school.

RESOURCES FOR CURRENT KNOWLEDGE IN HEALTH SCIENCE RELATED TO ADOLESCENT HEALTH

Resources for keeping informed about current knowledge in health science include the following:

- **Internet**: The government has many websites devoted to current knowledge, such as CDC.gov. A valuable online resource is the E-Updates and News in Adolescent Health provided by *the Office of Adolescent Health* (HHS). Major news sites, such as CNN.com, have daily health news. *Medical News Today* provides links to medical news articles.
- **Professional journals**: Journals such as the *Journal of School Health* and the *American Journal of Health Education* provide health information of particular interest to health educators.
- **Public health/Local health agencies**: These agencies provide updates to the community about issues of current concern, such as outbreaks or emerging infections.
- **Professional organizations**: Organizations such as the American School Health Association (ASHA) and the American Association for Health Education (AAHE) carry out research and provide information and support to members as well as sponsoring state and national conferences, various workshops, and informative websites.

ROLE OF HEALTH EDUCATORS IN ADVOCATING FOR HEALTHY SCHOOL ENVIRONMENT

The health educator has the primary role of communicating, promoting, and **advocating** for a healthy school environment and should take every opportunity to do so, beginning with **increasing awareness** within the classroom through a variety of means: panel discussions, guest speakers, demonstrations, project-based learning, debates, experiments, and role playing. The health educator should carry out an **assessment** and report to the school board about the school's environment, highlighting areas in which the school is performing well as well as those that need improvement. The health educator must also establish close working relationships with **administrators**, whose support is critical, and with teachers and other staff members, stressing how their roles are made easier in a healthy school environment and ways in which they can support taking steps to improve the situation at the school. The health educator should monitor and report progress.

Theories and Principles of Health Education

COMMUNICATING HEALTH EDUCATION INFORMATION TO DIVERSE AUDIENCES

The Centers for Disease Control and Prevention (CDC, 2009) has noted that **diversity** among audiences creates challenges for health communication. Differences preclude a "one size fits all" approach to developing effective materials. Among multiple factors, **literacy skills** and **cultures** are significant to keep in mind. The US Department of Education National Assessment of Adult Literacy (NAAL, 2006) found basic reading a struggle for 30 million American adults, meaning one-third of them have difficulty reading and acting upon health-related information; only 12 percent of consumers are proficient in health literacy skills. Thus, almost 90 percent of American adults may be inadequately equipped for managing their own health. Performing self-care, managing chronic disease, finding healthcare services and providers, completing health forms, and communicating personal health information to providers are all affected by insufficient health literacy. Even consumers with better health literacy skills want easily utilized, understandable, and personally relevant health information. The CDC advises health educators to develop an overall communication plan, with one step being designing health communication materials.

DEVELOPING USER-FRIENDLY, EVIDENCE-BASED HEALTH COMMUNICATION MATERIALS

According to the Centers for Disease Control and Prevention (CDC, 2009), health educators should first identify who their intended **audience** is, and define the primary health interests and problems to address. Then they should familiarize themselves with this audience to ascertain their essential characteristics, e.g., location, race and/or ethnicity, gender, culture, beliefs, behaviors, literacy skills, and current knowledge regarding the subject(s) they have identified. Next, health educators should define the main **messages** they want to communicate. Before including them in communication materials, they should test drafts of these messages with their prospective audience to determine if they will be properly received. They can then modify their drafts based on audience feedback. Then they should decide which **mode(s)**—e.g., print, video, audio, etc.—will best serve to communicate with their identified audience. They should then decide what **method(s)** they will use—e.g., websites, brochure displays, direct mail, etc.—to distribute their materials to the audience. Health educators can then publish their materials and distribute and market them. They should follow up by **evaluating** audience comprehension and satisfaction with the materials.

WRITING HEALTH EDUCATION MATERIALS FOR CLARITY, RELEVANCE, AND APPEAL TO DIVERSE AUDIENCES

The Centers for Disease Control and Prevention (CDC, 2009) offers guidelines for **clear health education materials**. For instance, try to engage the audience quickly by communicating the most important information first. Include the actions to take, and explain why these are important. An example of this from the CDC is, "Always wash hands with soap and warm water for 20 seconds before and after handling food. Food and water can carry germs that may make you and your family sick." Each section or document should limit the number of messages to three or four main ideas, concentrating only on what the audience really needs to know and do, avoiding extraneous material. Developing one idea completely at a time before moving on prevents confusing audiences by skipping back and forth among subjects. Lists should be short, e.g., three to seven items. Audiences with limited literacy skills will forget items in longer lists. Items should be marked by bullets, not separated by commas, for visual clarity. Active voice, imperative mood, and concrete nouns are best for stating action instructions. Positive statements are more effective than negative; e.g., "Wear a helmet every time you ride a bicycle," rather than "Do not ride a bicycle without a helmet."

PHILOSOPHIES, THEORIES, AND MODELS OF COMPREHENSIVE HEALTH EDUCATION

TRANSTHEORETICAL MODEL

The transtheoretical model focuses on changes in behavior based on the individual's (not society's or others') decisions and is used to develop strategies to promote changes in health behavior. This model outlines stages people go through changing problem behavior and having a positive attitude about change. **Stages of change** include the following:

- **Precontemplation**: The person is either unaware or underinformed about the consequences of a problem behavior and has no intention of changing the behavior in the next six months.
- **Contemplation**: The person is aware of the costs and benefits of changing the problem behavior and intends to change in the next six months but is procrastinating and not ready for action.
- **Preparation**: The person has a plan and intends to instigate change in the near future (within one month) and is ready for action plans.
- **Action**: The person is modifying the problem behavior, and change occurs only if behavior meets a set criterion (such as complete abstinence from drinking).
- **Maintenance**: The person works to maintain changes and gains confidence that he/she will not relapse.

HEALTH BELIEF MODEL

The health belief model (**HBM**) is a model used to predict health behavior with the understanding that people take a health action to avoid negative consequences if the person expects that the negative outcome can be avoided and that he/she is able to do the action. The HBM, as modified, is based on six basic **perceptions**:

1. **Susceptibility**: Belief that the person may get a negative condition.
2. **Severity**: Understanding of how serious a condition is.
3. **Benefit**: Belief that the action will reduce risk of getting the condition.
4. **Barriers**: Direct and psychological costs involved in taking action.
5. **Action cues**: Strategies used to encourage action, such as education.
6. **Self-efficacy**: Confidence in the ability to take action and achieve positive results.

This model attempts to encourage people to make changes or take action (such as stopping smoking) in order to avoid **negative consequences**, so this model—when used for education—focuses on the negative consequences (such as quitting smoking to avoid cardiovascular and pulmonary disease).

THEORY OF REASONED ACTION

The theory of reasoned action, developed in 1975 by Fishbein and Ajzen, is based on the idea that the actions people take voluntarily can be predicted according to their personal attitude toward the action and their perception of how others will view their doing the action. There are three basic concepts to the theory:

1. **Attitudes**: These are all of the attitudes about an action, and they may be weighted (some are more important than others).
2. **Subjective norms**: People are influenced by those in their social realm (family, friends) and their attitudes toward particular actions. The influence may be weighted. For example, the attitude of a spouse may carry more weight than the attitude of a neighbor.

3. **Behavioral intention**: The intention to take action is based on weighing attitudes and subjective norms (opinions of others), resulting in a choice to either take an action or avoid the action.

THEORY OF PLANNED BEHAVIOR

The theory of planned behavior, by Ajzen, evolved from the theory of reasoned action in 1985 when studies showed that behavioral intention does not necessarily result in action. The **theory of planned behavior** is more successful in predicting behavior. To the basic concepts of attitudes, subjective norms, and behavioral intentions encompassed by the earlier theory, Ajzen added the concept of **perceived behavioral control**, which relates to the individual's attitudes about self-efficacy and outcomes. Ajzen's theory shows that the following beliefs are central:

- **Behavioral beliefs** lead to attitudes toward a behavior/action.
- **Normative beliefs** lead to subjective norms.
- **Control beliefs** lead to perceived behavioral control.

All of these beliefs interact to influence intention and action. Basically, this theory relates to the person's **confidence**, based on beliefs and social influence of others, that he/she can actually do an action and that the outcome of this action will be positive. This theory looks at the power of emotions—such as apprehension or fear—when predicting behavior.

SOCIAL COGNITIVE THEORY

In the 1970s, Albert Bandura proposed the **social cognitive theory** (theory of social learning), in which learning develops from observation and organizing and rehearsing behavior that has been modeled. Bandura believed that people were more likely to adopt the behavior if they valued the outcomes, if the outcomes had functional value, and if the person modeling had similarities to the learner and was admired because of his or her status. Behavior is the result of observation of behavioral, environmental, and cognitive interactions. There are four **conditions** required for modeling:

1. **Attention**: The degree of attention paid to modeling can depend on many variables (physical, social, and environmental).
2. **Retention**: People's ability to retain models depends on symbolic coding, creating mental images, organizing thoughts, and rehearsing (mentally or physically).
3. **Reproduction**: The ability to reproduce a model depends on physical and mental capabilities.
4. **Motivation**: Motivation may derive from past performances, rewards, or vicarious modeling.

NATIONAL HEALTH EDUCATION STANDARDS

A comprehensive school health education program is often based on the **national health education standards**, which provide the framework for health education and outline what students should know and the skills they should have by grades 2, 5, 8, and 12. The eight standards are as follows:

1. Students will comprehend concepts related to health promotion and disease prevention to enhance health.
2. Students will analyze the influence of family, peer, culture, media, technology, and other factors on health behaviors.
3. Students will demonstrate the ability to access valid information, products, and services to enhance health.

4. Students will demonstrate the ability to use interpersonal communication skills to enhance health and avoid or reduce health risks.
5. Students will demonstrate the ability to use decision-making skills to enhance health.
6. Students will demonstrate the ability to use goal-setting skills to enhance health.
7. Students will demonstrate the ability to practice health-enhancing behaviors and avoid or reduce health risks.
8. Students will demonstrate the ability to advocate for personal, family, and community health.

CHARACTERISTICS OF EFFECTIVE HEALTH EDUCATION CURRICULUM

The CDC's characteristics of an effective health education curriculum provides guidelines for development of a comprehensive school health education program. **Characteristics** include the following:

- Focuses on health goals and behavioral outcomes.
- Is research based, driven by theories, and addresses individuals' values, attitudes, and beliefs.
- Addresses individual and group norms to support health behaviors.
- Reinforces protective factors and increases perceptions of personal risk in risk-taking behaviors.
- Addresses social pressure and influences and provides adequate time for teaching and learning.
- Builds skills for personal and social competence and self-efficacy.
- Provides basic and accurate health knowledge that contributes to health-promoting behaviors.
- Uses strategies to engage students and personalize information.
- Provides age-appropriate and developmentally appropriate information, strategies, materials, and teaching methods that are culturally inclusive.
- Provides opportunities and skills to enforce positive health behaviors and to make positive connections with others.
- Includes professional development and training for teachers.

PRECEDE-PROCEED MODEL

PRECEDE-PROCEED, a widely used model for developing health programs, focuses on outcomes and is used for analysis and program design. This model considers the educational and environmental influences on health behavior and attempts to diagnosis health concerns and aid in planning for interventions. The model includes four phases related to planning and diagnosis (social; epidemiological, behavioral, and environmental; educational and ecological; and administrative), one phase for implementation, and three phases for evaluation (process, impact, and outcomes). **PRECEDE** is an acronym for predisposing, reinforcing, and enabling constructs in educational diagnosis and evaluation. **PROCEED** stands for policy, regulatory, and organizational constructs in educational and environmental development.

INDIVIDUAL BEHAVIOR CHANGE FRAMEWORK

The individual behavior change framework is a model that has similar elements to PRECEDE-PROCEED in that it considers the predisposing, reinforcing, and enabling factors that influence knowledge, skills, and attitudes that lead to behavior change. This is a nonlinear model because all of these factors interact. For example, if the goal is to encourage students to avoid smoking, then the beginning point is to assess the students' knowledge about the effects of smoking, their self-regard (such as assertiveness and refusal skills), and their attitude toward smoking. Despite knowing the risks of smoking, if the student is part of a group that believes that smoking is "cool" behavior or lives in a family in which adults routinely smoke, then that student's attitude toward smoking is likely to override his or her knowledge. The student's attitude may be reinforced by peers or family members for positive or negative. If family members allow the student to smoke or provide no consequences for smoking, these enabling factors may influence his or her behavior.

STAGES OF PREVENTION AND INTERVENTION ALONG THE CONTINUUM OF CARE

The continuum of care includes all aspects of care that influence outcomes. The primary components are prevention, intervention, and recovery/maintenance during which the person is monitored for compliance.

Prevention	Intervention
May be aimed universally at the entire population, at selected groups, or at-risk individuals, and it usually involves long-term goals. Primary: Aims to prevent disease occurrence and may include educational campaigns (no smoking, use seatbelts), vaccinations. Secondary: Aims to identify and reduce impact (screening mammograms, BP checks). Tertiary: Aims to prevent/delay disease progression (support programs).	Usually aimed at specific groups or individuals and often involves specific treatments (such as surgery, chemotherapy, medications) to alleviate a problem or disorder. Goals may be long term, or they may be time limited with the aim to resolve the problem as quickly as possible.

CURRENT TRENDS IN HEALTH EDUCATION

RESILIENCY AND ASSET DEVELOPMENT

Resiliency is the ability to cope with risk factors such as poverty and to remain emotionally healthy. One of the current trends is to aid students in developing resiliency by providing a safe and supportive environment. Promoting **resiliency** also includes identifying problems early and taking steps to deal with them before they become ingrained as well as proving aid for severe or long-term problems. Holding students to high expectation and supporting them in attaining goals helps to build self-confidence and coping skills.

Asset development focuses on identifying and developing the assets that children and adolescents need in order to become physically and emotionally healthy. Traits that indicate good development include good grades, good health, diverse friends, leadership roles, avoidance of risk-taking behaviors, and the ability to delay gratification and deal with adversity. Children and adolescents need external assets (support, empowerment, boundaries, expectations, and meaningful activities) as well as internal assets (positive values, positive self-identity, social awareness and competency, and interest in and commitment to learning).

SKILLS-BASED INSTRUCTION AND EVIDENCE-BASED PROGRAMS

Skills-based instruction moves the focus of instruction from simple acquisition of knowledge to acquisition of **skills that promote acquisition of knowledge**: reading, writing, speaking, and problem solving. Students are taught reading, writing, and speaking skills in all content areas and are provided skill practice along with high expectations. The literacy skills that students master are transferrable to all areas of study. The student assumes an increasing responsibility for learning and learns through analysis and application rather than through rote learning.

Evidence-based instructional programs are based on scientific research using objective methods to determine the most effective method of instruction. Instructional practices are selected based on

success in multiple schools and tests verifying that success that have both reliability and validity as well as replicability. The strongest conclusions are based on studies that involve randomized controlled trials, although that is not always possible in education. Decisions should be based on **data** and not on previous misconceptions or biases.

Health Education Standards and Literacy

HEALTH LITERACY

The US Centers for Disease Control and Prevention (CDC) refers to Title V of the Patient Protection and Affordable Care Act of 2010, which defines **health literacy** as being able to acquire, process, understand, and communicate fundamental health information and services for making proper health decisions. Individuals needing health services and/or information need **health literacy skills** for communicating their needs and preferences, finding information and services, responding to them, understanding their contexts, choices, and consequences, processing their meaning and utility, and matching them to their needs and preferences to act. Providers of health information and services—physicians, dentists, nurses, pharmacists, public health employees, etc.—need these skills for communicating about healthcare and health; helping people find services and information; understanding how to provide useful services and information; processing what people are requesting, both explicitly and implicitly; and matching services and information to various individuals and circumstances to act. Organizations help people find, process, understand, and decide about health services and information. The CDC website, the *National Action Plan to Improve Health Literacy,* and the Institute of Medicine's commissioned papers and discussion (links on www.cdc.gov) are good resources for learning about and enhancing health literacy.

NATIONAL HEALTH EDUCATION STANDARDS
PURPOSES, GENESIS, AND DEVELOPMENT

The national Centers for Disease Control and Prevention (CDC, 2013) reports that in the early 1990s, educational leaders across America were developing **model standards** for various educational subject areas. Based on these endeavors, authorities in the fields of health education, physical education, public health, and school health saw a need to create similar standards for the subject area of health education. To do this, the Joint Committee on National Health Education Standards was formed with support from the American Cancer Society. Members of this committee were from the American Association for Health Education, American Public Health Association, American School Health Association, and Society of State Leaders of Health and Physical Education. They formulated the **National Health Education Standards (NHES)**, first publishing them in 1995. In ensuing years, the health education field came to embrace these standards as a reference supplying a structure for most US states to adopt health education standards. In 2004, authorities began a review process, producing revisions that recognized the original document's strength and impact and reflected over a decade of nationwide application. The revised version became the 2nd edition, *National Health Education Standards—Achieving Excellence.*

GENERAL CONTENT AND PURPOSE

The **National Health Education Standards (NHES)** are statements of what students are expected to know and be able to do to further personal, family, and community health by grades 2, 5, 8 and 12. They are designed to give educators a structure for developing and selecting curriculum, planning instruction, and conducting assessment of students in health education. **Standard 1** expects students to understand ideas about promoting health and preventing disease to improve health. **Standard 2** expects students to analyze how health behaviors are influenced by factors including culture, peers, family, technology, and media. **Standard 3** expects students to show they can obtain valid health-improving information, services, and products. **Standard 4** says students are expected to show they can promote health and decrease or avert health risks by using interpersonal communication skills. **Standard 5** expects students to show they can improve health by applying decision-making skills. **Standard 6** indicates students are expected to show they can improve health by applying goal-setting skills. **Standard 7** expects students to show they can limit or avert health risks, and practice behaviors that improve health. **Standard 8** expects students to demonstrate personal, family, and community health advocacy capacity.

DISTINCTION BETWEEN EDUCATIONAL STANDARDS AND PERFORMANCE INDICATORS

A **learning standard** is a verbal expression of what students should know, understand, or do. A **performance indicator (PI)** associated with the standard is a description of more specific behaviors students should perform to demonstrate that knowledge, understanding, and action. For example, Standard 2 of the NHES (2nd Edition) states: "Students will analyze the influence of family, peers, culture, media, technology and other factors on health behaviors." Among the associated performance indicators, PI 2.2.3 for grades Pre-K-2 is: "Describe how the media can influence health behaviors." For grades 3-5, PI 2.5.5 is: "Explain how media influences [sic] thoughts, feelings, and health behaviors." For grades 6-8, PI 2.8.5 is: "Analyze how messages from media influence health behaviors." For grades 9-12, PI 2.12.5 is: "Evaluate the effect of media on personal and family health." Performance indicators are also included regarding family, culture, peers, school and community, and technology respectively for each group of grade levels. As an analogy, learning standards are like goals and performance indicators are like objectives, with the former being more general and the latter more specific.

STATUTORY CURRICULUM POLICIES FOR BY STATE

Most states base **health education (HE) curriculum content** on the National Health Education Standards (NHES). **Alaska** does not require HE but requires one credit of HE *or* PE for graduation, encouraging district K-12 HE programs. **Alabama** requires K-8 HE, not specifying amount, but recommending 60 minutes a week for grades 1-6; and requires comprehensive, planned, sequential HE curriculum. **Arkansas** requires K-8 health and safety instruction, amount unspecified; and a 9-12 unit course to graduate. **Arizona** does not require HE to graduate or specify minimum amount, but includes HE or PE in its minimum course of study; and requires including skin cancer prevention in HE curricula. **California** has specific HE requirements for applicable grades including individual, family, and community health; HIV/AIDS prevention; parenting education; drug and substance effects; STIs; prenatal care; and gang prevention. **Colorado** does not require, but encourages voluntary pre-K-12 HE. **Connecticut** requires HE with no specified amounts. Washington, D.C. requires HE, specifying required content areas and amounts. **Delaware** requires HE, specifying amounts by grade. **Florida** requires comprehensive HE, including content and grades. **Georgia** requires HE and PE, specifying amounts and grades. **Hawaii** specifies standards-based HE amounts by grade but not content, not in its board policy but in its wellness guidelines.

Idaho requires K-8 HE and PE with content standards and a one-credit course to graduate. **Illinois** requires HE with amounts by grade and general curriculum topics. **Indiana** requires HE, one unit to graduate, without other amounts or grades; no specific curriculum, but certain required curriculum content. Iowa requires 1-12 HE but not amounts, with general pre-K curriculum standards and a list of resources and materials for other grades. **Kansas** requires HE and/or PE, one unit to graduate, e.g., safety, first aid, or physiology, requiring health and human sexuality instruction for accreditation, but no amounts or grades. **Kentucky** requires HE without amount, one HE and PE unit each to graduate, and encourages skin cancer risk instruction. **Louisiana** requires elementary HE, secondary substance abuse prevention instruction with amounts by grades, one-half credit for public HS graduation, two units of HE and PE for non-public HS graduation. **Maine** requires HE, amounts or grades unspecified; five HE credit-hours and one PE credit-hour to graduate, specifying curriculum content. **Maryland** requires comprehensive K-8 HE within county school health programs, amount unspecified, one-half credit to graduate. **Massachusetts** requires HE without amounts, grades, or graduation requirements, suggesting curriculum and specifying content topics. **Michigan** requires HE, PE, and one credit each to graduate.

Minnesota requires HE, mandating district curriculum standard development. **Mississippi** requires HE with amounts and grades and one-half unit to graduate, accepting Allied Health, heath science, JROTC substitution, with state minimum content standards. **Missouri** requires comprehensive standards-based elementary HE, and health and safety education including HIV/AIDS and substance abuse prevention, specifying amounts and a graduation requirement course; and requiring state standards-based curricula. **Montana** requires "health enhancement," combining HE and PE with amounts by grades. **North Carolina** requires K-9 comprehensive HE plus one credit for HS graduation, with recommended curriculum and standards. **North Dakota** requires HE, plus one-half unit of HE out of one PE unit, with content and achievement standards. **Nebraska** requires K-12 HE, specifying amounts for high school, without formal HE standards, but with required and recommended curriculum. **New Hampshire** requires K-12 HE, specifying topics, authorizing local amount requirements, and requiring credits to graduate. **New Jersey** requires 1-12 HE, specifying amounts, mandatory curriculum standards, and content. **New Mexico** requires 1-12 HE, plus an 8012 course before graduating, requiring district K-12 curriculum aligned with state content standards. **Nevada** requires HE in all public schools, also specifying grades and requiring credits for graduation, with state curriculum content standards.

New York requires HE, with a one-half unit graduation requirement and three-tiered HE learning standards. **Ohio** requires HE included in curriculum, not specifying grades or amounts, but requiring one-half unit to graduate. **Oklahoma** does not require HE for any grade level or to graduate, but "strongly recommends" two units of HE and PE in high school, with formalized curriculum standards by grade clusters. **Oregon** requires K-12 HE, plus one unit to graduate, with curriculum standards, benchmarks, and requiring common district HE curriculum goals and content standards. **Pennsylvania** requires planned HE aligned with each elementary grade's academic standards, amounts unspecified; requires HE in middle and high schools without amounts or grades, and one HE and PE credit to graduate, with no specific curriculum but mandatory curriculum standards. **Rhode Island** requires 1-12 HE and PE with amounts, graduation requirement, state standards-based curriculum, required CPR and blocked air passage training courses, and school health and wellness subcommittees. **South Carolina** requires annual K-8 HE and one-time 9-12 HE, specifying amounts by level without graduation requirements or specific curriculum, but with curriculum standards. **South Dakota** does not require HE, but requires one-half unit of health or health integration to graduate, with voluntary curriculum standards.

Tennessee requires annual K-8 HE, one 9-12 unit combining HE and PE, and one-and-a-half PE and wellness credits to graduate, with required curriculum standards. **Texas** requires K-12 HE and K-8 PE, one-half HE or health science credits to graduate; lets districts select from HE TEKS; and requires that TEA offers districts obesity, diabetes, and cardiovascular disease prevention curriculum programs and implementation training. **Utah** requires K-12 HE, 7-8 unit requirements and 9-12 graduation requirement units, standards and suggested curriculum. **Vermont** requires PE and comprehensive HE including substance effects, amounts, grades, and levels unspecified; no graduation requirement; and pre-K-12 curriculum standards. **Virginia** requires PE and HE at all levels, amounts and grades unspecified, specifying general curriculum topics; requires two HE and PE credits for graduating; provides HE learning standards, but leaves curriculum to schools. **Washington** requires HE, amounts and grade levels unspecified; no HE, but two health and fitness course credits as graduation requirements, with state standards and suggested curriculum framework. **West Virginia** requires HE, grades and amounts unspecified, one HE unit to graduate; curriculum content standards combining pre-K-4 HE and PE, and 5-12 HE. **Wisconsin** requires HE, with grades, amounts, and curriculum materials decided locally; 7-12 graduation requirement credit, voluntary curriculum standards. **Wyoming** requires including PE, amount and graduation

requirements unspecified but proficiency required; standards, no required or suggested curriculum.

Health Instruction and Assessment

PURPOSES OF PRE-TESTING

Before teaching any material to students, it is very important to **pre-test** them in the subject matter. First of all, pre-testing establishes a **baseline**. This determines what the students already know about the subject, informing where the teacher should start instruction. Beginning with what students already know well will not interest or challenge them; beginning too far beyond what they know will confuse them without the foundational knowledge needed to understand the new material. Moreover, this will leave large gaps in their learning. Another significant reason for establishing baseline levels of knowledge is for **assessing progress** after instruction has begun. One cannot determine what students have learned without establishing what they already knew before. With baseline information, the educator can compare their later knowledge to see what new information they have learned. This also facilitates evaluating the effectiveness of instruction. If student results on interim or post-tests are essentially similar to pre-tested baselines, instruction was unsuccessful and must be changed. Pre-testing also facilitates **monitoring student progress** during the course of instruction.

IDENTIFYING MEASURABLE LEARNING OBJECTIVES WHEN PLANNING HEALTH INSTRUCTION

"**SMART**" stands for specific, measurable, attainable, relevant, and targeted to learner and learning level. **Measurable** means an objective can be quantified or measured—numbers, amounts, distances, sizes, etc. To measure something, it must be **observable**. This excludes internal states. Therefore, objectives should generally avoid terms like *feel*, *think*, *understand*, or *learn*, which are internal states and also open to different interpretations. Criteria of observable, measurable behaviors are derived from behavioral learning theory, which states to change any behavior, it must be outwardly observable. Therefore, observable learning objectives should describe things that someone can see. A good way to identify such observable behaviors is using **action verbs**. Examples (cf. Fink's Taxonomy, 2003) include *explain, define, identify, describe, compare, associate, list, name, paraphrase, illustrate, indicate, predict, recite, recognize, restate, repeat,* and *tell.* Examples of objects on or with which these verbs can act include *facts, concepts, theories, models, relationships, structures, perspectives, organizations, proposals, purposes, problems, results, conclusions,* and *plans.* Fink also includes application verbs for critical—*analyze, classify, contrast,* etc.; practical—*answer, calculate, advise,* etc.; creative—*compose, design, create,* etc.; project management—*administer, assign, delegate,* etc.; performance skills—*demonstrate, operate, use,* etc.; and others.

ELEMENTS OF EFFECTIVE LESSON PLANS

Effective teachers are defined as those who teach to a learning objective at the right difficulty level, then monitors student progress and adjust his or her instruction for maximum student learning. Here is an approach with seven steps, divided into four categories (Hunter, 1982) for planning lessons:

Category 1 - **preparing students for learning**.

> Step 1: Review

> Step 2: "Anticipatory Set" – focus student attention, use a "hook" to get their interest, and connect new information to what students already know.

> Step 3: Tell students what the learning objective is.

Category 2 - **Instruction**.

Step 4: Give students instructional input and provide modeling for them.

Category 3 - **Monitoring for comprehension**.

Step 5: Check to determine whether students understand the material.

Step 6: Guided practice: have students practice with what they have learned, give them feedback on their practice, and do not grade their performance.

Category 4 - **Independent practice**.

Step 7: Typically, give students an assignment using what they have learned, and grade their completed work.

DEVELOPMENT, CHARACTERISTICS, AND COMPONENTS OF DIRECT INSTRUCTION

Two distinct types of **direct instruction** have developed:

- Mainly during the 1980s, teachers were trained to use specific instructional practices based on findings synthesized from multiple, independent researchers and studies, and learning outcomes compared to those of students not taught by those experimental methods. Researchers identified effective teaching functions common among experiments, including task analysis (teaching in small steps) with student practice between steps, initial guided practice, and assuring high practice success levels for all students. Also called explicit, systematic, or active teaching, it was named direct instruction (Rosenshine and Stevens, 1986). This type is a **generic instructional model**.
- The **more direct instruction**, pioneered by Siegfried Engelmann and colleagues, dictates detailed teaching programs and practices, based on specific analyses of comprehension and thinking skills required to perform successfully in given subjects; and learning theory regarding how students generalize from current knowledge to comprehend untaught new material. Classroom tasks are sequenced, including scripted teacher questions, comments, cues and individual or choral student responses in interactive and extended sessions informed by this theory's principles; and student written activity sheet or workbook tasks. Both types are teacher-directed, skills-oriented, face-to-face, small-group, broken into small units, deliberately sequenced, and explicitly taught.

COOPERATIVE LEARNING

In **competitive learning**, students work against each other to achieve the highest academic goals, and educators evaluate student performance using norm-referenced assessments, comparing it to that of other students. In **individualistic learning**, students work alone to achieve learning goals unrelated to other students' learning goals, and teachers evaluate their performance using criterion-referenced assessments comparing it against pre-established criteria. In **cooperative learning**, students work together interdependently to achieve shared learning goals that benefit all members, and teachers evaluate their performance using criterion-referenced assessment. Cooperative learning projects employ small groups of students who collaborate to research information, conduct experiments, and/or complete tasks and assignments. In **formal cooperative learning**, teachers make pre-instructional decisions including group size, grouping method, member roles, room and materials arrangement, and academic and social skills objectives. They explain tasks, criteria, and expected behaviors, operationalizing social skills objectives and desired interaction patterns; teach required concepts and strategies; and structure individual accountability and positive interdependence and cooperation. They monitor and assist group work, collecting data. They assess group function and learning, and guide group function self-assessment and closure.

FORMAL VS. INFORMAL COOPERATIVE LEARNING

Formal cooperative learning involves structured procedures by the teacher in assigning groups and roles, arranging space and materials, and creating objectives; teaching concepts, strategies, criteria, tasks, and behaviors; structuring group cooperation and interdependence and individual accountability; observing and monitoring group interaction and gathering data; assessing group functioning and learning; and guiding groups to self-assess their cooperative functioning and achieve closure. In contrast, **informal cooperative learning** involves forming ad-hoc, temporary student groups, lasting several minutes to a full class period, collaborating to accomplish a shared learning goal. Teachers can use informal cooperative learning during lectures, demonstrations, films or videos for defining expectations about what a class will cover; establishing moods conducive to learning; focusing student attention on learning material; assuring that students process cognitively and rehearse learning material; summarize learning; preview the following class; and give a lesson closure. Teachers "bookend" focused discussions before and after lessons and distribute intermittent paired discussion throughout to enhance students' active intellectual engagement. Precision and explicitness regarding tasks, and requiring a specific group product, are necessary elements.

COOPERATIVE BASE GROUPS

Cooperative base groups are long-term with heterogeneous, stable memberships. The main responsibilities of members are positive goal interdependence, assuring all members are progressing well academically; individual accountability, holding one another accountable for efforts to learn; and promotive interaction, giving one another encouragement, help, and support to complete tasks. Teachers assign three or four members per group, schedule regular meeting times, establish specific agendas with concrete tasks, oversee implementation of the basic elements of cooperative learning, periodically instruct them in necessary social skills, and guide them in assessing the effectiveness of their functioning. Members typically share common task orientation and achievement motivation; meet daily or biweekly; and continue throughout the semester, year, or several years. **Base groups** can include in their agendas **academic support tasks**, e.g., editing each other's essays, seeing everybody did and understood homework; **personal support tasks**, e.g., getting acquainted, helping solve non-academic problems; **routine tasks**, e.g., taking attendance; and **assessment tasks**, e.g., mutually checking individual test answer comprehension with individual testing and base group retesting. **Permanent base groups** increase caring relationships, social support, commitment to mutual success, and interpersonal influence to personalize educational experiences, augment achievement, and improve school life quality.

FORMAL, INFORMAL, AND BASE GROUP COOPERATIVE LEARNING CHARACTERISTICS

Formal cooperative learning involves more pre-instruction planning, structuring, and guiding by the teacher of groups to which the teacher assigns students in advance, typically for durations across multiple class periods to complete tasks and multiple assignments. **Informal cooperative learning** involves the teacher assigning students to temporary groups for one class period or less for specific learning task purposes, initiating focused discussions before and after the lesson, and assigning paired discussions intermittently throughout the lesson. **Base group cooperative learning** involves long-term groups; staying together and meeting regularly across a semester, year, or several years; and developing deeper group bonding and interdependence. A teacher can integrate all three types of cooperative learning into one class session. For example, the teacher can start class with a base group meeting. Then the teacher gives a brief lecture, applying informal cooperative learning techniques. Then the teacher gives a lesson using formal cooperative learning procedures. Shortly before the class period ends, the teacher may give another brief lecture incorporating informal cooperative learning. Finally, the teacher can end the class with another base group meeting.

NECESSARY COMPONENTS

- **Positive interdependence**: for students to believe they must succeed or fail as a team, teachers must give them a group goal and a clear task. Group members realize each of their efforts benefit themselves and all other members.
- **Individual and group accountability**: every member is responsible to contribute his or her share of work; nobody rides on another's coattails. Groups must clarify their goals, and measure both group progress and individual member efforts. Cooperative groups strengthen each individual member.
- **Promotive interaction**: members share resources and encourage, support, help, and praise one another's learning efforts. Cooperative groups are both academic and personal support systems. Face-to-face, mutual learning promotion enables significant, unique interpersonal dynamics and cognitive processes, including discussing concepts, connecting past to current learning, and teaching individual knowledge to classmates.
- **Teaching interpersonal and small-group skills**: cooperative groups require taskwork to learn academic material, and teamwork to learn group social skills. Engaging in both simultaneously makes cooperative learning more complex than individual or competitive learning. Students must demonstrate communication, decision-making, trust-building, leadership, and conflict-management skills and the motivation to use them.
- **Group processing**: discussing and analyzing helpful or unhelpful member actions, working relationship effectiveness, goal achievement; and decision-making about changing or continuing behaviors continuously improve learning processes.

POSITIVE RESEARCH FINDINGS

Extensive research in hundreds of studies, conducted internationally over 120+ years, shows powerful educational, personal, and social **benefits of cooperative learning**. These include higher effort to achieve, accomplishing higher achievement than individualistic or competitive learning; greater on-task behavior, productivity, use of higher-level reasoning strategies, generation of new solutions and ideas, and transfer of learning across situations; positive attitudes toward school, learning tasks, and taskwork experiences; greater engagement in activities, more motivation to succeed, and fewer off-task, disruptive, or apathetic behaviors. **Relationship quality**, including interpersonal attraction, emotional bonding, esprit de corps, social support, and cohesion, is enhanced by cooperative learning, reducing absenteeism and dropouts and increasing morale, satisfaction, personal group responsibility, group goal commitment, commitment to one another's success and growth, motivation and persistence for achieving goals, and willingness to undertake difficult tasks, endure frustration and pain on the group's behalf, defend the group from external attack or criticism, and listen to and be influenced by colleagues. Research also shows that cooperative learning correlates more strongly with **psychological health** than individualistic or competitive learning.

REFLECTION

Reflection is a self-observation and self-evaluation process whereby teachers consider what they do in the classroom, why, and whether it works. From gathering information about what happens in their classroom and analyzing and evaluating it, teachers can explore and identify their own practices and their beliefs underlying them, subsequently changing and improving their instruction. Though teachers often tell colleagues or think things to themselves about students' behaving badly one day or seeming not to understand a lesson, without additional time and attention focusing on and considering what happened, they may jump to conclusions or only notice certain student behaviors. **Reflection** is important by more systematically collecting, recording, and analyzing teacher and student observations and thoughts and making changes accordingly. For example, what did they do in a successful lesson? Why did students not understand? What were misbehaving students doing, when, and why? Teachers can begin by looking at their teaching in general, or focusing on a specific problem, class, or teaching feature. They can keep diaries or journals, ask colleagues to observe and give feedback, record audio or video of classes, and solicit student feedback. Thinking, talking, reading, and asking about information collected informs change. Reflection is **cyclical**: after implementing changes, reflection and evaluation resume.

PROCEDURES TO USE IN REFLECTIVE TEACHING PROCESS

- **Diaries**: discipline yourself to write regularly after each lesson or class what took place, the student reactions that you observed, your own reactions and feelings, and questions as they occur to you based on your observations.
- **Peer observations**: ask a colleague to observe your class and focus on such things as how you deal with mistakes, what patterns of interaction take place, and/or which students contribute the most.
- **Audio recordings**: observe and consider things like how much you talk, and what you talk about. Are your explanations and directions clear? How much time do you allow for the students to talk? How do you respond to what students say?
- **Video recordings**: where were you standing? Did you move around? To whom did you speak? How do you think you came across to your students?
- **Student feedback**: give students simple questionnaires to fill out, or ask them to write down their observations and feedback about your teaching and the learning of the class in learning diaries.

IMPLEMENTATION OF STEPS INVOLVED IN REFLECTIVE PROCESS OF TEACHING

- **Thinking**: you may have observed behaviors in yourself and/or students that you had not noticed before. You may have observed some patterns in your teaching of which you were previously unaware. Some of the feedback that you got from your students may have surprised you. You may already have some ideas for changes you want to make.
- **Talking**: discuss issues based on scenarios you describe that took place in your own classroom with colleagues who also want to use reflection as a tool to develop their instructional insight and effectiveness. Make a list of statements of teaching beliefs, e.g., nutrition is more important than exercise, or vice versa, or having students work in pairs is a valuable activity, etc.; discuss with colleagues which ideas you agree and disagree with, and which your teaching practices reflect based on your self-observations.
- **Reading**: look online, in libraries and bookstores for more information on specific topics.
- **Asking**: use websites and forums and professional association meetings to get other teachers' ideas, and request in-service trainings in areas of interest to you.

FORMATIVE ASSESSMENTS

Formative assessments are cyclical and interactive in nature. For example, **formative assessment** in the classroom during instruction enables teachers to gather information about student learning, adjust their teaching accordingly to improve its effectiveness, and then continue collecting more data. Some types include: teacher observation and recording of student academic behavior, affective behavior, and/or engagement level, which the teacher uses to develop and implement an action plan for student support, and then uses continued observation and recording to assess the plan's effectiveness. **Teacher feedback** about student work, oral or written, is another type of formative assessment. Teachers can have students use journals, checklists, etc. for self-assessment of their own progress, another formative assessment. Teachers may assign **self-assessment** in coordination with preset academic and/or behavioral goals, learning contracts, or **curriculum-based measurement (CBM)**. CBM is another formative assessment. While other types of formative assessment often seem informal, CBM is an example of standardized measures, e.g., oral reading fluency tests, used formatively. **Portfolios** of accumulated student products over time are also used formatively to record student progress as their skills develop.

SUMMATIVE ASSESSMENTS

Summative assessments are not conducted during instruction like formative assessment. Rather, they are made after classes, lessons, units, and courses are completed to evaluate what students have learned at individual student, classroom, and school levels. They yield data about whether students have achieved specified learning objectives or not. Familiar large-scale **summative assessments** are **standardized tests**. Student scores on these tests are often used to address state accountability requirements. They can indicate how effective classroom instruction has been, give information about overall student learning, reflect state content and performance standards, and show how many students are meeting grade-level expectations. They are most useful when combined with other information sources, and when used to inform instructional practices rather than justify or reward them. Additional types of summative assessments include **end-of-unit tests** or **final projects**. If these reflect identified learning objectives, they help determine whether they were met. **Course grades**, when based on specific criteria, define how well students have met a class or course's overall expectations. **Portfolios** of student products can be used both formatively and summatively. When included in comprehensive evaluations, they can show that students have met learning objectives.

FORMATIVE VS. SUMMATIVE ASSESSMENTS

Formative assessments are conducted during the course of instruction to monitor ongoing student progress. This allows teachers to adjust their instruction to better meet the needs and strengths of students. They can increase the pace if students are learning faster than expected, or slow it if they are taking longer to grasp concepts and/or skills. If one teaching method or strategy is proving ineffective with some students, then teachers can try others. They can stop spending unnecessary time on elements students have completely mastered, and devote more to areas students are struggling with or do not understand. Hence **formative assessment** informs **future instruction**. **Summative assessments**, conducted at the ends of lessons, units, semesters, and school years, do not inform ongoing assessment. They measure student achievement of standards determining curriculum and instruction they received. In addition to teacher or class-specific end-of-unit tests, prominent summative assessment types include national or state-standardized achievement tests. These compare student scores to average scores of representative samples of students across the country or state. They indicate the progress of a school's students relative to the larger population, and can be used to measure accountability, e.g., for **Adequate Yearly Progress (AYP)**.

> **Review Video: Formative and Summative Assessments**
> Visit mometrix.com/academy and enter code: 804991

PORTFOLIO ASSESSMENT

A portfolio assessment collects student work products over a period of time to provide concrete evidence of the student's learning experiences and accomplishments. Teachers can use **portfolio assessments** for **formative assessment** by examining the changes from one product to the next and the overall change to assess the progress they have achieved to date. They can also use the portfolio's contents to inform their future instruction of the student to focus on which elements of a subject the student needs to improve, and in which areas the student's work shows especial aptitude and interest, where they can offer enrichment activities and advanced projects. A portfolio can also be used for **summative assessment** by reviewing all of the student's cumulative work products over a unit, semester, or school year to evaluate what the student has learned and achieved in the class, subject, or year. A completed portfolio may be used to contribute to the student's final grade.

RUBRIC, NORM-REFERENCED TEST, AND CRITERION-REFERENCED TEST

A rubric specifies certain learning objectives a student should be able to demonstrate, and in what ways. Teachers should first review the **rubric** with students to inform them of what they are expected to learn. Then they have students use the rubric to guide their learning experiences and work. Finally, they use the rubric to assess whether students have met the learning objective(s). A **norm-referenced test** compares the student's scores to a previously established norm. For example, standardized tests commonly obtain samples of scores from students they have identified as representative of a given national or state population. They then calculate the average score of these students. Whenever other students take these standardized tests, their scores are then compared to these averages. The test authors and publishers provide statistical computations and tables whereby educators can determine how many standard deviations from the norm a student's score falls, and in what percentile of the population the student's score ranks. **Criterion-referenced tests** do not compare student scores to a norm, but against predetermined criteria of what learning they should demonstrate, determined by test authors, publishers, school districts, individual teachers, etc. They do not determine student rank, but whether or to what degree the student meets lesson, unit, class, course, or subject requirements.

MANAGING DISTRACTING OR DISRUPTIVE BEHAVIORS THROUGHOUT A CLASSROOM

By the end of the first school week, discuss with students and then write a **group contract** with classroom rules and procedures. Review these periodically until students succeed in following them. Address misbehavior with private, moderately toned, simple, to-the-point verbal reprimands, e.g., "Please stop talking and work on your math assignment." As often as possible, praise the entire class, e.g., "I'm so happy to see you all working so well today," or "Thank you for working so quietly." If one student constantly displays an unacceptable behavior, e.g., out of seat, make an **individualized contract** specifying reinforcing consequences, e.g., if the student stays in his/her seat throughout the class period, s/he will receive a specified reward or form of recognition. To prevent misbehavior, intervene as early as possible; for example, if a student is beginning to exhibit signs of frustration, ask "Can I help you with your assignment?" before it escalates to acting-out behavior. Move around the classroom regularly to prevent possible behavior problems. Use facial expressions to show students misbehavior was not overlooked completely.

Health Education Content

Exercise and Physical Fitness

HEALTH BENEFITS OF REGULAR PHYSICAL ACTIVITY

According to the US Department of Health and Human Services Office of Disease Prevention and Health Promotion, regular **physical activity (PA)** affords a myriad of benefits to cardiorespiratory health, musculoskeletal health, mental health, metabolic health, weight control, and life expectancy. It helps prevent high blood pressure, high cholesterol, heart disease, strokes, osteoporosis, falls and fractures, some cancers, cognitive decline, depression, anxiety, type 2 diabetes, obesity, and premature death. PA promotes **functional capacity** for activities of daily living. Some of these benefits, like greater muscle strength, cardiorespiratory fitness, lowered blood pressure and less depression can appear after only a few weeks. Moreover, only modest amounts and moderate intensity of PA, e.g., 150 minutes weekly of brisk walking, are needed to realize most health benefits. For children and adolescents, research finds strong evidence of better bone health, muscular and cardiorespiratory fitness, body composition, and cardiovascular and metabolic health biomarkers through regular PA. Studies also show moderate evidence that PA reduces child and teen **anxiety and depression** symptoms. Not only does PA help control weight, but even obese and overweight people who are physically active have lower premature death rates than those who are inactive.

Across numerous research studies, consensus has been established about the health benefits of regular physical activity (PA) for all people. As reported by the US Department of Health and Human Services Office of Disease Prevention and Health Promotion, regular PA lowers risks of many health problems. Although added benefits accrue as individuals increase the intensity, frequency, and/or duration of their PA, scientists also find even some PA is superior to inactivity. A person can spend as little as 30 minutes, five days a week, doing something simple like walking briskly, to obtain the majority of health benefits available. More PA realizes more benefits. Studies find both **aerobic activity** to increase endurance and **resistance activity** to increase strength beneficial. Research shows health benefits from PA to every racial and ethnic group studied, and every age group—children, teens; young, middle-aged, and older adults—including people with disabilities. Though some people fear injuries, researchers have determined the benefits of PA are far superior to its risks. Engaging in moderate PA regularly also achieves conditioning, lowering injury risk compared to sudden or unaccustomed, excessive exertion.

SERIES OF NATIONAL HEALTH INITIATIVES

The US Department of Health and Human Services (HHS) has launched a series of **Healthy People initiatives** in support of prevention endeavors across its divisions for making the national population healthier. More information is available on the website healthypeople.gov, including the latest news and events, health indicators, progress updates, and webinars. The **Healthy People 2010 initiative**, managed by HHS' Office of Disease Prevention and Health Promotion, had the primary goals of increasing life expectancy and quality, and eliminating demographic health disparities in the US population. The **Healthy People 2020 initiative**, launched in 2010 and addressing 42 areas of public health, has targeted the main goals of achieving longer, high-quality lives without premature death, preventable injury, disease, and disability; eliminating health disparities, attaining health equity, and improving all population groups' health; creating physical and social environments promoting good health for everybody; and furthering healthy development, behaviors, and quality of life across all ages and life stages.

PRIMARY HEALTH INDICATORS INVESTIGATED BY US RESEARCHERS

Scientists have studied 10 leading **health indicators** from 2000-2010, and have continued to assess these since 2010. These health behaviors have strong influences on American health:

- **Physical activity**: a goal is getting more teenagers to engage in vigorous physical activity.
- **Obesity and overweight**: a goal is to decrease numbers of obese and overweight teens and children.
- **Tobacco use**: the goal is to decrease teen cigarette smoking.
- **Substance abuse**: the goal is to augment the number of teenagers not using alcohol and other drugs.
- **Responsible sexual behavior**: the goal is to encourage more adolescents to abstain from engaging in sexual intercourse.
- **Mental health**: among adults with diagnoses of depression, the goal is to raise the proportion of people who receive treatment for it.
- **Injury and violence**: the goal is to decrease the number of motor vehicle deaths and homicides in the population.
- **Environmental quality**: the goal is to decrease non-smoker exposure to secondhand tobacco smoke.
- **Immunization**: a goal is to raise the percentage of young children receiving all recommended vaccinations for a minimum of five years.
- **Healthcare access**: the goal is to raise the percentage of people covered by health insurance.

BODY COMPOSITION

Body composition equals the proportions of fatty and muscular tissue that make up a person's body weight. The percentage of body fat an individual has is significant to health and fitness because people with excessive body fat have higher risks of many chronic diseases, including type 2 diabetes, hypertension, coronary artery disease, osteoarthritis, and many kinds of cancer. Recommended **body fat levels** differ by age and sex. Men are generally advised to have a maximum of 25 percent body fat, and women 30 percent. Somewhat higher levels are often allowed at older ages, because muscle mass decreases with aging. Women naturally have higher levels of essential body fat for reproductive purposes. One method of measuring body fat is by using calipers to measure skinfold thickness at the triceps, suprailiac (above the hip), male chest, thigh, abdomen, subscapular (below shoulder blade) and calf sites. The sum of these measurements can yield an estimate of body fat percentage.

CARDIORESPIRATORY ENDURANCE

"**Cardio**" refers to heart and "**respiratory**" to breathing. One definition of **cardiorespiratory endurance** is the ability to perform dynamic exercise using large muscles over long times. Cardiorespiratory endurance is determined by functioning of the cardiovascular (heart and blood vessel), pulmonary (lungs), and skeletal muscle systems. Higher risk of dying prematurely from all causes is associated with low cardiorespiratory endurance levels. Moreover, the leading cause of death in America is **coronary artery disease**, and high cardiorespiratory endurance levels protect strongly against this. To evaluate cardiorespiratory endurance, a stress test uses an electrocardiogram (ECG) and metabolic cart. First, resting blood pressure and heart rate are measured to obtain baselines and compare with normal values. Then the individual ambulates on a treadmill, pedals on a stationary bicycle, or repeatedly steps onto and off a step, with an ergometer measuring energy output. The ECG has 12 leads attached to the individual to measure heart function. The metabolic cart measures how much oxygen the person's body can consume during exercise—labeled **VO₂ max**, maximal oxygen consumption. Higher VO_2 max indicates higher cardiorespiratory endurance. This assesses cardiovascular fitness and informs planning safe, effective exercise programs.

BENEFITS OF ENHANCING FLEXIBILITY

Having or developing a good range of motion and **flexibility** can greatly improve an individual's **functional abilities** for many everyday living tasks. For example, when driving, turning to see the blind spot before changing lanes is highly difficult when one has poor upper-back and neck flexibility. But with improved range of motion, this common movement becomes simple. The same applies to everyday activities like getting out of bed, picking something up off the floor, or even fastening a seat belt. However, the benefits of flexibility are not only functional. Flexibility **prevents injuries** to joints and muscles, both in daily life and in sports. Stretching following exercise can decrease short-term muscular stiffness and soreness. Flexibility **improves performance** in sports and other exercise. Stretching relieves both general muscular tightness and specific muscle tightness from repetitive motions, ergonomic and/or occupational issues, and even sleeping in bad positions. Two main sources of **lower-back pain**, tightness and muscle spasms, can be treated by stretching; and its long-term benefits decrease future episodes. Neck and upper-back stretching can relieve **muscle-tension headaches**. Stretching can rehabilitate many soft tissue injuries and conditions.

SARCOMERE HYPERTROPHY

Sarcomere hypertrophy builds muscular strength. It apparently requires breaking down muscle fibers to build them up. When tension accumulates in muscle fibers during exercise, connections between actin and myosin protein filaments are damaged, and muscle cell plasma membranes (sarcolemma) rupture, leaking calcium between cells. Increased levels of **intracellular calcium ions** activate **calpains**, enzymes that remove damaged tissue. This activates monocytes, neutrophils, macrophages, and other immune system cells to remove and break down damaged fibers. Also, muscle cells near the damage site are stimulated by ruptured sarcolemma to make and release growth factors. **Satellite cells**, a type of myogenic stem cells activated by the damaged fiber cells' removal and the released growth factors, repair damaged muscle fibers and stimulate muscular growth. Satellite cells activated by muscle damage differentiate into myoblasts and then skeletal muscle cells, which fuse with existing muscle fibers in damaged areas. The fusion adds satellite cell nuclei to skeletal cell nuclei; the larger total number of nuclei then enables muscle fibers to make larger amounts of actin and myosin important to muscular contraction, enhancing muscle contractile ability and strength. Lifting heavier weights with fewer repetitions stimulates **sarcomere hypertrophy**, increasing muscular strength.

PRINCIPLES IN EXERCISE SCIENCE
DIMINISHING RETURN, VARIATION PRINCIPLE, AND ADAPTATION AND SPECIFICITY

In exercise science, the **principle of diminishing returns** means that, when unconditioned individuals start training, their fitness levels improve quickly because they have so far to progress. However, as their fitness increases, they improve less as they near their genetic limits and their fitness levels have plateaued. A corollary to this is that, as people's fitness levels grow, they must train harder to achieve equal gains. Both athletes and trainers designing training programs should remember fitness levels will not continue improving at constant rates as fitness progresses. The **variation principle** means that athletes should alternate hard with light training every several days. Light days enable bodies to recover. Varying training volume and intensity enables attaining peak fitness levels for competing, prevents overstressing or injuring body parts, and sustains athlete interest and motivation for training. Variation relates to **adaptation** because routines must be varied because the body adjusts and adapts to the same routines, stopping challenge and progress. Variation and **specificity** appear to conflict—sport and activity improvement requires more sport- and activity-specific training, while variation dictates training variety—but these can be balanced between enough sport- and activity-specific training for improvement, and some variety using the same muscle groups.

FITT

FITT is a good mnemonic device, homonymous with "fit." It makes it easier to remember exercise variables, which we can manipulate to keep our bodies from adapting and ceasing to progress, and also keep our minds from becoming bored. "FITT" stands for frequency, intensity, time, and type. **Frequency** represents how often we exercise; **intensity** how hard; **time** how long; and **type** the kind of exercise, e.g., walking, running, bicycling, etc. When we work out often enough, hard enough, long enough, and using exercise types appropriate for our individual physiological makeup, body composition, fitness levels, skill levels, mental and psychological dispositions, and preferences, we begin seeing changes in our aerobic capacity, cardiovascular endurance, strength, body fat percentage, and weight. When our bodies adapt to current FITT levels, we can manipulate one or more variables every four to six weeks for ongoing training effects. For example, if someone stops seeing improvement after walking for 20 minutes three times a week, they can: add another day each week; add short bursts of speed-walking, jogging, or hill training; add 10-15 minutes to the duration; or switch to swimming, cycling, or aerobics.

Personal Health and Wellness

PERSONAL HYGIENE

Good personal hygiene promotes good health by preventing and limiting exposure to bacterial and viral microorganisms. In addition to **physical benefits**, good bodily hygiene also supports good **mental health** by promoting psychological well-being and feeling good about oneself. When people neglect their personal hygiene, they develop body odors, bad breath, damaged and lost teeth, and unkempt hair and clothing. Other people then view them as unhealthy; as a result, they can encounter social and employment discrimination. Some components of good personal hygiene include bathing, nail care, and foot care. Not everybody needs to bathe or shower daily; for some people, this can remove too many body oils, exacerbating dry skin. However, individuals should wash their bodies and hair regularly as often as they find necessary. The skin is continually shedding dead cells, which must be removed. If it accumulates, it can cause health problems. Trimming the fingernails and toenails regularly averts problems like hangnails and infected nailbeds. Keeping the feet clean and dry, and wearing clean flip-flops at public facilities, gyms, health clubs, spas, and around swimming pools prevents contracting athlete's foot and other fungal infections.

ORAL HYGIENE, HAND WASHING, AND SLEEP

Ideally, we should brush our teeth after every time we eat. Health professionals recommend brushing and flossing the teeth twice a day at a minimum. **Brushing teeth** removes plaque and reduces mouth bacteria, inhibiting tooth decay. This prevents not only tooth cavities, but also gum disease. **Flossing and gum massage** keep gums healthy and strong. If oral bacteria build up, it can cause gum disease. Gum disease not only causes irreversible bone loss in the jaw; the bacteria can travel from the gums directly to the heart, causing serious heart valve disorders. Unhealthy gums can loosen teeth, causing difficulty chewing, eating, and tooth loss. Most people need dental cleanings and checkups twice yearly, some more often. **Hand washing** prevents bacteria and viruses from spreading. We should wash our hands after using the bathroom; before preparing food and eating; after sneezing or coughing; and after handling garbage. Having alcohol-based hand sanitizing gels on hand is recommended when water is inaccessible. **Sleeping** enough and well must not be overlooked as a component of personal hygiene: insufficient or inadequate sleep impairs the immune system, inviting illness.

RELATIONSHIP BETWEEN PERSONAL HYGIENE AND MENTAL AND EMOTIONAL STATUS

Physicians and other experts advise that if a friend or acquaintance is neglecting his or her **personal hygiene**, especially if this is unaccustomed, or has an unkempt appearance, this can be a sign of underlying **depression**. When people are depressed or feeling sad, they tend to neglect taking care of themselves and their bodies. This has multiple sources: depression commonly causes low energy and fatigue, making even routine hygiene practices seem to require too much effort. Depression also lowers self-esteem; people do not feel good enough about themselves to show their bodies and health the self-respect or attention they deserve. Additional depression symptoms are feelings of helplessness, inhibiting motivation to control personal care and health; and hopelessness, removing motivation to take any positive action for self-care. Preoccupation with other concerns can also make people forget hygiene. One should not always assume depression is the cause, however; some people simply lack awareness, particularly if poor hygiene is habitual. Honest yet sensitive conversations about hygiene's importance in disease prevention can help some friends and acquaintances. If not, it is best to encourage their seeing a physician, therapist, or counselor.

DECREASING TOBACCO USE

WHO recognizes tobacco as "the most widely available harmful product on the market." Therefore, it negotiated the first international, legally binding treaty, the **WHO Framework Convention on Tobacco Control (FCTC)**, providing protocols and guidelines for evidence-based interventions to decrease tobacco supply and consumption. Raising tobacco prices and taxes is a documented cost-effective method that substantially increases quitting and decreases starting smoking, particularly among poor and young people. With proper implementation, enforcing smoke-free public place and workplace laws obtains high compliance levels: fewer youths start smoking; smokers are supported in quitting or reducing smoking; and smoke-free policies prevent perpetuating addiction at earlier stages, especially in youth. Informing and educating the public is another cost-effective measure. Studies in multiple countries find graphic health warnings on cigarette and tobacco packaging and creative media campaigns succeed in powerfully decreasing consumer demand, despite opposition from wealthy tobacco companies and health officials' comparatively limited resources. Another cost-effective measure is providing smoking cessation assistance, combining pharmaceutical and behavioral therapies, through primary medical care and public health providers. Though a minority of the global population has received these measures, research finds them affordable in all world nations.

ROLE OF PHYSICAL ACTIVITY IN PREVENTING AND REDUCING HEALTH RISKS

Studies demonstrate regular **physical activity (PA)** lowers risks of heart disease, strokes, diabetes, colon cancer, and breast cancer. Thirty to 60 minutes daily of PA decreases breast and colon cancer risks significantly; 150 minutes weekly of PA commonly reduces cardiovascular disease and diabetes risks. The World Health Organization (WHO) finds media promotion of combined PA and healthy diet very cost-effective, inexpensive, and feasible. **Schools** should include physical education with trained teachers and parental involvement in supportive environments. Successful **workplace** strategies include furnishing fitness spaces and signs encouraging staircase use; engaging employees in planning and implementing fitness programs; engaging families via festivals, newsletters, self-learning programs, etc.; and supplying self-monitoring and individual behavior change strategies. Effective **community** interventions include group PA classes and programs; community development campaigns concentrating on shared goals like reducing cardiovascular disease risk; and lifestyle modification advice regarding diet and physical activity, which research has proven to prevent diabetes with effectiveness similar to pharmacological therapy in people with impaired glucose tolerance.

MEASURES FOUND GLOBALLY TO DECREASE HARMFUL ALCOHOL CONSUMPTION

To be effective, strategies for prevention of cardiovascular disease, cirrhosis of the liver, and certain cancers secondary to **harmful alcohol consumption** must change both amounts and patterns of use. Based on evidence from research in Brazil, China, Mexico, Russia, Vietnam, and other countries, the World Health Organization (WHO) recommends these interventions to reduce harmful alcohol use: raising alcoholic beverage taxes; government monopolies of retail alcohol sales where applicable; restricting sales times and outlet density; regulating alcoholic beverage availability and minimum legal purchasing age; comprehensive advertising bans and/or effective marketing regulations limiting exposure to alcoholic drink advertising and marketing; measures to counter drinking and driving including lower (a half-gram per liter) driver blood alcohol concentration limits, zero tolerance or limits lowered further for younger drivers, sobriety checkpoints, and random breath testing; brief interventions for harmful and hazardous drinking, and treatment for alcohol abuse disorders. Isolated classroom and public education, mass media campaigns, and consumer warning messages and labels have not been found effective by research; however,

informational and educational campaigns supporting the aforementioned effective measures can enhance their public acceptance.

HEALTHY DIET COMPONENTS FOR PREVENTING AND REDUCING HEALTH RISKS

To prevent and reduce risks of cardiovascular disease, diabetes, and some cancers, healthy diets should balance calorie intake and expenditure for healthy weight maintenance; limit intake from total fats to 30 percent; eliminate trans fats, and substitute unsaturated fats for saturated; limit consumption of free sugars; increase consumption of vegetables, legumes, fruits, whole grains, and nuts; make all salt iodized; and limit sodium intake from all sources. Although studies find multiple nutritional interventions more cost-effective with greater potential health gains than individual interventions, the World Health Organization (WHO) also identifies **salt reduction** for preventing noncommunicable diseases. A major cause of death is high blood pressure, frequently caused or exacerbated by excess dietary sodium. About 75 percent of salt intake in North America and Europe comes from sodium added to manufactured meals and foods. Most sodium consumed in many Asian and African countries is from soy sauce and salt added at home during cooking and eating. WHO estimates decreasing salt to recommended levels could prevent up to 2.5 million deaths annually. Finland, France, Ireland, Japan, and the United Kingdom have successfully implemented salt reduction initiatives, preventing thousands of premature deaths and saving billions in healthcare and other expenses annually.

Chronic and Communicable Diseases

LIFE CHOICES TO PREVENT CHRONIC DISEASES AND HEALTH CONDITIONS, AND CONTRASTING HEALTH RISK BEHAVIORS

Regular **aerobic exercise** or **physical activity** can prevent cardiovascular disease. Weight-bearing exercise strengthens bones, preventing osteoporosis which leads to fractures. Exercising, limiting sodium intake, not smoking, eating diets low in saturated and trans fats and high in fiber, and losing or controlling weight all reduce risks for strokes and heart disease by strengthening the heart and blood vessels and reducing blood pressure, cholesterol and arterial plaque. **Not smoking** also prevents lung cancer and other respiratory, oral, and digestive system cancers. **Eating vegetables and fruits** accesses antioxidants protecting against many cancers, and fibers protecting against colorectal cancers, as does eating whole grains. Binge drinking kills many Americans, most of whom are not alcohol-dependent; hence **avoiding binge drinking** prevents deaths. According to the CDC, more than half of adults do not get recommended levels of aerobic or muscle-strengthening exercise or physical activity. Most Americans consume **excessive sodium**, risking hypertension. Almost half have other major heart-disease risk factors, i.e., uncontrolled hypertension and/or high LDL cholesterol. Over one-third of adults reported (2011) eating fruit less than once daily, almost one-fourth vegetables less than once daily; over one-third of teens ate fruit and vegetables less than once daily. Nearly 20 percent of adults smoked in 2012.

TREATMENT FOR MANY TYPES OF CANCER

Whether they involve localized solid tumors or diffuse conditions like leukemia and other cancers of the blood, all **cancer** is, by definition, an uncontrolled growth of abnormal cells. Therefore, treatment typically involves removing and/or killing the cancerous cells, growths, or masses. One treatment is **surgically removing** cancerous tissue. Some inoperable cancers would require removing needed healthy tissue, as with sarcoidosis wrapped around the spinal cord, or aggressive tumors having invaded too much of vital organs. In some cases, an entire organ may be surgically replaced by **donor transplantation**. Surgical removal of a cancerous growth is often followed by **radiation treatment**—exposure to radioactive elements—to eliminate any remaining cancer cells and/or prevent new regrowth. Side-effects include burns or other damages to the treatment site. Another treatment method to kill cancer cells is **chemotherapy**. Various drugs, administered orally or intravenously, are toxic to cancer growths. Unfortunately, most treatments toxic enough to kill cancer cells are also toxic to the patient. Chemotherapy side effects include severe nausea, vomiting, debilitating fatigue, hair loss, skin damage, and osteoporosis. Some treatment protocols combine methods, e.g., surgery followed by radiation and chemotherapy, radiation to shrink a tumor followed by surgery, etc.

HEALTH EDUCATION PROGRAM FOR MANAGING CHRONIC DISEASES AND HEALTH CONDITIONS

Stanford University's School of Medicine Patient Education Research Center offers a chronic disease self-management program called the **Better Choices, Better Health® Workshop**. Facilitated by two trained leaders, one or both non-health professionals with their own chronic diseases, this workshop is held in hospitals, libraries, senior centers, churches, and other community settings. Weekly classes are two-and-a-half hours each for six weeks. The workshop covers subjects including techniques for coping with pain, fatigue, frustration, and isolation; exercises appropriate for preserving and enhancing endurance, strength, and flexibility; using medications appropriately; nutrition; decision-making; effective communication with health professionals, family, and friends; and how to evaluate new treatments. Participants are given the accompanying *Relaxation for Mind and Body* audio CD and *Living a Healthy Life with Chronic Conditions, 4th edition* book. Sessions involve high participation levels, mutual success, and support. This course was developed based on federally- and state-funded research. Researchers included Stanford psychologist Albert Bandura, originator of self-efficacy, i.e., self-confidence for mastering new skills or influencing one's health. Bandura and colleagues deemed **self-management skills instruction** instrumental in managing chronic disease; program evaluation yielded positive outcomes. Stanford offers healthcare organization representatives program training four to five times yearly.

HIV/AIDS

The **human immunodeficiency virus** (HIV) impairs or destroys an infected individual's immune system, raising infection risk and ruining infection defenses. As HIV advances, its final stage is **AIDS**, acquired immune deficiency syndrome. The World Health Organization (WHO) estimated that by the end of 2013, 35 million humans were living with HIV. Of these, 23.4-26.2 million lived in sub-Saharan Africa. Global health community efforts include research and development of new medications to address symptoms for people already infected, as well as preventing new infections; outreach and education to stop HIV spread; and supporting children and families who have lost parents to AIDS deaths. **Anti-retroviral therapy (ART) drugs** have enabled many HIV patients to survive 15+ years before developing AIDS symptoms. WHO estimated 12.9 million people were receiving these by the end of 2013, 11.7 million of them in low-income and middle-income nations. The most successful global health effort, this program has been significantly helped by the **President's Emergency Plan for AIDS Relief (PEPFAR)**. Additionally, the US Department of Health and Human Services (HHS), National Institutes of Health (NIH) offices, Gates Foundation, and Centers for Disease Control and Prevention (CDC) are all actively involved in global HIV/AIDS research, researcher training, coordination, and vaccine development.

Cystic Fibrosis

In cystic fibrosis (**CF**), a defective gene produces a protein causing the body to secrete mucus that is much thicker and stickier than normal. This mucus clogs up the lungs, resulting in infections that can cause or threaten death. It also blocks the pancreas from delivering enzymes that help break down and absorb necessary nutrients from foods. Over 75 percent of CF patients are diagnosed by age 2. Today, almost half of CF patients are aged 18 or more. Around 1,000 new CF cases are diagnosed annually. Symptoms include shortness of breath; wheezing; chronic persistent coughing, including phlegm-productive coughs; slow weight gain and inadequate growth despite good appetite; frequently developing lung infections; difficult, bulky, greasy, and/or frequent bowel movements; and skin with an extremely salty taste. Most children with CF died before entering elementary school during the 1950s. Today, significant progress in the understanding and treatment of CF has dramatically improved longevity and life quality in CF patients. Many now live into middle adulthood or older; life expectancy has doubled in the past three decades. The **Cystic Fibrosis Foundation**, whose support has enabled almost all available CF treatment medications, views research for a cure as "promising."

Sickle Cell Anemia

Anemia means the blood has fewer **red blood cells (RBC)** than normal. RBCs, which transport oxygen in **hemoglobin** (an iron-rich protein) through the bloodstream and remove the waste product carbon dioxide, are produced in the bone marrow, normally living about four months. **Sickle cell** is one genetic type of anemia, inherited when both parents have the gene. When one parent has this gene but the other's is normal, children inherit sickle cell trait; they do not have the disease, but pass the sickle hemoglobin gene to their children. In America, sickle cell anemia is commonest in African-Americans (around one in 500). It also affects Hispanic-Americans (around one in 36,000); and people of Caribbean, Mediterranean, Indian, and Saudi Arabian descent. Normal RBCs are disc-shaped and travel easily through blood vessels. Sickle cells are crescent-shaped, sticky, and stiff, impeding blood flow. This causes organ damage, pain, and increased risk of infections. Some patients have chronic fatigue and/or pain. A few patients may receive future cures through stem cell transplants, but no widespread cure currently exists. Symptoms and complications are managed through treatments. Improved care and treatments enable some patients to live into their 40s, 50s, or older.

TAY-SACHS DISEASE

Tay-Sachs disease is a rare genetic disorder, inherited through an **autosomal recessive pattern**; i.e., both parents carry copies of a mutated gene and are usually asymptomatic, but pass these to their children. **Tay-Sachs** is rare overall, and more common among Eastern/Central European Jewish, certain Quebec French-Canadian, Old-Order Pennsylvania Dutch/Amish, and Louisiana Cajun populations. The genetic defect prevents an enzyme from breaking down a toxic substance, which builds up in the brain and spinal cord, progressively destroying neurons. The commonest form appears in infancy, typically around 3-6 months. A typical sign is a "cherry-red spot" eye abnormality, detectable through eye examination. Babies' motor muscles weaken; development slows; they lose motor skills like turning over, sitting up, and crawling; and develop exaggerated startle reactions to loud sounds. As it progresses, this disease causes seizures, loss of vision and hearing, intellectual impairment, and paralysis. Most children with the commoner infantile form of Tay-Sachs disease typically only survive until early childhood. Later-onset forms of the disease are extremely rare, typically with milder, highly variable symptoms including muscular weakness, poor coordination, other motor symptoms, speech difficulties, and mental illness.

TYPE 2 DIABETES

Historically, type 1 diabetes, which has a greater genetic component, was called "juvenile diabetes" because symptoms appeared during childhood, contrasting with type 2 "adult-onset diabetes." However, these terms were abandoned as more cases of **type 2 diabetes** are occurring in childhood and adolescence—evidence of the contributions of **lifestyle factors** including obesity, poor nutrition, and physical inactivity. When people consume large amounts of refined carbohydrates (simple sugars and starches processed to remove all fibers) with no fiber slowing digestion, these enter the bloodstream rapidly, causing a sudden spike in blood sugar, experienced by some as an energy rush. However, with quick metabolism and the pancreas' secretion of extra insulin to neutralize excessive blood sugar, sugars exit as fast as they entered, causing a precipitous blood-sugar drop, or "crash," with fatigue, sleepiness, irritability, depression and cycle-perpetuating cravings for more sugar or starch. Moreover, **metabolic syndrome** eventually develops—insulin resistance to the pancreas' attempts to neutralize repeated artificial blood sugar elevation. In type 1 diabetes, the pancreas fails to produce insulin; in type 2, the body becomes immune to insulin, causing chronically high, unstable blood sugar. Blindness, limb loss, shock, coma, and death are a few of many sequelae from uncontrolled diabetes.

CHRONIC, NONCOMMUNICABLE DISEASES

According to the World Health Organization (WHO, 2013), over 36 million people die annually from **noncommunicable diseases (NCDs)**, with almost 80 percent (29 million) in low-income and middle-income nations. Of these, over 9 million are before age 60. Of these premature deaths, 90 percent are in low-income and middle-income nations. Roughly 80 percent of all NCD deaths are due to four disease types: **cardiovascular diseases**, e.g., strokes and heart attacks, which cause the majority (17.3 million yearly); **cancers** (7.6 million yearly); **respiratory diseases** like asthma and chronic obstructive pulmonary disease (COPD) (4.2 million yearly); and **diabetes** (1.3 million yearly). These four disease groups have four **risk factors** in common: tobacco use, physical inactivity, harmful alcohol use, and poor nutrition. WHO projects the greatest increases in NCD mortality by 2020 will be in African countries, where NCDs are also predicted to surpass maternal and infant mortality from childbirth and nutritional and communicable diseases combined as the most common killers by 2030. Behavioral risk factors for NCDs that can be modified are tobacco use, physical inactivity, unhealthy diets, and harmful alcohol consumption.

MEASURES TAKEN BY WHO TO PREVENT NCDS

WHO's *Action Plan of the global strategy for the prevention and control of noncommunicable diseases* gives member states and international partners steps for preventing and addressing NCDs in world nations. WHO is also working to reduce **NCD risk factors**, including: implementing anti-tobacco measures identified in the WHO Framework Convention on Tobacco Control in world nations to decrease public tobacco exposure; helping world communities lower rates of death and disease from physical inactivity and unhealthy diets through the WHO *Global strategy on diet, physical activity and health aims to promote and protect health;* identifying action areas with priority and recommending measures of protection against the harmful consumption of alcohol through the WHO *Global strategy to reduce the harmful use of alcohol;* responding to the United Nations Political Declaration on NCDs by developing a comprehensive framework for global NCD prevention, monitoring, and control, which includes a group of global voluntary targets and a list of indicators; and responding to the World Health Assembly's resolution (WHA 64.11) by developing a 2013-2020 **Global NCD Action Plan** with comprehensive guidance for implementing the United Nations High-Level Meeting's political commitments. WHA endorsed this plan, urging member state, Director-General and Secretariat implementation and future WHA progress reports.

DISEASE ETIOLOGY

Etiology is defined in medicine as the study of origins or causes of diseases or pathological conditions. Early writings attributed diseases to various unproven "causes" including spells, curses, and imbalances in bodily humors. Ancient Greek physicians Galen and Hippocrates often associated disease with unidentified components in the air, influencing miasmatic perspectives on disease etiology of Medieval European physicians. Ancient Roman scholar Marcus Terentius Varro suggested **microorganisms** caused diseases in his book *On Agriculture* in the 1st century BC. German physician Robert Koch (1843-1910), modern bacteriology founder, discovered scientific evidence of microorganisms causing the infectious diseases anthrax, cholera, and tuberculosis. As in all experimental science, in **epidemiology**, statistical correlation between/among variables does not prove causation. Sir Austin Bradford-Hill, the epidemiologist who proved causal relationship between tobacco smoking and lung cancer, defined criteria for showing causation. American epidemiologist Alfred Evans proposed the **Unified Concept of Causation**, synthesizing previous thinking. **Etiology** can contribute to causal chains including independent co-factors and promoters. For example, stress, once believed to cause peptic ulcer disease, was belatedly identified as a promoter, with excess stomach acid a prerequisite and *Helicobacter pylori* infection the primary etiology.

RELATIONSHIPS AMONG AND WITHIN DISEASE ETIOLOGIES

Certain diseases, e.g., hepatitis or diabetes, can be diagnosed according to their symptoms. However, these diseases can also develop from **different etiologies**, and can co-exist with, result from, or result in various other conditions. For instance, type 1 diabetes includes a strong genetic component in its etiology, though it also appears to involve complex interactions of genetic and environmental influences; whereas type 2 diabetes more often appears to result from environmental (i.e., lifestyle) influences to a greater extent. Hepatitis (liver inflammation) has separate etiologies: hepatitis A, B, and C are each caused by distinct viruses; autoimmune hepatitis is not infectious, but caused by the patient's own immune system attacking the liver. On the other hand, several different diseases can also result from one **single etiology**. For example, the Epstein-Barr virus can cause the infectious disease mononucleosis, or either of two types of cancer—Burkitt's lymphoma or nasopharyngeal carcinoma—under different conditions.

INFLUENZA

Influenza (flu) is an infectious viral respiratory illness. Its symptoms can range from mild to fatal. Young children, seniors, and people with some health conditions have greatest risk for serious complications. Annual **vaccination** is the best way to prevent it. The US Department of Health and Human Services' (HHS) Office of Global Affairs, International Influenza Unit (IIU) is an international partnership to enhance global flu identification and response, coordinated by HHS personnel and Operation Divisions including National Institutes of Health (NIH); Centers for Disease Control and Infection (CDC); Food and Drug Administration (FDA); Office of the Assistant Secretary for Preparedness and Response, Biomedical Advanced Research and Development Authority (ASPR/BARDA); the US Departments of State (DOS), Defense (DOD), Agriculture (USDA), Commerce, and Treasury; the US Agency for International Development (USAID); foreign governments; the international World Health Organization (WHO), World Bank, International Partnership on Avian and Pandemic Influenza (IPAPI), Global Health Security Action Group (GHSAG), UN System Influenza Coordination (UNSIC), Pan-American Health Organization (PAHO); and nonprofits like PATH and the Gates Foundation. **Influenza pandemics**—world outbreaks—occur when a new virus with little or no human immunity emerges. There were three in the 20th century and one so far in the 21st.

RELATIONSHIP BETWEEN COMMUNICABLE DISEASES AND EMERGENCY AND DISASTER CONDITIONS

According to the World Health Organization (WHO), **natural disasters** and **war conditions** can break water and sewer pipes and sewage treatment mechanisms, and disrupt electricity for pumping water. This can lead to **waterborne** and **vector-borne diseases**. When disaster or war survivors live in crowded temporary arrangements with inadequate personal hygiene and laundry facilities and poor ventilation, personal contact can spread highly contagious diseases into **epidemics**. Disaster victims are also more susceptible to communicable diseases as unsanitary living conditions, stress, fatigue, and malnutrition lower their resistance. An additional disease transmission factor is how long refugees live in temporary shelters: mass settlement for extended times can cause epidemic outbreaks. Famine relief camps particularly involve many people already weakened, potentially ill, and staying there for long durations. Storms, floods, earthquakes, mudslides, etc. can both contaminate water supplies with sewage and waste and create standing water where insect disease vectors breed. **Communicable disease control** requires adequate shelter, sanitation, clean water, vector control, health workers trained in early diagnosis and treatment, and immunization which combine to produce healthy environments.

PREPARING FOR AND PREVENTING COMMUNICABLE DISEASE OUTBREAKS

Research by the World Health Organization (WHO) has identified the five commonest **causes of mortality** related to emergency and disaster conditions: malaria (in certain areas), malnutrition, diarrhea, measles, and acute respiratory infections. While not a communicable disease, **malnutrition** is made significantly worse by communicable diseases; the others, all communicable diseases, are related directly to environmental health conditions. When conditions preceding disasters are **unsanitary**, as in large cities with dense populations in developing nations, disease problems following disasters are more likely. Therefore, advance measures to alleviate poverty, raise awareness, improve organization, and establish sanitary and health services offer greater community protection in the event of disaster. **Preparedness** includes training outreach and health personnel to identify and manage specific disease threats; stocking equipment and supplies locally for environmental health; diagnosis and treatment for potential disease outbreaks; applying protocols for information management practices regarding particular diseases; raising local awareness of communicable diseases and the importance of early health facility referral;

strengthening health-surveillance systems; promoting hygiene; and providing adequate clean water supplies, suitable shelter, sanitation facilities, and advance vaccination campaigns.

PUBLIC HEALTH SURVEILLANCE

Public health surveillance involves collecting, analyzing, and distributing health information for the purpose of taking prompt and appropriate action. As reported by Doctors Without Borders, during emergency and disaster situations, affected populations are more susceptible to diseases; the instability of the circumstances causes sudden changes in health; and to take effective action quickly, health workers must share quantitative data with a variety of partners. The World Health Organization (WHO) emphasizes the importance of designating certain health personnel to conduct public health surveillance. Hospital staff, temporary relief center workers, and community and neighborhood health personnel must be vigilant for unusual numbers of malaria cases, food poisoning, other toxicity, encephalitis, meningitis, cholera, plague, typhus, typhoid fever, paratyphoid fever, and other ailments or diseases. Workers should take patient histories, identify contacts, and isolate disease sources. **Public health surveillance** can be conducted to some degree even in large-scale population movement's worst circumstances. Health workers can extend existing reporting systems to area-wide surveillance systems addressing sanitation- and water-related epidemics and other high-priority diseases. **Active population movement pattern surveillance** affords data for predicting future settlement patterns, general disease surveillance, and emergency intervention planning.

Mental and Emotional Health

EQ

Components, Aspects of Life Effected, and Development Skills

Emotional intelligence (EQ) includes self-awareness, self-regulation (self-management), social awareness, and relationship management. EQ affects physical health, mental health, school and work performance, and relationships. Five **skills to develop EQ** are:

- ability to reduce stress quickly in various contexts
- ability to recognize our emotions and prevent their overwhelming us
- ability to relate to others emotionally through nonverbal communication
- ability to maintain connections during challenging circumstances through playfulness and humor
- ability for confident, positive conflict resolution

To function well under stress, identify your **physiological responses to stress** (e.g., shallow/rapid breathing, tight stomach, muscle tension/pain, clenched hands). Recognition enables **regulation**. Identify your individual stress response: those who become agitated or angry can relieve stress with calming, quieting activities. Those who become withdrawn or depressed can relieve stress through stimulating activities. Those who slow down in some ways and speed up in others, causing paralysis, need activities combining stimulation and comfort. Sensory engagement rapidly decreases stress. Individuals should discover which sense(s) (vision, hearing, touch, smell, taste) and technique(s) are most energizing and/or soothing personally.

To recognize your emotions and stay focused and calm during stressful interactions, ask yourself about the quality of your **relationship with your emotions**. Do your emotions flow from one to another along with your changing momentary experiences? Do you feel physical sensations in your body associated with your emotions? Do you feel distinct emotions, e.g., joy, sadness, anger, and fear; and do your subtle facial expressions show each of these? Are you able to feel intense emotions, strong enough to capture both your and others' attention? Do you attend to your emotions? Do they affect your decision-making? If any of these are unfamiliar, you may have shut your emotions off. Many people do this in reaction to negative childhood experiences. Reconnecting with, becoming comfortable with, and accessing **core emotions** are necessary to emotional intelligence and health. Mindful meditation can facilitate these.

To interact well with others, **nonverbal signals** can be more important than words—i.e., how you say things more than what you say. This includes body posture, muscle tension, physical gestures, facial expressions, eye contact, vocal tone, etc. Nonverbal cues convey interest or disinterest, trust or mistrust, excitement or apathy, confidence or fear, clarity or confusion, and connection or disconnection. Nonverbal communication requires both conveying what you intend, and reading others' subtle nonverbal signals. To improve it, attend to others rather than planning what to say next, thinking about other things, or daydreaming so as not to miss cues. Make eye contact to gauge others' responses, maintain conversational flow, and convey interest. Attend to nonverbal signals you are sending and receiving—not only face, body, touch, and tone of voice, but also the pace, timing and rhythm of conversation. If what you say does not reflect what you feel, your body will contradict your words.

Being able to **laugh** and make others laugh can relieve stress, improve moods, rebalance nervous systems, lighten mental loads, place things in perspective, and increase EQ. Laughing and playing enable us to take setbacks and difficulties in stride. Gentle humor enables communicating messages that could otherwise offend, anger, or provoke defensiveness in others. Humor also soothes **interpersonal differences**. Communicating playfully both energizes and relaxes, simultaneously alleviating fatigue and dissipating physical tension. It moreover loosens rigid thinking, enabling creativity and new perspectives. To develop playful communication, experts recommend practicing by interacting often with outgoing, playful people; playing with young children, babies, and animals; discovering activities you enjoy that access your playful qualities and loosen you up; and setting aside time regularly for quality playing, joking, and laughing.

Conflict is inevitable, but when constructively managed, it can promote relationship safety, trust, freedom, and creativity. When interpersonal conflicts are not viewed as punitive or threatening but managed positively to build trust, they can strengthen relationships. This skill is informed by the previous four: stress management, emotional awareness, nonverbal communication, and playfulness and humor facilitate skillful handling and defusing of emotionally charged interactions. To develop positive, trust-building **conflict-resolution skills**, focus on the present and acknowledge current reality as an opportunity to resolve old reactions to conflicts, rather than clinging to old resentments and wounds. Regarding arguments, pick your battles: arguing, particularly toward positive resolutions, uses energy and time. Decide whether an issue is worth or not worth arguing over. Forgiveness is also necessary: we must let go of desires for revenge or punishment for others' past hurtful actions to resolve conflicts. Even when a conflict cannot be resolved, continuing it takes two people; although disagreeing, you can end the conflict by disengaging from it.

MENTAL OR EMOTIONAL HEALTH

Mental or emotional health describes an individual's overall **psychological well-being**. This incorporates a person's self-esteem, i.e., the way s/he feels about herself/himself, a person's ability to manage her/his emotions and ability to cope with stress and problems in life, and the quality of an individual's relationships. **Mental and emotional health** are analogous to physical health in the sense that, just as we must make conscious efforts to maintain or build up our physical health, we must equally make conscious efforts to sustain or establish our mental and emotional health. Good mental and emotional health is not simply an absence of anxiety, depression, or other mental health problems. It is moreover the presence of positive attributes. It is not merely the absence of feeling bad, but the presence of feeling good. Some people may not experience any overtly negative feelings, yet it is still necessary for them to do things that afford them positive feelings to attain emotional and mental health.

CHARACTERISTICS ASSOCIATED WITH BEING MENTALLY AND EMOTIONALLY HEALTHY

When people are **healthy**, both emotionally and mentally, they feel and demonstrate **positive personal characteristics**, enabling them to engage in meaningful, productive activities and relationships that promote full participation in life. These include: high self-esteem, i.e., they feel good about themselves. They feel and demonstrate self-confidence in themselves and their abilities. They are able to have fun and laugh, and they experience and display a zest for life. They are able to cope with stress and can bounce back from the impacts of any adverse events they encounter. They feel a sense of contentment. They demonstrate flexibility for adapting to changes and learning new things. They are able to develop and sustain satisfying relationships. In both their relationships and their activities, they experience senses of purpose and meaning. In living their lives from day to day, they achieve a balance between opposites like activity and rest, work and play, waking and sleeping, exercising and eating, physical and mental activity, etc.

RESILIENCE

It is a normal part of life to experience **changes**; disappointments; losses; difficult times; and emotional problems that can provoke anxiety, sadness, and stress. While all people encounter these, some cope better than others. Some people experience a very traumatic event and never recover from it. Some suffer permanent damage, significantly impairing their ability to live normal lives. Others carry on, but with major impingements on their ability to participate in and enjoy life fully. **Resilience** is the ability to bounce back from stress, trauma, and other adverse experiences. People with good emotional and mental health have resilience. One component of resilience is having **personal tools** to keep a positive perspective and cope with difficulties. While some people begin developing these early in life, those who did not can still acquire them later with effort and help. Resilient individuals maintain focus, flexibility, and creativity through good and bad times. Additional components of resilience are stress management and emotional self-regulation skills. Being able to recognize our feelings and appropriately express them prevents becoming lodged in negative emotional states like anxiety or depression. Another component of resilience is a strong **network** of supportive people.

EFFECTS OF PHYSICAL HEALTH ON MENTAL AND EMOTIONAL HEALTH

The body and mind are interdependent and constantly interact. Better **physical health** automatically confers better **mental and emotional health**. For instance, when we exercise, we not only make our hearts and lungs stronger, but the activity also releases endorphins, i.e., neurotransmitters in the brain that relieve pain, elevate mood, energize, and promote euphoria or feelings of well-being. Physical health practices supporting mental and emotional health include adequate **sleep**, about 7-8 hours for most individuals. Learning about and practicing good **nutrition** is also important; it is complex and sometimes not simple to implement, but the more we learn about how what we eat affects mood as well as energy, strength, endurance, etc., the easier it can become to eat for physical and psychological health. **Exercise** not only promotes physical fitness; it powerfully relieves anxiety, depression, and stress. Restricting it to going to a gym is unnecessary: regularly incorporating physical activity into daily life, e.g., taking the stairs, walking more, etc. has enormous benefits. Ten to 15 minutes of sunshine daily improves mood (longer durations require sunscreen to prevent skin damage and cancer). Alcohol, tobacco, and other drugs may produce short-term good feelings, but long-term they impair mood and both mental and emotional health, and so should be avoided.

LIVING STRATEGIES TO SUPPORT MENTAL AND EMOTIONAL HEALTH

Attending to our own emotions and needs is necessary to mental and emotional health by preventing buildup of negative feelings and stress. Striking a balance between duties and enjoyable pursuits is important. **Self-care** enables better coping when encountering challenges. **Endorphins** (brain chemicals promoting well-being) are released not only by physical exercise and activity, but also by the following: helping or positively affecting others, which also enhances self-esteem; practicing self-control and discipline, which counters negative ideas, helplessness, and despair and promotes hope; discovering and learning new things—taking classes, learning languages, attending museums, traveling ("mind candy"); enjoying nature, e.g., walking paths through woods or gardens, sitting by a lake or on a beach, hiking, etc., which research proves not only releases endorphins but also lowers blood pressure and dissipates stress; enjoying art, e.g., art galleries, architecture, etc., which have the same effects; managing stress levels; and consciously avoiding absorption in mental habits like excessive worrying or negative thoughts about the world and/or oneself.

The following practices are strategies recommended to care for ourselves that promote good **mental and emotional health**: do things appealing to the senses, like listening to mood-elevating music; looking at beautiful scenes of nature, art and craft objects, and animals; looking at and smelling flowers; savoring the flavors and temperatures of foods and beverages; massaging one's hands and feet, or giving and receiving these to and from partners; scented baths; petting animals, etc. Adopt a pet. Though they incur responsibilities, caring for pets makes us feel loved and needed; pets give unconditional love, and some promote going outside, exercising, and finding new places and people. Do creative, meaningful work, for pay or not. Building things, playing musical instruments, composing music, drawing, painting, sculpture, pottery, writing, gardening, etc. stimulate creativity, engender feelings of productivity, and result in products we can feel proud of, enjoy, and share. Prioritizing leisure time is not self-indulgent; playing and doing enjoyable things for their own sake, e.g., reading, watching movies, visiting or talking with friends, or enjoying nature are necessary to mental and emotional health. Meditating, praying, reviewing reasons for gratitude, watching sunrises and sunsets, etc. are ways to take time to contemplate and appreciate life.

INFLUENCE OF SUPPORTIVE SOCIAL INTERACTIONS AND RELATIONSHIPS ON MENTAL AND EMOTIONAL HEALTH

Humans are naturally **social**, with emotional needs for connections and relationships with others. Improving mental and emotional health includes social as well as private activities. **Social interactions** provide companionship, intellectual stimulation and exchanges, intimacy, humor and laughter; talking to others about problems and feelings can decrease stress. People who are supportive and listen well without criticizing or judging benefit our psychological health; reciprocally, so do listening well to and supporting others. Some ways to engage in social interactions include: periodically walking away from the screens of our computers, tablets, smartphones, and TV sets for the real world to engage in face-to-face, direct interaction that includes nonverbal communication. Another strategy is to make it a priority to spend face-to-face time with friends, co-workers, neighbors, relatives, and other people that we like and enjoy, and who have positive attitudes and interest in us. When we meet people we like, we can make it a point to ask about them. Volunteering benefits both recipients and ourselves, expanding and enriching our lives. Many organizations rely on volunteers to function. Another way to meet potential friends is joining groups that share our interests and meet regularly.

RISK FACTORS THAT CAN THREATEN MENTAL AND EMOTIONAL HEALTH

Experiences in life, particularly in early childhood, influence mental and emotional health. While genetic and biological influences are involved, these interact with and are affected by **environmental experiences**. Some **risk factors** that can threaten mental and emotional health include: inadequate attachment to one's parent or primary caregiver in infancy or early childhood; feeling unsafe, isolated, lonely, confused, or abused early in life; serious traumas or losses, e.g., parent death, hospitalization, or war, particularly in early childhood; negative experiences whereby an individual develops learned helplessness, i.e., the belief that one has little or no control over the circumstances of one's life; serious illness, particularly disabling illness, chronic illness, or illness that isolates the individual from other people; medication side-effects, which can often become hazardous for older people taking multiple medications that interact unfavorably; and substance abuse. Abusing alcohol and/or other drugs can both exacerbate pre-existing mental health disorders, and cause new mental health or emotional problems.

WARNING SIGNALS THAT PROFESSIONAL HELP FOR EMOTIONAL OR MENTAL HEALTH PROBLEMS IS NEEDED

Some behaviors, feelings, or thoughts to pay attention to as signals to seek **professional help** for emotional or mental health problems include: you are unable to sleep, not just for one night but recurrently. You feel discouraged, sad, helpless, or hopeless a majority of the time. You have trouble concentrating, such that it interferes with work and/or life at home. You are using food, tobacco, alcohol, or other drugs to cope with problematic emotions. You are having negative or self-destructive thoughts or fears you cannot control. You think more often than normal about death and dying. You have thoughts about suicide. Even if you think these are only speculative and you would never act on them, any thoughts of suicide are serious warning signs. If you have consistently worked to improve your mental and emotional health without success, this is reason to pursue professional help. Our natural **human social orientation** makes us amenable to input from caring, knowledgeable professionals. Their knowledge, training, experience, expertise, perspective, techniques, advice, and counsel can help us do things we could not do on our own to help ourselves.

Stress, Depression, and Suicide

CONSERVATION OF RESOURCES THEORY

Conservation of resources (**COR**) theory (Hobfoll, 1988, 1989, 1998, 2001) views the main element in stress as **resource loss**. People lose resource and also use additional resources during stress. Hence throughout the process, they accumulate greater susceptibility to **negative stress impacts**. While many theorists view stress as either environmental/external or psychological/internal, COR is an integrative theory equally incorporating both orientations. Its essential premise is that people endeavor to get, keep, cultivate, and protect things they value. To combat perceived environmental threat, they need a combination of cultural belonging, social attachments, and personal strengths. These attributes are **resources**: energy, condition, personal characteristic, and object resources. They are both cultural products and cross-cultural in nature. When individuals lose resources, resource loss is threatened, or individuals invest significant resources without gaining resources, stress ensues. COR theory principles are: (1) resource loss is disproportionately more impactful than resource gain. (2) To prevent resource loss, recover from loss, and gain resources, people must invest resources. Proactive coping and positive stress outcomes are also aspects considered in COR theory.

Two **conservation of resources (COR) theory principles** are: losing resources has disproportionately more impact than gaining resources; and people have to invest resources to prevent losing them, recover from losing them, and acquire additional resources. There are also four corollaries to these principles. **Corollary 1**: those with more resources are more able to gain and less vulnerable to lose resources; conversely, those with fewer resources are less able to gain and more likely to lose resources. **Corollary 2**: initial loss causes future loss. **Corollary 3**: initial gain causes additional gain. **Corollary 4**: lacking resources engenders defensive responses of conserving what resources one does possess. One example of a **loss spiral** is in research (Lane & Hobfoll, 1992) with people suffering chronic obstructive pulmonary disease (COPD). They experienced a series of increasing resource losses. The more resources they lost, the angrier they became. The angrier they became, the more they alienated possible support givers, increasing their resource loss vulnerability. Another study (Rini et al, 1999) reported lower self-esteem, mastery, and optimism—i.e., personal resources—in lower-income, less-educated Hispanic mothers-to-be, causing greater stress, which caused major infant risk factors of shorter gestation and low birth weights—predicting greater ongoing resource demands and stress.

STRESS MANAGEMENT AND COMMON UNHEALTHY REACTIONS TO LIFE STRESSORS

Stress is inevitable; however, effective **stress management skills and techniques** enable healthy coping. According to the Mayo Clinic, individuals begin stress management by understanding how they currently react to stress, and then adopting new stress management techniques or modifying existing ones to keep life stressors from leading to health issues. There are several unhealthy but common reactions to stress:

- **Pain**: internalized or unresolved stress can trigger headaches, backaches, upset stomachs, shortness of breath, insomnia, and muscular pain from unconsciously tensing the shoulders and neck and/or clenching jaws or fists.
- **Eating and/or activity**: some people skip eating from stress, thereby losing weight; others overeat or eat when not hungry and/or skip exercise, gaining weight.
- **Anger**: some people lose their tempers more easily over minor or unrelated things when stressed.
- **Crying**: some people cry over minor or unrelated things when stressed; experience unexpected, prolonged crying; and/or feel isolated and lonely.

- **Depression and anxiety**: stress can contribute to depressive and anxiety disorders, including problem avoidance, calling in sick, feeling hopeless, or giving up.
- **Negativity**: individuals not coping effectively with stress may exaggerate the negative qualities of undesired circumstances and/or always expect the worst.
- **Smoking and/or substance use**: people may escalate current smoking, drinking, or drug use under stress; those who had previously quit may relapse.

STRESS MANAGEMENT TECHNIQUES

- **Cut back**: when overextended, examine duties and delegate, eliminate, or limit some.
- **Prepare**: set realistic goals for major and minor tasks; improve scheduling; allow time for unexpected events like traffic jams, car trouble, minor medical emergencies, extra work, etc. to prevent stress from accumulating.
- **Reach out**: revisit lapsed relationships; form new ones; volunteer. Surrounding oneself with supportive friends, relatives, colleagues, and spiritual leaders enhances psychological well-being, boosting capacity for coping with stress.
- **Hobbies**: enjoyable activities that do not stimulate competitiveness or anxiety are soothing. These vary individually. Some choices include crafts, music, reading, dance classes, gardening, woodworking and carpentry, electronics, fishing, sailing, etc.
- **Relaxation techniques**: these include meditation, yoga, massage therapy, physical activities, etc. The technique selected is less important than increasing body awareness and refocusing attention onto calmness.
- **Adequate sleep**: lack of sleep exacerbates stress. Insufficient sleep impairs judgment and the immune system. Sleep-deprived individuals are more prone to overreacting to minor irritants. Most of us require eight hours of sleep nightly. Interrupted or irregular sleep impedes REM sleep, dreaming, and deep sleep-enabling physical and neurological repairs.
- **Professional help**: if stress management techniques are insufficient, see a physician before uncontrolled, ongoing stress causes health problems.

LIFE SKILLS TO USE FOR STRESS MANAGEMENT AND STRESSFUL LIFE EVENTS DURING LIFE STAGES

Four major life skills that people can apply to cope with common life stressors are values clarification, decision-making, communication skills, and coping skills. The following are typical life stressors in early childhood, adolescence, middle adulthood, and later adulthood; and coping mechanisms they can apply from the life skill perspective of **values clarification**.

- Early childhood: a pet's death – according to values clarification, reviewing the pet's **positive qualities** (similarly to adults' celebrating the life of the deceased) and considering getting another pet can address stressors.
- Adolescence: unwanted pregnancy – discussing **feasible alternatives** and their ramifications for the teen, unborn baby, family, and society is not only required to make decisions, but also provides positive coping.
- Middle adulthood: divorce – evaluating its **impact** on the couple and their relatives and friends; and the roles played by marital status, social expectations outside home, and religion inform values clarification coping mechanisms.
- Later adulthood: retirement – when people retiring from careers or employment view retirement in terms of their **values**, this can facilitate their ability to choose feasible options for post-retirement living.

Among life skills that enable coping with the stress of common life events are values clarification, decision-making, communication skills, and coping skills. Common stressors in four life stages follow, accompanied by coping mechanisms utilizing the **decision-making** life skill.

- Early childhood: a pet's death – helping the child discuss the **pros and cons** of each alternative for disposing of the pet's remains is a decision-making-oriented way to cope with the loss.
- Adolescence: unwanted pregnancy – careful consideration and evaluation of such **alternatives** as abortion; carrying the baby to term and surrendering it for adoption (and open or closed, public or private adoption, etc.); carrying to term and keeping the baby, etc. are necessary decisions to make and cope proactively with stressors. Decisions about future birth-control methods are also indicated.
- Middle adulthood: divorce – from the decision-making perspective, considering alternatives, risks, and consequences and making **choices** among career options, life roles, and future social relationships have major impacts on post-divorce living.
- Later adulthood: retirement – the decision-making life skill enables the retiree to consider **alternatives** and their advantages and disadvantages, e.g., not retiring, pursuing leisure activities, embarking on a second career, volunteering, realizing a long-deferred dream, etc.

Four major life skills are values clarification, decision-making, communication skills, and coping skills. Examples of common stressors in each life stage, plus ways to cope using **communication skills**, follow.

- Early childhood: a pet's death – when a child feels sadness and anxiety over the loss, encouraging the child to **communicate** his or her feelings and thoughts can mediate psychic distress.
- Adolescence: unwanted pregnancy – teenage mothers need support from various sources including family, friends, counselors, educators, and health professionals. Effectively utilizing communication skills enables them to know how, where, and from whom to **solicit help and advice** to cope with their situation.
- Middle adulthood: divorce – adults undergoing divorces often have to assume various new life roles, including some that their former spouses may always have addressed. As a part of the process of divorce, adults need to apply communication skills to seek out **supportive friends, relatives, and professionals** as they establish and adjust to these new roles and experiences.
- Later adulthood: retirement – when older adults retire, they may lose some of their autonomy. Using communication skills assertively can help them maintain their **independence**.

Four life skills for coping with stressors are values clarification, decision-making, communication skills, and coping skills. Following are stressors common in each of four life stages, and corresponding coping methods associated with the **coping skills** portion of stress management.

- Early childhood: a pet's death – children can emerge from early loss experiences to discover personal abilities and strengths. From the coping skills perspective, they can prevent normal grief becoming depression through **developing aptitudes and interests**.
- Adolescence: unwanted pregnancy – before and after processes of values clarification and decision-making, teen mothers should examine their personal response to pregnancy for its **significance** in the context of their life.

- Middle adulthood: divorce – it is not unusual for adults to experience lowered self-concept and self-esteem during and after divorce. From the coping skills perspective, the individual can cope better with the stressor of divorce through engaging in behaviors that **enhance self-esteem and self-concept**. Personal and/or professional activities that affirm or reaffirm one's skills, talents, abilities, accomplishments, and sense of self facilitate coping.
- Later adulthood: retirement – retirees often encounter changing responsibilities and roles. Physical activity and exercise, hobbies, social activities, traveling, etc. are **positive coping behaviors** to enhance post-retirement life.

Human Sexuality

ADVISING STUDENTS ABOUT WAYS UNPROTECTED SEX CAN CAUSE UNWANTED PREGNANCY, AND PREGNANCY PREVENTION

Some teens may not know how **pregnancy** occurs; others may believe it can only happen when a male ejaculates inside a female's vagina. However, a few drops of pre-ejaculate released before and during sex, which can be almost undetectable, also contains sperm. Though the probability of conception from this small amount is lower, it is still possible. Though less common, conception can also result from semen on the vulva without penetration. Males cannot control pre-ejaculate release; therefore, they should be advised to put on a condom *before*, and wear it continuously during, sex. Though the point is not to encourage sex among immature students, educators can inform those harboring misunderstandings that kissing, body rubbing, masturbating, and oral and anal sex cannot cause pregnancy without vaginal or vulvar contact with sperm; and that abstaining from sex, or using both a condom and birth control continuously during sex, are the ways of preventing pregnancy. Teen couples contemplating sex should discuss birth control with each other and a parent or trusted adult, and see a physician, nurse, or healthcare provider.

INFORMATION TO GIVE STUDENTS ABOUT STIS

Over half of Americans contract an **STI** during their lives. Practicing **safer sex** can include using condoms, having strictly monogamous sex, and engaging in sexual activities that do not transmit STIs. Vaginal and anal intercourse are high-risk activities. Without condoms, they are likely to transmit chancroid, chlamydia, cytomegalovirus (CMV), genital warts, gonorrhea, hepatitis B, herpes, HIV, human papilloma virus (HPV), molluscum contagiosum virus, pelvic inflammatory disease (PID), pubic lice ("crabs"), scabies, syphilis, and trichomoniasis. Unprotected oral sex is high-risk for transmitting CMV, gonorrhea, hepatitis B, herpes, syphilis, and HPV. Skin-to-skin contact without intercourse is risky for transmitting CMV, herpes, HPV, molluscum contagiosum, pubic lice, and scabies. Many STIDs are often asymptomatic.

RAPE

An estimated 80-90 percent of **rapes** go unreported. Recent trends project one-third of American women will be assaulted sexually in life. Typical assailants usually choose women of their race, and at least casually know victims almost half the time from living or working near them. Over one-third of rapes involve alcohol. Over half happen in victims' homes, via break-ins or entry by false pretenses. Expressed via sex, rape is primarily violent, not sexual. Prostitutes and prisoners with reduced credibility, those with limited language or disabilities who cannot call for help, and those facing discrimination are more vulnerable. **Prevention** includes locking doors and windows in homes and cars; checking car backseats before entering; parking in well-lit, open areas; not jogging or walking in isolated or secluded areas at night or when alone; displaying confidence, security, awareness, and strength in surroundings; sitting near drivers or in the front in public transportation; avoiding proximity to young male groups; self-defense training; carrying personal alarms or whistles; screaming loudly or blowing whistles if assaulted; actively resisting attacks and not being passive; and not hitchhiking. PTSD is a common complication. Over half of rape victims have difficulty re-establishing existing relationships or establishing new ones. Victims should avoid urinating, changing clothes, bathing, or douching pre-ER to preserve evidence; should be allowed to interview dressed, not hospital-gowned; and not left alone unless desired. **Treatment** includes examining for and addressing STIs, pregnancy, and physical injury; and providing emotional support.

DEVELOPMENT OF FEMALE REPRODUCTIVE SYSTEM

Because females do not have a Y-chromosome, during embryonic and fetal development they are not affected by **testosterone** to develop male reproductive organs. Without testosterone stimulation, reproductive organs develop into ovaries, a uterus, and other female organs. Most internal female organs are formed by the end of the first trimester. Immature eggs (ova) form in the ovaries in utero; all of a female's eggs are produced before birth. Female infants are born with all **reproductive organs** formed, but immature and not functional. These do not grow much in childhood, but rapidly mature and grow during puberty. Girls typically start **puberty** one or two years before boys; and take around four years to complete, whereas boys take around six years. The primary female sex hormone is **estrogen**. In the brain, the hypothalamus stimulates the pituitary gland to secrete **luteinizing hormone (LH)** and **follicle-stimulating hormone (FSH)**, which stimulate the ovary to produce estrogen. (The same hormones stimulate the testes' testosterone production in males.) Estrogen stimulates uterus and breast growth; pubic hair growth; bone development; the adolescent growth spurt, which begins and ends earlier than in males; and menarche (menstrual cycle onset).

GROWTH AND DEVELOPMENT OF HUMAN MALE REPRODUCTIVE SYSTEM

While a male fetus develops in utero, the **testes** begin to develop. Around two months before birth, the testes begin descending into the scrotal sacs outside of the main body cavity, allowing slightly lower temperatures aiding sperm production. The testes additionally produce hormones enabling development of secondary male sex characteristics. **Puberty** activates an increase in brain hormones, triggering the pituitary gland's increased production and release into the bloodstream of **luteinizing hormone (LH)** and **follicle-stimulating hormone (FSH)**. In the bloodstream, LH stimulates testes cells to produce and release **testosterone**, which enlarges and develops the penis and other sex organs, promotes skeletal and muscular growth, and deepens the voice. Testosterone and FSH stimulate **sperm production** in seminiferous tubules within the testes. Each sperm cell takes 65-75 days to form; about 300 million are produced daily, stored in the epididymis, wherefrom the vas deferens carries sperm through the prostate gland below the bladder to the urethra. The male urethra releases both sperm and urine. The prostate gland and seminal vesicles—accessory sex glands—produce specialized fluids, mixing with sperm during transport, creating **semen** which exits from the urethra through the penis during ejaculation.

INFLUENCE OF MEDIA MESSAGES ON ADOLESCENT SEXUALITY

Researchers find that, although any age group can be influenced by sexual media content, teens can be especially vulnerable to **media messages**. Adolescence is a developmental time when individuals are forming their sexual attitudes, behaviors, and gender roles. Teenagers have recently developed the ability to think abstractly and critically; however, their **cognitive skills** are still not completely developed for critical analysis of media messages and decision-making that takes into account future potential consequences. This places them at higher risk for **media influence**. Researchers have found (Gruber, 2000) that teens viewed an average of 143 instances of sexual behavior on TV weekly during prime time. Activities between unmarried partners were depicted three to four times more often than between spouses. Network and cable TV channels show movies, an estimated 80 percent of which include sexual content. Researchers analysis of music videos estimated that 60 percent included sexual impulses and feelings. Sexual TV messages are found to be nearly always presented in positive terms, with scarce treatment of negative consequences or risks of unprotected sex. High school students have reported substantial access to and viewing of TV and video. Over 80 percent of teens report peer discovery about sex from entertainment media.

RESEARCH FINDINGS ABOUT ADOLESCENT SEXUAL ATTITUDES AND BEHAVIORS

Various studies find teens' sexual attitudes influenced by variables including their parents' attitudes regarding teen sex, religiosity, the media, bonding in school relationships, and adolescents' perceptions of social norms among their peers. According to some experts, such research demonstrates the necessity of considering the wide range of **sexual attitudes** teenagers consider. Warning of **negative consequences** is insufficient; adults must provide **information** enabling teens to weigh positive and negative aspects of both engaging in and abstaining from sex to make their own best decisions as they mature and develop physically, intellectually, emotionally, and socially. While many models of teen risk behaviors emphasize perceptions of possible consequences in decision-making, studies also find positive motivations for having sex. Some investigators found teens valued sexual goals and expectations of intimacy, then social status, then pleasure in that order; but then expected sex to result in pleasure, then intimacy, then social status in that order. Male adolescents valued pleasure more; females valued intimacy more. The National Adolescent and Young Adult Health Information Center (NAHIC, 2007) found almost half of high school students reported having sex. CDC's Youth Risk Behavior Surveillance (YRBS, 2008) found sexual intercourse most prevalent in black, then Hispanic, then white, then Asian teens.

SIGNIFICANT ASPECTS OF THE STAGES OF PREGNANCY

In the **first trimester**, a zygote transforms into an implanted embryo; organs, hair follicles, nail beds, muscles, white blood cells, and vocal cords form; and the baby starts moving around week eight. While pregnancy does not show externally, mothers awash in **pregnancy hormones** feel many symptoms. However, every woman and pregnancy are different; no two necessarily have the same symptoms, but most diminish further into pregnancy (though others develop). During the **second trimester**, babies grow hair; begin sucking and swallowing; and their eyes and ears reposition. They have fingerprints and can hiccup and yawn by week 18. Their limbs are coordinated and their senses develop by week 21. Weight gain, capillary formation, and opening eyes occur by six months. By seven months, fetal weight doubles to two pounds. Babies perceive light and dark, taste what mothers eat, and hear their voices by week 31. Transparent skin becomes opaque by week 32; length may increase an inch during week 33. Weight reaches around six pounds by week 36; waxy vernix and hairy lanugo shed in week 38. By week 40, fetal weight is 6-9 pounds, length 19-22 inches; babies dream, blink, and regulate their body temperatures.

HUMAN LABOR AND CHILDBIRTH

In late pregnancy, symptoms can mask labor signs, or some contractions can be false labor. If contractions persist, become stronger, last longer, and occur closer together, this usually indicates **labor**. The "411" method is one way to judge: contractions 4 minutes apart, lasting 1 minute each, continuing for at least 1 hour. Labor's **first stage** is typically the longest, marked by contractions and gradual cervical dilation. The first stage has three phases: the **early phase**, usually comfortable, with contractions 20 minutes apart progressing to 5 minutes apart. The second, **active phase** generally involves 1-minute contractions every 4-5 minutes. The third, **transition phase** is among the shortest (1-2 hours) but hardest. Contractions are 2-3 minutes apart; some women shake and may vomit. This phase ends with complete dilation. Some women temporarily cease contractions but feel no need to push. Labor's **second stage** involves a need to push. It can last 3+ hours, but often less. Contractions spread out again to around every 4 minutes. This stage culminates in **childbirth**. Then the mother must push out the **placenta**; nursing the newborn aids uterine contractions to expel it. The fourth labor stage is **postpartum**.

CONTRACEPTION METHODS

Some young (or uninformed older) people assume **condoms** worn by males are sufficient for **contraception**. However, condoms can break, leak, or slip off during or following intercourse. Ideally, foam, gel, or other spermicide should accompany condoms. Female contraception includes IUDs, diaphragms, and birth control pills. **IUDs** are typically inserted by physicians and worn continuously. They can periodically require removal and replacement. While effective, they can have undesirable side-effects for some women including irritation, inflammation, cramping, spotting, tissue damage, etc. **Diaphragms** are typically self-inserted by women before intercourse, often with spermicidal gel applied to the surface, and removed afterward. They are also effective, but some women have difficulty inserting them properly and/or cannot tolerate their presence. They can also sometimes shift position, impeding contraception. **Birth control pills** are very effective, though a very small percentage of women using them might still get pregnant. Oral hormones cause some women undesirable side effects like weight gain and symptoms resembling pregnancy. Lower-dose pills have fewer side effects; different dosages affect individual women differently. More extreme measures include **tubal ligation** (reversible but not always) and **hysterectomy** (irreversible) for women, and **vasectomy** (reversible but not always) for men.

HIV/AIDS

The first known case of **human immunodeficiency virus/acquired immunodeficiency syndrome (HIV/AIDS)** occurred in 1951 in the Congo, but the first U.S. case occurred in 1981. Dr. Robert Gallo of the National Cancer Institute identified the cause in 1984. The first cases were in the gay population, resulting in the disease being initially labeled a "gay disease," although it later became clear that it was not limited to gays. AIDS resulted in the deaths of millions of people worldwide before the first Food and Drug Administration (FDA)-approved treatment was available in 1995. By 2002, home testing kits were available. Currently, although males having sex with males are most at risk and African American have the highest rate of racial groups, HIV/AIDS affects all populations, races, and socioeconomic groups with about 50,000 new infections in the United States each year. About 25% of cases are female, and 25% are older than age 50. Modes of transmission include oral, anal, and vaginal sex as well as the sharing of needles and contact with infected blood, semen, vaginal fluids, and breast milk.

PREVENTION AND TREATMENT

Treatment for HIV/AIDS should begin with **diagnosis** and includes medication management, mental health counseling, and supportive and social care as needed. The first step after diagnosis is to undergo a number of **laboratory tests** to determine the viral load and CD4 count (measures the CD4 T lymphocytes to determine the strength of the immune system). Although **antiretroviral therapy (ART)** does not cure HIV/AIDS, it can slow the progression. Six classes of drugs are currently used to treat HIV with initial treatment usually involving three drugs from at least two different drug classes. Several drug regimens are available, depending on the patient's condition, drug resistance, and comorbid diseases. **HIV/AIDS prevention** includes universal testing, needle exchange programs, sex education, consistent and correct use of latex condoms, substance abuse prevention, and treatment programs. Individuals should understand that risk increases with multiple sexual partners, and males having sex with males are particularly at risk.

Conflict Resolution and Violence Avoidance

CONFLICT IN RELATIONSHIPS

Many people try to avoid **conflict** at all costs because they find it unpleasant and feel threatened by **confrontation**. However, conflict is normal and integral to healthy relationships. Its source is differences between and among people, whether major or minor. No two (or more) people can agree about everything 100 percent of the time. Anytime that people disagree, conflict results. Though some disagreements seem unimportant, any conflict that evokes strong emotions indicates some deep personal need at its core—e.g., to be valued or respected, to be closer or more intimate, or to feel safety or security. As one example, young children need to explore and take risks to learn and develop normally, while parents need to protect children's safety, and this can present a child-parent conflict. Conflicts in **personal relationships** can cause discord and even end them when members do not understand each other's different needs. Conflicts in **workplaces** can ruin deals, lower profits, and end jobs. Acknowledging needs that conflict, and a willingness to examine them in understanding, compassionate environments enable team-building and creative problem-solving. Both avoiding and mismanaging conflict can damage relationships, but positive and respectful conflict management can improve them.

CHARACTERISTICS OF CONFLICT PEOPLE NEED TO KNOW IN ORDER TO RESOLVE THEM

According to experts, a **conflict** is not simply a disagreement, but a situation wherein both or either party perceives a real or imagined **threat**. Because such perceived threats are to people's survival and well-being, conflicts continue; ignoring them does not make them go away. **Confronting** and **resolving** conflicts stop them from going on indefinitely, or until the relationship ends. People do not necessarily (or usually) respond to conflicts based on objectively considering the facts, they react to them based on their personal values, beliefs, cultural backgrounds, and life experiences. Hence individual reactions to conflict are according to individual perceptions of the situation. Conflicts naturally provoke strong feelings. Therefore, people who cannot manage their emotions under stress or who are uncomfortable with them will be unable to succeed at resolving conflicts. Another characteristic of conflicts is that they present opportunities for **growth**. When members of a relationship succeed at resolving interpersonal conflict, they build **trust** between themselves. They gain direct experience that their relationship can withstand disagreements and challenges. This proof enables them to feel more secure about their relationship's existence and future.

UNHEALTHY VS. HEALTHY WAYS OF RESPONDING TO, MANAGING, AND RESOLVING CONFLICT

When conflict inevitably arises, one **unhealthy** reaction is being unable to recognize and respond to things that are most important to the other person. A **healthier** response is being able to identify and address things that matter most to another. Emotional reactions that are resentful, angry, explosive, or designed to hurt the other person's feelings are unhealthy. Healthier responses involve staying calm, not becoming defensive, and showing respect for the other person. When one person reacts to conflict by rejecting the other, withdrawing his/her affection, isolating himself/herself, saying or doing things to shame the other, or showing or expressing fears of being abandoned, these are unhealthy reactions. Healthier responses are being willing to forgive the other person; forget undesirable reactions, words and deeds; and progress beyond the conflict without retaining anger or resentment. Being unable to see the other person's viewpoint or make any compromises is unhealthy; being able to compromise instead of punishing the other person is healthier. Fearing and avoiding conflict due to expected negative outcomes is unhealthy; believing in the mutual benefit of confronting conflict head-on is healthier.

EFFECTS OF STRESS

Excessive stress and/or not coping effectively with stress impede the ability to understand other people's nonverbal communications. **Stress** interferes with people's ability to hear what another person is really saying, to be aware of and in touch with their own emotions, and to connect with their deepest personal needs. Moreover, being affected by stress makes a person much less able to **communicate** his or her own needs clearly. These abilities are all required for positively resolving conflict, so when stress interferes with them, it interferes with conflict resolution. Some people become so habituated to stress that they lose recognition of it. Some ways to identify if it is a problem in life are to observe whether conflict preoccupies their attention and time, whether they cannot feel movement in their chests or stomachs while breathing, and/or whether they often feel tightness or tension in certain body parts. Excessive stress limits how many emotions one can attend to, preventing understanding and thus communicating one's needs. Hence stress interferes with **emotional awareness**, which interferes with communicating problems and resolving conflicts.

DOMESTIC VIOLENCE

Domestic violence is domestic or spousal abuse, wherein one relationship partner dominates and controls another, that incorporates physical violence. Some **violent behaviors** include having an unpredictable, bad temper; harming, threatening harm, or threatening to kill the partner; threatening to hurt or take children; threatening suicide if the partner leaves; forcing sex; and destroying the partner's belongings. **Manipulative power tactics** abusers employ include: dominance, humiliation, isolation, threats, intimidation, denial, and blame. The cycle of domestic violence follows a common **pattern**: one partner abuses the other with violent behavior to exhibit dominance. The partner appears guilty, but really fears being caught and punished rather than feeling remorse. The abuser avoids responsibility by making excuses for the violent behavior, rationalizing it, and/or blaming the other partner for it. The abuser, trying to keep the victim in the relationship and regain control, behaves contritely, "normally," or with great affection and/or charm, often fooling the victim into hoping s/he has changed or will change. The abuser fantasizes and plans further abuse to make the victim pay for perceived wrongs. The abuser then places the victim in a situation to justify further abuse, and the cycle repeats all over again.

Family Relationships

RELATIONSHIP PATTERNS IN MURRAY BOWEN'S FAMILY SYSTEMS THEORY

MARITAL CONFLICT

Bowen's concept of the nuclear family emotional system consists of four basic relationship patterns that determine where family problems develop. Clinical symptoms or problems typically emerge during times of intensified and protracted tension in a family. Stress levels, family adaptations to stress, and family connections with extended family and social support networks determine tension levels. In the **marital conflict pattern**, spouses project their increasing anxiety into the marital relationship. Each partner becomes preoccupied with the other's shortcomings, tries to control him or her, and resists being controlled. For example, a couple with a young child conceives a second child. The wife becomes anxious about meeting two children's needs. The husband questions his wife's ability to cope in order to avoid facing his own anxieties. After the second child's birth, the husband, observing his wife's stress, helps out more at home and is more controlling of her. He starts to feel neglected and disappointed in his wife's inadequate coping. The wife, who used to drink but quit while pregnant, resumes drinking.

DYSFUNCTION IN ONE SPOUSE

In Bowen theory, the relationship pattern of **dysfunction in one spouse** involves one partner pressuring the other to behave in certain ways, and the other acceding to that pressure. While both partners accommodate for maintaining harmony, eventually one does more than the other. Both are comfortable with this interaction for some time; however, if family tensions increase, the subordinate partner gives up enough self-control, yielding to the dominant partner to become significantly more anxious. Combined with other factors, this **anxiety** contributes to a psychiatric, social, or medical problem. For example, a couple with one young child has a second child. In the relationship pattern of marital conflict, the husband projects his own anxiety into criticizing his wife's coping abilities, taking on more household duties, and controlling her while the wife addresses her anxiety by drinking. The husband accuses her of selfishness and lack of effort. She agrees with but resents his criticism, feeling more dependent on him. Feeling increasingly unable to cope and make decisions, she escalates her drinking. He calls her an alcoholic. The wife becomes increasingly under-functional, the husband increasingly over-functional, functioning for her—all in an effort to avoid direct conflict and maintain harmony.

IMPAIRMENT OF ONE OR MORE CHILDREN

In the pattern of impairment of a child or children, parents project their own anxieties onto their child/children. They view the child **unrealistically**—either negatively or idealistically. The child **reciprocates** excessive parental focus by focusing excessively on the parents, overreacting to parental expectations, needs, and attitudes. This undermines the child's differentiation of self from family, increasing his or her susceptibility to either internalizing or acting out family tensions. **Anxiety** can disrupt the child's social relationships, school progress, and health. For example, a couple with one young child has another baby. Anxieties over the added stress of raising another child cause marital conflict and a dysfunctional relationship, developing into greater dysfunction in one spouse or parent. This causes emotional distance between spouses, who focus anxiously on the older child. She reacts by regressing, making immature demands of the parents, especially her mother. The mother externalizes her anxiety onto the child, worrying the new baby will displace her, acceding increasingly to her demands. The father avoids conflict with his wife by supporting her focus on the child, relieving her by giving the child attention when he gets home from work. Parents and child unwittingly conspire in seeing and creating **dysfunction in the child**.

EMOTIONAL DISTANCE

In Bowen's family systems theory, the four basic relationship patterns are marital conflict, spousal dysfunction, child impairment, and emotional distance. Whichever pattern predominates will dictate which family members will manifest familial tensions by developing psychological, social, or medical symptoms. The pattern of **emotional distance** consistently occurs in relation to the other three patterns. When interactions between family members become too intense, they develop emotional distance to decrease intensity. However, the drawbacks of emotional distance are that distanced members can become overly isolated, and can lose intimacy in their relationship. For example, when a couple with one child has another baby, they first project their anxieties onto each other and experience marital conflict. They then withdraw from one another emotionally to reduce the intensity of the conflict. They react to the emotional distance between them by externalizing their anxieties onto the first child, worrying she will feel left out with the new baby. The child reacts to the obsessive parental emotional over-involvement with her, reciprocating their emotional focus and overreacting to real or imagined parental withdrawal—creating impairment of a child. Thus, emotional distance **interacts** with the other patterns.

INFLUENCE OF SOCIOECONOMIC AND HEALTH VARIABLES ON PARENT-ADULT CHILD RELATIONSHIPS

Some sociological researchers investigating relationships of parents in their mid-50s to mid-70s with their adult children found **intergenerational exchanges** were characterized by strong **reciprocity** in both the United States and Great Britain. Contrary to stereotypical views of elderly adults becoming "burdens" on adult children, researchers have seen instead that married parents who gave help and support to at least one adult child were twice as likely to receive support from another adult child as parents who did not provide such support. Investigations showed when researchers controlled for various other parent and child variables, parents who owned homes, had higher incomes, and were married or widowed were more likely to help adult children than divorced parents. Conversely, parents with homes and higher incomes were less likely to receive help from adult children. Parental disability and advanced age **correlated positively** with adult children's responding to parent needs. Investigators inferred socioeconomic variations in support exchange balances between parents and adult children. Researchers predicted in 2005 that demographic trends would likely increase adult children's demands for support from older parents in the future.

TALKING ABOUT PROCREATION WITH CHILDREN

Many parents feel squeamish about "The Talk" or discussing "the birds and bees" with their maturing children. This is not just discomfort over an intimate topic; parents frequently fear that discussing sex with preadolescent and adolescent children is akin to giving them **permission** to engage in it. However, research studies find the opposite is true: teens are more prone to sexual behaviors when their parents have *not* talked about sex with them. When uninformed of possible **consequences**, they are more likely to act, not knowing of any disadvantages; they may experiment to get knowledge their parents have not imparted; and/or sexual behavior may be a reaction against parental avoidance and lack of openness. Communications researchers say sex is a continuing, two-way conversation that starts when very young children see pregnant women and ask questions. They advise parents to use Socratic questions, e.g., "What do you think the right time is for having sex?" and sharing their own thoughts after children do. **Open, receptive attitudes** are critical: if children bring up sex and perceive avoidant or shocked parental reactions, they will stop approaching parents, shutting down this vital conversation.

ROLES AND RESPONSIBILITIES OF EFFECTIVE PARENTING
RESPONSIBILITIES

Effective parenting includes ensuring the safety and well-being of one's children by providing adequate shelter and food as well as the following:

- **Helping the child build self-esteem**: Encouraging the child to become self-sufficient and demonstrate skills.
- **Providing positive reinforcement**: Recognizing and rewarding the child for doing something right rather than focusing on negatives.
- **Setting limits**: Establishing reasonable rules and discipline.
- **Providing consistent discipline**: Following through by providing consequences.
- **Spending quality time with the child**: Engaging one on one with the child. Scheduling activities and time together and being available when the child wants to talk or interact.
- **Providing a good role model**: Modeling the type of behavior that is expected of the child.
- **Communicating with the child**: Being open, honest, and willing to listen and stating expectations directly.
- **Exhibiting flexibility in the parenting role**: Recognizing that children have different needs at different times in their lives and allowing the child to have increasing autonomy with age.
- Providing unconditional love and support: Being nurturing and kind.

DISCIPLINE

Parents use a number of different approaches to discipline adolescents:

Strategy	Parent action
Behavior modification	Uses positive reinforcement to encourage appropriate behavior and ignores inappropriate behavior.
Consequences	Inappropriate behavior results in a consequence, such as losing privileges or a specified punishment.
Corporal punishment	Spanks or otherwise inflicts pain on the adolescent to force appropriate behavior but may have serious negative impacts on self-esteem of adolescent and, in some cases, may cause injury.
Scolding	Uses harsh, often loud, language to express unhappiness with an adolescent's behavior.
Time-out	Uses a specified period of time-out away from activities or time-out from phone, Internet, or other desired activity.
Reasoning	Discusses problem behavior and the reason that it is not appropriate.

PROMOTING GOOD BEHAVIOR

Discipline entails more than punishing or correcting inappropriate behavior. A good parent also uses strategies to **promote good behavior**. Strategies include the following:

- Being realistic about what the adolescent can do and understand, depending on the child's age and maturity level.
- Modeling appropriate behavior.
- Discussing appropriate behavior in new situations, such as before a family event or an outing.
- Attending to inappropriate behavior immediately, including discussion of more appropriate actions.

- Reprimanding the adolescent for bad behavior and not for being a bad person.
- Anticipating circumstances that may encourage inappropriate behavior, such as when the adolescent is stressed or tired.
- Providing reminders to help the adolescent control his/her own behavior.
- Providing rationale for appropriate behavior in accordance to the adolescent's ability to understand.
- Helping the adolescent to understand that different situations require different standards of behavior and language, such as partying with friends as opposed to attending a wedding.

Interpersonal Relationships

BIG FIVE THEORY OF PERSONALITY TRAITS

In a very popular theory developed by a series of researchers (Fiske, 1949; Norman, 1967; Smith, 1967; Goldberg, 1981; McCrae & Costa, 1987; Costa & McCrae, 1994, etc.), the **Big Five universal personality traits** are extraversion, agreeableness, conscientiousness, neuroticism, and openness. **Extraversion** is characterized by sociability, assertiveness, emotional expressivity, talkativeness, and excitability. **Agreeableness** features affection, kindness, trust, altruism, and similar prosocial behaviors. **Conscientiousness** includes organization, detail-orientation, goal-directed behaviors, good impulse control and thoughtfulness. **Neuroticism** includes anxiety, irritability, moodiness, emotional instability, and sadness. **Openness** has characteristics of broad interests, insight, and imagination. Each trait is a continuum, with individuals demonstrating various degrees of each trait between two extremes, e.g., between extreme extraversion and extreme introversion. Some researchers examining the interaction of personality traits with young adult social relationships have found that, while personality traits predict numbers and qualities of peer relationships, relationships do not reciprocally predict personality traits. Also, major relationship changes do not affect personality traits. Extraversion, agreeableness and conscientiousness affected quality and number of social relationships. Longitudinal study found agreeableness influenced later but not initial peer conflict; and conscientiousness influenced later but not initial family contact. Personality traits are more stable than relationship characteristics.

INFLUENCE OF SOCIAL CONTEXT FACTORS ON CHILDREN'S PEER RELATIONSHIPS

In studying the peer interactions of children with **attention deficit hyperactivity disorder (ADHD)**, multiple researchers have found peers dislike children with ADHD within hours of first meeting them, across situations and over time; and ADHD plus peer difficulties cumulatively predict **adolescent psychopathology**. These collected findings indicate serious social problems for ADHD populations. One social context factor is **parental influence**. Though disruptive ADHD behaviors cause conflict in parent-child relationships, one lead investigator (Mikami et al, 2010), questioning whether these parenting problems then also worsened children's peer conflicts, found parents indeed more critical of their ADHD children and less likely than other parents to have strong support networks—even after controlling for disruptive child behaviors. While parental warmth toward children, skilled adult-adult interactions, and modeling and coaching of children's peer interactions normally correlate with children's acceptance by peers, both parental criticism and—unexpectedly—praise predicted ADHD children's *poorer* peer interactions (again, after controlling for disruptive behaviors). Possible influences include parental ADHD; peer observations of parent-child interactions; and effects of parent-child relationships on the accuracy of children's self-perceptions of peer competence.

SOCIAL CONTEXT FACTOR OF TEACHER INFLUENCES OF PEER RELATIONSHIPS AMONG CHILDREN

Children typically develop likes and dislikes among school peers. Some research has revealed children's observations of **teacher responses** contribute to their **social peer preferences**. Some studies found children with ADHD did not gain better peer acceptance even when they improved their behavior because peers continued rejecting them based on their established negative reputations. But others have found teachers can mitigate these bad reputations by directing **positive attention** to children with ADHD. Multiple researchers concur that children's ADHD behaviors cause many teachers difficulty relating to them. Dislike of children with high levels of ADHD symptoms tends to progress over the school year. However, investigators also find teachers who use instructional practices communicating their belief that all children can learn, and who form positive relationships with all students, can change the association of peer difficulties with

200

ADHD symptoms. Researchers speculate such outcomes may support the possibility that teachers can promote **better peer relationships** through shaping classroom environments. Although studies continue to show peer dislike predicted by children's ADHD symptoms, they also find teacher practices can influence that interaction, making it less invariable.

DISCLOSING UNCOMFORTABLE TOPICS IN INTERPERSONAL COMMUNICATION

Communications experts observe that even in healthy relationships, people avoid bringing up some topics. They often do so strategically. Experts point out that constantly expressing every little criticism and stressor can destroy a relationship. Instead, we protect our personal identities and preserve the peace in our relationships by setting **thresholds of privacy**. Researchers studying motivations for **topic avoidance** identify self-protection or protecting the relationship as potential reasons. For example, bringing up a desire to solidify a relatively new relationship risks the partner's rejection. We may avoid broaching other topics to avoid the other's judgmental response. Researchers find that people avoiding topics for self-protection feel less satisfaction than those who do it to protect their relationship. Experts also note that, in romantic relationships, a delicate balance is necessary between avoidance and direct sharing. For example, sharing about past relationships can inform a new partner's understanding of the person, but only to a point; beyond that, too many details offer no benefit. On the other hand, overly repressing feelings and thoughts is found detrimental to health. Studies find habitually avoiding difficult subjects correlates with exacerbation of **irritable bowel syndrome symptoms**; and when families avoid discussing a member's cancer, patient illnesses become worse.

MAIN GOALS INVOLVED IN INTERPERSONAL CONVERSATIONS

According to communications researchers who have analyzed interpersonal conversations, people frequently strive, consciously or unconsciously, to meet three main goals during serious conversations. (1) **Task goals**. These represent the official purpose or point of the conversation. For example, a conversation with an aging parent may have the purpose of deciding who will make decisions for him/her when s/he is no longer able to make them. (2) **Identity goals**. These are tacit methods of preserving both one's own and another's sense of self. For example, in the preceding example, the family member(s) consider that by bringing up this topic, they are being caring and responsible, and that the aging parent wants to experience continued autonomy despite deteriorating health. (3) **Relationship goals**. These are directed to maintaining interpersonal connections. For example, in the foregoing examples, the parties in the conversation perceive that their open discussion is enabled by their closeness. Conversations with the highest quality entail both (or all) parties' observing these three goals concurrently, which is cognitively very challenging. It requires taking another's perspective, and then composing messages acknowledging that viewpoint while achieving our own goals for the conversation at the same time.

RELATIONSHIP BETWEEN INTERPERSONAL COMMUNICATION AND STRESS

Experts in communications note that research studies show stress is generated by **avoiding discussion** of important subjects, damaging the immune system and personal well-being over time. Conversely, they comment that we are able to achieve some **control** over a problem when we are able to explain it. Therefore, it more often than not benefits us to talk about subjects we find difficult to discuss. Another consideration is that we tend to **expect worse outcomes** of disclosing sensitive information than what really occurs. Research shows that we overestimate how much our negative perceptions coincide with those of our family members or significant others because we project our own beliefs onto them. In reality, it is often both more productive and safer emotionally than we think to bring up a touchy topic. However, another aspect highlighted by communications researchers is that **quality supersedes quantity** in communication. They find when discussing important issues, like serious illness or end-of-life wishes, it can be more harmful to discuss it in the wrong way than not discuss it at all, and that more is not necessarily better. Some research initiatives in healthcare communications have failed by emphasizing the quantity of communication rather than its quality.

EFFECTIVE INTERPERSONAL COMMUNICATION

Among elements making interpersonal conversations effective, experts in communications and clinical psychology include these:

- Ask yourself "**Why**?" Clarify whether you are sharing to benefit the relationship or yourself. Disclosure for the relationship's benefit supersedes self-interest.
- Affirm you **deserve to communicate**. Many people are concerned it is not their place to raise certain issues. However, experts point out a close relationship is not close unless each member speaks up sometimes.
- Use a **less personal approach** first to test another's response. To determine whether to avoid discussing how a topic relates to yourself and/or another, mention a less personal example of it (e.g., "My cousin once had an abortion.").
- Use **natural openings**. To discuss something naturally, be alert to times when another is willing and able to hear it. As a clinical psychologist puts it, waiting for a door to open is better than breaking down the door. Initiating conversation succeeds more when someone is responsive.
- Do not raise touchy subjects when **upset**. This is inconvenient, because this is when we most want to talk about them. But experts advise calming down before resuming difficult conversations.

ELEMENTS RECOMMENDED FOR DIFFICULT SUBJECTS

- **Aim for productive, quality conversations**. A clinical psychologist says hinting at a subject at ten different times is less productive than one productive talk. However, a communications expert also points out that conversation is more typically a process than a single, conclusive discussion. When people reveal information or feelings in one conversation, this frequently requires additional conversations.
- **"I" statements**. It is more useful to say "This is how I feel," than "This is how you are." While this advice is common, psychologists caution people not to use it mechanically as a conversational "trick." They should be authentic acknowledgements of our responsibility: when we are hurt, even when it is not our fault, it is still our hurt and our responsibility to find ways of assuaging it.
- **Take others' points of view**. Empathize to balance honesty; be responsible for your role in a situation. Moreover, be prepared for diverse responses: others can be more sensitive *or* more resilient than we thought.
- **Stick to the subject**. When others introduce distracting issues, defer discussion. Sometimes neutral third parties (e.g., couples or family counselors) can narrow conversational scope.
- **Lighten up**: humor can bring perspective and balance to tense situations and ease expressing resentment, anger, sadness, and frustration.

DISCUSSING SEX IN RELATIONSHIPS

Most people's egos are very sensitive to threats regarding their lovemaking abilities. Conversations about **sex** can be particularly difficult for spouses, because rejection from one's lifelong partner hurts most. Experts advise members of couples not to make the assumption that their partners automatically know they are experiencing dissatisfaction. They discourage saying something like "Lately it seems you are tired a lot of the time," and instead saying something like "Lately I have been feeling like I am being ignored, and I want to find out together how we can make our sex life better." Experts also say that after a couple has such a conversation, they should mutually decide on a specific time in the future when they will talk about the subject again and evaluate what progress they have made. Moreover, they should not bring up the subject again or complain about it until the time they have chosen: if the partner perceives such behaviors as nagging, they become self-fulfilling prophecies. The partner thinks, "S/he thinks I can't change, so why should I try?"

INTERPERSONAL CONVERSATIONS ABOUT DEATH

Most of us understandably do not want people we love to **die**. Moreover, we do not want loved ones to think we welcome this inevitable life passage, and we often fear this is how they will perceive our talking about death with them. Experts suggest taking advantage of **less personal examples** available about third parties to test loved ones' responses and/or bring up the subject. For example, if a news story reports about an individual in a coma, adult children might use that topic to find out what their aging parents think and feel about end-of-life decisions like DNR (do not resuscitate), living wills, using heroic measures to preserve or prolong life, etc. Communications experts point out that rather than introducing the subject of a living will at Christmas dinner, Easter brunch, or similar family celebrations, it is not as threatening to use relevant third-party examples like news stories to initiate the conversation. A general rule for families is not to wait for an "official Big Conversation," but to start **early** and **regularly**, frequently discussing this important topic.

DISCUSSING RELATIONSHIP STATUS

When people are involved in relationships they have established fairly recently, they frequently have not yet determined how they feel about them. They fear bringing up where the relationship is headed too soon could sabotage its future unnecessarily. This is one reason they avoid talking about **relationship status**, especially early. Another reason is gender differences. Researchers find women want more to **evaluate relationship status**; men tend to allow relationships to unfold **passively** without wanting to talk directly about them. Experts in communications say that in new relationships, partners wanting to assess their status should get information through more **indirect means**. For example, if one asks another, "What are you doing this weekend?" and gets an answer like "I'm incredibly busy," one can assume the other is not very interested; both parties can save face without more pointed questions. When relationships have lasted longer, it is normal to want to know whether they are exclusive. Partners should then more explicitly state their own **rules** so they are not broken, their **expectations** so they are not unmet, and their **questions** so they are not unanswered.

SIGNS OF ABUSIVE RELATIONSHIPS AND BELITTLING BEHAVIORS

People who want to determine if they are in an **abusive relationship** should consider whether they think or feel the following: they feel afraid of their partner often, they avoid mentioning certain subjects for fear of making their partner angry, they feel they cannot do anything right with their partner, they believe being mistreated is what they deserve, they wonder whether they are the member of the relationship who is crazy, and they feel helpless and/or emotionally numb. To consider whether their partner engages in **belittling behaviors** toward them, they should consider the following: whether their partner yells at them often; whether the partner says or does things to humiliate them; whether the partner insults them or criticizes them regularly; whether the partner treats them so poorly they find it embarrassing for family, friends, or others to witness it; whether the partner dismisses, disparages, or ignores their successes and/or opinions; whether the partner blames them for the partner's abusive behaviors; and whether the partner views and/or treats them as a sexual object or property instead of a human being.

BEHAVIOR OF ABUSIVE PARTNERS

Victims in abusive relationships should consider whether their partner behaves in an overly possessive and jealous manner toward them; whether the partner controls what they do or where they go; whether the partner prevents them from seeing their family or friends; whether the partner limits their access to the car, the phone, and/or money; and whether their partner is continually checking up on what they are doing and where they are going. These are all behaviors intended to **control** the other person, and are not normal or healthy. Threats of **violence or violent behaviors** to watch for in a partner include: the partner has a bad temper, and is unpredictable about losing his or her temper; the partner threatens to harm or kill them, or actually does harm them; the partner threatens to hurt their children, actually hurts them, or threatens to take them away; the partner threatens that if they leave, the partner will commit suicide; the partner forces them to engage in sex when they do not want to; or the partner takes away or destroys their personal belongings.

DOMESTIC ABUSE

Domestic violence is domestic abuse including physical violence. Physical force that injures or endangers someone is **physical abuse**. Physical battery or assault is a crime: police have the authority and power to protect individuals from physical attacks, whether outside or inside a family or home. **Sexual abuse** is an aggressive, violent act and a type of physical abuse. This includes forced sex, even by a partner with whom one also has consensual sex. Victims of physical and sexual abuse are at greater risk of serious injury and death. Even if incidents seem minor, e.g., being pushed or shoved, they are still abuse, and also can still cause severe injury or death. Even if incidents have only happened once or twice in a relationship, they are still abuse and are likely to continue and escalate. If physical assaults stop when the victim becomes passive, this is not a solution: the victim has given up his/her rights as a partner and a person to independence, self-expression, and decision-making. Even when no physical violence exists, victims may suffer from **verbal and emotional assault and abuse**.

EMOTIONAL AND FINANCIAL DOMESTIC ABUSE

People often associate the idea of domestic abuse with physical battery. However, many partners are victims of **emotional abuse**. Without physical bruises, the victim, abuser, and other people unfortunately overlook or minimize emotional abuse. The intention and result of emotional abuse are to erode the victim's independence, control, and feelings of self-worth. Victims come to feel they have nothing without the abusive partner, or have no way to escape the relationship. Emotional abuse includes **verbal abuse** like blaming, shaming, name-calling, insulting, and yelling. It also includes **controlling behaviors**, **intimidation**, and **isolating** the victim. Threats of punishment, including physical violence, frequently enter into psychological or emotional abuse. Emotional abuse scars are less visible than physical ones, but are equally or more damaging. **Financial or economic abuse** is another way to control the victim. It includes withholding money, checkbooks, credit or debit cards; withholding shelter, food, clothing, medications, or other necessities; making victims account for every cent they spend; rigidly controlling the victim's finances; restricting the victim to an allowance; sabotaging the victim's job by constantly calling there and/or causing the victim to miss work frequently; preventing the victim's working or making career choices; and stealing from or taking the victim's money.

CHOICE AND SELF-CONTROL IN ABUSIVE PARTNERS

Some people observe that abusive individuals lose their tempers; apparently have some psychological disorder; and some also abuse substances (though others do not), and, equating their problems with the illness or disease model of substance abuse, mistakenly assume that abusers cannot **control their behavior**. However, experts point out that abusive behaviors and violence are deliberate **choices** that the abusers make to control their victims. Evidence that they can control their behavior includes that they do not abuse everybody in their lives—only those they claim to love who are closest to them; that they choose carefully where and when to abuse, controlling themselves in public but attacking the victim once they are alone; that they can stop the abusive behavior when it is to their benefit, e.g., when their employer calls or the police arrive; and that they frequently aim physical attacks to parts of the victim's body where they are hidden by clothing, so others cannot see them.

TACTICS EMPLOYED BY DOMESTIC ABUSERS TO EXERT POWER OVER AND MANIPULATE VICTIMS

- **Dominance**: abusers, needing to feel in control of victims and relationships, dominate by making decisions for victims and family, giving them orders, and expecting unquestioning compliance. They often treat victims as children, servants, slaves, or possessions.
- **Humiliation**: to keep victims from leaving, abusers make them feel worthless and that nobody else will want them. To make victims feel inadequate, they insult and shame them publicly and privately, making them feel powerless and destroying their self-esteem.
- **Isolation**: abusive partners make victims dependent on them by cutting off their contact with others. They may stop victims from visiting with friends and relatives, or even going to school or work. Victims may have to ask permission to see anybody, go anywhere, or do anything.
- **Threats**: to frighten victims into dropping charges and/or prevent their leaving, abusers typically threaten to: harm or kill victims, children, other family, or pets; commit suicide; report victims to child services; and file false charges against them.
- **Intimidation**: threatening gestures and looks, property destruction or smashing objects in front of victims, hurting pets, or displaying weapons are tactics signaling violent consequences for noncompliance to frighten victims into submission.
- **Denial and blame**: abusers minimize or deny abuse or blame it on circumstances or, commonly, the victim. "You made/make me do it" is a frequent accusation used by abusers.

WARNING SIGNS OF DOMESTIC ABUSE, PHYSICAL VIOLENCE, AND ISOLATION

Warning signs of **domestic abuse**: the person agrees with everything the partner does and says; frequently checks in with the partner, reporting what they are doing and where they are; often receives harassing phone calls or texts from the partner; appears anxious or afraid to please the partner; and/or mentions the partner's jealousy, possessiveness, or temper. Warning signs of **physical violence**: the person often misses school, work, or social events without explaining; often has injuries, excusing them as "accidents" or "clumsiness"; and/or wears sunglasses indoors, long sleeves in summer, or other means of hiding injuries. Warning signs of **isolation**: the person never or seldom goes out in public without the partner; is unable to see friends and family; and/or has limited access to the car, money, or credit or debit cards. Psychological warning signs of being abused: someone who used to be confident displays significantly lowered self-esteem. An outgoing person becomes withdrawn; or an individual shows other major personality changes. The person appears anxious; depressed; despondent; or suicidal, verbalizing suicidal ideations or displaying suicidal behaviors.

ADVICE FOR PEOPLE WHO SUSPECT SOMEBODY THEY KNOW IS A VICTIM OF DOMESTIC ABUSE

Abusers are experts at **manipulating** and **controlling** victims. Victims are drained, frightened, ashamed, depressed, and confused. They need to escape the situation, but frequently have been isolated from others. Those suspecting abuse should be alert to warning signs, offer support to victims for extricating themselves, getting help, and starting the healing process. Some people may hesitate, thinking they could be mistaken; learn the victim does not want to discuss it or have them interfere; or simply be told that it is none of their business. In these cases, experts advise people to **speak up** regardless: expressing concern not only informs a victim somebody cares, it moreover could save that person's life. They should speak with the person privately, identifying signs they have observed and explaining why they are concerned, reassure the individual they will keep all conversation confidential, that they are there whenever s/he is ready to talk, and will help in any way possible. Regarding dos and don'ts, **do** the following: express concern, ask whether something is wrong, listen, validate the person's communications, offer help, and support the individual's decisions. **Don't**: wait for the person to approach you, blame or judge the individual, give advice, pressure the person, or attach conditions to your support.

CHILD ABUSE

Many things can precipitate child abuse, including stress related to poverty, unemployment, divorce, single parenting, and lack of support. Other causes include parental substance abuse, mental illness, and sociopathic/psychopathic personalities. Child abuse occurs across all socioeconomic levels. **Indications of child abuse** include the following:

- **Physical**: Unexplained bruises and burns, frequent injuries (including fractures), unkempt appearance, and delayed medical treatment. Sexual abuse may result in difficulty sitting or walking, frequent urination, and pain in the genital area.
- **Emotional/Psychological**: Aggressive behavior toward others; shy, withdrawn behavior; fearful of parents and other adults; low self-esteem; poor school performance; marked depression; and anxiety. A child experiencing sexual abuse may refuse to participate in exercises or gym class and may show a precocious interest in sex or sexualized behavior. The child may run away from home, be truant, and show a sudden decline in academic performance. Adolescents who are abused often turn to substance abuse.

PREVENTION OF CHILD ABUSE AND ABDUCTION

Prevention of child abuse and abduction includes a variety of approaches:

- **Parent education**: Includes developmental milestones, positive discipline techniques, age-appropriate behaviors and skills, child safety, and methods to improve parent-child interactions.
- **Support groups**: Parent groups to help members discuss problems and develop coping strategies.
- **Mental health programs**: Support for the child and other family members to help manage symptoms and life challenges.
- **Respite care**: Short-term childcare to allow parents/caregivers to remove themselves from the situation and the stress in order to avoid behaving abusively.
- **Home visiting programs**: Provide guidance for parents/caregivers regarding good health practices, positive parenting, home safety, and community resources.
- **Family resource centers**: Provide education and resources for parents/caregivers, including job training, parenting classes, violence prevention, substance abuse prevention, literacy programs, crisis intervention, respite care, and child care.
- **Law enforcement programs**: Abduction prevention education for parents focusing on how to educate and protect children regarding possible stranger abduction.

AGENCIES AND PROGRAMS DEALING WITH CHILD ABUSE AND ABDUCTION

Agencies and programs that deal with child abuse and abduction include the following:

- **Law enforcement agencies** - They arrest and bring criminal charges against those who abuse and/or abduct children.
- **Government agencies** - State and local child protective services. They investigate charges of child abuse and can remove a child from the home and place in foster care or provide ongoing monitoring of parent(s). They monitor foster children.
- **Children's advocacy centers** - They investigate and collect evidence regarding child abuse and coordinate with law enforcement and child protective services.
- **Nonprofit organizations** - Examples: The International Society for the Prevention of Child Abuse and Neglect, Child Welfare League of America, and National Children's Alliance. These organizations advocate for children, support those working to protect children, and increase public awareness.
- **Professional organizations** - Example: The American Academy of Pediatrics provides guidelines for recognizing, reporting, and dealing with abuse.
- **The National Center for Missing & Exploited Children** - This nonprofit organization established by Congress provides a hotline and tip line, posts pictures and information, raises awareness, and works with law enforcement and families. Serves as a clearinghouse of resources.

SEXUAL HARASSMENT, ABUSE, AND RAPE

Sexual harassment can take many forms, including making unwanted personal comments about appearance or lifestyle, pressing the person to date, promoting offensive material (such as showing pornography or telling off-color jokes), making unwanted physical contact (hugging, kissing, touching, standing very close), and behaving inappropriately (leering, catcalling, whistling, bullying). **Sexual abuse** can include all types of harassment as well as inappropriate and unwanted sexual contact. **Rape** involves coerced or violent sexual contact as well as sexual contact with a person who is impaired and unable to give consent (such as a person who is inebriated or under the influence of drugs). **Prevention** requires education about what constitutes harassment, abuse, and rape; prompt response to reports; having support systems in place; bystander intervention; enlisting others to assist; contacting authorities; avoiding alcohol and drugs; and using distraction. Adolescents and adults should have a clear understanding of date rape and the repercussions for both the perpetrator and the victim and should keep social media sites private and avoid tagging people.

PHYSICAL AND EMOTIONAL/PSYCHOLOGICAL EFFECTS

Sexual harassment, abuse, and rape may result in similar long-term results:

- **Physical**: The victim may experience vaginal or anal tearing that may result in long-term painful intercourse. Chronic urinary infections may occur. STIs may be transmitted, including HIV/AIDS. Some victims may become pregnant and have to make a difficult decision about aborting or carrying the child and then another decision about keeping the child or placing it for adoption.
- **Emotional/Psychological**: The victim often engages in self-blame and may experience deep guilt. Posttraumatic stress disorder is common with flashbacks, especially with violent encounters. The victim often distrusts others and suffers from unexplained bouts of anger and severe depression. The victim may feel powerless and afraid, feeling as though he or she has lost control of life. Some may become very reclusive, afraid to leave their house or apartment, and become unable to work, resulting in increased stress.

AGENCIES, PROGRAMS, AND REGULATIONS

Sexual harassment is covered under **Title VII of the Civil Rights Act** (1964), which prohibits sexual harassment but applies only to employers with 15 or more employees. Complaints are submitted to the Equal Employment Opportunity Commission (EEOC). Employers with fewer employees are covered by various state laws and regulatory agencies. Some nongovernmental agencies have limited programs to assist victims of sexual harassment, including the Legal Advocacy Fund of the American Association of University Women (AAUW). **Sexual abuse and rape** are criminal offenses covered by laws against sexual violence and involve law enforcement agencies, usually the local police, although federal authorities may intervene in sex trafficking and online stalking. Many organizations now have workplace violence prevention programs that include strategies to prevent sexual abuse, stalking, and rape. The National Sexual Assault Hotline refers people to the nearest services. The National Sex Offender Public Website links state, tribal, and territorial sexual offender registries. Numerous organizations provide assistance to victims, including the National Organization for Victim Assistance.

COMMUNICATION SKILLS

ACTIVE LISTENING

Active listening requires more than passively listening to another individual. **Active listening** includes observing the other individual carefully for nonverbal behaviors, such as posture, eye contact, and facial expression, as well as understanding and reflecting on what the person is saying. The listener should observe carefully for inconsistencies in what the individual is saying or comments that require clarification. **Feedback** is critical to active listening because it shows the speaker that one is paying attention and showing interest and respect. Feedback may be as simple as nodding the head in agreement but should also include asking questions or making comments to show full engagement. Listening with **empathy** is especially important because it helps to build a connection with the speaker. The listener should communicate empathy with words: "You feel (emotion) because (experience)" because the speaker may not be sensitive to what the listener is comprehending.

ASSERTIVENESS

Assertive communication occurs when the individual expresses opinions directly and actions correlate with words. **Assertive communicators** are respectful of others and do not bull, but they are firm and honest about their opinions. They frequently use **"I" statements** to make their point: "I would like. . . ." Communication usually includes **cooperative statements**, such as "What do you think?" and distinguishes between fact and opinion. Assertive communicators often engender trust in others because they are consistent, honest, and open in communicating with others. The assertive communicator feels free to express disagreement and anger but does so in a manner that is nonthreatening and respectful of others' feelings. Assertive communication requires a strong sense of self-worth and the belief that personal opinions have value. Assertive communicators tend to have good **listening skills** because they value the opinions of others and feel comfortable collaborating.

"I" MESSAGES AND REFUSAL SKILLS

Using "I" messages is a method of communication in which the speaker focuses on personal feelings rather than characteristics or actions of the listener. For example, if an adolescent stays out late, an **"I" message** would be "I worry that you have been in an accident when you come home late" rather than focusing on the adolescent: "Why are you late?"

Refusal skills are those that help people refuse to participate in activities and to say "no" to situations that are dangerous or unwanted, such as drug taking and sexual contact. The person needs to stand up straight, make eye contact, and say "NO" forcefully and support this statement with the appropriate body language and facial expression. The person should avoid making excuses but remain firm and repeat the same message if necessary. Young people may need to practice these techniques in role-playing activities.

NEGOTIATION SKILLS

Negotiating may be a formal process (such as negotiating with the administration for increased benefits) or an informal process (such as arriving at a team consensus), depending on the purpose and those involved.

- **Competition** - In this approach, one party wins and the other loses, such as when parties state that their positions are nonnegotiable and are unwilling to compromise. To prevail, one party must remain firm, but this can result in conflict.
- **Accommodation** - One party concedes to the other, but the losing side may gain little or nothing, so this approach should be used when there is a clear benefit to one choice.
- **Avoidance** - When both parties dislike conflict, they may put off negotiating and resolve nothing, and the problems remain.
- **Compromise** - Both parties make concessions to reach a consensus, this can result in decisions that suit no one, compromise is not always the solution.
- **Collaboration** - Both parties receive what they want, a win-win solution, often through creative solutions, but collaboration may be ineffective with highly competitive parties.

SELF-ASSESSMENT OF BEHAVIORAL RISK FACTORS

Self-assessment of behavioral risk factors begins with identifying risk factors (drinking, sexual activity, dishonesty, drug abuse) that may be an issue and then assessing the **degree of risk**. Although self-reflection may be helpful, in most cases a **self-assessment tool** is the easiest and most effective way to carry out self-assessment. Examples include the student sexual risks scale and suicide risk screening tools. The National Institute on Drug Abuse provides links to a number of evidence-based screening tools that can be used for the assessment of alcohol and drug use for adolescents and adults. Although the results of self-assessment may be enlightening, they do not necessarily lead to **changes** unless the person is motivated to change. If self-assessment indicates behavioral risk, the person should seek help in making changes, such as through a support group or therapist. The person may also enlist family and friends to help in monitoring and assessing change.

DIFFERENTIATING AMONG SAFE, RISKY, AND HARMFUL BEHAVIORS IN RELATIONSHIPS

A **safe** relationship is one in which the individuals have mutual respect and maintain appropriate boundaries. It can be difficult to differentiate between **risky** and **harmful** behaviors in a relationship because risky behaviors are often a precursor to harmful behaviors. The following behaviors are warning signs that the behaviors are not safe:

Risky behaviors	Harmful behaviors
Critical—Public or private criticism, purposefully humiliating the person.	Aggressive/Abusive—Any type of hitting, shoving, pushing, or physical violence.
Irresponsible/Immature—Constant problems (social, financial) and discord.	Controlling/Possessive—Attempts to control another person's life and to isolate the person from others.
Noncommunicative—Difficulty expressing feelings and being open with others.	Volatility—Unpredictable bouts of anger and rage.
Self-centered—thinks only in terms of personal needs.	Manipulative—Pressuring someone to do something or using guilt or threats to get one's way.

Community Health

INFLUENCING PUBLIC POLICY TO IMPROVE COMMUNITY HEALTHCARE

One example of individuals who can **affect public healthcare policy** is nurses, who can draw on hundreds of experiences with patients. Researchers (Maryland and Gonzalez, 2012) find **nurses** can use hands-on patient experience to advocate in their communities regarding healthcare and educational systems and economic issues; and in legislative systems for public healthcare policy. Nurses can use real-life examples they have experienced to illustrate patient needs, and public policy impacts on patient morbidity and mortality, to influence patient access to effective, efficient, appropriate, quality healthcare. In addition to firsthand experience of healthcare system advantages and disadvantages, research (Porter-O'Grady and Malloch, 2011) finds nurses rank highest among the most trusted professions. This respect enables them to advocate for greater immunization access, greater educational funding, etc. by persuading elected officials to make necessary changes in services and care. Nurses need abilities for analyzing their experiences to recommend effective changes, and skills for participating in public policymaking processes. In communities, nurses can advocate, for example, by sharing information with patients about resources for reducing prescription drug costs, relieving the economic burdens of cancer treatment, and informing elected officials of the need to alleviate expenses.

MEDIA STRATEGIES FOR LOCAL HEALTH DEPARTMENTS TO ADVOCATE FOR PUBLIC HEALTH

21st-century **public health issues**—climate change; chronic disease; emerging diseases; healthcare inequities, disparities, and access; and disease control—encourage local health departments to transcend traditional roles as health education and individual service providers, and focus more on environmental, social, political, and physical factors determining individual and community health. They can change the media's typical approach of individual responsibility and behavior to establish wider understanding of environmental and social influences on community health. A **credible source communication strategy** targets individuals, policymakers, and the public. Its spokesperson is a trained program expert. The pace is medium; outcomes are raising awareness and possible behavior changes. **Risk communication** targets individuals, institutions, and the public. A credible, respected official is the spokesperson. Its pace is rapid; outcomes are individual awareness and compliance with health recommendations. Media advocacy targets policymakers and the public. A trained program expert is a spokesperson. The pace is slow; outcomes include norm and policy changes. **Social marketing** targets individuals. A marketing expert is a spokesperson. The pace is slow, the outcome individual behavior change. **Counter advertising** targets policymakers and the public. Spokespersons are a marketing expert and trained program expert. The pace is slow; the outcome is behavior change.

FEDERAL EMPLOYEES AND DEPARTMENTS RESPONSIBLE FOR INFECTIOUS DISEASE CONTROL

The **Secretary of the US Department of Health and Human Services** is legally responsible to prevent introduction, transmission, and spreading of communicable diseases in the US. The **Division of Global Migration and Quarantine** is delegated the authority for meeting this responsibility via activities that include operating quarantine stations at entry ports; establishing standards for medical examinations of people coming to the US; and administering foreign and interstate quarantine regulations of the international and interstate movements of people, animals, and cargo. These activities are legally founded in Titles 8 and 42 of the US Code, and pertinent supporting regulations. The US federal government is authorized for isolation and quarantine through the US Constitution's Commerce Clause. US Code 42, Section 264 – Regulations to control communicable diseases, authorizes the **Surgeon General** to make and enforce regulations including inspection, fumigation, disinfection, sanitation, pest extermination, and destruction of articles or animals contaminated or infected with sources of dangerous infections to humans.

Individuals may not be apprehended, detained, conditionally released, or examined under this regulation except for preventing introduction, transmission, and spread of communicable diseases. Amendments include executive orders for public health authority evaluation, and a revised list of quarantinable communicable diseases.

FEDERAL AND STATE REGULATIONS CONCERNING IMMUNIZATIONS

There are no federal-level **immunization laws** in the US; however, certain vaccinations are required for children to enter **public schools** in all 50 states, varying by state. Children are required to be vaccinated for some or all of the following diseases to enter public schools: diphtheria, measles, mumps, pertussis, poliomyelitis, rubella, and tetanus. Because each state has its own requirements, the US Centers for Disease Control and Prevention (CDC) provides a database of state immunization laws, with results from a legislative review of laws in all 50 states requiring vaccination status assessment and vaccine administration for patients, residents, and healthcare workers. The CDC conducted this review in 2005, collecting data on laws for hospitals, individual provider practices, ambulatory care facilities, facilities for the developmentally disabled, and correctional facilities. The CDC also provides data on requirements for school entry by disease and by state. This includes a tool with state vaccination requirements for school and childcare, state exemptions, and links to state websites; a tool listing diseases preventable by vaccines; and state mandates for immunizations required in prenatal, daycare, childcare, kindergarten, elementary, secondary, K-12, college and university, and long-term care facilities.

MEDICAL AND HEALTH MYTHS

For many years, some people believed that drinking milk caused certain individuals' bodies to secrete more mucus. Even some doctors believed this, considering it a type of lactose intolerance that is not necessarily concentrated in the digestive system. Physician authors (Carroll and Vreeman, 2009) report that in a study of over 300 patients, almost two-thirds of them believed in such a relationship between milk and phlegm. However, in an experiment with volunteers who had cold viruses, some drank a lot of milk and were found to have no more nasal secretions, congestion, or coughing than those who did not drink as much milk. Another popular **misconception** is the idea that one can develop arthritis from repeatedly cracking one's knuckles. Scientists find no correlation between cracking the knuckles having arthritis, although one study found it could affect soft tissue around the knuckle joint. It can also decrease hand grip strength and increase hand swelling. However, people who crack their knuckles were not found likelier to develop osteoarthritis.

OCCUPATIONAL POSITIONS IN THE HEALTHCARE FIELD

Physicians diagnose and treat illnesses; perform, order, and interpret diagnostic tests and procedures; prescribe medications; perform surgeries; specialize in specific patient populations and diseases and treatments; and counsel patients. **Physician assistants (PAs)** assist with surgical procedures rather than performing surgeries; counsel patients under physician direction; prescribe medication in most US states; diagnose and treat illnesses; and perform, order, and interpret diagnostic tests and procedures. **Registered nurses (RNs)** treat patients, administer medications, execute physician orders, and advise and educate patients. **Medical assistants** obtain medical histories and vital signs; draw blood; collect laboratory specimens; prepare patients for examination; assist physicians during examinations; and perform administrative duties like filing charts, scheduling appointments, answering phones, and medical coding and billing. **Surgical technologists** prepare patients for surgery, organize operating room instruments and equipment, and assist physicians during surgical operations and procedures. **Pharmacists** fill prescriptions; compound medications; educate patients about medications; advise physicians and other clinical personnel about drug selection and dosages; and conduct drug experiments, tests, and research.

Clinical psychologists evaluate and treat mental and emotional disorders. There are many more professions.

EDUCATIONAL REQUIREMENTS FOR DIFFERENT HEALTHCARE PROFESSIONS

Physicians must complete undergraduate degrees plus 4 years of medical school, 3-8 years of residency or internship, and pass a national licensure test. **Physician assistants** must complete a 2-4-year PA certification program and pass a national licensure test. **RNs** must complete a bachelor's/associate's degree or diploma and pass a national licensure test. **Medical assistants** must attain a 1-year diploma or certificate or a 2-year associate's degree, and in some US states pass a national certification test. **Surgical technologists** must receive a 9-month diploma/certificate or 2-year associate's degree and pass a national certification test. **Pharmacists** must complete a 6-8-year Doctor of Pharmacy degree and pass a national licensure test. **Clinical psychologists** must complete a doctoral (Ph.D. or Psy.D.) degree and pass a national licensure test. **Audiologists and speech-language therapists** must each complete Master's degrees and pass national licensure tests; in some US states, audiologists must pass an additional licensure test for dispensing hearing aids.

EXAMPLES OF HEALTH ORGANIZATIONS USING COMMUNITY AND SCHOOL EVENTS TO DELIVER HEALTH EDUCATION

Healthcare system leaders recognize the importance of **prevention** and **early detection** to sustaining health and reducing illness. For example, physicians and health teams at the leading nonprofit comprehensive healthcare system **WellStar** demonstrate their belief in prevention and early detection by providing screenings, health fairs, and educational opportunities in a diverse range of settings to help people improve individual and family health and well-being. They produce community events free of charge or low in cost. Throughout communities, health fairs feature medical screenings, community education, and basic preventive medicine through interactive educational events. Some health fairs have particular themes, e.g., weight loss and fitness, diabetes, or heart health. Well*Screen Events offer affordable, convenient screenings for early detection of diabetes, prostate conditions, thyroid disorders, high cholesterol, and other medical issues. Multiple WellStar facilities and other locations like senior centers, religious organizations, and YMCAs host **screening events** throughout the year. WellStar also offers educational events and classes for schools, community groups, local businesses, and religious organizations; and the nationally recognized Safe Sitter babysitter education program for ages 11-13, teaching personal safety, behavior management, injury prevention, first aid, CPR, choking care, and business and ethical aspects of babysitting.

PLANNING SCHOOL HEALTH FAIRS AS A MEANS OF HEALTH EDUCATION ADVOCACY

Fuel Up to Play 60 (© 2013), a program of Play 60, the NFL Movement for an Active Generation supported by the National Dairy Council, offers these tips to educators and parents: work with the school nurse and other health professionals to produce a list of potential **health fair presenters**. Invite community members to set up tables with physical activity and healthy eating information, give presentations, and even just attend to learn more. Guests could include local chefs, health news broadcasters or other local celebrities, and local pediatricians and hospital staff. Plan space and time for an event, including events such as family contests, races, and other fun activities; space for presentations; and healthy picnic foods to eat. Form a team and decide the best place, day, and time with the principal. Indoor and outdoor activities combined enable greater attendee movement to derive the most from the event. Collaborate with **school nutrition professionals** to choose healthy foods, and **physical educators** to choose and organize fun physical activities. Enlist student and parent volunteers to manage activity stations. Contact local organizations and businesses for donations of tables, food, equipment, prizes, etc. Invite the donors.

HEALTH EDUCATORS SERVING AS LIAISONS BETWEEN SCHOOL PERSONNEL, STUDENTS, PARENTS, AND COMMUNITIES

Many health educator activities connect different education stakeholders. For example, when they identify and request resources from school administrators for meeting learning goals and objectives they have developed, they are acting as **liaisons** between students and administrators. When they develop processes to **integrate health education** into other programs across the curriculum, they liaise with school administrators, curriculum coordinators, other school subject teachers, and students. By training others to implement health education, they liaise between trainees and students. When developing and conducting research, they liaise between the school and the research community. They are liaisons between support providers and students when requesting program support; and liaisons among all stakeholders when promoting their collaboration. As resource persons, they are liaisons communicating health information from resources to stakeholders, between existing resources and trainees when providing training, and between other trainers and trainees when they implement training programs and sessions. As consultants, they may liaise between or among different personnel whom they provide consultative assistance. As advocates, they are liaisons between students and parents and families to promote healthy home practices and parental school involvement in health education, and between policymakers and schools and communities when advocating health promotion policies.

SKILLS AND ABILITIES

Health educator skills for assessing community as well as individual needs enable them to **liaison** between the school and the community to **promote school and community health**. Their skills for planning health education programs mean they can interact with other educators, school administrators, curriculum coordinators, etc. Skills for coordinating health education programs naturally require them to liaison among different school personnel, as do skills for managing health education programs and personnel. Coalition-building skills mean they can liaise among the diverse stakeholders they recruit to form coalitions for health promotion, advocacy, and health education advocacy. Skills for making referrals make them liaisons between students and parents and various agencies and service providers to whom they refer them. Skills for developing mass media and social marketing campaigns enable them to liaison between media representatives and the public. Abilities for mobilizing and organizing communities make them liaisons among various community members, and school and community. Abilities to encourage healthy behaviors, and to manage controversial health content and issues, enable them to liaise between parents and students.

GSHS

The **Global School Health-based Student Health Survey** (GSHS), developed in a joint effort by the World Health Organization (WHO), the United Nations organizations UNAIDS, UNESCO, and UNICEF with technical assistance from the Centers for Disease Control and Prevention (CDC), is a school-based survey of **health behaviors and health-protective factors** in students 13-17 years old in over 120 countries. Over 450,000 students had participated through 2013. The data gleaned from this survey is intended to assist world nations in setting priorities, developing programs, and advocating for youth and school health policies and programs; help nations, international agencies, and others compare the prevalence of protective factors and health behaviors across different countries; and determine trends in protective factor and health behavior prevalence according to each nation to utilize for evaluating youth health advocacy and school health. GSHS core questionnaire modules cover hygiene and diet; alcohol, drug, and tobacco use; physical activity; mental health; protective factors; sexual behaviors; unintentional injury; and violence. WHO and CDC offer technical support and continuing capacity-building via training, materials, data analysis, and software. Country reports, data, documentation, bibliography, and fact sheets are available online.

PROMOTING STUDENT PARTICIPATION IN SCHOOL-/COMMUNITY-BASED EFFORTS TO ADDRESS HIGH-RISK BEHAVIORS ASSOCIATED WITH SUBSTANCE ABUSE

Promoting student participation in school-/community-based efforts to address high-risk behaviors associated with substance abuse often begins by recruiting **student leaders** to participate and lead these efforts because students look to their peers for guidance. **Sports coaches** are also often role models and can influence athletes to participate, and athletes often are admired by other students, who may follow their lead. The leaders of school clubs, such as the honor society or chess club, should also be recruited because they can positively influence club members. The school can also include **families** in prevention methods through such programs as Family Matters, in which parents receive booklets and telephone guidance by the health educator. Programs for adolescents that have proven successful include Life Skills Training (focuses on decision making, problem solving, and critical thinking); Lions Quest Skills for Adolescence (focuses on civic responsibility, social skills, and resisting peer pressure); ALERT Plus (Adolescent Learning Experiences Resistance Training), a 9–10th-grade extension of the middle school program; and the Project Toward No Drug Abuse (an interactive classroom project that focuses on motivation, life skills, and decision making).

HEALTH-RELATED CAREERS AND EDUCATIONAL REQUIREMENTS

Health-related careers:

- **Physicians** - Requires a bachelor's degree, four years of medical school, internship, and residency and licensure.
- **Nurses (RNs, LVN, APNs)** - Registered nurses (RNs) require two- to five-year training programs (ASN, BSN) and licensure as well as additional training for advance practice nurses (APNs). Licensed vocational nurses (LVNs) require an 18-month to 2-year training period, licensure, and work under RN supervision.
- **Nutritionists** - Requires bachelor's or master's degree.
- **Certified nurse assistant (aide)** - Requires six to eight weeks of training. Work under the supervision of RNs and LVNs.
- **Physician assistant** - Requires a two-year master degree program. PAs carry out many of the tasks of physicians.
- **Technicians** - Technicians include x-ray technicians, laboratory technicians, ultrasound technicians, dental hygienists, pharmacy technicians, emergency medical technicians, echocardiogram technicians, and phlebotomists. Training varies but is often approximately for two years, whereas those that require one skill, such as phlebotomists, may be trained in a matter of weeks. Some require licensure.
- **Medical assistant** - Programs vary from one to two years and include a certificate and/or associate's degree.

WHO'S WORLD HEALTH SURVEYS

The World Health Organization (WHO) began the **World Health Surveys (WHS)** in 2002-2004, partnering with 70 world nations to gather information about adult health populations and health systems through cross-sectional survey studies. More than 300,000 people aged 18 years and older participated in the studies, yielding a very large sample size. The WHS extended the results of WHO's 2000-2001 Multi-country Survey Study. The purpose of the WHS was to use a valid, reliable survey instrument to reinforce national capacities for monitoring **health systems** and **critical health outcomes**. WHO used statistical probability to select nationally representative samples from countries chosen to represent all of the world's regions. They adjusted the weights of sampling according to population distribution, and corrected for non-response following stratification. The surveys covered household data including household members, health insurance coverage, health expenditures, and permanent wealth or income indicators. On the individual level, the survey information included sociodemographic data, descriptions of health states, valuations of health states, health risk factors, chronic health conditions, healthcare use, mortality, social capital, and responsiveness of healthcare systems.

Nutrition

ENTERTAINING PRESENTATIONS TO TEACH NUTRITION EDUCATION AT SCHOOL ASSEMBLIES

Jump with Jill, an interactive instructional program designed by Jill Jayne, MS, RD, a registered dietitian and professional musician, is "the world's only rock and roll nutrition show." Research proves its effectiveness: a 2013 study found 92.4 percent of students very excited and happy, 75 percent of students surveyed reported trying to be more active, 81 percent of 4th-graders trying to drink more water afterward, and teachers found student engagement and entertainment value excellent. With live original music, a professional sound system and lighting and "hip" costumes, songs help students remember healthy messages; structured dance breaks enable singing and dancing along with performers, providing kinesthetic learning and exercise. Students learn to value healthy eating and b as fun ways of expressing individuality, recall healthy behaviors through song and dance, describe energizing healthy choices, and recognize their personal health impacts. Studies show results of measurable positive emotional affect and self-reported behavior improvements. Recommended for grades K-6 in groups of 300-600, the 1-hour show is adaptable to preschool, middle school, and professionals. The follow-up CD and website resources inform future and continuing lessons. Faculty and staff participate for modeling. By inviting parents and community members, educators can shape not only individual health habits, but also health culture.

DEVELOPMENTALLY APPROPRIATE INSTRUCTION IN NUTRITION
PIAGET'S PREOPERATIONAL COGNITIVE STAGE

Preoperational children "**centrate**" on one property at a time: if you say, "Eating many different vegetables like peas, carrots, and corn is healthy," they only hear, "Eating peas is healthy." Inability to **categorize** means not differentiating "food" from "snacks," or including "peas" among "vegetables." Lacking **reversibility** means they cannot reverse "Overeating makes you fat" to "Not overeating keeps you from getting fat." They can repeat certain words, phrases, and sentences without understanding their meanings; e.g., "Vegetables are good for us," but they cannot explain how, or name specific vegetables. If told foods contain vitamins, they may object by saying, "Vitamins are pills, not things in food." They think **intuitively**, not logically, not understanding cause-and-effect relationships or changes and transformations. Asked how foods give our bodies nutrients, they might respond, "Little pieces of broccoli go into your arms and legs." For this age group, focus on one simple concept or subject at a time. Postpone trying to explain logical sequences. Animistic and intuitive ideas, like certain foods making a happy, smiling tummy or Popeye's biceps popping out when he eats spinach, are understandable and appealing. Sorting concrete food-group members may help and can be fun.

PIAGET'S CONCRETE OPERATIONS AND FORMAL OPERATIONS STAGES

Concrete operational children can follow **concrete** cause-and-effect; reversibility, e.g., being well, getting sick, and recovering; event chains, e.g., growing crops, harvesting, selling, shipping, processing, and selling in stores; classification, e.g., beef, chicken, and pork are all meats, food vs. snacks, and good vs. bad foods. However, they are still **present-oriented**, not considering future health effects of nutrition. Educators can now teach digestion and energy processes, weight gain and loss, cycles of the food chain, and the food groups, all using concrete objects and illustrations. They should emphasize current, not future, benefits of healthy eating, e.g., feeling better now, running faster today, etc. **Formal operational** students start understanding **abstract** concepts, e.g., dietary fat contributes to heart disease; formulating hypotheses, e.g., "If I stop eating so much junk food, then I'll lose weight"; taking others' perspectives, e.g., "Other kids teasing him about his weight must make him feel bad"; considering multiple consequences, e.g., "Eating healthy foods may or may not make me better at sports"; and informing decisions with their values, e.g., choosing

foods and behaviors relative to independence, appearance, and peers. Educators can now discuss protein, vitamins, and minerals; classification of foods by nutrients; processes whereby foods affect health; and chronic disease risks.

CHOOSEMYPLATE.GOV

ChooseMyPlate.gov is the current federal healthy eating guide, formerly the Food Pyramid. Since replacing the Food Pyramid with MyPlate, the US Department of Agriculture (USDA) eliminated oils and sugars. The **five food groups** are: fruits, vegetables, grains, proteins, and dairy. USDA advises that in a meal, half the plate should be fruits and vegetables. **Vegetables** are categorized as dark green, red and orange, legumes (beans and peas), starchy, and other, according to nutrient content. **Whole grains** include whole wheat and whole-wheat flour; cracked or bulgur wheat; oatmeal; whole rye; whole barley; cornmeal; brown rice; amaranth; millet; quinoa; sorghum; triticale, etc. White flour and bread, white rice, and de-germed cornmeal are refined grains. USDA advises at least half the grains we eat be whole grains, not processed or refined, which have beneficial fiber removed. **Proteins** include meats, poultry, seafood, eggs, soy, nuts, seeds, and legumes (also in the vegetables group). USDA recommends eating a variety of lean proteins. **Dairy** includes milk and milk products and calcium-fortified soymilk. Recommended dairy foods are fat-free or low-fat. Milk products retaining calcium content (cheeses, yogurt, etc.) are in the dairy group; cream, butter, cream cheese and others having little or no calcium are not. Oils are not a USDA food group, but included for essential nutrients.

HISTORY OF AMERICAN DIETARY GUIDELINES FROM 1977-1980

Early in 1977, the US Senate Select Committee on Nutrition and Human Needs, then chaired by Senator George McGovern, following extensive reviews of science and discussions, recommended dietary goals consisting of recommendations concerning food and nutrients. The first goal recommended Americans only eat as much energy from food—i.e., calories—as they expended. This goal addressed obesity through **balanced consumption**. Regarding nutrients, the committee recommended eating more complex carbohydrates and fewer simple (i.e., processed or refined) carbohydrates and decreasing total fat, saturated fat, cholesterol, and sodium. Food goals also included eating more vegetables, fruits, and whole grains and replacing more saturated fats with unsaturated fats. Due to controversy and skepticism from industrial and scientific groups, the US Departments of Agriculture and Health and Human Services (formerly Health, Education, and Welfare) jointly issued a nutrition and health brochure in 1980, partly based on the Surgeon General's 1979 report on health promotion and disease prevention and reflecting research findings about relationships between diet and health. However, this too met with debate.

AMERICA'S FEDERAL HISTORY OF DIETARY GUIDELINES AFTER 1980 INTO 2010

Despite their straightforward, scientific basis, **US Dietary Guidelines** issued in 1980 encountered arguments from various industrial and scientific quarters. In response, Congress directed the Departments of Agriculture (USDA) and Health and Human Services (HHS, formerly HEW) to form an advisory committee to solicit formal and informal outside and private-sector advice for subsequent editions. Though the 1985 edition of the Guidelines did not incorporate extensive changes, adding non-federal scientists' input resulted in far less controversy and wider adoption. HHS and USDA formed a second scientific advisory committee in 1989 to review and revise the Guidelines. The 1990 edition reinforced earlier editions' principles, but additionally suggested **numerical targets** for saturated and total fat amounts—emphasizing these did not apply to a single food or meal, but to eating choices over multiple days. While these first three editions were voluntarily issued, the 1990 National Nutrition Monitoring and related Research Act first legally mandated the **Dietary Guidelines report**, required a new report every five years, and established a **Dietary Guidelines Advisory Committee** for that purpose. The 2005 committee adopted systematic methods to review scientific evidence and literature. The 2010 committee extended these, also establishing the **Nutrition Evidence Library** to support its work with a comprehensive, evidence-based review process.

CARBOHYDRATES, FATS, PROTEIN, VITAMINS, AND MINERALS FOUND IN FOODS

Carbohydrates are starches, fibers, and sugars in foods from which the body manufactures glucose, the blood sugar used to fuel all activities of the body, including the brain. Glucose is accessed immediately, or stored in the muscles and liver for future use. **Fats** are necessary to normal bodily functions, but only 20-35 percent of the human diet need be from fats—preferably oils, not solid fats; and unsaturated, not saturated or trans fats. USDA recommends eating below 10 percent of calories in saturated fats, and avoiding trans fats. (Trans fats are found in partially hydrogenated oils.) We need to eat foods with protein, which our bodies digest into amino acids to rebuild all organs, tissues, and cells, which contain protein that is continually broken down and replaced. **Animal proteins** are complete protein sources with all essential amino acids. **Vegetable proteins** are incomplete sources, but combining complementary vegetable proteins can yield complete protein. Ten to 35 percent of daily calories should be protein; Americans typically eat enough. **Vitamins and minerals** are important to health; for instance, vitamin D aids calcium absorption, and calcium promotes strong bone formation. Supplements are available, but eating a nutritious and varied diet usually provides enough vitamins and minerals.

RELATIONSHIP BETWEEN DIET AND EXERCISE

Diet and exercise are **interdependent**. For example, it can be difficult to achieve optimal energy, effort, or results from exercising after eating nothing but junk food. Alternatively, people who do eat healthy diets but never exercise may find it hard to maintain optimal weights. According to the American Council on Exercise, only about five percent of people losing weight exclusively through diet maintain the loss. Weight loss requires a **negative balance of calories**, attained by either burning more calories from exercising, eating fewer calories, or a combination of the two. The individuals most successful in losing weight and maintaining weight loss both **exercise more** and **eat fewer calories** than people who cannot lose weight or who lose it and then regain it. Snacks containing complex carbohydrates and some protein afford energy before exercising. Afterward, water, milk and juice rehydrate; carbohydrates replenish energy; and protein supports muscle repair and growth. Nutritional experts recommend eating 15 percent of calories from protein, 55 percent from carbohydrates, and 30 percent from fat for optimal exercising.

FAD DIETS

Fad diets are extreme, unbalanced, and ultimately **unhealthy**. Some **fad diets** fail to provide all necessary nutrients. Some contain insufficient calories to support normal life functions. Some eliminate certain food groups, causing unbalanced nutrition. Some may cause weight loss initially; however, this typically does not last, and because these diets are impossible to maintain long-term, any weight lost is usually regained soon after ending the diet. Many people not only regain what they lost, but also gain beyond their starting weights as their bodies rebound from nutritional deprivation. Moreover, fad diets do not establish healthy eating habits for **maintaining** ongoing healthy weight and nutrition. Nine common characteristics of many fad diets include:

- sounding "too good to be true"
- promising "quick fix" results
- banning certain regimens and/or products
- oversimplifying complex science
- making dramatic claims rejected by science
- basing claims on isolated testimonials and/or a single research study

- basing claims on studies lacking independent expert reviews
- promoting product sales
- eliminating food groups. Moderate portions of varied, whole or unprocessed foods and regular, moderate exercise are better for losing and controlling weight

Safety and Accident Prevention and Emergency Response

MEDICAL EMERGENCIES

Medical emergencies are those in which the person is at severe risk and needs prompt medical attention. For life-threatening **emergencies**, the most appropriate response is to call 9-1-1, but some first-aid procedures may be used if necessary, such as applying pressure to a bleeding wound, while waiting for assistance. In less acute cases (such as severe diarrhea), the person may be transported to an emergency department directly without calling 9-1-1 if he or she appears stable. Medical emergencies include the following:

- Shortness of breath, severe wheezing, difficulty breathing.
- Sudden onset of dizziness and fainting or unexplained weakness.
- Sudden changes in vision.
- Sudden onset of severe pain.
- Chest pain or pressure or pain radiating to neck, shoulders, and arms.
- Severe gastrointestinal problems with vomiting and/or diarrhea.
- Severe uncontrolled hemorrhage.
- Vomiting blood or coughing up blood.
- Difficult speaking or swallowing.
- Threats of suicide.

BASIC FIRST-AID PROCEDURES IN VARIOUS SITUATIONS

The following are first-aid procedures in various situations:

- **Anaphylaxis (allergic shock)** - Immediately call 9-1-1. Administer epinephrine (EpiPen) per autoinjector if the person has one. Begin cardiopulmonary resuscitation (CPR) if in respiratory arrest.
- **Animal bites**
  - *Minor* (if no concern about rabies): Wash with soap and water and apply antibiotic cream/ointment and bandage.
  - *Major*: Apply pressure to stop the bleeding with a dry clean bandage, and transport to the emergency department, or call 9-1-1 if severe.
- **Black eye** - Apply cold compress, avoiding pressure on eye. If blood is noted in the eye itself or if vision is impaired, transport to the emergency department.
- **Chemical burns/eye splashes** - Remove contaminated belongings and flush the burn area with a copious amount of tap water for at least 10 minutes. Transport to the emergency department or call 9-1-1 if burns are severe, the patient feels faint, or the burn is more than three inches in diameter. Flush the eyes for at least 20 minutes, and then transport to the emergency department.
- **Cut/Scrapes** - Apply pressure with a clean bandage to stop the bleeding. Rinse with clear water and wash around the wound with soap and water. Apply antibiotic ointment and dressing. If the wound is deep and requires suturing; transport to the emergency department.
- **Heat cramps, heat exhaustion, heat stroke**
  - *Heat cramps and exhaustion*: Remove the person to the shade, lay flat, and elevate legs; cool by spraying with cold water, and have the person drink cool water.
  - *Heat stroke*: Call 9-1-1. Spray or immerse in cool water and fan; administer CPR if necessary.

- **Hypothermia** - Call 9-1-1. Remove wet clothing, warm gradually with warm compresses to the trunk; give warm drinks. Do not warm too quickly, and do not massage limbs.
- **Insect bites/stings** - Remove stingers, wash with soap and water, and apply a cool compress. Apply cortisone cream to reduce itching. If a severe reaction or bite with a known dangerous insect (such as a scorpion), call 9-1-1. Administer an EpiPen if the person has one for allergies to insects.
- **Bleeding**
  - *Minor*: Apply pressure with a clean bandage to stop the bleeding and apply dry dressing.
  - *Severe*: Call 9-1-1. Remove any large debris from the wound. Apply pressure with a clean bandage to stop the bleeding but not if debris is imbedded in the wound, and don't apply pressure to an eye. In these cases, simply cover with a clean dressing. Lie the person flat and elevate the feet. Apply a tourniquet for bleeding that is life-threatening only if trained to do so.
- **Snakebites (venomous)** - Call 9-1-1. Position the injury below the level of the heart if possible. Cover the wound with a dry dressing. DO NOT apply ice, cut the skin, or apply a tourniquet. Report a description of the snake to first responders.
- **Spider bite** - Cleanse the bite with soap and water, and apply antibiotic ointment and cool compress. Transport to the emergency department if a poisonous spider, such as a black widow or brown recluse, is suspected.
- **Sprains/Fractures/Dislocations**
  - *Sprains*: RICE (rest, ice, compress, elevate). Transport to the emergency department if unable to bear weight or use the joint.
  - *Fractures*: Call 9-1-1 or transport to the emergency department. Apply pressure to stop any bleeding, cover with a dry dressing, immobilize the injured limb, and apply an ice pack.
  - *Dislocation*: Transport to the emergency department. Do not attempt to move the joint. Apply an ice compress to the joint.
- **Shock (any cause)** - Call 9-1-1. Lay the person flat, elevate the legs and feet, and keep still. Loosen clothing. Begin CPR if cardiac or respiratory arrest exist.
- **Stroke** - Call 9-1-1. Keep the head elevated.
- **Nosebleeds** - Sit the person upright and pinch nostrils for 5 to 10 minutes. Transport to the emergency department if bleeding follows an accident or if it persists for more than 20 minutes.

CPR

Hands-only **cardiopulmonary resuscitation** (CPR) is recommended for nonmedical rescuers for unconscious teens or adults who have no pulse or respirations. The rescuer should call 9-1-1 and place the victim supine on a hard surface. To find the correct hand position, run two fingers along the ribs to the center chest, place two fingers over the xiphoid process, and place the palm of the other hand on the sternum directly above the fingers. Then place the other hand on top of the first, fingers linked and elbows locked, to begin **compressions**, which should be done in a rocking movement, using the body to apply pressure. (Note: Use two fingers for infants.) The rate of compressions is at least 100 per minute and at least two inches deep (one-third chest depth for infants and small children). This rate corresponds roughly to the beat of the Bee Gees' song "Staying Alive" (dum, dum, dum, dum, stayin' alive, stayin' alive....). With two trained rescuers, **rescue breathing** may be added at a compression to breathing rate of 30:2.

HEIMLICH MANEUVER

The universal sign of choking is when a person clutches his or her throat and appears to be choking or gasping for breath. If the person can speak ("Can you speak?") or cough, the **Heimlich maneuver** is not usually necessary. The Heimlich maneuver can be done with the victim sitting, standing, or supine. The Heimlich procedure for children (≥1 year) and adults is as follows:

- Wrap arms around the victim's waist from the back if sitting or standing. Make a fist and place the thumb side against the victim's abdomen slightly above the umbilicus. Grasp this hand with the other and thrust sharply upward to force air out of the lungs.
- Repeat as needed and call 9-1-1 if there is no response.
- If the victim loses consciousness, ease him or her into a supine position on the floor, place hands similarly to CPR but over the abdomen while sitting astride the victim's legs. Repeat upward compressions five times. If no ventilation occurs, attempt to sweep the mouth and ventilate the lungs mouth to mouth. Repeat compressions and ventilations until recovery or emergency personnel arrive.

Indications of **choking** in infants younger than one year include lack of breathing, gasping, cyanosis, and inability to cry. Procedures for the **Heimlich chest thrusts** include the following:

- Position the infant in the prone (face-down) position along the forearm with the infant's head lower than the trunk, being sure to support the head so the airway is not blocked.
- Using the heel of the hand, deliver five forceful upward blows between the shoulder blades.
- Sandwich the child between your two arms, turn the infant into the supine position, and drape him or her over your thigh with the head lower than the trunk and the head supported.
- Using two fingers (as in CPR compressions), give up to five thrusts (about 1.5 inches deep) to the lower third of the sternum.
- Only do a finger sweep and remove any foreign object if the object is visible. Repeat five back blows, five chest thrusts, repeating until the foreign body is ejected or until emergency personnel take over.
- If the infant loses consciousness, begin CPR. If a pulse is noted but spontaneous respirations are absent, continue with ventilation only.

HEALTH AND SAFETY OF INDIVIDUALS RESPONDING TO MEDICAL EMERGENCIES

When responding to a medical emergency, it's important to take measures to **prevent self-injury or infection**. Precautions include the following:

- Assess the **safety risks** of the situation before rendering aid (gunshots, gang activity, fire, fallen electrical wires, severe storm conditions), and do not give aid unless the situation is safe.
- Avoid contact with **body fluids** (blood, urine, feces, semen), and use gloves if available; otherwise, attempt to find some type of barrier (plastic bag, towel) to use to prevent direct contact.
- Use a face mask if possible if in danger of **airborne pathogens**, such as when a person has a severe cough.
- **Standard precautions**: Hand hygiene with soap and water or alcohol scrub should be carried out if possible before touching a person, but this is not always possible in an emergent situation. Hands and any contaminated body parts should be washed with soap and water as soon as possible after contact, especially if contaminated by body fluids.

AMERICAN RED CROSS CERTIFICATION COURSES IN FIRST AID, CPR, AND AED

The American Red Cross states on its website that knowing what to do in the event of an emergency involving respiratory or cardiac problems, or requiring first aid measures, could help save somebody's life. The Red Cross offers course options among hands-on learning of **first aid**, cardiopulmonary resuscitation (**CPR**), and automated external defibrillator (**AED**) use. These courses are all aligned with the *Best Practices for Workplace First Aid Training Programs* issued by the Occupational Safety and Health Administration (OSHA). They are available in both classroom versions, and blended (i.e., combined classroom and online) formats. Depending on the option chosen, courses last from two to five hours. Upon completing a course successfully, people receive a two-year **certification**. The Red Cross offers refresher courses free of charge for all course options, and short classes for renewing current certification. The first aid course, including a pediatric version, teaches people how to respond to common emergencies including cuts, burns, head injuries, neck injuries, back injuries, and other situations requiring first aid. The CPR and AED courses teach how to respond to breathing and heart emergencies, including using AEDs, for adults, children, and infants.

PRACTICING HEIMLICH MANEUVER AND CPR

For choking, quick response is necessary to prevent unconsciousness, even death. For adults and children (procedures for infants differ), perform the **Heimlich maneuver**: first, remember panicky victims may unintentionally strike out, and protect yourself. Do not perform the Heimlich on someone who is speaking, coughing, or breathing—someone who can do these things is not choking. Stand behind the victim. Wrap your arms around him or her as if hugging. Make a fist with your right hand; put it above the victim's navel. Grasp your right fist with your left hand; thrust in and up forcibly. Repeat thrusting until the victim can breathe. If the victim loses consciousness, begin child **CPR** for children aged 1-8 years, adult CPR above 8 years. Practice universal precautions and use protective equipment if available to avoid contagious or infectious diseases. "Shake and shout" trying to wake the victim. If he or she does not awaken, call 911. If nobody is available, perform CPR for two minutes, then call 911. On children, do two chest compressions per second 30 times; repeat until help arrives. On adults, do chest compressions at least 100 times a minute, 30 times in 18 seconds; repeat until help arrives.

COURSES FOR EMERGENCY RESPONSE AND FIRST AID

The American Red Cross offers a course specifically designed for high school and college students. Students who successfully complete this class receive **certification** in first aid, cardiopulmonary resuscitation (CPR), and using automated external defibrillators (AEDs). The course also provides students with a comprehensive array of skills that prepares them for responding to a varied range of **emergencies** that can occur to adults, children, and infants. By learning these skills and applying them in an emergency situation, students might be able to save a life. This course involves 30 hours of instruction with an emphasis on hands-on learning, and awards a two-year certification to students upon its satisfactory completion. The class includes modules that cover first aid techniques, adult and pediatric CPR and AED use, how to manage various injuries, and how to prevent the transmission of different diseases. The American Red Cross website includes a search engine whereby students can enter their city, state, and ZIP code to find and register for classes available in their areas.

GUIDELINES FOR CALLING 911

Emergencies requiring **911 calls** are defined as any situations that need immediate help from an ambulance, the fire department, or the police. Some examples of such emergencies include medical emergencies needing immediate medical attention, like uncontrollable bleeding, chest pains, allergic reactions, someone not breathing or struggling to breathe, or someone who is unconscious. Automobile accidents, particularly including injuries, are emergencies. Crimes, particularly in progress, are emergencies. Fires are 911 emergencies. Officials recommend if a person is not sure whether a situation is a real emergency or not, he or she should call 911 and let the call-taker help determine this. Callers should be prepared to **answer questions** from the dispatcher like the street address and location of the emergency; the phone number they are calling from; the nature of the emergency; and details, like descriptions of symptoms or injuries in a medical emergency, descriptions of fires in progress, or descriptions of persons who may have committed crimes. Callers should also be prepared to **follow any instructions** given by call-takers, including step-by-step CPR or Heimlich maneuver directions. Callers should not hang up until instructed by the call-taker.

Today **911** can be called using landline and wireless phones. Enabling text messages to 911 is expected in the near future. The National Emergency Number Association (NENA) and 911.gov advise if adults call 911 accidentally, or a child dials 911 with no emergency, callers or parents should briefly explain the mistake, not simply hang up: call-takers may assume there is an emergency and dispatch responders unnecessarily, diverting them from real emergencies. Separate phone numbers exist for non-emergency services. Call-takers can identify emergencies and non-emergencies and direct unsure callers to proper non-emergency numbers. Prank calls to 911 are illegal in most states; local law enforcement agencies address them. Callers should know cross street names, signs, neighboring buildings and other landmarks: 911 centers answering calls may not be those servicing the caller's area. Callers should post their addresses on both mailboxes and houses. Parents should teach young children what 911 is and how to dial from landlines and wireless phones, ensuring they can reach at least one phone in the house. Children must know their name, parents' names, address, and phone number. Parents should teach children to trust 911 call-takers, answer their questions, and not hang up until instructed.

SHI

The Centers for Disease Control and Prevention (CDC) collaborated with school health experts, administrators and staff, parents, and national non-government health and education agencies to develop the *School Health Index: Self-Assessment & Planning Guide 2012* (**SHI**), an online, confidential, and easy-to-use tool available on the CDC website's SHI page—one PDF for elementary schools and another for middle and high schools—that helps schools identify their health and safety policy and program strength and weaknesses; develop student health-enhancing action plans to incorporate into School Improvement Plans (SIPs); and involve students, teachers, parents, and communities in promoting better health and health-enhancing behaviors. The SHI uses the CDC's research-based guidelines for school health programs as its basis. These guidelines identify policies and practices found most effective for **decreasing health risk behaviors** by students. The SHI covers sexual health topics, including teen pregnancy, HIV and other STI prevention; cross-referential health services, mental health services, and family and community involvement modules; and updated nutritional information aligned with Institute of Medicine recommendations and USDA requirements. The SHI can be customized and used interactively online, and/or downloaded and printed.

BEHAVIORAL CHANGE THEORIES APPLICABLE TO HEALTH EDUCATION PROGRAMS FOR PREVENTING AND CONTROLLING INJURY

Behavioral change theories applicable to health education injury prevention and control programs include: community organization theory, diffusion of innovations theory, the ecological/social ecological model, the extended parallel processing model, the health belief model, health promotion models, integrated models, the PRECEDE/PROCEED model, the public health model, social-cognitive theory, the theory of reasoned action/planned behavior, and the stages-of-change or transtheoretical model. **Community organization theory** concentrates on community strengths. Main concepts include community capacity, critical consciousness, empowerment, participation, relevance, and issue selection. The federal Health Start program is an example. **Diffusions of innovation theory** focus on processes whereby new ideas are spread through society. Main concepts include social networks, communication channels, innovations, and time to reach members. Examples include collaboration between the Alzheimer's Association and police to augment Alzheimer's patient safety through a community-based initiative, and Australian public hospital prenatal smoking cessation programs. **Ecological/social ecological models** emphasize multilevel approaches to sociological and environmental influences on individual behavior. Applications include road traffic injury prevention, unintentional injury prevention, world violence and health reporting, and needs assessment for community intervention planning.

The **extended parallel processing model of behavior change** is a theory of fear appeal. It describes how people process messages and respond to them to increase their awareness of personal health risk, and how health education program planners can design methods for overcoming health risks. One application of this model has been to prevent noise-induced hearing loss in Appalachian coal miners (Murray-Johnson et al, 2004). The **health belief model** focuses on perceptions of disease threat and the net benefits of behavior change to ascertain whether and why an individual will change his or her behavior. **Health promotion models** have had actual and proposed applications, including to drinking and driving, preventing violence and injuries, increasing bicycle helmet use, prevention of alcohol-related traffic injuries, and improving fire escape behaviors when responding to smoke alarms. **Integrated models**, including the public health model with the social-ecological model and the PRECEDE framework with the Haddon Matrix, have been applied to injury control and health education, epidemiology and disease prevention, interventions in male violence against females, urban violence, and unintentional injury prevention. The **PRECEDE/PROCEED model** includes epidemiological, ecological, environmental, social, behavioral, educational, policy, and administrative assessments; and evaluations of process, implementation, outcomes, and impacts.

Drugs and their Use, Misuse, Abuse, and Addiction

RISKS OF DRINKING AND DRIVING

According to the National Council on Alcoholism and Drug Dependence, Inc. (NCADD), 32 percent of deadly auto crashes are estimated to involve a driver or pedestrian **intoxicated by alcohol**. The influence of alcohol slows reaction time and impairs attention; judgment; the ability to make quick decisions; reactions to environmental changes; and executing precise, difficult maneuvers while driving. Therefore, **driving** is dangerous and can be deadly under the influence of alcohol and other drugs. Though public awareness has increased, many people still drive under the influence. Almost 13,000 individuals die annually in alcohol-related accidents, and hundreds of thousands are injured. These crashes cost over $100 billion to American taxpayers. Yearly arrests for driving while intoxicated number above 1.4 million, representing below one percent of 159 million self-reported instances of drinking and driving. Of those arrested, 780,000 are convicted; two-thirds of those sentenced to prison are repeat offenders. Most deaths are caused by drivers with at least 0.10 **blood alcohol concentration (BAC)**—the common criterion for intoxication. However, even 0.02 BAC impairs driving ability.

RISKS FROM SMOKING TOBACCO

More than 480,000 Americans, i.e., around one in five, die annually from **smoking cigarettes**. Smoking causes more mortalities than drinking alcohol, using illegal drugs, auto accidents, gunshots, and human immunodeficiency virus (HIV) *combined.* Compared to all war casualties in US history, smoking cigarettes has killed over 10 times as many citizens. More women die annually from **lung cancer** than breast cancer. Of all lung cancer deaths in women and men, 90 percent are caused by smoking. Eighty percent of **chronic obstructive pulmonary disease (COPD)**, including chronic bronchitis and emphysema) deaths are from smoking. Over the past 50 years, risk of death from smoking has risen in American men and women. Smoking raises death risk from all causes. Smokers are at an estimated two to four times the risk for coronary heart disease and stroke; male smokers have 25 times the risk of lung cancer, and female smokers 25.7 times the risk. COPD deaths are 12-13 times more likely in smokers. Fewer than five cigarettes daily can cause cardiovascular disease. Smoking causes bladder, blood, cervical, colorectal, esophageal, kidney, ureter, laryngeal, liver, oropharyngeal, pancreatic, stomach, tracheal, bronchial, and lung cancer. Smoking causes one of every three cancer deaths in the US.

SMOKING CIGARETTES IN ADDITION TO CARDIOVASCULAR DISEASE AND CANCERS

In addition to cardiovascular disease and cancers, smoking cigarettes decreases overall health. Researchers questioning smokers find they self-report **poorer health status**. Smokers are absent from work more often. They require more health care and cost more to themselves, the government, and American taxpayers in healthcare expenses. In addition to the cardiovascular effects of strokes, heart attacks and heart disease—the foremost American killers—plus blood clots, reduced blood flow, blood vessel damage, high blood pressure, multiple cancers, and chronic obstructive lung diseases, smoking can trigger and exacerbate asthma attacks. It damages almost everybody organ. Smoking makes conceiving children more difficult. It also raises risks of miscarriage, premature delivery, stillbirth, low birth weight, sudden infant death syndrome (SIDS), ectopic pregnancy (extrauterine implantation), infant orofacial clefts, and other birth defects. Smoking can lower sperm counts, decreasing fertility. Post-menopausal women smokers have weaker bone density, risking fractures. Smoking damages tooth and gum health and causes tooth loss. Higher risks of eye cataracts and age-related macular degeneration are also associated with smoking. Smoking causes type 2 diabetes, raising risk 30-40 percent, and impedes its treatment. Smoking causes rheumatoid arthritis, other inflammatory conditions, and impairs immune function.

BENEFITS OF SMOKING CESSATION

The Centers for Disease Control and Prevention (CDC) reports smoking has been estimated to raise a person's risk of heart disease, including heart attacks, to between double and quadruple those of a nonsmoker's risk; but also has found that risk drops greatly only one year after **quitting smoking**. A stroke or cerebrovascular accident (CVA) happens when either a blood clot blocks blood flow to a part of the brain (an ischemic stroke), or a blood vessel in or near the brain leaks/bursts (a hemorrhagic stroke). Whereas smoking also increases the risk of stroke to two to four times a nonsmoker's risk; two to five years after quitting smoking, that risk can be similar to that of someone who never smoked. Whereas smoking raises an individual's risks for mouth, throat, esophageal, and bladder cancers, these risks decrease by one-half within five years after quitting smoking. While smoking increases a person's risk for lung cancer by 25 times or more, that risk is cut in half by 10 years after the person has quit smoking. Smoking cessation can extend **life expectancy**.

COCAINE AND CRACK COCAINE

Cocaine is derived from the coca plant and available in powdered form. It is either injected intravenously or snorted nasally. **Crack cocaine** is produced by processing powdered cocaine, altering its chemical composition. It is available in the form of "rocks" which are smoked. One distinction is that, while powdered cocaine is typically quite expensive, crack cocaine is comparatively cheap, making it more accessible and hence more dangerous. Either form of cocaine is in the **stimulant** drug class and is extremely addictive. Using any amount of either incurs physical risks, including: elevated heart rate, respiratory rate, body temperature, and blood pressure; respiratory failure; heart attack; stroke; seizures; reduced capacity to resist and fight infections; hepatitis and/or AIDS from sharing needles for injections; and burn injuries from smoking crack. Psychological risks include: hallucinations, including tactile hallucinations of "coke bugs," i.e., the sensation of insects crawling on the skin; paranoid, erratic, and/or violent behavior; loss of appetite; loss of sexual interest; anxiety; depression; confusion; and "cocaine psychosis," i.e., losing interest in family, friends, hobbies, sports, and all other usual activities; and losing touch with reality.

METHAMPHETAMINE

Methamphetamine is a drug in the **stimulant** class. Chemically it is related to the stimulant amphetamine, but it affects the central nervous system more powerfully. Street names for the drug include speed, crank, and meth. It is available in pills for taking orally, or in powder for injecting or snorting. Through a chemical process ("cooking"), it can be crystallized into an even stronger form, called crystal meth, ice, or glass, which is smoked. **Methamphetamine** use produces physiological and psychological effects including: euphoria; insomnia; elevated blood pressure and heart rate; an increase in physical activity; severe anorexia (lack of appetite); irritability; anxiety; confusion; paranoia; violent behavior; tremors; respiratory difficulties; cardiovascular disruptions, which can be fatal; hypothermia; convulsions; and irreversible damage to blood vessels in the brain, causing strokes. In addition, users who inject methamphetamine and share needles with others have the risk of contracting HIV/AIDS.

ALCOHOL ABUSE AND ALCOHOLISM

According to a publication by the US Department of Health and Human Services' Substance Abuse and Mental Health Services Administration (SAMHSA), citing the National Institute on Drug Abuse (NIDA, 2004), a division of the National Institutes of Health (NIH), as its source, **alcohol abuse** is a problematic drinking pattern that causes social problems, health problems, or both. The term **alcoholism**, or alcohol dependence, however, indicates an illness whose symptoms include abnormal behaviors for the purpose of obtaining alcohol, which causes impairment in an individual's control over his or her drinking. Regular, substantial use of alcohol has short-term effects that include impaired judgment, altered emotions and perceptions, impaired coordination, distorted vision and hearing, halitosis, and hangovers. Heavy use of alcohol has long-term effects that include skin problems; vitamin deficiencies; stomach disorders; loss of appetite; sexual impotence; liver damage; loss of memory; and damage to the central nervous system, heart, and cardiovascular system.

PRESCRIPTION DRUG ABUSE

The most commonly abused **prescription drugs** are opiate and opioid painkillers like Vicodin and Oxycontin; anxiolytic and anti-anxiety and sedative medications like Valium and Xanax; hypnotics like Ambien, prescribed for insomnia and anxiety; and stimulants like Ritalin, prescribed for ADHD and some sleep disorders. These are popular for their consciousness-altering effects. Signs of abuse include asking multiple doctors for prescriptions; repeatedly "losing" prescriptions, requiring replacements; forging, selling, and/or stealing prescriptions; abnormally sedated, energetic, or altered behaviors; extreme mood swings; hostility; decreased or increased sleeping; higher-than-prescribed dosing; and reduced decision-making capacity. **Opiates and opioids** cause symptoms including depression, low blood pressure, constipation, lowered respiration, perspiration, incoordination, and confusion. **Anxiolytics** cause confusion, dizziness, drowsiness, unstable gait, rapid involuntary eye movements, and poor judgment. **Stimulants** cause restlessness, insomnia, irritability, agitation, high blood pressure, heart arrhythmia, weight loss, and impulsivity. Reasons for abuse include to relieve tension or relax; increase alertness; improve concentration, school, or work performance; decrease appetite; get high and feel good; experiment with mental effects; prevent withdrawal once addicted; and/or facilitate socialization and peer acceptance.

Although many patients prescribed pain medications following surgery are afraid they will become addicted to them, this seldom happens when they take them as prescribed. **Addiction** is more likely when potentially addictive drugs are not taken as directed. Some **risk factors** for abusing prescription drugs include: youth, i.e., adolescence or early 20s; some pre-existing psychiatric disorders; current or past addictions to alcohol and other substances; lack of adequate knowledge or information regarding prescription medications; social environments with drug use; peer pressure; and working in healthcare settings or other situations with easier access to prescription drugs. Older adult abuse of prescriptions is an increasing problem: an aging population includes multiple health problems and multiple medications. This creates greater risk for misusing drugs; combining prescriptions with other prescriptions, over-the-counter medications, alcohol, and/or illegal drugs; and addiction. Some serious medical dangers of abusing prescriptions include: memory problems from anxiolytics and sedatives; choking risk; lowered blood pressure; slowed or stopped breathing; coma; and death by overdose from opiates, opioids, anxiolytics, and sedatives. Sudden withdrawal from sedatives and anxiolytics can cause nervous system hyperactivity and seizures. Abusing stimulants can cause paranoia, aggression, tremors, hallucinations, high blood pressure, dangerously high body temperatures, cardiac problems, and seizures.

LEGAL AND SOCIETAL IMPACTS OF SUBSTANCE ABUSE

The National Drug Intelligence Center's National Drug Threat Assessments find millions of people, many aged 18-25, have injected **illegal drugs**. Among adult Americans with AIDS, the CDC reports those contracting it from injecting drugs have lower survival rates than those contracting it from all other forms of transmission. Thousands of Americans die every year from the effects of drug use. **Drug abuse** frequently causes parents to neglect or abuse their children physically and/or emotionally. Children with parents or family members abusing substances are often deprived of shelter, water, food, medical and dental care, and necessary immunizations. Parents manufacturing drugs like methamphetamine pose even higher risks to children for hazardous chemical exposure, neglect, injury, and death. Employee substance abuse causes significant economic impacts on businesses through productivity loss; absenteeism; escalated medical insurance use; workplace accidents; workplace theft; and catastrophic accidents caused by drug impairment in employees like bus drivers, train conductors, air traffic controllers, and airline pilots. Methamphetamine lab operations not only severely strain taxpayer, local, state, and federal government resources, but moreover injure and kill neighbors, police, emergency responders, and children. Meth users seriously increase social services and law enforcement expenses.

Prevention, Intervention, and Treatment of Substance Abuse

STAGE-OF-CHANGE APPROACH TO SUBSTANCE ABUSE TREATMENT

The stages of change are precontemplation, contemplation, preparation, action, and maintenance. In the **action stage**, clinicians should support realistic approaches to change via small steps; acknowledge early-stage change difficulties; engage clients in treatment; emphasize the importance of staying in recovery; help clients use functional analysis to identify high-risk situations, and develop corresponding suitable coping strategies; and help clients find new reinforcers for positive change. In **maintenance**, clinicians should help clients identify and try new, non-substance reinforcers; affirm client self-efficacy and determination; support lifestyle modifications; help clients practice and apply new coping skills to prevent relapse; and maintain supportive contact. Some competing **reinforcers** for clients include: involvement in self-help or 12-step activities and groups; setting goals for educational, employment, nutritional, and fitness improvements; volunteer work to enhance self-efficacy, interact with socially acceptable friends, occupy time, and help others; cultural and spiritual activities; interacting more with significant others and families; learning new hobby skills or improving existing ones; and socializing with non-substance abusers.

PREVENTION STRATEGIES FOR USE AND ABUSE OF ALCOHOL, TOBACCO, AND OTHER LEGAL AND ILLEGAL DRUGS

Prevention strategies for the use and abuse of alcohol, tobacco, and other legal and illegal drugs include the following:

- **Enlist the parents/caregivers**: Provide them with information about the signs of use and abuse of alcohol, tobacco, and drugs and guidelines about how to talk to their children about these issues as well as lists of community and Internet resources.
- **Promote self-esteem**: Identify and recognize individuals' talents and skills and encourage them to develop their talents.
- **Develop critical thinking skills**: Focus on problem-solving and values in class discussions and assignments.
- **Educate regarding risks**: Include facts, dangers, and laws related to drug and alcohol use. (However, education alone without skills training has not proven to be effective.)
- **Provide skills training**: Focus on specific skills, such as assertiveness, refusal methods, and methods of withstanding peer pressure.
- **Provide alternatives**: Engage students in activities such as sports, music, and computer clubs. Provide after-school programs/activities for high school students.

PROMOTING INDIVIDUAL RESPONSIBLE DRUG/ALCOHOL USE

Strategies for promoting individual responsible drug/alcohol use include the following:

- **Education**: Include facts about drug/alcohol effects, dangers, and clearance as well as laws related to drugs and alcohol. Outline the effects of mixing drugs with other drugs or alcohol and review safety measures such as the use of designated drivers.
- **Assertiveness training**: Teach the child how to say "no" and how to handle peer pressure to avoid risk-taking behaviors.
- **Designated driver**: One person who uses no drugs or alcohol is designated to drive those using drugs/alcohol to prevent accidents.
- **Sober/Safe ride programs**: Free rides on request for those using drugs/alcohol are available in some communities.

- **Sober friend**: One person is designated to watch over other friends who are using drugs/alcohol to prevent them from risk-taking behavior (such as sexual contact or severe intoxication, or making public displays of risk-taking behavior on social media) and who remains alert to prevent the use of date-rape drugs.

INTERVENTION AND TREATMENTS FOR SUBSTANCE ABUSE

INTERVENTIONS

Interventions substance abuse include the following:

- **Personal intervention**: Friends and/or family may confront the person and explain how the person's substance abuse is affecting them. Interventions are best done with a small group rather than with one individual confronting the abuser; adolescents should generally include adults in the group and not attempt to handle the intervention without assistance. If the drug abuser has overdosed, then 9-1-1 should be called.
- **Tell a responsible adult**: Young people especially are often not prepared to confront others who are participating in substance abuse but should seek help from a parent, counselor, spiritual advisor, or teacher whom they trust and who can help them deal with the problem. Adolescents are often reluctant to divulge others' "secrets," so it's important to have discussions in class about health and safety issues taking precedence over confidentiality.

TREATMENT

Treatments for substance abuse include the following:

- **Drug rehabilitation**: Addicted and alcoholic substance abusers may require inpatient or outpatient treatment in a drug rehabilitation center. Many programs are covered by insurance, although some may be prohibitively expensive for some students, and others may have waiting lists.
- **Smoking cessation programs**: These include support groups, online programs, and nicotine replacement (such as transdermal patches).
- **Counseling**: Substance abusers often have unresolved problems that require professional intervention, so referral for counseling is often indicated.
- **Detoxification**: This should be carried out under medical supervision because of the potential for life-threatening complications. Adolescents should not attempt detoxification by themselves or under the supervision of friends.
- **Medications**: Methadone or buprenorphine may be used for maintenance after detoxification for drug addicts. Naloxone is administered in emergent conditions for opioid overdose.

ROLE OF PEER PRESSURE IN DECISION MAKING AND PROBLEM SOLVING RELATED TO SUBSTANCE ABUSE

Peer pressure is the pressure to conform to the behavior or ideals of a group that is approximately the same age and social class. Most adolescents are introduced to drugs and alcohol by peers, and **peer pressure** to participate in high-risk behavior, such as substance abuse, is very strong because the adolescent wants to be accepted as part of the group. Groups that use drugs or alcohol tend to view others as abnormal, not themselves, so adolescents that refuse to participate may find themselves ostracized. Thus, although an adolescent may be aware of the dangers of drugs and alcohol and doesn't want to participate in use, he or she may feel compelled to do so. **Assertiveness training** and **refusal skills** can help the adolescent to deal with peer pressure, but the reality is that the person may need to align with a **different group of peers** in order to make good decisions about avoiding substance abuse.

Handwritten notes at top of page:

$\frac{103}{130} = \frac{n}{100}$

$130n = 10300$

$\frac{130n}{130} = \frac{10300}{130}$

$n = 79\%$

Praxis Practice Test

Want to take this practice test in an online interactive format?
Check out the bonus page, which includes interactive practice questions and
much more: **mometrix.com/bonus948/priihpeck5857**

SCAN HERE

1. The National Health Education Standards (NHES) were developed in response to what?

    a. Standards being developed in hospitals
    b. Standards being developed in education
    c. Standards being developed in public health
    d. Standards being developed in private practice

2. Which of the following is MOST accurate regarding the components of a coordinated school health program?

    a. School health education should be comprehensive.
    b. Physical education is separate from such a program.
    c. School health services are only for emergency care.
    d. Community and family are not part of this program.

3. Of the following diseases, which one is NOT caused by the Epstein-Barr virus?

    a. Infectious hepatitis
    b. Burkitt's lymphoma
    c. Infectious mononucleosis
    d. Nasopharyngeal carcinoma

4. According to Piaget's developmental theory, when do children first achieve mental operations?

    a. During the sensorimotor stage
    b. During the preoperational stage
    c. In the concrete operations stage
    d. In the formal operations stage

5. About 80 percent of all deaths from noncommunicable diseases are caused by four types of disease. Which of these four types causes the majority of these deaths?

    a. Diabetic
    b. Cancerous
    c. Respiratory
    d. Cardiovascular

6. Which statement is MOST accurate regarding the nature of decision-making for teenagers?

    a. The decisions teens make are unlikely to affect their long-term futures.
    b. Social contexts change; hence, teens must evaluate and adjust decisions.
    c. Teens generally have enough life experience to make difficult decisions.
    d. Intervention programs to improve decision-making skills are ineffective.

7. What is true about the privacy of records protected under Family Educational Rights and Privacy Act (FERPA)?

    a. Student health but not immunization records are protected by FERPA.

    b. Student health and immunization records are protected under FERPA.

    c. Student health but not public school nurses' records are protected under FERPA.

    d. Student special education records are protected under Individuals with Disabilities Education Act (IDEA), not FERPA.

8. What is a valid claim when comparing Rosenshine and Stevens' model of direct instruction with the Direct Instruction method of Engelmann and colleagues?

    a. Both are teacher directed, but only one is skills oriented.

    b. Both are face-to-face, but only one uses small groups.

    c. Both use task analysis, but only one is sequenced.

    d. Both teach explicitly, but only one is generic.

9. Of the following research methods for gathering health-related data, which one is most applicable to collecting aggregate information on large population groups?

    a. Questionnaires

    b. Observations

    c. Interviews

    d. Surveys

10. Among the life skills of values clarification, decision-making, communication, and coping skills, which of the following responses to stressful life events MOST reflects decision-making skills?

    a. Considering positive aspects of the situation

    b. Evaluating the pros and cons of the situation

    c. Expressing your feelings about the situation

    d. Positive behaviors to deal with the situation

11. According to Erikson's theory of psychosocial development, which ability must be achieved during the period of adolescence?

    a. Identity

    b. Intimacy

    c. Industry

    d. Autonomy

12. How is cardiorespiratory endurance best defined?

    a. The ability to perform dynamic exercise using large muscles over long times

    b. The ability to perform dynamic exercises using small muscles for short times

    c. The ability to perform static exercises using all muscles for average durations

    d. The ability to perform any kind of exercising using any muscles for any time

13. What is a common misconception among teenagers that health educators should correct?

    a. That conception cannot occur by body rubbing without vaginal or vulvar sperm contact

    b. That conception will not occur without penetration and ejaculation inside the vagina

    c. That teenage males should put on condoms before sex and wear them continuously

    d. That kissing or oral or anal sex will not cause pregnancy if no sperm touches the vulva or vagina

14. Within personal hygiene, which of these is a fact about oral care?

a. Gum disease can cause serious disorders of the heart valves.
b. Unhealthy gums can cause gum infections but not tooth loss.
c. Brushing one's teeth prevents tooth decay, not gum disease.
d. Gum disease affects soft tissues rather than the jaw's bones.

15. We get _____ from _____ in our diet and _____ from _____.

a. Energy, protein; amino acids, carbohydrates
b. Energy, vitamins; muscle repair, amino acids
c. Energy, carbohydrates; amino acids, protein
d. Energy, minerals; tissue repair, saturated fat

16. Which of the following correctly sequences the stages of change in the stages of change model of health behavior?

a. Precontemplation, contemplation, preparation, action, maintenance
b. Preparation, precontemplation, contemplation, action, maintenance
c. Maintenance, preparation, precontemplation, contemplation, action
d. Preparation, action, maintenance, precontemplation, contemplation

17. Of the four types of diseases—cancers, cardiovascular diseases, diabetes, and respiratory diseases—that cause the majority of deaths from noncommunicable diseases, which risk factors do they all share in common?

a. Smoking and drinking
b. Poor diet and inactivity
c. All of these risk factors
d. None of these factors

18. Teaching the idea that saturated fat in the diet contributes to heart disease is MOST developmentally appropriate to which stage of Piaget's theory of cognitive development?

a. Sensorimotor
b. Preoperational
c. Formal operations
d. Concrete operations

19. Which statement is accurate concerning U.S. laws governing immunizations?

a. Federal laws specify immunizations for children to enter public schools.
b. Laws regulating child immunizations for public school vary in each state.
c. Certain states have laws about immunizations for school; others do not.
d. As laws vary by state, there is no central data repository for these laws.

20. Which of the following major muscles controls the chewing functions of the jaws?

a. The orbicularis oris muscle
b. The zygomaticus muscles
c. The trapezius muscles
d. The masseter muscles

21. What is correct about the hormones that stimulate male and female organs to produce male and female sex hormones?

 a. Female organs are stimulated by female hormones and male organs by male hormones.
 b. The same hormones that produce male or female sex characteristics stimulate the organs.
 c. The same hormones stimulate both male and female organs to produce sex hormones.
 d. The hypothalamus stimulates the pituitary gland's secretion of male and female hormones.

22. What is true about guidelines for making emergency 911 calls?

 a. Call 911 for uncontrollable bleeding or unconsciousness but not allergic reactions or chest pains.
 b. Situations needing immediate help from police, fire departments, or ambulances merit 911 calls.
 c. Prank calls to 911 are a great nuisance and interfere with actual emergencies but are not illegal.
 d. When a person calls 911 in an emergency, he or she should hang up immediately to free up the lines.

23. What has been found by research into teacher influence on children's peer relationships as a social context factor?

 a. Teachers who believe in and relate positively with attention deficit hyperactivity disorder (ADHD) children can modulate peer dislike of them.
 b. Teachers have difficulty relating to children with ADHD; therefore, they cannot change peers' dislike.
 c. Teachers cannot affect dislike of ADHD children by peers rejecting them despite improved behavior.
 d. Teachers who create classrooms improving peer relationships eliminate all dislike of ADHD children.

24. When comparing the federal Healthy People 2000, 2010, and 2020 initiatives, which applies MOST?

 a. The 2000 initiative aimed to decrease health disparities, 2010 to eliminate them, and 2020 to establish health equity.
 b. The 2000 initiative aimed to eliminate health disparities, 2010 to establish health equity, and 2020 to improve health.
 c. The 2000 initiative aimed to improve American health, 2010 to reduce health disparities, and 2020 to eliminate them.
 d. The 2000, 2010, and 2020 Healthy People initiatives all have aimed to improve health for all Americans.

25. Which of the following is MOST appropriate concerning extracurricular activities for student health needs?

 a. A student should expect to feel overextended when participating in activities.
 b. A student should discontinue an activity if he or she cannot keep up with all things.
 c. A student should join only those activities that he or she already knows how to do.
 d. A student should consider trying new things but not the time that is available.

26. Of the following, which is accurate regarding personal hygiene in adolescence?

    a. The majority of teens experience acne regardless of skin care habits.
    b. Teens should not need to shampoo hair more but do so out of vanity.
    c. The same oral hygiene they used as children should suffice for teens.
    d. Teens who learned good bathing habits as children need not change.

27. Of the following, which is accurate regarding modes of human immunodeficiency virus (HIV) transmission?

    a. HIV cannot be transmitted by oral sex.
    b. HIV cannot be transmitted genetically.
    c. HIV cannot be transmitted via nursing.
    d. HIV cannot be transmitted perinatally.

28. Of the following, which is NOT a sign that an individual may need to get help from a professional for emotional or mental health problems?

    a. Persistent insomnia
    b. Pervasive depression
    c. Difficulty concentrating
    d. Any or all of these are signs

29. Among signs of domestic abuse, physical violence, isolation, and psychological symptoms of being abused, which of the following is more specifically a sign of domestic abuse than of the others?

    a. Constantly reporting one's locations and activities to the partner
    b. Often exhibiting or trying to hide injuries, claiming accidents
    c. Marked changes in a person's personality traits or behaviors
    d. Few or no public outings, no car or money use alone, or no visiting with others

30. Which of the following are used as formative assessments?

    a. Student final class projects
    b. Tests given at the ends of units
    c. Curriculum-based measurement
    d. Standardized state examinations

31. What is a result of regular and substantial alcohol use?

    a. It impairs judgment over the long term but not in the short term.
    b. It distorts the perceptions but not the senses of vision or hearing.
    c. It damages both the cardiovascular and central nervous systems.
    d. It causes liver damage but not impotence or stomach disorders.

32. Which of the following correctly identifies the big five personality traits?

    a. Introversion, detail-orientation, responsibility, psychoticism, and kindness
    b. Extraversion, agreeableness, conscientiousness, neuroticism, and openness
    c. Oral traits, anal traits, phallic tendencies, latency tendencies, and genital traits
    d. Assertiveness, prosocial behaviors, impulse control, moodiness, and imagination

33. Among tactics typically employed by domestic abusers to control their victims, what is destroying the victim's property an example of?

    a. Isolation
    b. Humiliation
    c. Dominance
    d. Intimidation

34. In a coordinated school health program, which of the following is a factor?

    a. Psychological, counseling, and social services are parts of a different program.
    b. This program is for promoting the health of students, not of school personnel.
    c. Healthy physical, emotional, and social school environments support learning.
    d. Coordinated school health programs incorporate physical education but not nutrition services.

35. In professional development (PD) for health educators, which of the following organizations offers a national PD conference for educational support professionals (ESPs)?

    a. Society of Health and Physical Educators (ShapeAmerica)
    b. The Centers for Disease Control and Prevention (CDC)
    c. The American Public Health Association (APHA)
    d. The National Education Association (NEA)

36. When health educators teach their students eight steps for establishing and meeting health goals, which of the last four is MOST related to monitoring progress for accountability?

    a. Asking friends to help or forming a club
    b. Using journals, diaries, charts, or graphs
    c. Healthy self-rewards for meeting goals
    d. Making revisions in plans and time lines

37. Which of the following is accurate regarding the history of U.S. regulations addressing pollution?

    a. The Environmental Protection Agency (EPA) first developed standards, laws, and regulations in the 1980s.
    b. The EPA's focus shifted from the remediation of existing pollution to preventing it during the 2000s.
    c. Congress's policy to prevent and reduce pollution is declared in the Pollution Prevention Act of 1990.
    d. National policy shifted in the 1990s from reducing pollution sources toward treatment and disposal.

38. In which human body system do the white cell blood cells function?

    a. Respiratory
    b. Circulatory
    c. Lymphatic
    d. Endocrine

39. Which statement accurately reflects recommended refusal strategies for children and teens?

    a. Walking away from a pressure situation is avoidant.
    b. Standing up for others being pressured is meddling.
    c. Proposing alternative activities is coping effectively.
    d. To say "no," one often needs to be very aggressive.

40. Of the following, which correctly reflects how teenagers make decisions?

    a. Internal, not external, variables influence teen decisions.
    b. Adolescents usually make decisions in isolated conditions.
    c. Feedback influences the decisions that adolescents make.
    d. External, not internal, variables influence teens' decisions.

41. According to research studies, what is true about the impact of physical activity (PA) on health risks?

    a. PA lowers heart disease, stroke, diabetes, and colon and breast cancer risks.
    b. PA reduces risks of heart disease and stroke but not of diabetes or any cancer.
    c. PA reduces risks of all these diseases, but amounts of PA needed for each disease vary greatly.
    d. PA in adequate amounts improves overall well-being but does not lower disease risks.

42. According to current research, what is true related to diabetes prevention?

    a. Supplements and foods control blood sugar equally well.
    b. Overall hours of sleep are unrelated to insulin sensitivity.
    c. Research does not connect stress with insulin resistance.
    d. Exercise in cooler temperatures can help glucose control.

43. From birth to three years, children typically grow to reach _____ of their previous height; during puberty, they typically attain around _____ of their growth in height.

    a. 175 percent; 50 percent
    b. 300 percent; 75 percent
    c. 200 percent; 25 percent
    d. 150 percent; 30 percent

44. How many deaths does smoking cigarettes cause annually in America compared to other causes?

    a. More than alcohol and drug use, car accidents, human immunodeficiency virus (HIV), and gunshots together
    b. More than alcohol and drug use combined or more than HIV and gunshots
    c. More than alcohol and drug use and HIV combined, not including gunshots
    d. More than gunshots and HIV combined, but less than alcohol and drug use

45. Which of the following accurately represents findings about how stress interacts with interpersonal communications on health care and other important subjects?

    a. We can control a problem better by limiting discussions of it.
    b. Being able to explain a problem affords more control over it.
    c. Sensitive discussions have outcomes worse than we expect.
    d. Quantity supersedes quality for discussing important issues.

46. Which statement is MOST accurate concerning differences between type 1 and type 2 diabetes?

    a. Type 1 involves children and teens; type 2 involves onset in adulthood.
    b. Type 1 involves more lifestyle factors; type 2 involves genetic elements.
    c. Type 1 involves insulin insufficiency; type 2 involves insulin insensitivity.
    d. Type 1 involves obesity and inactivity; type 2 involves nutrition deficits.

47. Among domains of development throughout life stages, what does Piaget's theory focus MOST on?

    a. Emotional development
    b. Developing relationships
    c. Intellectual development
    d. Developing independence

48. Which of the following is recommended for teachers to deal with an individual student who is always misbehaving in class?

    a. Speaking with the student in private
    b. Disciplining the student during class
    c. Differentiating behavior versus the student
    d. (A) and (C) but not (B) unless necessary

49. Regarding contraception methods, which of the following is correct?

    a. A condom or spermicide is effective enough by itself.
    b. Vasectomy is never reversible; tubal ligation always is.
    c. None of these choices is correct about contraception.
    d. Women insert IUDs, diaphragms, and pills themselves.

50. Which of Howard Gardner's multiple intelligence styles would learn best through group instructional activities?

    a. Interpersonal
    b. Intrapersonal
    c. Visual-spatial
    d. Mathematical

51. What is the School Health Index (SHI)?

    a. A tool that the Centers for Disease Control (CDC) uses to rate school health policies
    b. A tool that the CDC uses for (C) and (D) but not for (A)
    c. A tool to help schools in their health self-assessments
    d. A tool to help schools create health policies and plans

52. Among the following instructional techniques, which is equally amenable to individual or multiple student work and also to student work with or without the teacher's active involvement?

    a. Role-playing
    b. Brainstorming
    c. Guided discovery
    d. Cooperative learning

53. In his developmental theory, what did Erikson identify as the positive outcome of successfully resolving the nuclear conflict of basic trust versus mistrust?

    a. Will
    b. Hope
    c. Purpose
    d. Competence

54. Which of the following foods is classified in two food groups by the U.S. Department of Agriculture (USDA)?

    a. Legumes
    b. Seafood
    c. Cheese
    d. Eggplant

55. In the majority of U.S. states and territories, which of these professions are identified as mandated reporters of child maltreatment?

    a. Probation or parole officers, substance abuse counselors, and film processors
    b. Camps and recreation and youth center employees, directors, and volunteers
    c. School, health care, child care, mental health, and law enforcement employees
    d. Domestic violence workers, humane or animal control officers, and college faculties

56. To write learning objectives in planning health instruction, which of the following verbs represents a measurable student action?

    a. Learn
    b. Explain
    c. Understand
    d. Any of these

57. In the nuclear family emotional system Dr. Murray Bowen describes in his Family Systems Theory, which basic relationship pattern is represented if a parent shows excessive anxiety about a child, and the child responds by regressing to increased dependence and immature demands on the parent?

    a. Dysfunction in one spouse
    b. Impairment of a child(ren)
    c. Emotional distance pattern
    d. The marital conflict pattern

58. In the reflective process of teaching, which tools would MOST help a teacher to self-analyze his or her own body language and movement within the classroom and adjust these to be more effective?

    a. Journals and diaries
    b. Video recordings
    c. Audio recordings
    d. Peer observation

59. What is a definition of body mass index (BMI)?
- a. The ratio of weight to height squared
- b. The ratio of abdominal fat to total fat
- c. The ratio of body fat to muscle cubed
- d. The ratio of total fat to overall weight

60. What have physical education teachers found about using apps like Coach's Eye, iCoachview, and so on with their students?
- a. Student enthusiasm helps them appreciate constructive criticism.
- b. Students typically cannot use apps after only brief demonstration.
- c. Students are uncomfortable seeing their performance postgame.
- d. Students experience delayed feedback when teachers play videos.

61. Which of the following body systems controls fluid loss, protects deep tissues, and synthesizes vitamin D?
- a. The skeletal system
- b. The muscular system
- c. The lymphatic system
- d. The integumentary system

62. What is true about how teachers can engage community members and groups in physical education (PE) programs?
- a. It would be inappropriate to solicit funds from local health agencies to buy sports equipment.
- b. Local trophy companies are in business to make money and will not donate for school events.
- c. Local governments lack departments that could talk to students about community resources.
- d. When PE teachers plan Olympics-themed events, they may find volunteers from local colleges.

63. The frog kick is used in which swimming stroke(s)?
- a. The breaststroke
- b. The butterfly
- c. The crawl
- d. All these

64. Which of the following describes the most appropriate physical education self-assessment activity for kindergarten through Grade 2 students?
- a. Students write entries in journals describing the fitness activities they are doing.
- b. Students pictorially illustrate their activities in each of several fitness categories.
- c. Students keep notebooks of progress notes and give them to teachers regularly.
- d. Students record their progress on index cards they give to teachers at intervals.

65. Regarding perceptual-motor abilities, which is a performance skill that would be MOST affected by individual differences in control precision?

    a. Playing quarterback in football
    b. Handling a hockey puck
    c. Dribbling a basketball
    d. Driving a race car

66. Compared to naturalistic observations, structured observations are _____ in physical education assessment.

    a. more objective and less subjective
    b. more subjective and less objective
    c. more to see social than motor skills
    d. more realistic regarding behaviors

67. For cooperative learning activities to be more productive than competitive or individual learning activities, one of five necessary elements is positive interdependence among the members of a student group, including student awareness of it. What is accurate about the other four required elements?

    a. The students occasionally engage in productive, face-to-face interactions.
    b. The students are accountable for group goals collectively, not individually.
    c. The students use task-relevant interpersonal and group skills frequently.
    d. The students process group functioning to sustain current effectiveness.

68. A physical education teacher addresses a wide range of skill levels in one class by setting up several learning stations to teach a lesson in throwing. Which station activity represents the highest student skill level?

    a. Throwing lead passes
    b. Throwing at a stationary target
    c. Throwing to teammates while defended
    d. Throwing all these ways equally

69. Regarding communication with athletes, which statement is recommended by experts for coaches to consider?

    a. Coaches must not only get athlete attention but also explain, so athletes understand easily.
    b. Coaches must determine if athletes understood them but not whether they believed them.
    c. Coaches must get athletes to understand and believe, not necessarily accept, what they say.
    d. Coaches must disregard athletes' individual and group nonverbal cues for controlling them.

70. Which of these locomotor activities is most appropriate for children younger than five years old?

    a. Blob tag
    b. Musical hoops
    c. Follow the leader
    d. Any of these equally

71. Relative to spatial awareness, which movement concept involves vertical, horizontal, and circular paths of movement?

   a.   Locations and levels
   b.   Personal space
   c.   Directions
   d.   Planes

72. A physical education teacher has included an objective for student heart rates to reach a target range when they play a sport. The teacher discovers the majority of students did not reach that target. Which teacher response to this discovery is the best example of using reflection to inform instruction?

   a.   The teacher decides students were not playing hard enough and gives them a pep talk.
   b.   The teacher experiments with having the students play the next game at faster speeds.
   c.   The teacher changes the rules of the game so all students will participate more actively.
   d.   The teacher might do either (B) or (C) or even both of these but is less likely to use (A).

73. Compared to regular baseball, softball has a _____ ball, a _____ infield, _____ innings, and _____ pitch.

   a.   smaller; bigger; more; the same
   b.   bigger; smaller; fewer; a different
   c.   bigger; bigger; fewer; a different
   d.   smaller; smaller; more; the same

74. For a student who has joint problems but wants to be physically active, which is the best extracurricular activity?

   a.   Skiing
   b.   Swimming
   c.   Skateboarding
   d.   Playing soccer

75. Which statement about physical education (PE) class safety and teacher liability is a valid one?

   a.   PE classes can include advanced gymnastics safely by having group spotters.
   b.   PE classes as well as extracurricular activities can include trampolines safely.
   c.   PE teachers must instruct students in calling for and backing away from fly balls.
   d.   PE teachers commonly and safely discipline students with strenuous exercise.

76. Regarding indications that a student should be evaluated to determine eligibility for adapted physical education (APE), which of the following (in addition to referral) correctly states a criterion?

   a.   The student performs at his or her ability level in group settings but not on an individual basis.
   b.   The student's social behaviors impede his or her or others' learning more than half of class time.
   c.   The student has scored below average in at least one part of the state physical fitness test.
   d.   The student scored at least one standard deviation low on the norm-referenced test used.

77. One teaching method for managing kindergarten through Grade 12 physical education classes uses three steps to address student noncompliance with class rules. In which of the following sequences should these steps be applied?

    a. An oral warning; a brief time-out; a time-out with written response
    b. A brief time-out; a time-out with written response; an oral warning
    c. A time-out with written response; an oral warning; a brief time-out
    d. A brief time-out; an oral warning; a time-out with written response

78. Of the following, which elementary school activity best integrates physical education skills with English language arts (ELA) skills within the same lesson?

    a. Students perform movements and then look up adverbs and write synonyms and antonyms.
    b. Students look up and write adverbs, synonyms, and antonyms and then perform movements.
    c. Students identify adverbs in teacher-read sentences and describe movements using adverbs.
    d. Students perform movements in ways described by recently learned adverbs on given cards.

79. Within the TARGET model, which physical education teaching strategy is an example of the R in the acronym?

    a. Varying the difficulty levels among several different activities
    b. Giving students some responsibility for the choice of activities
    c. Acknowledging process and improvement rather than product
    d. Avoiding peer comparison through rapid and variable grouping

80. Of the following statements, which is true about aerobics?

    a. Aerobics originally focused on the flexibility of the body.
    b. Aerobics originally focused on the strength of the muscles.
    c. Aerobics originally focused on cardiorespiratory endurance.
    d. Aerobics originally focused on one thing as it still does today.

81. Which of the following is a recommended strategy for physical education teachers to plan effective class behavior management?

    a. Announce at least ten expectations to the students in oral format.
    b. Enforce expectations occasionally for intermittent reinforcement.
    c. Define expectations in terms of what they want students not to do.
    d. Define expectations in terms of what they want the students to do.

82. According to national physical education (PE) standards, to show respect, which of the following should PE teachers do to address a student's behavior problem?

    a. The teacher describes the student's behavior, why it was disruptive, and solutions for the problem.
    b. The teacher has a classmate describe the behavior, why it was disruptive, and solutions for the problem.
    c. The teacher has the student describe the behavior, why it was disruptive, and solutions for the problem.
    d. The teacher avoids discussing it but provides concrete consequences and solutions for the problem.

83. When someone bench presses weights to strengthen the arms and upper body, this is an example of which exercise science principle?

a. Overload
b. Specificity
c. Adaptation
d. Progression

84. What advantages does Fitbit technology include for physical education teachers and students?

a. Weight control but not sleep quality
b. Self-monitoring but not competition
c. Fashion appeal as well as motivation
d. Stand-alone fitness progress tracking

85. The respiratory system _____ oxygen for and _____ carbon dioxide from the circulatory system.

a. creates; filters
b. provides; removes
c. ionizes; absorbs
d. eliminates; destroys

86. Among the following divisions of biomechanics that involve physics concepts, which one is MOST closely related to Newton's first three laws of motion?

a. Coplanar vectors
b. Kinematics
c. Kinetics
d. Forces

87. Among the following common areas of negligence in physical education, in addition to first aid emergencies, which one can teachers and coaches MOST mitigate by enlisting the help of students?

a. Instruction
b. Supervision
c. Transportation
d. Class environments

88. Of the following assessment approaches, which one is traditional rather than alternative?

a. Students write down their personal fitness plans.
b. Students perform a series of dance movements.
c. Students show learning by playing a sports game.
d. Students label the team's positions on a diagram.

89. Research finds that motor skills training, endurance training, and strength training all share which neuroplasticity effects in common?

a. New blood vessel formation
b. Motor map reorganization
c. Spinal reflex modification
d. New synapse generation

90. When a physical education teacher gives a defense cue of "Match up" to students during basketball practice, what does this mean?

    a.   Students always should pair up with another player on the court for defense.

    b.   Students should stay near to offensive players that they defend on the court.

    c.   Students should defend players more like them in size than fitness or skill level.

    d.   Students should defend players similar to them in size, fitness, and skill level.

91. Concerning the impacts of various resources on student physical education (PE) outcomes, what has research found?

    a.   Class size and student–teacher ratio correlate inversely with activity levels, time, safety, and learning.

    b.   Students receive a higher quantity and quality of PE from teachers who also teach different subjects.

    c.   Student physical activity is the same whether PE curriculum is based on educational standards or not.

    d.   PE facilities and equipment are valuable resources but do not change the amount of student activity.

92. Among the most prevalent challenges to kindergarten through Grade 12 physical education, which has recently become even more challenging than the others?

    a.   Inadequate resources and parental support

    b.   Overly large class sizes and teacher burnout

    c.   Violence, student drug abuse, and discipline

    d.   Reductions in school curriculum times for physical education

93. Regarding feedback that physical education teachers and coaches give students and athletes, which of the following is an example of prescriptive feedback rather than descriptive feedback?

    a.   "You can do this!"

    b.   "Follow through!"

    c.   "That was great!"

    d.   "Way to play ball!"

94. Among fundamental movement skills (FMS), which two are both part of the same main category?

    a.   Locomotor and manipulative

    b.   Manipulative and rotation

    c.   Rotation and balance

    d.   Balance and stability

95. Related to summation of forces, which is accurate about how body parts move?

    a.   The largest body parts are the slowest and move last.

    b.   The smallest body parts are the fastest and move first.

    c.   The largest body parts are the slowest and move first.

    d.   Regardless of speed, all parts move at the same times.

96. According to experiences reported by physical education teachers, what are some characteristics of technology in applications such as GradeBookPro?
    a. Apps like this enable physical education teachers to use most of their time for teaching.
    b. Apps like this reduce final grade disputes by consolidating student data.
    c. Apps like this can exponentially speed up the task of taking attendance.
    d. Apps like this streamline all these and a great many more teacher tasks.

97. Which of the following is an example of the short-term effects of exercise on health?
    a. Exercising releases endorphins, generating euphoria.
    b. Exercising regularly prevents and relieves depression.
    c. Exercising lowers the risk of heart attacks and strokes.
    d. Exercising can reduce one's blood pressure and pulse.

98. Which non-English language is shared in common by some of the terminology in both ballet and ballroom dancing?
    a. French
    b. Italian
    c. Spanish
    d. Russian

99. Which kinds of physical education activities are both appropriate for boys and girls to participate in together and are less dependent on team assignment by student skill levels?
    a. Activities that involve participant body contact
    b. Activities that require more upper-body strength
    c. Activities that require agility and lower-body strength
    d. Activities of all these types

100. Which of these describes a function of formative assessments?
    a. They enable teachers to show accountability for adequate yearly progress and similar requirements.
    b. They enable teachers to compare student achievement to population averages.
    c. They enable teachers to adjust instruction in progress to address student needs.
    d. They enable teachers to see if they helped students meet curriculum standards.

101. Which development in human manual skills emerges the earliest?
    a. Successfully reaching for objects
    b. Coordinated arm–hand movements
    c. Arm flapping and jerky arm extensions
    d. Changing hand shapes before touching objects

102. Of the following, which is a valid principle of physical education (PE) coaching for teaching movement and sport skills to students?
    a. Asking think-about questions gives an advantage to students.
    b. Reading tasks or steps aloud only will delay the setup of players.
    c. PE teachers should alternate practice plan sequence for variety.
    d. PE teachers should either describe or demonstrate but not both.

103. Compared to the amount of time in moderate to vigorous physical activity (MVPA) the Institute of Medicine recommends for children to spend daily, how much do research studies find they actually spend in school physical education classes?

   a. About one-sixth of what is recommended
   b. About one-third of what is recommended
   c. About one-half of what is recommended
   d. About the same as is recommended

104. What amount of quality physical education time most reflects the National Association for Sport and Physical Education (NASPE) recommendation for elementary school students?

   a. A minimum of 15 minutes per day
   b. A maximum of 30 minutes per day
   c. A minimum of 30 minutes per day
   d. A maximum of 60 minutes a week

105. Regarding appropriate physical education (PE) teaching practices, which statement is MOST valid?

   a. PE teachers must use extrinsic motivations to teach student responsibility for learning.
   b. PE teachers should ignore certain inappropriate student behaviors to extinguish them.
   c. PE teachers do not necessarily need to obtain or renew certification in cardiopulmonary resuscitation (CPR) or automated external defibrillator (AED) use.
   d. PE teachers must regularly and consistently inspect facilities and equipment for safety.

106. Regarding physical education teacher communication with parents, what is MOST effective related to posting and communicating class rules to students at the beginning of the school year?

   a. Giving rules to students, but not parents, so students feel they can trust teachers
   b. Giving copies of rules to students with instructions to take them home to parents
   c. Sending the rules by postal mail with a cover letter asking parents to review them
   d. E-mailing the rules to the parents with a cover letter asking them to review them

107. Which of the following is true about center of gravity (COG)?

   a. COG is in the same location for each human body.
   b. COG varies according to the body parts' positions.
   c. COG varies among bodies but is constant for each.
   d. COG is the same as center of mass or of pressure.

108. The MyFitnessPal, Endomondo, and Fitbit digital fitness apps all share what in common?

   a. Sync
   b. Recipes
   c. Audio feedback
   d. Social networking

109. Of the following, which most accurately represents an aspect of the relationship between nutrition and fitness?

    a. Exercising regularly and energetically enables you to eat anything you want.
    b. Eating a diet rich in calcium prevents bone density loss, but exercise cannot.
    c. Eating right provides energy for exercise, while exercise can control appetite.
    d. Exercising prevents high blood pressure and cholesterol more than diet does.

110. Among examples of how physical education (PE) teachers can collaborate with other educators, which one applies most to taking advantage of administrator support to improve student motivation and learning?

    a. Reading *A River Runs Through It* to study fly-fishing and character development and relationships
    b. Watching *Footloose* to study dance movements and themes of freedom, rebellion, and repression
    c. Designing a joint PE and Family and Consumer Sciences unit that combines nutrition and exercise
    d. Developing a morning walk/run project together with the principal to help students focus better

111. Regarding individual differences that affect physical education activity performance, which of these sports is most appropriate for the ectomorphic somatotype (body type)?

    a. Wrestling
    b. Gymnastics
    c. Shot-putting
    d. High jump

112. When using an assessment instrument meant to measure aerobic endurance, physical education teachers find that maximum student repetitions are limited not by their becoming winded but by specific muscle fatigue. After obtaining the same results over repeated administrations, they conclude that this test measures muscular endurance instead. What have they discovered about this test?

    a. The test is neither a reliable nor valid test.
    b. The test is a valid test, but it is not reliable.
    c. The test is a reliable test, but it is not valid.
    d. The test is valid and reliable, but misused.

113. Among physical proficiencies that affect individual performance, which type of strength is most involved in the activity of kayaking?

    a. Static strength
    b. Trunk strength
    c. Dynamic strength
    d. Explosive strength

114. A physical education teacher designs a student volleyball activity to meet National Association for Sport and Physical Education (NASPE) standards for setting, spiking, forearm passing, defensive strategies, officiating; aerobic capacity; and cooperating and accepting challenges. Which of the following represents the correct sequence of steps in this activity?

a. Rotational positions; serve; base positions; defend against attack
b. Base positions; rotational positions; defend against attack; serve
c. Serve; base positions; defend against attack; rotational positions
d. Defend against attack; serve; rotational positions; base positions

115. In three stages of motor learning, which of these is characteristic of the associative stage?

a. Understanding an activity's goal and nature
b. Making attempts that include major errors
c. Making fewer and more consistent errors
d. Effortless automaticity in performance

116. If a student has the condition of atlantoaxial instability, which of the following activities would be safe for a physical education teacher to assign to the student?

a. A log roll would be safest for this student.
b. A forward roll would be better for this student.
c. No kind of roll should be assigned to this student.
d. It is irrelevant because atlantoaxial instability is so rare.

117. According to experts, what is true about the primary functions of nonverbal communication?

a. Nonverbal communication serves a function of performing social rituals.
b. Nonverbal communication shows personalities rather than relationships.
c. Nonverbal communication is used to replace, not help, verbal interaction.
d. Nonverbal communication is not used like words for expressing feelings.

118. A physical education teacher writes an entry task on the board before class. How does this relate to teacher communication toward student understanding and ownership of high expectations for themselves?

a. This is not recommended because the teacher will not be supervising the students for this activity.
b. This supports high classroom expectations because students can begin the activity independently.
c. This supports student independence for activities but not student comprehension of expectations.
d. This is not recommended because the teacher did not structure the learning activity for students.

119. In quality of movement, _____ is bound/interrupted or free/sustained.

a. flow
b. effort
c. speed
d. rhythm

120. Professional development at its best accomplishes which of these?
- a. Improves primarily the teacher's own knowledge and skills
- b. Improves both a teacher's and his or her colleagues' expertise
- c. Improves primarily the expertise of the teacher's colleagues
- d. Improves teaching practices primarily at the classroom level

121. Which statement best characterizes the role of posture in theories of motor development?
- a. As evidence of growing cerebral control, posture was more important to classical theories.
- b. As the biomechanical basis of action, posture is more important to contemporary theories.
- c. For different reasons, posture has been equally important to both earlier and later theories.
- d. In both classical and contemporary theories, posture is a minor part of motor development.

122. Which of the following biomechanics subjects are based on calculus?
- a. Vector composition and resolution
- b. Differentiation and integration
- c. The parallelogram method
- d. None of these topics

123. Which of these is a typical effect of substance abuse on student behavior?
- a. A shy student becomes more sociable.
- b. An outgoing student becomes withdrawn.
- c. An inhibited student becomes more impulsive.
- d. These are all typical effects of substance abuse.

124. Of the following, which accurately reports research findings related to how physical fitness affects academic achievement?
- a. Cardiovascular fitness and body mass index (BMI) correlate positively with test scores in achievement.
- b. More physically fit children react more quickly but not necessarily more accurately.
- c. Children burn more calories during active gaming than teacher-led fitness activities.
- d. Intense exercise is followed by a significant temporary decline in cognitive function.

125. In one instructional method to promote psychomotor learning, a physical education teacher clearly explains learning goals and skills to be learned to the students; demonstrates the skills for the students; and provides the students with practice time, frequently and regularly monitoring their progress during practice. This describes which of the following methods?
- a. The contingency or contract method
- b. The command or direct method
- c. The task or reciprocal method
- d. None of these methods

126. When is performing the Heimlich maneuver on a student indicated?
- a. The student says he or she is having trouble breathing.
- b. The student is choking and is not able to breathe.
- c. The student has trouble breathing and is coughing.
- d. The Heimlich should not be done until cardiopulmonary resuscitation (CPR) is tried.

127. Which of these is an effective strategy for physical education teachers to enhance students' perceived physical competence?

    a. Specify the number of trials to complete during a certain time period.
    b. Specify the length of time for practicing but not the number of trials.
    c. Specify the technical errors students make in instructional feedback.
    d. Specify a certain activity without varying it to keep students on task.

128. When students learn to fall sideways and land using their hands, which of the following should be the last activity they do in a sequence of increasing difficulty?

    a. Falling sideways from kneeling
    b. Rolling sideways down a wedge
    c. Falling, rolling, and standing up
    d. Running, falling, rolling, and standing

129. When does physical education instruction necessarily require giving feedback to students?

    a. When a skill requires specific correction
    b. When a skill gets environmental feedback
    c. When a student has experience with a skill
    d. When a teacher can comprehensively demonstrate a skill

130. What is MOST accurate about how physical education teachers can use bulletin boards to communicate instructional information to students?

    a. Schools must provide real bulletin boards for physical education teachers to utilize them.
    b. A time-lapse bulletin board accesses student participation and creativity.
    c. A time-lapse bulletin board is a project only the physical education teacher can complete.
    d. Physical education teachers must communicate orally, as students ignore bulletin boards.

Answer Key and Explanations

1. B: The original impetus for the National Health Education Standards (NHES) was that health education, physical education, public health, and school health authorities observed standards being developed for other subject-area content in education (B) and decided that the subject area of health education needed similar standards developed. Health educators were not influenced by standards developed in hospitals (A), public health (C) agencies, or private medical practice (D).

2. A: A coordinated school health program includes comprehensive school health education addressing physical, cognitive, affective, and social health domains, differentiated for every developmental and age level to promote health knowledge, skills, and attitudes, decrease health risk behaviors, and enhance student health. Physical education is not separate (B) but is an essential component of a coordinated school health program. So are school health services, which include not only emergency care (C) but also prevention, education, referral, and acute and chronic health condition management. Another essential component of a coordinated school health program is family and community involvement (D).

3. A: Infectious hepatitis is caused by different viruses depending on which type it is: three separate viruses cause hepatitis A, B, and C. Burkett's lymphoma (B), infectious mononucleosis (C), and nasopharyngeal carcinoma (D) all can be caused by the Epstein-Barr virus under different conditions.

4. A: During the latest part of the sensorimotor stage, from around 18 to 24 months of age, Piaget said children develop early representational thought when they begin using symbols to represent other things, like playing make-believe by pretending to be adults or fictional characters and using objects to represent other things or beings, for example, pretending a broom is a horse, a block is a phone, and so on. This is the first instance of mental operations. In the preoperational stage (B), children display more intuitive than logical thinking. Though capable of basic mental operations, they do not perform logical ones. In concrete operations (C), they begin performing logical mental operations but only concerning concrete objects or events. In formal operations (D), they begin performing mental operations that are abstract as well as logical.

5. D: Cardiovascular diseases like strokes and heart attacks were found in 2013 by the World Health Organization (WHO) to cause 17.3 million deaths yearly. Diabetes (A) was found to cause 1.3 million deaths yearly. Cancers (B) were found to cause 7.6 million deaths annually. Respiratory (C) diseases like asthma and chronic obstructive pulmonary diseases (COPD) were found to cause 4.2 million deaths a year. Thus (D), (B), (C), and (A) is the order of most to least causes of mortality, with (D) far exceeding all the others.

6. B: Because the social contexts in which teenagers make decisions are subject frequent change, they must learn to evaluate and adjust those decisions in response to such changes. A challenging paradox for teens is that the decisions they make are frequently critical, with long-term consequences affecting their futures (A); yet they commonly lack enough life experience to inform these decisions (C). Research has found intervention programs to improve teen decision-making skills effective (D) in enhancing positive, responsible, prosocial, constructive and self-sufficient behaviors and decreasing negative, irresponsible, antisocial, destructive and self-destructive behaviors.

7. B: Student health records in educational institutions and agencies receiving federal Department of Education funding are protected under the Family Educational Rights and Privacy Act (FERPA);

255

immunization records are not excluded (A). Neither are records kept by public school nurses (C) on students, whose privacy is also protected under FERPA. Student special education records, including records of services they receive under the Individuals with Disabilities Education Act (IDEA), also are defined as "education records" by FERPA; hence, their privacy is also protected by FERPA (D).

8. D: The model described and named *direct instruction* (lower-case) by Rosenshine and Stevens in 1986 is a generic instructional model; the Direct Instruction (capitalized) model pioneered in the 1960s by Siegfried Engelmann and his colleagues is a specific instructional model. However, both share in common the characteristics of teacher-directed, skills-oriented (A), face-to-face, small-group (B) instruction that uses task analysis, deliberate sequencing (C), and explicit teaching (D).

9. D: While questionnaires (A) can be sent to large groups of people, they also can be used to collect data on an individual and small group basis equally well or better (i.e., not all recipients return mailed questionnaires, whereas individuals and small groups, when given these directly in clinical, public health, or other settings, are obligated to complete them). Observations (B) are most useful for gathering data about individuals or small groups as they require researchers to watch their actions and interactions directly (overtly or covertly). Interviews (C) typically require one-to-one question-and-answer interactions between researchers and respondents. The survey (D) method enables researchers to collect large-scale data on entire population groups, often through a combination of these other methods, by obtaining the same information from a much greater number of respondents.

10. B: Carefully weighing and evaluating the pros and cons of a stressful life situation facilitates making decisions that aid coping with stress and most reflects the decision-making life skill. Considering the positive aspects of the situation (A) most reflects the life skill of values clarification. Expressing feelings about the situation (C) most reflects the life skill of communication skills. Engaging in positive behaviors that raise self-esteem or develop interests to enable dealing with the situation (D) most reflects the life skill of coping skills.

11. A: Erikson identified a nuclear conflict to be resolved in each stage of psychosocial development. Babies confront basic trust versus mistrust, toddlers autonomy (D) versus shame and self-doubt, preschoolers initiative versus guilt, school-aged children industry (C) versus inferiority, adolescents identity (A) versus role confusion, young adults intimacy (B) versus isolation, middle adults generativity versus stagnation, and older adults integrity versus despair.

12. A: Cardiorespiratory endurance is best defined as the ability to perform dynamic, that is, movement, exercise rather than static (C) or passive exercise using the large, that is, limb and trunk muscles, not small (B) muscles like those in the hands and feet, or both large and small, that is, all muscles (C), or any muscles (D) for extended time periods. Cardiorespiratory means involving the heart and breathing. Endurance requires long, not short (B), average (C), or any (D) durations.

13. B: A common misconception among teenagers is that only vaginal penetration and ejaculation will cause pregnancy. Health educators should inform them that small drops of pre-ejaculate they may not detect can be released before as well as during sex. Pre-ejaculate also contains sperm; males cannot control its release; and vulvar contact alone can cause conception. Thus, there is a smaller but real chance of impregnating a girl without penetrating or ejaculating inside her vagina [a reason to do (C)]. Choices (A), (C), and (D) are all facts, not misconceptions, of which health educators can inform teens.

14. A: Gum disease can develop when oral bacteria build up due to poor oral hygiene and can cause serious heart valve disorders when the bacteria travel from the gums directly to the heart. Unhealthy gums cannot only lead to periodontal (gum) infections; they also can cause loosening and loss of teeth (B). While flossing and gum massage are important for preventing gum disease, brushing the teeth also prevents both tooth decay and gum disease (C). Gum disease not only affects the soft tissues of the gums but also causes irreversible bone loss in the jaw (D).

15. C: Carbohydrates in our diet (e.g., from fruits, vegetables, and grains) are sources whereby our bodies make glucose, which supplies energy. Our bodies get amino acids, which they use to repair cells, muscle and other tissue, and organs by breaking down protein in our diet (e.g., from meats, poultry, seafood, dairy, and beans). Our bodily functions require 20 to 35 percent of our diet from fats but not saturated fat (D). Unsaturated fats are healthier for the heart, blood vessels, body composition, weight, and organs.

16. A: In precontemplation, individuals have no plans to act anytime soon. This can be caused by lack of information, lack of motivation, and resistance. In contemplation, individuals plan to make changes within roughly six months but are not ready to act immediately. They have acquired awareness of both the costs and benefits of change, causing ambivalence that fuels procrastination. In preparation, individuals usually have made some significant action in the last year; plan to act within a month; and have developed some plan of action. In action, people have accomplished obvious lifestyle changes in the last six months, sufficient to reduce disease risk according to professional and scientific criteria, for example, quitting smoking. In maintenance, people devote more effort to preventing relapse than initiating change processes, which they have already largely done. This stage can last six months to five years.

17. C: Smoking tobacco, drinking alcohol (A), poor nutrition, and lack of physical activity (B) are all risk factors shared in common by all four types of illnesses that cause the majority of deaths from noncommunicable diseases. Therefore, (D) is incorrect.

18. C: The idea that saturated fat in the diet contributes to heart disease is an abstract concept. This would be most appropriate to teach to students in Piaget's stage of formal operations (typically preadolescent and adolescent ages), who can understand abstract concepts. Babies in Piaget's sensorimotor (A) stage and toddlers in Piaget's preoperational (B) stage cannot grasp abstract concepts. Preschoolers are best taught using single, simple subjects one at a time and intuitive or animistic ideas. Middle childhood students in Piaget's concrete operations (D) stage can think logically and perform mental operations but only related to concrete objects and events; they still have not developed the facility for comprehending completely abstract ideas that emerge during the formal operations stage. They are best taught using concrete illustrations of food groups, digestion and energy processes, the food chain cycle, weight gain and loss, and so on rather than future nutritional benefits or abstract relationships.

19. B: There are no federal laws in the United States concerning immunizations required for children to enter public schools (A). These laws vary from state to state (B). However, all 50 U.S. states do have such laws (C). Because the laws vary by state, the U.S. Centers for Disease Control and Prevention (CDC) does offer a database of all state immunization laws (D) for schools, hospitals, health care facilities, provider practices, child care providers, long-term care facilities, facilities for the developmentally disabled, and correctional facilities.

20. D: The masseter muscles in the sides of the face connect the jaws and control their chewing functions. The temporalis muscles in the side of the head also are involved in chewing. The orbicularis oris muscle (A) encircles the mouth and is used to make facial expressions, open and close the mouth and pucker the lips to kiss, and blow trumpets and other musical horns, but not to chew. The zygomaticus major and minor muscles (B) are in the cheekbones, running between the cheek below the eye and the corners of the mouth; they control smiling, not chewing. The trapezius muscles (C) are large, triangular muscles extending from the neck, across each shoulder, and down the upper back and thus not in the jaws or face.

21. C: In both females and males, the brain's hypothalamus stimulates the pituitary gland to secrete luteinizing hormone (LH) and follicle-stimulating hormone (FSH). In females, these two hormones stimulate the ovaries to produce estrogen; in males, they stimulate the testes to produce testosterone. Hence, female and male organs are stimulated by the same hormones, not by separate hormones for each (A). LH and FSH, the hormones that stimulate the male and female sexual organs, are not the same as estrogen and testosterone, which respectively stimulate the male and female organs to produce these sex hormones (B). The pituitary gland does not secrete these (D); it secretes LH and FSH.

22. B: Emergencies that warrant 911 calls are identified as any situations needing immediate help from the police, a fire department, or an ambulance. People should call 911 not only for uncontrollable bleeding or unconsciousness but also for allergic reactions, which can be fatal; for chest pains (A), which can indicate heart attacks; and if someone is not breathing or having trouble breathing. Prank calls to 911 are not only nuisances and interfere with actual emergencies; they are also illegal (C) in most U.S. states and subject to law enforcement. When a person calls 911 in an emergency, he or she should not hang up until instructed to do so by the call taker, who will first need to get information from or give instructions to the caller.

23. A: Research has found that, although teachers do have difficulty relating to children with attention deficit hyperactivity disorder (ADHD), this does not mean they cannot change peer dislike of these children (B). Peers do tend to continue rejecting ADHD children based on their existing negative reputations, even after those children improve their behavior, but this also does not mean teachers cannot affect this (C). Teachers who create classroom environments that promote better peer relationships do not eliminate all dislike of ADHD children (D), which classmates continue to display; however, they do influence peer interactions to enable more variation and less consistent dislike.

24. A: The federal Healthy People 2000 initiative had as its main goal to decrease health disparities in America. The Healthy People 2010 initiative made its main goal to eliminate those disparities rather than just decrease them. The Healthy People 2020 initiative established goals not only to eliminate health disparities but moreover to establish health equity and improve health for all Americans.

25. B: When students engage in extracurricular activities, if they begin to feel overextended, they should not expect (A) or consider this normal; it is a sign that they should quit at least one activity (B). Students should consider not only the abilities and skills they already have (C) and familiar interests but also trying new things in which they are interested as well as the time they have available (D) before they choose extracurricular activities.

26. A: At least 80 percent of adolescents develop acne. This is not due to inadequate or incorrect facial skin care but to hormonal changes. Health educators should inform teen students how to treat and not treat acne. Hormonal changes in puberty also frequently make teens' hair oilier, so they are likely to need to shampoo it more often (B). Many teenagers have to wear braces, which makes oral hygiene more complicated and challenging; additionally, fresh breath becomes more important to them in adolescence. Therefore, the same oral hygiene they practiced in childhood usually will not suffice (C). Hormonal changes also cause increased perspiration, so adolescents need to bathe more often than in childhood (D).

27. B: It is impossible for parents to pass the human immunodeficiency virus (HIV) genetically to their children as it is not a genetic disease. However, HIV can be transmitted by oral sex (A) as well as genital and anal sex. Infected nursing mothers can transmit HIV to their babies (C) in breast milk. Infected mothers also can transmit HIV perinatally (D) to their unborn children.

28. D: If an individual has insomnia, not just occasionally but persistently (A); feels sad, depressed, discouraged, or hopeless more of the time than not (B); or has enough difficulty concentrating to impede home or work functioning (C), these are signs that the person should probably consult a mental health professional. Uncontrollable fears, negative thinking, or self-destructive thoughts are additional signs. Preoccupation with death and suicidal ideations are also warning signals to seek professional help. Qualified professionals can help when self-help measures cannot.

29. A: Constantly reporting one's locations and activities to the partner is a sign of being domestically abused as well as appearing desperate to please the partner; agreeing with all the partner's words and actions; often receiving harassing partner contacts; and mentioning partner possessiveness, jealousy, or temper. Often exhibiting or trying to hide injuries or excusing them as accidents (B) or clumsiness is a sign of being physically abused. Marked personality and behavioral changes (C) are psychological symptoms of being abused. Making few or no public outings, use of the car or money, or visits with friends and family (D) are signs of being isolated by an abuser.

30. C: Curriculum-based measurement (CBM) is a standardized measure that is used as a formative assessment to evaluate student progress during instruction. Final projects (A), end-of-unit tests (B), and standardized state examinations (D) are used as summative assessments to evaluate student learning after instruction.

31. C: The short-term effects of regular, substantial alcohol use include impaired judgment (A); distortion of perceptions, vision and hearing (B), and emotions; impaired coordination; bad breath; and hangovers. The long-term effects of heavy alcohol use include liver damage, sexual impotence, stomach disorders (D), vitamin deficiencies, skin problems, loss of appetite, loss of memory, damage to the heart and entire cardiovascular system, and damage to the central nervous system (C).

32. B: The big five personality traits are extraversion, agreeableness, conscientiousness, neuroticism, and openness. All people are said to possess some greater or lesser degree of each along a continuum; for example, very introverted (A) people are low in extraversion; very irresponsible people are low in conscientiousness; very emotionally stable individuals are low in neuroticism, and so on. Detail-orientation (A) is a characteristic of conscientiousness. Kindness (A) is a characteristic of agreeableness. Assertiveness (D) is a characteristic of extraversion. Prosocial behaviors (D) are characteristic of agreeableness. Good impulse control (D) is characteristic of conscientiousness. Moodiness (D) is characteristic of neuroticism. Imagination (D) is characteristic of openness. Oral, anal, phallic, latency, and genital traits or tendencies (C) are concepts from Freud's psychosexual theory of personality, not the big five trait theory of personality.

33. D: Destroying the victim's property is an example of domestic abusers' typical tactics of intimidation, which they use to frighten victims into submission by indicating the violent consequences they will suffer if they do not comply with the abuser. Examples of isolation (A) include cutting their victims off from contact with family and friends to make the victims dependent on the abusers. Examples of humiliation (B) include making victims feel worthless, undermining their self-esteem by shaming them both in private and public. Examples of dominance (C) include giving their victims orders, treating them like children, servants, slaves, or even possessions and expecting them to comply unquestioningly.

34. C: Components of a coordinated school health program include psychological, counseling, and social services (A); health promotion for school personnel as well as for students (B); healthy school environments that support learning through physical, emotional, and social safety and health (C); and school nutrition services as well as physical education (D).

35. D: The National Education Association (NEA) offers a national professional development (PD) conference for educational support professionals (ESPs), its Leaders for Tomorrow program, and various other PD trainings. ShapeAmerica (aka American Association of Health, Physical Education, Recreation, and Dance [AAHPERD]) (A) offers a PD webinar series on various topics, a Researcher's Toolkit, a Distinguished Lecture Series, and workshops. The Centers for Disease Control (CDC) (B) has a Division of Scientific Education and Professional Development (DSEPD), its Learning Connection containing thousands of public health learning products and continuing education (CE) courses through CDC TRAIN, online resources, Quick-Learn lessons for mobile devices, and Facebook and Twitter links to public health topics. The American Public Health Association (APHA) (C) has a Center for PD, Public Health Systems, and Partnerships.

36. B: Students can use journals, diaries, charts, or graphs to keep track of their progress toward their health goals and ensure accountability. Asking friends to help or forming a club (A) is related to developing a support system for meeting health goals. When students give themselves healthy rewards for meeting their goals (C), this is related to positive reinforcement. Revising their action plans or time lines (D) is related to ensuring success in meeting health goals by adjusting the means or time by which they need to achieve them.

37. C: The Environmental Protection Agency (EPA) first developed standards, laws, and regulations to address environmental pollution during the 1970s, not the 1980s (A). Its focus shifted from remediation in the 1970s toward prevention in the 1980s and 1990s, not the 2000s (B). In 1990, Congress's national policy to prevent and reduce pollution was declared in the Pollution Prevention Act (C). This law called for the national policy to shift away from emphasizing treatment and disposal and toward emphasizing source reduction, not vice versa (D).

38. C: White blood cells are known as lymphocytes, a clue to the fact that they function in the lymphatic system to produce antibodies and destroy virally affected or foreign cells. While they are also found within the circulatory (B) system, that is, in the bloodstream, they do not function there but are only in transit from the bone marrow to the lymphatic system. The endocrine (D) system includes the pancreas, male testes, female ovaries and uterus, and all of the body's glands, which secrete hormones regulating bodily function, metabolism, and growth.

39. C: Experts advise children and teens particularly to use refusal strategies when others try to pressure them, including walking away from the situation (A); standing up for others who are being pressured (B); proposing alternatives to whatever unwanted activity others are pressuring them to engage in (C); and not being overly aggressive when saying "no" (D).

40. C: Teenagers' decisions are influenced by both internal variables (A), like self-concept and locus of control, and external variables (D), like their relationships with their parents and friends. They do not make decisions in isolated conditions (B); rather, their decision-making is influenced by the feedback they receive (C).

41. A: Multiple research studies repeatedly demonstrate that cardiovascular diseases, diabetes, and colon and breast cancer risks are lowered by regular physical activity (PA). Researchers recommend 30 to 60 minutes a day of PA to reduce the risks of breast and colon cancer significantly, and 150 minutes a week to decrease risks of cardiovascular diseases and diabetes. Thirty minutes a day for five days a week equals 150 minutes a week; therefore, the amounts needed are similar to lower the risks of these diseases. (Sixty minutes is double this and may afford some people greater cancer risk reduction.) Hence, risks for all these diseases are lowered, not some. The amounts necessary to reduce risk do not vary greatly among these diseases. Regular PA in adequate amounts does lower disease risk.

42. D: Current (2014) research finds that exercising in temperatures up to 62 to 65 degrees Fahrenheit maximum increases the odds of producing and activating healthy brown fat, which promotes building lean muscle tissue and burning more calories and keeps the internal organs warm. New research suggests brown fat may enhance glucose control and decrease insulin resistance. Studies find whole foods effective as opposed to supplements (A) for controlling blood sugar and weight because vegetables and fruits contain enzymes that activate antioxidants the body needs for controlling blood sugar and weight (as well as preventing cancers). Supplements lack these enzymes. A meta-analysis of multiple studies recently found people 28 percent more apt to develop diabetes when sleeping below 5 to 6 hours nightly, compared to those sleeping 6 to 8 hours. Insulin sensitivity also improved greatly in people who slept 6 hours on weeknights but caught up by sleeping 10 hours on weekend nights (B). Studies also show stress raises levels of the hormone cortisol and of inflammatory cytokines, which both cause insulin resistance (C).

43. C: Milestones of physical growth and development include that, from birth to three years, children typically grow to twice their previous height and that, during puberty, they typically attain around 25 percent of their growth in height.

44. A: The seriousness of health risks from smoking cigarettes is driven home by the statistic that it causes more deaths in America every year than alcohol use, drug use, car accidents, human immunodeficiency virus (HIV), and gunshots combined—that is, around one in five people, exceeding 480,000. Another statistic to put smoking deaths in perspective is that they equal more than ten times the number of all casualties of war in American history. Moreover, one of every three deaths from cancer in America is caused by smoking.

45. B: Researchers find that, over time, avoiding discussion of important issues causes stress, damaging health and well-being, rather than affording more control over them (A). Instead, they find we attain more control over problems when we can explain them (B). Studies also find we overestimate the outcomes of sensitive discussions, which are emotionally safer and have more productive outcomes than we expect (C). Investigators also find quality supersedes quantity of discussion (D); that is, more is not better. They also find discussing important issues in the wrong way (e.g., by emphasizing quantity over quality) can cause more harm than not discussing them at all.

46. C: Whereas historically, type 1 diabetes involved children and teens more and type 2 involved onset in adulthood, today this is not true (A): More and more children and adolescents are developing type 2 diabetes due to lifestyle factors. Both types of diabetes are influenced by genetic and lifestyle factors; however, genetic elements contribute more to type 1, while lifestyle behaviors contribute more to type 2 (B). In type 1, the pancreas fails to produce insulin; in type 2, the pancreas produces insulin, but the body loses its sensitivity (C) and fails to respond to it. Obesity, inactivity, and poor nutrition all contribute to type 2 diabetes (D).

47. C: Piaget's theory identifies progressive stages of cognitive development; hence, it focuses most on intellectual development. While cognitive development interacts with and affects emotional development (A), relationship development (B), and the development of independence (D), and Piaget does explain how it does, his primary concern is how the intellect develops from birth to adulthood.

48. D: It is recommended that the teacher speak with the student in private (A) if at all possible rather than discipline the student in front of the whole class (B). This can backfire in two ways: (1) Humiliating the student in front of the entire class can have a negative impact on the student's attitude, making the misbehavior worse, or (2) making the student the center of attention can reinforce the misbehavior if it is motivated by attention seeking. It is also important for the teacher to make clear to the student that it is the behavior, not the student him- or herself, which the teacher finds unacceptable.

49. C: None of these is correct. Neither a condom nor a spermicide by itself is effective enough (A); the two should be used in combination. Vasectomy is often reversible, but not every time; tubal ligation is often reversible, but not in every case (B). While some women may ask a physician to insert a diaphragm for them, at least initially, they usually insert diaphragms themselves prior to intercourse once they have learned how. However, intrauterine devices (IUDs) are inserted for long-term use by physicians and removed by physicians as needed. Women swallow birth control pills orally rather than inserting them (D).

50. A: Students high in Gardner's interpersonal intelligence style learn best through social interactions with others. Those high in intrapersonal (B) intelligence prefer to be alone and would not learn best through group activities. Those high in visual-spatial (C) intelligence learn best through visual instructional activities and materials, for example, looking at, using, and making drawings, charts, graphs, photos, images, models, videos, multimedia, illustrations, and jigsaw puzzles and using videoconferencing and TV. Those high in logical-mathematical (D) intelligence learn best through solving mysteries and puzzles, conducting experiments, learning and formulating concepts, learning and applying logic, identifying and exploring patterns and relationships, and performing calculations.

51. B: The School Health Index (SHI) was developed jointly by the Centers for Disease Control (CDC) and national health and education nongovernmental organizations (NGOs), school staffs, school health experts, and parents as a self-assessment (C) and planning (D) guide. Schools use it to help conduct needs assessments to identify the strengths and weaknesses of their health and safety policies and programs, develop action plans for enhancing health to include in their School Improvement Plans (SIPs), and engage students, teachers, parents, and communities in health-promoting, health-enhancing behaviors.

52. B: Brainstorming can be done alone by individual students, or together by more than one student, and with or without the teacher's active involvement. Role-playing (A) can be done with or without the teacher's active involvement but requires more than one student. Guided discovery (C) can be done by individual or multiple students but requires the teacher's active involvement to guide students. Cooperative learning (D) may be done with or without active teacher involvement but requires more than one student. (Note: For all techniques that can be done without active teacher involvement, it is assumed that the teacher has previously instructed the students in the procedures involved when necessary, e.g., if students were not already familiar with them.)

53. B: Erikson described the nuclear conflict of infancy as basic trust versus mistrust: A baby whose needs are met fully and consistently develops trust in the world, while a baby whose needs are inadequately or inconsistently met develops mistrust. Erikson found that the positive outcome of this stage was hope. He identified will (A) as the positive outcome of successfully resolving the nuclear conflict of autonomy versus shame and self-doubt during toddlerhood. He identified purpose (C) as the positive outcome of successfully resolving the nuclear conflict of initiative versus guilt during the preschool years. He identified competence (D) as the positive outcome of successfully resolving the nuclear conflict of industry versus Inferiority during the elementary school years.

54. A: Legumes, that is, beans, split peas, and lentils, are classified in both the vegetables and the proteins food groups by the U.S. Department of Agriculture (cf. ChooseMyPlate.gov) because they have much higher protein content than other vegetables. Seafood (B) is in the protein food group only. Cheese (C) is in the dairy food group only. Eggplant (D) is in the vegetable food group only.

55. C: As of 2014, 48 U.S. states, the District of Columbia, plus Puerto Rico, the Virgin Islands, Guam, American Samoa, and the Northern Mariana Islands school, health care, child care, mental health, social services, and law enforcement employees are all mandated reporters of child maltreatment. Probation or parole officers are mandated reporters in 17 states; substance abuse counselors are in 14 states; and commercial film processors are in 12 states, Guam, and Puerto Rico (A). Employees, directors, and volunteers of camps and recreation and youth centers (B) are mandated reporters in 11 states. Domestic violence workers and humane or animal control officers are mandated reporters in 7 states and Washington, D.C.; college and university, technical and vocational school faculties, administrators, and other employees and volunteers (D) are mandated reporters in 4 states. Clergy are mandated reporters in 27 states and Guam.

56. B: *Explain* is an observable behavior that others can see and hear a student do; hence, it is also measurable. *Learn* (A) and *understand* (C) are verbs that refer to internal states, which others cannot observe students doing and which are also open to variable interpretations. The SMART acronym lists the characteristics of ideal learning objectives: specific, measurable, attainable, relevant or results oriented, and targeted (to learner and learning level). *Identify*, *define*, *describe*, *compare*, *contrast*, *analyze*, *classify*, *list*, and so on are some additional examples of measurable verbs. Therefore, (D) is incorrect.

57. B: This scenario describes the relationship pattern involving impairment of one or more children. The parent projecting anxiety onto the child becomes overly concerned that something is wrong with the child; this becomes a self-fulfilling prophecy as the child comes to believe something is indeed wrong with him or her and behaves accordingly. The dysfunction in one spouse (A) pattern involves one spouse overcompensating for, criticizing, and dominating the other, who becomes more dependent and dysfunctional in response. The emotional distance pattern (C) involves emotional withdrawal or isolation by one or more family members when their interactions with others become too intense for comfort. The marital conflict pattern (D) involves projection of their unmanageable personal anxiety by both partners into their marital relationship.

58. B: For teachers to self-analyze and adjust their own body language and movements within the classroom, video recordings would enable them to observe where they were positioned in the classroom; whether and how they moved around; and their posture, body language, and so on and make changes accordingly. Journals or diaries (A) help teachers reflect on what took place during class, their own reactions and feelings, student reactions they observed, and related questions that occur to them. Teachers may or may not recall their physical positions and movements, but they cannot view them as they can in videos. Audio recordings (C) give teachers a record of what was said but no visual recording. Peer observation (D) allows teachers to hear observations from colleagues about their physical positions and movements but not to observe and analyze these themselves.

59. A: Body mass index (BMI) is the ratio of weight to height squared, which shows the relationship between a person's weight and height. It is not the ratio of abdominal to total fat (B), fat to muscle (C), or fat to weight (D). Healthy BMIs are generally between 18.5 and 24.9. Below 18.5 is considered underweight, and 25 to 29.9 is considered overweight (with a few exceptions; e.g., some people with very high muscle mass rather than fat may have higher BMIs). A BMI of 30 or above is considered obese.

60. A: Physical education (PE) teachers find that their students are enthusiastic about apps that allow them to view their and classmates or teammates' athletic performance. This enthusiasm makes it easier for teachers to create positive learning environments wherein students are more appreciative of constructive criticism and more motivated to improve their performance. PE teachers find that, after only a brief demonstration, students can easily use them (B) for recording one another, viewing the recordings, and giving each other feedback. Teachers find student athletes really enjoy watching their performance postgame (C) in the locker room. They can much more easily identify which strategies and tactics they used were most and least effective through this viewing. Also, when PE teachers use apps to record video and they play it back, students get much more immediate feedback (D).

61. D: The skin is a part of the integumentary system, along with the hair, nails, and glands. The skin controls fluid loss, protects deep tissues, and synthesizes vitamin D. The skeletal system gives the body its supporting structure, protects vital organs, assists muscles in body movement, stores calcium, and produces red blood cells. The muscular system maintains posture, collaborates with the bones in body movement, uses energy, and generates heat. The lymphatic system contains white blood cells, which aid in immune responses, and retrieves fluids leaked from capillaries.

62. D: When physical education (PE) teachers want to hold events with Olympics themes for students, their local colleges are good places for them to find students willing to volunteer their time and work to help. PE teachers whose schools are short on funds for sports equipment can solicit financial assistance from local health and wellness agencies, which is not inappropriate (A) as these organizations may be able and often want to help. PE teachers also can ask local trophy companies to donate some of their products—and even refreshments as well—to student athletic events; these businesses frequently welcome the good public relations and advertising they can get by helping out schools (B). Local governments do have a department where PE teachers can recruit representatives to present to students about the use of community resources (C): their county and city Parks and Recreation Departments.

63. A: The breaststroke uses the frog kick. The frog kick is also used in self-contained underwater breathing apparatus (SCUBA) diving and can be used for treading water. The butterfly (B) stroke uses the dolphin kick. The crawl (C) typically uses the flutter kick. Therefore, (D) is incorrect.

64. B: Physical education (PE) teachers can provide kindergarten through Grade 2 (K–) students with log sheets with a prepared left column and an empty right column. The left side uses simple statements like "I have a strong heart," "I have strong muscles," "I can do movements over and over again," and "I can stretch," accompanied by graphic pictures (a heart, a bicep, a figure with arrows indicating repeated movement, and a figure with arrows or lines depicting stretching) to represent cardiovascular endurance, muscular strength, muscular endurance, and flexibility, respectively. In the blank right side, children make drawings or cut and paste pictures illustrating their activities (e.g., running, lifting, dancing, stretches, etc.) in each category. Teachers can guide this activity and collect the products to get assessment information. Writing journal entries (A), notes (C), or cards (D) is inappropriate for students with the limited writing skills of K–2 levels, as is independently turning in records regularly (C) or periodically (D) on a schedule at these ages.

65. B: Handling a hockey puck is an example of a performance skill that would be affected most by individual differences in the perceptual-motor ability of control precision. Football quarterbacking (A) is an example of a performance skill that would be affected most by individual differences in the perceptual-motor abilities of response orientation or choice reaction time. Dribbling a basketball (C) is an example of a performance skill that would be affected most by individual differences in the perceptual-motor ability of manual dexterity. Driving a race car (D) is an example of a performance skill that would be affected most by individual differences in the perceptual-motor ability of rate control.

66. A: Structured observations involve informing both teacher and student of the observation and applying specific criteria for evaluating student performance in physical education (PE) assessment. Naturalistic observations involve not informing students of the observation to capture typical student behavior, such as during their daily practice in regular PE classes. Though naturalistic observations are more realistic regarding behaviors than structured observations, not vice versa (D), they have been criticized for being more subjective, whereas structured observations are more objective, not vice versa (B). Structured observations are equally good for assessing social skills, motor skills (C), and movement skills.

67. C: In effective cooperative learning activities, the students engage in productive, face-to-face interactions frequently and substantially, not occasionally (A). They are accountable and responsible for their group goals not only collectively but also personally and individually (B). They frequently do apply their interpersonal and small-group skills that pertain to their specific cooperative learning activity (C). They regularly, frequently conduct group processing of how their group currently functions in order to improve their group's future effectiveness, not simply to sustain its current effectiveness (D).

68. C: Throwing at a stationary target (B) represents a beginner level of throwing skill. Throwing lead passes (A) represents an intermediate level of throwing skill. Throwing to teammates while being defended (C) by another player represents an advanced level of throwing skill. Therefore, these do not all represent similar levels of throwing skill (D).

69. A: Experts advise coaches that they must first determine whether they have athletes' attention before communicating with them successfully, and second, whether they are explaining in a way that athletes can understand easily. Third, coaches must determine whether the athletes have in fact understood what they said, and fourth, whether the athletes believed what they told them (B). Fifth, coaches must determine whether their athletes have accepted what they told them (C) as well as understanding and believing it. To control a team or group of athletes, coaches also must be sensitive to the nonverbal cues they give (D), while the coaches are talking. These cues communicate whether the athletes are puzzled, confused, disbelieving, bored, resentful, disrespectful, and so on toward a coach and what he or she is saying.

70. B: Musical hoops is played like musical chairs, except children must jump into hoops instead of sitting on chairs when the music stops. This is appropriate for younger children. Freeze tag or blob tag is more appropriate for children older than 5 years, up to 12 years old. Children must try to tag others while holding hands with those in their blob. This demands higher levels of coordination than younger children have. Follow the leader is better as a warm-up activity for children age 5 to

12 years, as younger children can have difficulty with leading and following and with the variations in leaders and locomotor skills that teachers can use with older children.

71. D: In spatial awareness, locations and levels (A) of the body or body parts can be high, middle, or low. Personal space (B) refers to the space immediately surrounding an individual person, as opposed to general space, which refers to the total space available or playing area. Directions (C) of movement in space include forward, backward, up, down, and sideways. Planes of movement in space include vertical, horizontal, and circular paths (D).

72. D: A teacher using reflection to inform instruction is less likely to use (A) as placing the responsibility for meeting the objective entirely with the students betrays a lack of reflection. Reflective teachers evaluate how students respond to their instruction, analyze their own design and implementation of lessons, evaluate the results, and determine how they can change what they do to promote the best outcomes for their students. Thus, the teacher using reflection might see whether having the students play the next game faster (B) will increase their heart rates to the target range, or change the game rules to enhance more active participation by all students (C), or even both of these.

73. B: Compared to regular baseball, softball has a bigger ball, a smaller infield, fewer innings, and a different pitch. Softballs are 11 to 12 inches around, whereas baseballs are 8 to 9 inches around. Softball infields have their bases 60 feet apart, whereas baseball infields have their bases 90 feet apart. Regulation softball games consist of seven innings, whereas regulation baseball games consist of nine innings. Softball requires underhand pitching, whereas baseball typically uses overhand pitching.

74. B: Of the activities named, swimming is ideal for students with joint problems because it puts no weight or stress on the joints. The buoyancy of the body in water keeps weight and impact off the joints. Students can be active and get exercise without aggravating joint conditions or pain. Skiing (A) requires a lot of knee bending and turning, hip swiveling, and bearing weight on the joints, so it is not compatible with joint problems. Skateboarding (C) also involves much knee bending and turning, as well as jumping and landing, and would be hard on joint problems. Playing soccer (D) requires running and kicking, again putting too much impact on the joints. These other sports also are done on the ground and subject to gravity, whereas swimming relieves the joints of weight.

75. C: When physical education (PE) classes involve a baseball, for example, injuries are much more likely when fielding teams include 30 or more students instead of only 9 as in regulation games. Teachers must instruct students wanting to field fly balls to call for them and other students to back away from them. Experts with legal and PE experience warn teachers to limit any gymnastics to only basic vaulting and tumbling and these only with individual spotters (A). Most average students cannot support their bodies or hang by their arms, making falls likely; falling from inverted positions risks spinal damage, paralysis, and death. Experts additionally warn PE teachers never to include trampolines in PE classes and also not in extracurricular activities (B) like gymnastics, cheerleading, and so on unless school insurance includes trampoline accidents, which are often not covered or incur excessive premiums. PE teachers should never discipline students using strenuous exercise (D), which is unsafe.

76. B: In addition to referrals, criteria indicating that a student should be evaluated to determine eligibility for adapted physical education (APE) include that the student performs below his or her ability level in group settings (A); has social behaviors that interfere with his or her or others' learning more than one-third of class time (B); has scored below average in two or more parts of the state physical fitness test used by the school district (C); and scored 1.5 or more standard deviations below the norm on the norm-referenced test used (D) by the school or district.

77. A: These steps are sequenced in order of ascending severity: First, the teacher gives the noncompliant student an oral warning that he or she is not following class rules. If the student fails to comply, second, the teacher gives the student a brief time-out from class to refocus his or her attention. If the student is still not complying upon returning, third, the teacher assigns another time-out wherein the student must write a response, for example, identifying the rules he or she broke and what he or she will do now to follow the class rules.

78. D: Teachers can give students cards with adverbs they recently learned, have them look up synonyms and antonyms for these, and write them on the cards. The teacher then directs the students to perform movements in ways described by the adverbs on their cards. The teacher then has students pass their cards to classmates and repeat the activity with new words. This lesson integrates physical education (PE) and English language arts (ELA) skills. Performing movements and then working with words separately or vice versa, (A) and (B), do not integrate PE and ELA skills together into the same activity. Describing movements using the adverbs (C) makes a mental connection between words and movement, but the students are not actually performing any body movements; they are only describing them verbally, so this is an ELA activity rather than an integrated PE and ELA activity.

79. C: TARGET stands for task, authority, recognition, grouping, evaluation, and timing. Varying difficulty levels (A) refers to task. Giving students some responsibility for choice of activities (B) refers to authority. Acknowledging process and improvement rather than product (C) and outcome refers to recognition. Avoiding peer comparison through strategies that get students to form groups quickly and switch groups frequently (D) refers to grouping.

80. C: When Cooper and Potts developed and named aerobics in the late 1960s, it originally focused on the ability of the heart and lungs to use oxygen in sustained physical activity. Cooper was the first to differentiate aerobic capacity from body flexibility (A) and muscular strength (B) and to notice that some people who were very flexible or very strong still did not have good endurance for running, biking, or swimming long distances. Although aerobics initially focused on cardiorespiratory endurance exclusively, today's aerobics classes combine all the elements of fitness (D), incorporating stretching for flexibility and strength training for the muscles along with movements that raise heart and breathing rates for cardiovascular fitness in their exercises.

81. D: For effective class behavior management plans, physical education (PE) teachers should define their expectations positively in terms of what they want the students to do, not negatively in terms of what they want them not to do (C). They should limit expectations to five at most, as students will be unable to remember more than that, and put them in writing, not orally (A), posted visibly in locker rooms and on classroom bulletin boards. They also should enforce their stated expectations consistently, not just occasionally (B).

82. C: The National Board for Professional Teaching Standards (NBPTS) include creating an environment of respect and rapport with students. The board provides an example for addressing student problem behaviors of having the misbehaving student describe his or her behavior, state what made it disruptive, and identify solutions for the problem. This standard's example does not advise for the teacher to do these things (A): The student must do them for ownership, responsibility, and understanding of his or her behavior. Neither should the teacher ask a classmate (B) to do them for the same reasons. The standard does not recommend giving concrete consequences and solutions instead of discussing the problem (D).

83. B: In exercise science, the principle of specificity means that, to improve certain body parts, muscles, or sports movements and techniques, one must exercise those specific parts, muscles, or movements and techniques. Exercising the lower body will not strengthen the upper body or vice versa. Specificity also means that one must practice football skills, for example, to improve in football rather than only exercising for general body conditioning: The latter may be required for and benefit playing football but will not improve specific football skills; only practicing those skills specifically will. The principle of overload (A) means extra or unaccustomed stimuli are required to make the body respond beyond its normal levels. If the question had said someone bench presses more weight than usual to make the upper body stronger, this would illustrate overload as well as specificity. The principle of adaptation (C) means the body adjusts to processes and demands, making activities easier over time and eventually requiring variation for continuing progress. The principle of progression (D) means individuals must progress at certain rates natural to them to achieve results and avoid injuries.

84. C: Fitbit devices can help physical education teachers to support and increase student motivation and also include a line of designer fashion accessories. They can be used for both controlling weight and monitoring sleep quality (A). Students can self-monitor their own progress using Fitbit devices; they also can use them to challenge and compete with friends (B). They are not just stand-alone progress trackers (D); they also sync wirelessly with mobile smartphones and tablets and with charts, graphs, and badges available online for documenting improvements and gaining insights about physical fitness.

85. B: The respiratory system inhales air, of which oxygen is one component. From that inhaled air, the respiratory system delivers oxygen to the circulatory system through gas exchange. It then removes carbon dioxide (CO_2) from the circulatory system as we exhale. The respiratory system does not create or destroy anything (A, D). It also does not ionize the oxygen (C).

86. C: Kinetics is the division of biomechanics that studies the forces causing motion. Newton's First Law of Inertia, Second Law of Momentum, and Third Law of Reaction are most closely related to kinetics. Coplanar vectors (A) belong in the biomechanics division of vector algebra. Kinematics (B) is the biomechanics division that describes motion. Kinematics involves physics concepts including mass, center of gravity, inertia, displacement, linear and angular motion, linear and angular velocity, and acceleration. The biomechanics division of forces (D) involves concepts including center of pressure; force line; resultant force; muscular forces, joint forces, joint reaction forces, ground reaction forces, resisting forces, inertial forces, and gravitational forces; and fulcrums, levers, rotation, couples, equilibrium, weight, friction, and mechanical advantage.

87. B: Physical education (PE) instructors can address negligence in instruction (A) by ensuring they teach students the correct procedures and protocols for safety and for equipment setup, use, and takedown and ensuring students understand and practice how to execute sport and movement activities beforehand. Because PE classes often are large and getting larger, they can address negligence best in supervision (B) by ensuring they continually and actively supervise students throughout all activities and enlisting students to practice peer supervision in addition to supplement teacher supervision. In transportation (C), teachers and coaches are liable outside of school and must obtain written parental consent; follow all school policies, practices, and procedures; and supervise student behavior on buses. In class environments (D), teachers and coaches must be alert for possible dangerous conditions, which can vary daily, and space students to limit hazards.

88. D: Labeling a diagram is an example of a traditional assessment approach. Other traditional approaches include short-answer, constructed-response, and fill-in-the-blank written questions;

written matching tests or worksheets; and written multiple-choice or true–false questions. Writing down a personal fitness plan (A) is an example of a written alternative assessment. Additional examples include research papers, essays, stories, poems, anecdotes, journals, logs, checklists, rating scales, brochures, advertisements, rubrics, performance records, newspapers, magazines, projects, pre-assessment inventories, surveys, questionnaires, interviews, editorials, and reflections. Performing dance movements (B) and playing sports games (C) are examples of alternative performance task assessments. Additional examples include locomotor or gymnastics routines, officiating games, making fitness assessments or oral reports, teaching lessons, warm-up routines, showcases, debates, skits, role-plays, or interviews.

89. C: Research studies find that motor skills, endurance, and strength training all modify the spinal reflexes according to the specific behaviors each task requires. New blood vessels are formed (A) through endurance training but not motor skills or strength training. Motor maps are reorganized (B) through motor skills training but not endurance or strength training. New synapses are generated (D) through motor skills and strength training but not endurance training.

90. D: "Match up" as a defense cue in basketball means that students should defend other players who are as similar to them in size, fitness, and skill level as possible—not just in size (C). This cue does not mean to pair up with another player (A). Staying near to the offensive players they are defending wherever they move on the court (B) is indicated to students with a cue of "Shadow" rather than "Match up."

91. A: Researchers have found that smaller class sizes and student–teacher ratios correlate with larger quantities of activity time, activity level, safety, and learning for students, whereas larger class sizes and student–teacher ratios correlate with smaller quantities of student activity times, levels, safety, and learning—that is, an inverse correlation. Studies show that students receive more and better physical education (PE) from teachers who teach only PE rather than dividing their teaching time and attention between PE and other subjects (B). Researchers are coming to increasing consensus that standards-based PE curriculum results in greater student physical activity (C). Well-maintained, safe, appropriate, and aesthetically appealing PE facilities and equipment also are found to increase and improve student activity (D).

92. D: Recently, the issue that has become the greatest challenge to kindergarten to Grade 12 (K–12) school physical education (PE) is that time in school curricula for PE classes and activities has been reduced significantly to make time for other academic classes. Inadequate resources and parental support (A); overly large class sizes and teacher burnout (B); and violence, student drug abuse, and discipline problems (C) are also challenges to K–12 PE, but these are also equal challenges to other school subjects and to education in general.

93. B: "Follow through!" is an example of prescriptive feedback, which is specific. It specifies an instruction that corrects or improves what the student or athlete is doing or needs to do. In this example, it tells the student or athlete that, when batting, kicking, throwing, and so on, he or she must follow the movement through for it to be effective rather than stopping it abruptly upon contact or release. The other examples are all descriptive feedback, which is general. It gives students or athletes positive social reinforcement by encouraging or praising their performance in general but does not specify exactly what it was that they did well or need to do better or differently.

94. C: The three main categories of fundamental movement skills (FMS) are locomotor (A), manipulative, (A and, (B), and stability (D). Within the main category of stability are included the subcategories of rotation, (B) and (C), and balance, (C) and (D). Activities like spinning, twirling, rocking, bending, and turning demonstrate rotation. Balance can involve both stationary and movement activities. Both rotation and balance are components of stability. Locomotor skills involve activities like walking, running, and so on. Manipulative skills include activities like throwing, catching, hitting, batting, kicking, and transporting objects.

95. C: Summation of forces refers to producing the maximum possible force from any movement using multiple muscles. Adding up the forces generated by each individual muscle yields the total force or summation of forces. Related to this, the order of use is that the largest body parts are slowest, and being stronger and hence the initiators of power, they move first; the smallest body parts are fastest, and being in charge of coordination and refinement, they move last. Thus, the largest, slowest parts do not move last (A), and the smallest, fastest parts do not move first (B). Therefore, (D) is also incorrect.

96. D: Physical education teachers report that apps like Apple's GradeBookPro enable them to spend much more of their class time actually teaching by reducing the time it takes them to perform administrative tasks like taking attendance (C); using standard or weighted grading systems; and displaying assignment, absence, percentage, and other student data all on one page, making disputes at the end of the course or year less likely (B). This app and similar ones enable teachers to create reports and assignments easily; e-mail current attendance and grade status to students; send copies of assignments across classes; quickly take and attach student photos to files, helping them learn students' names sooner; record grades with far greater speed and ease; and overall, streamline and make more efficient all of the tasks that used to be cumbersome, even irrelevant, yet are necessary.

97. A: When we exercise, our bodies access their stored glycogen supplies for energy; glycogen depletion triggers the release of endorphins, hormones that generate feelings of euphoria. These feelings of well-being are short-term effects of exercise. The prevention and relief of depression through regular exercise are long-term effects. So are lower risks of heart attacks and strokes (C), which result from consistent aerobic exercise over time. While a short-term effect of exercise is an immediate increase in blood circulation, a reduction of blood pressure and pulse (D) can be a long-term effect of exercising regularly for at least a few months.

98. A: Other than terms that have been translated into English for use by English-speaking people, a great deal of ballet terminology is in French because, historically, the dance form was popularized in France. While ballroom dance uses many Spanish (C) terms, especially related to Latin ballroom styles and techniques, ballroom also incorporates many French terms taken from ballet to describe steps also taken from ballet, for example, the passé step, chaîné turns, pirouettes, and so on. Italian (B) is not shared in common by ballet and ballroom dance. Although ballet technique was highly developed in Russia later in its history after its early popularization in France, and Russia remains a stellar center of the ballet discipline today, ballet does not use Russian (D) terms, and neither does ballroom dance.

99. C: Activities that require agility and lower-body strength, which do not involve body contact (A), are most appropriate for coed participation and are less dependent on team assignment by student skill levels. For activities that require more upper-body strength (B), it is more important for physical education teachers to assign teams according to individual student skill levels to prevent injuries. Therefore, (D) is incorrect.

100. C: Formative assessments measure student progress during the instructional process. They enable teachers to use the assessment results to inform ongoing instruction and adjust it to meet their students' particular needs and strengths, for example, making their pace faster or slower according to student learning rates; spending more or less time on different skills or areas according to which students have already mastered or are struggling with more; or replacing teaching methods that are ineffective for some students with different ones. Showing accountability (A), comparing student achievement to state or national population averages (B), and assessing whether instruction has helped students meet curriculum standards (D) are all functions of summative assessments rather than formative assessments.

101. B: Human babies actually display coordinated arm–hand movements in the womb before birth, such as moving their thumbs to their mouths. The amniotic fluid provides buoyancy to make this easier. After birth, gravity makes arm and hand movements harder for newborns, who initially exhibit arm flapping and jerky arm extensions (C) before progressing to successfully reaching for objects (A) around four to five months old. At this age, they only adjust their hand shapes to object shapes after touching them. They develop the ability to use visual information to change their hand shapes before touching objects (D) around the age of eight months.

102. A: When physical education (PE) teachers pose think-about questions to students, for example, asking them what the pros and cons are of certain playing formations, positions, or strategies or where they should be aiming their shots, and so on, they give the students a mental advantage by getting them to consider, analyze, and then plan their playing strategies. Thinking about what they just did in one practice session enables them to plan ahead for the next one and improve their game. When PE teachers read aloud the tasks or steps of a practice session, they ensure that player setup is timely rather than delayed (B). They should not alternate the sequence of practice plans (C) but always follow them in the sequence they are written. PE teachers should both verbally describe and physically demonstrate movements or actions, not do only one or the other (D).

103. A: The Institute of Medicine recommendation is for children to spend an hour a day in moderate to vigorous physical activity (MVPA). But studies show that, in actual schools, physical education (PE) classes last about 23 minutes a day, with only 10 of those minutes spent in MVPA. In other words, children get about one-sixth the MVPA that is recommended from school PE classes. Researchers conclude that not only must children be physically active outside of PE classes, but also schools must increase how much children are active during PE class times.

104. C: National Association for Sport and Physical Education (NASPE) recommends that elementary school students should receive a minimum of 150 minutes per week of quality PE time in schools, meaning that somewhat more than this would not be too much. Thirty minutes per day most reflects the recommendation of 150 minutes per week as school is in session five days per week. A minimum of 15 minutes per day (A) is not enough. A maximum of 30 minutes per day (B) implies that more than this is bad, which does not reflect the NASPE recommendation. A maximum of 60 minutes for an entire week (D) is also far too little: This would break down to only 12 minutes daily, or two 30-minute classes per week, or three 20-minute sessions, four 15-minute sessions, and so on.

105. D: Physical education (PE) teachers must always conduct regular safety inspections of facilities and equipment on a consistent basis. Rather than using extrinsic motivations (A) like external punishments or rewards, PE teachers are advised to enhance intrinsic student motivations to be responsible for learning. When student behaviors are inappropriate, PE teachers should not ignore them (B) but address them immediately. PE teachers do need to obtain and regularly renew certification in cardiopulmonary resuscitation (CPR) and automated external defibrillator (AED) use (C).

106. D: It is not a good idea to keep class rules from parents in a misguided attempt to gain student trust (A). Parents need to be informed of the rules, so they know what is expected of their children and can make sure their children understand the rules. Teachers also protect themselves by informing parents of rules in advance: In the event of student behavior problems, injuries, or disputes, parents cannot subsequently deny knowledge or accuse teachers of not informing them. Giving the students copies of the rules to take home to parents (B) often means the parents never receive them. Postal mail (C) is much slower when today's technology enables almost instant transmission of e-mails (D), eliminating the potential for events to occur before parents receive the information.

107. B: Center of gravity (COG) is not in the same location in every human body (A); neither is it always in a certain location of every individual body (C). Rather, it shifts corresponding to changes in the positions of the body parts (B). COG is not precisely the same as center of mass, but their difference is negligible, so for all practical purposes they are considered synonymous; however, center of gravity or mass is not the same as center of pressure (D).

108. A: MyFitnessPal is an app that features healthy recipes (B) and an extensive food database, whereby users can enter meals to calculate caloric and nutritional content. The Endomondo Sports Tracker features Audio Coach feedback (C) on user exercise performance. Endomondo and Fitbit both include social networking (D) capabilities for sharing fitness motivation, goals, progress, support, and reinforcement with friends. One thing these apps share in common is that they all sync (A) with each other as well as with other apps, devices, and online tools. MyFitnessPal and Endomondo sync with heart-rate monitors as well as with each other and Fitbit.

109. C: Good nutrition provides the body with more energy, which enables and motivates people to exercise. Reciprocally, getting regular exercise can help to control the appetite and prevent overeating. Exercising does not mean you can eat anything you want (A). Both calcium and other nutrients in the diet and weight-bearing exercise can prevent loss of bone density and osteoporosis (B). A combination of exercise and a nutritious diet, not one or the other, prevents high blood pressure, high cholesterol (D), diabetes, and other diseases that unhealthy lifestyles often contribute to or cause.

110. D: Working together with the principal to develop an exercise program that benefits student learning by enhancing the environment is an example of using administrator support and collaboration. (A) is an example of collaborating with an English language arts (ELA) teacher by using a novel to study a sport for the physical education (PE) component and character development and relationships for the ELA component. (B) is also an example of how to collaborate with an ELA teacher by watching a movie, studying its dance movements for the PE component and its themes for the ELA component. (C) is an example of collaborating with a Family and Consumer Sciences teacher by combining nutrition with exercise—a very natural and valuable combination as good nutrition and physical activity interact and mutually support one another in healthy lifestyles.

111. D: Ectomorphs have long, narrow, thin body shapes with little muscle or fat. The high jump (D) and long-distance running are examples of appropriate sports for this somatotype. Wrestling (A) and shot-putting (C) are more suitable for endomorphic body types, which tend to be pear-shaped with more fat on the torso and limbs but small wrists and ankles. Gymnastics (B) is more appropriate for mesomorphs, who tend to have triangular shapes and strong limbs with more muscle and less fat.

112. C: According to the description, the test is reliable, meaning that it gives the same results every time it is administered, but it is not valid, meaning that it does not measure what it was intended to measure. Therefore, it is not correct that the test is neither reliable nor valid (A). It is not true that the test is valid but not reliable (B) but, rather, vice versa. The test is not both valid and reliable, and it is not simply misused (D); it is actually not valid because it does not test what it means or claims to test but assesses something else instead.

113. C: Kayaking is an activity that most involves the physical proficiency of dynamic strength. Static strength (A) is most involved in an activity like weight lifting. Trunk strength (B) is most involved in an activity like pole-vaulting. Explosive strength (D) is involved most in an activity like the standing long jump.

114. A: The first step in the volleyball activity is for students to assume rotational positions, that is, with one setter in front and one in the back row, without overlapping. The second step is for a student to serve the ball. In the third step, following the serve, students move from their rotational positions to their base positions. The fourth step is for players to defend against attack by watching, calling, and passing the ball.

115. C: In the first, cognitive stage of motor learning, learners understand the activity's goal and nature (A) and make initial attempts to perform it that include major errors (B). In the second, associative stage, learners engage in practice to master the timing of the skill, and they make fewer errors that are more consistent in nature (C). In the third, autonomous stage, learners perform the activity effortlessly and automatically (D), enabling them to redirect their attention to other aspects of the skill.

116. A: Atlantoaxial instability consists of excessive movement at the junction of the atlas, or first cervical vertebra (C1), and axis, or second cervical vertebra (C2), due to bone or ligament abnormality. It includes neurological symptoms when the spinal cord also is involved. This condition would make it unsafe for a student to perform a forward roll (B). However, to meet a learning objective, a physical education teacher could substitute a log roll, which would be safe for a student with this condition (A). Therefore, it is incorrect that no kind of roll should be assigned (C). Atlantoaxial instability is not necessarily that rare (D): It is caused by Down syndrome, a number of metabolic diseases, birth defects, traumatic spinal injuries, upper respiratory infections, rheumatoid arthritis, and surgeries to the head or neck. With so many different etiologies, the chances for a student to have this condition are not so remote.

117. A: According to social psychologists, nonverbal communication has these primary functions: performing social rituals (A) like greetings, farewells, and so on; revealing personalities as well as interpersonal relationships (B); supporting verbal interactions (C); and expressing feelings (D).

118. B: When the teacher writes a task on the board that students can begin upon entry to physical education (PE) class, this supports high expectations for students to take responsibility for classroom procedures and routines. While it encourages their independence in starting the activity, this does not mean the teacher will not be supervising them (A) thereafter. This teacher practice not only supports student independence in initiating activities; it also helps them comprehend their learning objectives and expectations (C) by the teacher's structuring the learning activities (D) he or she has provided for them.

119. A: In quality of movement, the flow of movement can be bound, that is, interrupted, or free, that is, sustained. Effort (B), or the amount of force in a body movement, can be strong, medium, light, or other increments within each of these. Speed (C) of movement can be quick, slow, or any degree in between these. Rhythm (D) of body movement can be constant, accelerating, or decelerating.

120. B: The best professional development not only improves a teacher's own expertise (A) and that of the teacher's colleagues (C) but both mutually as well as enabling physical education teachers to promote their own discipline. It enables teachers to improve instruction not only at the classroom level (D) but also at schoolwide and districtwide levels.

121. C: Posture has played an equally significant role in classical and contemporary theories of motor development. In classical theories attributing motor skill development to neuromuscular maturation, increasingly vertical posture was evidence of babies' progress as their cerebral cortices developed more control over their abilities to overcome gravitational pull. In contemporary theories attributing motor development to dynamic systems and relationships between perceptions and actions, posture became the stable biomechanical basis for action and was evidence of learning about new perception–action systems. Hence, posture was not more important to either classical theories (A) or contemporary theories (B). Neither did these theories regard its role in motor development as minor (D).

122. B: Differentiation is a calculus technique for finding a quantity's rate of change, used in biomechanics to get derivatives of curves or functions like velocity, acceleration, and jerk, which are derivatives of displacement. Integration is a calculus technique to determine the area between an x-axis and a curve, used in biomechanics to obtain integrals like velocity as an integral of acceleration, displacement as an integral of velocity, and work as an integral of power. Composition and resolution of vectors (A) in biomechanics are ways of combining coplanar and concurrent vector quantities by using vector algebra, not calculus. The parallelogram method (C) is a method for resolving vectors in different directions in biomechanics that is based on geometry, not calculus: The parallelogram is a geometric shape. Because (B) is correct, (D) is incorrect.

123. D: Alcohol, cocaine, Prozac, and other substances temporarily can reduce inhibitions so that students who are usually shy or introverted behave more sociably around peers (A). When students see substance use as a solution to being socially awkward and unpopular, they repeat it, which can lead to addiction. Conversely, students who were normally extroverted often withdraw socially when they become addicted to substances (B). Students who normally demonstrate self-control often behave more impulsively under the influence of substances (C).

124. A: Large-scale state research has found that student cardiovascular fitness achievement and healthy body mass index (BMI) scores correlate positively with student scores on the state academic achievement test of knowledge and skills. Other research has found that children who are more physically fit demonstrate not only quicker reaction times but also more accurate responses (B). Another investigation found that children burn more calories and take nearly twice as many steps during teacher-led fitness activities as during active gaming, not vice versa (C). Other studies show that intense exercise is followed by improvement in cognitive function (D).

125. B: This is a description of the command or direct method, which uses teacher-centered task instruction to promote psychomotor learning. The contingency or contract method (A) is a behavioral approach that uses specified rewards that are contingent on student task completion to reinforce psychomotor behaviors. The task or reciprocal method (C) uses stations whereby student learning of specific psychomotor tasks is integrated into the learning setup. Because (B) is correct, (D) is incorrect.

126. B: The Heimlich maneuver should be performed only on someone who is choking and cannot breathe. This means the person cannot speak, so the Heimlich maneuver should not be performed on a student who says he or she is having trouble breathing (A). Someone who is choking and cannot breathe also cannot cough, so the Heimlich maneuver should not be performed on a student who is coughing (C), which means he or she can breathe. The Heimlich maneuver should be done first if someone is choking; cardiopulmonary resuscitation (CPR) should be started after that if the victim loses consciousness (D).

127. B: To enhance students' perceived physical competence, it is better for physical education (PE) teachers not to specify how many trials to complete during a certain time period (A) but rather to specify the time period for practicing without requiring any specific number of trials (B). This allows students to focus not on how many times they complete the actions but rather on perfecting their technique. Rather than emphasizing technical errors they make (C), it is better to emphasize which things students do well technically, providing positive reinforcement that increases their motivation to practice. Varying assigned activities is more effective to minimize off-task student behavior than not varying them (D).

128. D: When learning to fall sideways and land on the hands, students should first learn to fall sideways from a kneeling position (A). Then they can practice rolling sideways down a wedge (B) to simulate falling down an incline. Then they learn while moving to fall, roll sideways, stand up (C), and keep moving. They begin this exercise from a walking speed and gradually increase to jogging then running (D). Thereafter, they can practice this activity with dodging. After mastering these activities, students can try in pairs to pull each other off balance and take turns tipping each other sideways from an all-fours position.

129. A: While feedback is important in physical education (PE) instruction, knowing when and when not to provide feedback is equally important to effective teaching. PE teachers need to give feedback to give students specific corrections to incorrectly performed techniques, for example. However, when a task furnishes inherent environmental feedback (B),—for example, a student throws a basketball, and it goes through the hoop—additional feedback may be unnecessary. When a student already has enough experience with a skill (C), sometimes PE teachers need not give them feedback. Also, when a teacher's demonstration enables students to see easily how to perform a skill correctly (D), they may need little or no additional feedback.

130. B: A time-lapse bulletin board can begin with the physical education (PE) teacher labeling a board's theme (e.g., balance, strength, speed, teamwork, sportsmanship, a certain sport, etc.) posting about a dozen pictures to provide examples and ideas for students and get them started. The teacher then assigns students to bring in pictures—drawings, photos, diagrams, art, and so on that they have found or made—that apply to the board's identified theme. Over time, student contributions fill the board with pictures, which students can view, discuss, and use as illustrations to help them understand aspects of a learning unit or topic. PE teachers need not even have schools provide (A) or have to buy their own real bulletin boards; they simply can create a board by hanging large pieces of paper, poster board, or fabric on the wall. This project is completed by students, not just teachers (C). Students do not ignore such boards (D), especially when they contain their own and classmates' contributions.

How to Overcome Test Anxiety

Just the thought of taking a test is enough to make most people a little nervous. A test is an important event that can have a long-term impact on your future, so it's important to take it seriously and it's natural to feel anxious about performing well. But just because anxiety is normal, that doesn't mean that it's helpful in test taking, or that you should simply accept it as part of your life. Anxiety can have a variety of effects. These effects can be mild, like making you feel slightly nervous, or severe, like blocking your ability to focus or remember even a simple detail.

If you experience test anxiety—whether severe or mild—it's important to know how to beat it. To discover this, first you need to understand what causes test anxiety.

Causes of Test Anxiety

While we often think of anxiety as an uncontrollable emotional state, it can actually be caused by simple, practical things. One of the most common causes of test anxiety is that a person does not feel adequately prepared for their test. This feeling can be the result of many different issues such as poor study habits or lack of organization, but the most common culprit is time management. Starting to study too late, failing to organize your study time to cover all of the material, or being distracted while you study will mean that you're not well prepared for the test. This may lead to cramming the night before, which will cause you to be physically and mentally exhausted for the test. Poor time management also contributes to feelings of stress, fear, and hopelessness as you realize you are not well prepared but don't know what to do about it.

Other times, test anxiety is not related to your preparation for the test but comes from unresolved fear. This may be a past failure on a test, or poor performance on tests in general. It may come from comparing yourself to others who seem to be performing better or from the stress of living up to expectations. Anxiety may be driven by fears of the future—how failure on this test would affect your educational and career goals. These fears are often completely irrational, but they can still negatively impact your test performance.

Elements of Test Anxiety

As mentioned earlier, test anxiety is considered to be an emotional state, but it has physical and mental components as well. Sometimes you may not even realize that you are suffering from test anxiety until you notice the physical symptoms. These can include trembling hands, rapid heartbeat, sweating, nausea, and tense muscles. Extreme anxiety may lead to fainting or vomiting. Obviously, any of these symptoms can have a negative impact on testing. It is important to recognize them as soon as they begin to occur so that you can address the problem before it damages your performance.

The mental components of test anxiety include trouble focusing and inability to remember learned information. During a test, your mind is on high alert, which can help you recall information and stay focused for an extended period of time. However, anxiety interferes with your mind's natural processes, causing you to blank out, even on the questions you know well. The strain of testing during anxiety makes it difficult to stay focused, especially on a test that may take several hours. Extreme anxiety can take a huge mental toll, making it difficult not only to recall test information but even to understand the test questions or pull your thoughts together.

Effects of Test Anxiety

Test anxiety is like a disease—if left untreated, it will get progressively worse. Anxiety leads to poor performance, and this reinforces the feelings of fear and failure, which in turn lead to poor performances on subsequent tests. It can grow from a mild nervousness to a crippling condition. If allowed to progress, test anxiety can have a big impact on your schooling, and consequently on your future.

Test anxiety can spread to other parts of your life. Anxiety on tests can become anxiety in any stressful situation, and blanking on a test can turn into panicking in a job situation. But fortunately, you don't have to let anxiety rule your testing and determine your grades. There are a number of relatively simple steps you can take to move past anxiety and function normally on a test and in the rest of life.

Physical Steps for Beating Test Anxiety

While test anxiety is a serious problem, the good news is that it can be overcome. It doesn't have to control your ability to think and remember information. While it may take time, you can begin taking steps today to beat anxiety.

Just as your first hint that you may be struggling with anxiety comes from the physical symptoms, the first step to treating it is also physical. Rest is crucial for having a clear, strong mind. If you are tired, it is much easier to give in to anxiety. But if you establish good sleep habits, your body and mind will be ready to perform optimally, without the strain of exhaustion. Additionally, sleeping well helps you to retain information better, so you're more likely to recall the answers when you see the test questions.

Getting good sleep means more than going to bed on time. It's important to allow your brain time to relax. Take study breaks from time to time so it doesn't get overworked, and don't study right before bed. Take time to rest your mind before trying to rest your body, or you may find it difficult to fall asleep.

Along with sleep, other aspects of physical health are important in preparing for a test. Good nutrition is vital for good brain function. Sugary foods and drinks may give a burst of energy but this burst is followed by a crash, both physically and emotionally. Instead, fuel your body with protein and vitamin-rich foods.

Also, drink plenty of water. Dehydration can lead to headaches and exhaustion, especially if your brain is already under stress from the rigors of the test. Particularly if your test is a long one, drink water during the breaks. And if possible, take an energy-boosting snack to eat between sections.

Along with sleep and diet, a third important part of physical health is exercise. Maintaining a steady workout schedule is helpful, but even taking 5-minute study breaks to walk can help get your blood pumping faster and clear your head. Exercise also releases endorphins, which contribute to a positive feeling and can help combat test anxiety.

When you nurture your physical health, you are also contributing to your mental health. If your body is healthy, your mind is much more likely to be healthy as well. So take time to rest, nourish your body with healthy food and water, and get moving as much as possible. Taking these physical steps will make you stronger and more able to take the mental steps necessary to overcome test anxiety.

Mental Steps for Beating Test Anxiety

Working on the mental side of test anxiety can be more challenging, but as with the physical side, there are clear steps you can take to overcome it. As mentioned earlier, test anxiety often stems from lack of preparation, so the obvious solution is to prepare for the test. Effective studying may be the most important weapon you have for beating test anxiety, but you can and should employ several other mental tools to combat fear.

First, boost your confidence by reminding yourself of past success—tests or projects that you aced. If you're putting as much effort into preparing for this test as you did for those, there's no reason you should expect to fail here. Work hard to prepare; then trust your preparation.

Second, surround yourself with encouraging people. It can be helpful to find a study group, but be sure that the people you're around will encourage a positive attitude. If you spend time with others who are anxious or cynical, this will only contribute to your own anxiety. Look for others who are motivated to study hard from a desire to succeed, not from a fear of failure.

Third, reward yourself. A test is physically and mentally tiring, even without anxiety, and it can be helpful to have something to look forward to. Plan an activity following the test, regardless of the outcome, such as going to a movie or getting ice cream.

When you are taking the test, if you find yourself beginning to feel anxious, remind yourself that you know the material. Visualize successfully completing the test. Then take a few deep, relaxing breaths and return to it. Work through the questions carefully but with confidence, knowing that you are capable of succeeding.

Developing a healthy mental approach to test taking will also aid in other areas of life. Test anxiety affects more than just the actual test—it can be damaging to your mental health and even contribute to depression. It's important to beat test anxiety before it becomes a problem for more than testing.

Study Strategy

Being prepared for the test is necessary to combat anxiety, but what does being prepared look like? You may study for hours on end and still not feel prepared. What you need is a strategy for test prep. The next few pages outline our recommended steps to help you plan out and conquer the challenge of preparation.

STEP 1: SCOPE OUT THE TEST

Learn everything you can about the format (multiple choice, essay, etc.) and what will be on the test. Gather any study materials, course outlines, or sample exams that may be available. Not only will this help you to prepare, but knowing what to expect can help to alleviate test anxiety.

STEP 2: MAP OUT THE MATERIAL

Look through the textbook or study guide and make note of how many chapters or sections it has. Then divide these over the time you have. For example, if a book has 15 chapters and you have five days to study, you need to cover three chapters each day. Even better, if you have the time, leave an extra day at the end for overall review after you have gone through the material in depth.

If time is limited, you may need to prioritize the material. Look through it and make note of which sections you think you already have a good grasp on, and which need review. While you are studying, skim quickly through the familiar sections and take more time on the challenging parts.

Write out your plan so you don't get lost as you go. Having a written plan also helps you feel more in control of the study, so anxiety is less likely to arise from feeling overwhelmed at the amount to cover.

STEP 3: GATHER YOUR TOOLS

Decide what study method works best for you. Do you prefer to highlight in the book as you study and then go back over the highlighted portions? Or do you type out notes of the important information? Or is it helpful to make flashcards that you can carry with you? Assemble the pens, index cards, highlighters, post-it notes, and any other materials you may need so you won't be distracted by getting up to find things while you study.

If you're having a hard time retaining the information or organizing your notes, experiment with different methods. For example, try color-coding by subject with colored pens, highlighters, or post-it notes. If you learn better by hearing, try recording yourself reading your notes so you can listen while in the car, working out, or simply sitting at your desk. Ask a friend to quiz you from your flashcards, or try teaching someone the material to solidify it in your mind.

STEP 4: CREATE YOUR ENVIRONMENT

It's important to avoid distractions while you study. This includes both the obvious distractions like visitors and the subtle distractions like an uncomfortable chair (or a too-comfortable couch that makes you want to fall asleep). Set up the best study environment possible: good lighting and a comfortable work area. If background music helps you focus, you may want to turn it on, but otherwise keep the room quiet. If you are using a computer to take notes, be sure you don't have any other windows open, especially applications like social media, games, or anything else that could distract you. Silence your phone and turn off notifications. Be sure to keep water close by so you stay hydrated while you study (but avoid unhealthy drinks and snacks).

Also, take into account the best time of day to study. Are you freshest first thing in the morning? Try to set aside some time then to work through the material. Is your mind clearer in the afternoon or evening? Schedule your study session then. Another method is to study at the same time of day that you will take the test, so that your brain gets used to working on the material at that time and will be ready to focus at test time.

STEP 5: STUDY!

Once you have done all the study preparation, it's time to settle into the actual studying. Sit down, take a few moments to settle your mind so you can focus, and begin to follow your study plan. Don't give in to distractions or let yourself procrastinate. This is your time to prepare so you'll be ready to fearlessly approach the test. Make the most of the time and stay focused.

Of course, you don't want to burn out. If you study too long you may find that you're not retaining the information very well. Take regular study breaks. For example, taking five minutes out of every hour to walk briskly, breathing deeply and swinging your arms, can help your mind stay fresh.

As you get to the end of each chapter or section, it's a good idea to do a quick review. Remind yourself of what you learned and work on any difficult parts. When you feel that you've mastered the material, move on to the next part. At the end of your study session, briefly skim through your notes again.

But while review is helpful, cramming last minute is NOT. If at all possible, work ahead so that you won't need to fit all your study into the last day. Cramming overloads your brain with more information than it can process and retain, and your tired mind may struggle to recall even previously learned information when it is overwhelmed with last-minute study. Also, the urgent nature of cramming and the stress placed on your brain contribute to anxiety. You'll be more likely to go to the test feeling unprepared and having trouble thinking clearly.

So don't cram, and don't stay up late before the test, even just to review your notes at a leisurely pace. Your brain needs rest more than it needs to go over the information again. In fact, plan to finish your studies by noon or early afternoon the day before the test. Give your brain the rest of the day to relax or focus on other things, and get a good night's sleep. Then you will be fresh for the test and better able to recall what you've studied.

STEP 6: TAKE A PRACTICE TEST

Many courses offer sample tests, either online or in the study materials. This is an excellent resource to check whether you have mastered the material, as well as to prepare for the test format and environment.

Check the test format ahead of time: the number of questions, the type (multiple choice, free response, etc.), and the time limit. Then create a plan for working through them. For example, if you have 30 minutes to take a 60-question test, your limit is 30 seconds per question. Spend less time on the questions you know well so that you can take more time on the difficult ones.

If you have time to take several practice tests, take the first one open book, with no time limit. Work through the questions at your own pace and make sure you fully understand them. Gradually work up to taking a test under test conditions: sit at a desk with all study materials put away and set a timer. Pace yourself to make sure you finish the test with time to spare and go back to check your answers if you have time.

After each test, check your answers. On the questions you missed, be sure you understand why you missed them. Did you misread the question (tests can use tricky wording)? Did you forget the information? Or was it something you hadn't learned? Go back and study any shaky areas that the practice tests reveal.

Taking these tests not only helps with your grade, but also aids in combating test anxiety. If you're already used to the test conditions, you're less likely to worry about it, and working through tests until you're scoring well gives you a confidence boost. Go through the practice tests until you feel comfortable, and then you can go into the test knowing that you're ready for it.

Test Tips

On test day, you should be confident, knowing that you've prepared well and are ready to answer the questions. But aside from preparation, there are several test day strategies you can employ to maximize your performance.

First, as stated before, get a good night's sleep the night before the test (and for several nights before that, if possible). Go into the test with a fresh, alert mind rather than staying up late to study.

Try not to change too much about your normal routine on the day of the test. It's important to eat a nutritious breakfast, but if you normally don't eat breakfast at all, consider eating just a protein bar. If you're a coffee drinker, go ahead and have your normal coffee. Just make sure you time it so that the caffeine doesn't wear off right in the middle of your test. Avoid sugary beverages, and drink enough water to stay hydrated but not so much that you need a restroom break 10 minutes into the test. If your test isn't first thing in the morning, consider going for a walk or doing a light workout before the test to get your blood flowing.

Allow yourself enough time to get ready, and leave for the test with plenty of time to spare so you won't have the anxiety of scrambling to arrive in time. Another reason to be early is to select a good seat. It's helpful to sit away from doors and windows, which can be distracting. Find a good seat, get out your supplies, and settle your mind before the test begins.

When the test begins, start by going over the instructions carefully, even if you already know what to expect. Make sure you avoid any careless mistakes by following the directions.

Then begin working through the questions, pacing yourself as you've practiced. If you're not sure on an answer, don't spend too much time on it, and don't let it shake your confidence. Either skip it and come back later, or eliminate as many wrong answers as possible and guess among the remaining ones. Don't dwell on these questions as you continue—put them out of your mind and focus on what lies ahead.

Be sure to read all of the answer choices, even if you're sure the first one is the right answer. Sometimes you'll find a better one if you keep reading. But don't second-guess yourself if you do immediately know the answer. Your gut instinct is usually right. Don't let test anxiety rob you of the information you know.

If you have time at the end of the test (and if the test format allows), go back and review your answers. Be cautious about changing any, since your first instinct tends to be correct, but make sure you didn't misread any of the questions or accidentally mark the wrong answer choice. Look over any you skipped and make an educated guess.

At the end, leave the test feeling confident. You've done your best, so don't waste time worrying about your performance or wishing you could change anything. Instead, celebrate the successful completion of this test. And finally, use this test to learn how to deal with anxiety even better next time.

> **Review Video: Test Anxiety**
> Visit mometrix.com/academy and enter code: 100340

Important Qualification

Not all anxiety is created equal. If your test anxiety is causing major issues in your life beyond the classroom or testing center, or if you are experiencing troubling physical symptoms related to your anxiety, it may be a sign of a serious physiological or psychological condition. If this sounds like your situation, we strongly encourage you to seek professional help.

Tell Us Your Story

We at Mometrix would like to extend our heartfelt thanks to you for letting us be a part of your journey. It is an honor to serve people from all walks of life, people like you, who are committed to building the best future they can for themselves.

We know that each person's situation is unique. But we also know that, whether you are a young student or a mother of four, you care about working to make your own life and the lives of those around you better.

That's why we want to hear your story.

We want to know why you're taking this test. We want to know about the trials you've gone through to get here. And we want to know about the successes you've experienced after taking and passing your test.

In addition to your story, which can be an inspiration both to us and to others, we value your feedback. We want to know both what you loved about our book and what you think we can improve on.

The team at Mometrix would be absolutely thrilled to hear from you! So please, send us an email at tellusyourstory@mometrix.com or visit us at mometrix.com/tellusyourstory.php and let's stay in touch.

Additional Bonus Material

Due to our efforts to try to keep this book to a manageable length, we've created a link that will give you access to all of your additional bonus material:

mometrix.com/bonus948/priihpeck5857

Strength
Static
Dynamic
Explore

Reflex
disappears
over time

Made in the USA
Columbia, SC
20 March 2024

33382022R00161